The History of the French Revol

Louis Adolphe Thiers

Introduction

As one of the seminal social revolutions in human history, the French Revolution holds a unique legacy, especially in the West. The early years of the Revolution were fueled by Enlightenment ideals, seeking the social overthrow of the caste system that gave the royalty and aristocracy decisive advantages over the lower classes. But history remembers the French Revolution in a starkly different way, as the same leaders who sought a more democratic system while out of power devolved into establishing an incredibly repressive tyranny of their own once they acquired it.

The height of Republican France's tyranny came during a 10 month period forever known as the Reign of Terror, the most notorious and arguably most memorable part of the French Revolution. One of the first victims of the Reign of Terror was its most famous: former French Queen Marie Antoinette. But Antoinette was followed by thousands more, including everyone from aristocrats to clergy to prostitutes and even instrumental revolutionaries like Danton, Desmoulins, and, most notably, Robespierre. It was Robespierre whose position on the Committee of Public Safety made him the Reign of Terror's instrumental figure until he himself became a victim of it in July 1794. Robespierre's date with the guillotine is often considered the official end of the Reign of Terror, but by then it is estimated that at least 16,000 people were guillotined in that time and possibly 25,000 more were summarily executed across the country.

Although Robespierre is almost singlehandedly associated with the Reign of Terror and is typically blamed for it, many factors influenced the actions and beliefs of Paris and the remainder of France during late 1793 and 1794. Robespierre and the Committee of Public Safety believed passionately in the Revolution and fought to eliminate any threat to the young French Republic. Robespierre envisioned a Republic of Virtue, with no room for anyone who did not abide by his rules and morality. Counterrevolutionaries certainly did threaten the Revolution; however, most of those killed during the Reign of Terror were not counterrevolutionaries and posed no serious threat to the Revolution or Republic.

PREFACE BY THE AUTHOR.

I PURPOSE writing the history of a memorable revolution, which has profoundly agitated the minds of men, and which still continues to divide them. I disguise not from myself the difficulties of the undertaking; for passions, which were supposed to have been stifled under the sway of military despotism, have recently revived. All at once men bowed down by age and toil have felt resentments, which, according to appearance were appeased, awaken within them, and they have communicated them to us, their sons and heirs. But if we have to uphold the same cause, we have not to defend their conduct, for we can separate liberty from those who have rendered it service or disservice; whilst we possess the advantage of having observed those veterans, who, still full of their recollections, still agitated by their impressions, reveal to us the spirit and the character of parties, and teach us to comprehend them. Perhaps the moment when the actors are about to expire is the most proper for writing this history; we can collect their evidence without participating in all their passions.

Be this as it may, I have endeavoured to stifle within my own bosom every feeling of animosity: I alternately figured to myself that, born in a cottage, animated with a just ambition, I was resolved to acquire what the pride of the higher classes had unjustly refused me; or that, bred in palaces, the heir to ancient privileges, it was painful to me to renounce a possession which I regarded as a legitimate property. Thenceforward I could not harbour enmity against either party; I pitied the combatants, and I indemnified myself by admiring generous deeds wherever I found them.

PREFACE TO THE PRESENT EDITION.

FIFTEEN years have elapsed since we first introduced M. Thiers' "History of the French Revolution" to our readers, in an English translation. The value of such a work can only he tested by time and popularity. The subject, although of the deepest interest, had been so repeatedly handled by previous writers, that novelty, either in fact or inference, was scarcely to be expected. In France, the book was received with enthusiasm, and adopted without hesitation, as the standard authority. This might have been looked for, from the impulsive character of the people, the known abilities of the author, and his political eminence. It was felt at once that he was able to grapple with the question, and examine its minute details with searching fidelity. His mind was practical more than speculative. He was a man of business rather than a dreaming philosopher; an adroit, keen, clear-headed, worldly statesman, with no strong passions or prejudices to mislead his judgment, and entirely uninfluenced by fanciful theories to obscure his meaning. His history is a narrative of facts, seldom interrupted by episodes or parenthetical reflections. He has no tendency to enter into long investigations of causes, which he leaves the reader to discover for himself. In his delineations of character, he seizes obvious points and prominent features. In this he is directly contrasted with Mignet, who refines with metaphysical nicety, and halts to dissect a feeling, when he should hasten on to relate an event. Mignet is subtle, and frequently obscure. Thiers is frank, and always intelligible. Hence the secret of his superior attraction; and, on this ground, independent of others, his work has established itself as a classic, and rises in value on repeated perusal. It may justly be pronounced the best that has been written on a very momentous period: the safest, as well as the most entertaining; and when we refer to the long list of eminent authors who have employed their pens in the description of this gigantic moral earthquake, it is no slight commendation to be placed at the head of the phalanx. We have said why we prefer Thiers to Mignet,—although in literary composition their merits are equally balanced. In England, the reputation of M. Thiers' History has increased gradually. Received at first with caution, perhaps with distrust, it has forced its way by intrinsic weight, and obtains, with each succeeding year, an additional circulation. A new edition has therefore become necessary, which we now present in a more convenient form, and, as we trust, with many additional recommendations.

It has been objected that Thiers is a partial historian, and writes with a natural bias in favour of his own country. If so, a reasonable allowance must be made for a fault inseparable from humanity. But this tendency, when it occurs, is amply corrected by the Editor, in this edition, for he has supplied a series of illustrative notes from every available source, so that the reader is thereby enabled to balance conflicting opinions, and regulate his own judgment on a comparison of evidence.

Lord Byron has said, "It has long been the fashion to ascribe every thing to the French Revolution, and the French Revolution to everything but the real cause.

That cause is obvious. The government exacted more than the people could bear, and the people neither could nor would bear any longer." There is truth is this short summary; but the question is too complicated to be dismissed in a sentence. The storm had long been brewing, and many agencies were concerned in bringing it to a head. The catastrophe was foreseen and predicted, not only by profound thinkers, but by casual observers. Many were the warning voices, but all were unheeded until the explosion took place. The chain of causes, immediate and secondary, have been amply discussed; but it is to be regretted that an author, so well versed in the annals of France as M. Thiers, has not entered more into detail in his introductory dissertation. After a few brief paragraphs, didactic rather than historical, he breaks at once into his subject, as if he took it for granted that all his readers were as well acquainted as himself with the origin of that memorable event. The climax was gradual of approach, and long in preparation. What Dr. Johnson says in his tragedy of "Irene" of the fall of Constantinople, applies strongly to the destruction of the French monarchy:—

> "A thousand horrid prodigies foretold it;
> A feeble government, eluded laws,
> A factions populace, luxurious nobles,
> And all the maladies of sinking states."

To complete the catalogue, may be added, and foremost in the list, the deficiency of the public revenue, the preposterous salaries of the officers of the Crown, and the unbridled speculations of the Encyclopædists,—brilliant but dangerous sophists, who promulgated visionary doctrines, utterly subversive of religion, law, policy, or morality. These were the most formidable pioneers of the Revolution. As soon as they were listened to, the end became certain. They exposed the wrongs, and pointed out the privileges of all classes; but while they did this, they, at the same time, advocated principles incompatible with the interests of civilised society. The executive energy of Cromwell, and the financial ability of Colbert, might, even at a late hour, have opposed an effectual barrier; but no such men were accorded. The lesson was intended to be taught; and well will it be for future generations if they lay it to their hearts, and imbibe wisdom from the study.

Foremost amongst those whose writings tended to inflame and pervert the public mind, were Voltaire and Rousseau. The first of these had every possible requisite for such a task. Shrewd, calculating, and cunning as a fox; a wit without heart, an innovator without conscience, an expert handler of paradoxes, the light thin soil of whose mind could not nourish the tree of knowledge; acquainted with society in all its grades, from the highest to the lowest; a contemner, less from sound conviction, than from the instincts of overweening self-conceit, of all systems of religion, government, and morals—this ready unprincipled satirist was just the man to precipitate the grand crisis of the Revolution. All who read, could understand him. There was no affected mysticism in his manner; he was uniformly concise, lucid, and plausible; and set off his style by all the graces of the most sparkling wit and cutting sarcasm. His favourite mode of commencing an attack is by insinuation. He sneers away a moral system in a sentence, and disturbs faith in religion and humanity by a terse and sparkling allegory. That he effected some good in his generation, is unquestionable. He denounced the avarice and negligence of the higher orders of the priesthood; lashed the insane rage for war, then so general on the continent; exposed the vices and imbecility of the *noblesse*; and did not spare even the throne itself. Had he stopped here, he would have deserved praise; but his restless intellect spurned all decent restraints, perversely confounding the distinctions between truth and falsehood—absurdity and common sense. Cynical by nature, the crimes and utter callousness which he observed amongst the higher classes made him a sceptic to all generous emotions; as the corruption of the privileged clergy made him reject all belief in Christianity. Hazlitt, who of all men in the world was the least likely to underrate him, has well observed that "the poisoned wound he inflicted was so fine as scarcely to be felt, until it rankled and festered in its mortal consequences; and he loved to reduce things below their level, making them all alike seem worthless and hollow!"

Of a far different order of intellect, but in his way equally influential, was Voltaire's great rival, Rousseau. The object of this insidious sentimentalist was—in politics, to bring about republicanism; in ethics, to subvert the entire frame-work of society, and introduce universal licence; in religion, to do away with faith grounded on the convictions of reason, and to substitute in its stead the cant of instinct and sensibility. His specious, shallow, tinsel eloquence, which was mistaken for the sterling ore of thought, turned the brain of all France. Because his ideas were eccentric, they were accounted profound; and his studied indecency was received as the prompting of a healthy and impassioned temperament. We who live in more enlightened times, when the public mind is able to detect the true from the false, and, if crazed for a season by some pet crotchet, never fails soon to right itself, can scarcely imagine the effect which Voltaire and Rousseau, assisted by the Encyclopædists, produced in their day. That a convulsion would have taken place, even without their aid, is unquestionable; but equally certain is it that they greatly contributed to hurry on the crisis. The effects of their writings may easily be traced in the wild speculations of the unworldly Girondins—the republican cant of the Dantonists—and the unblushing atheism of the worshippers of the Goddess of Season.

The radical defect of all Rousseau's writings was the substitution of sentiment for principle. Never was man so glaringly deficient in what may be called the moral sense. His mind "wore motley," and was made up of inconsistencies. While he professed to inculcate a system of the purest ethics, he lived in avowed adultery with a woman old enough to be his mother; and wrote upon the duties owing by parents to their children, while he sent his own to the Foundling Hospital! That he was actuated throughout his literary career by no better feeling than a mere morbid craving for notoriety, is evident from one of his published conversations with Burke, wherein he observes that, finding that the ordinary vehicle of literature was worn out, he took upon himself the task of renewing the springs, repainting the panels, and gilding the whole machine afresh. In other words, he was solely anxious to create a sensation, no matter how eccentric were the means which he employed for that purpose.

Voltaire and Rousseau lived and wrote exclusively for effect. Yet it has been urged by those, who, seduced by their talents, would fain make excuses for their sophistries, that both acted from the best intentions. This is pure cant—the plea urged by every knave for his offences against society. The bar of the Old Bailey is filled every session with the best intentions; they figure unequivocally in the police-offices; people the vast pasturages of Australia, and form—says the quaint old Spanish proverb—the pavement of hell itself!

While these, and other malign influences were at work, the grand struggle for independence took place in America. This event startled

France like a thunder-clap. Adieu now to all hope of escape from Revolution! The heather is on fire, and nothing can check the progress of the conflagration. Within the precincts of the palace, in the saloons of fashion, and universally among the *Tiers-état*, nothing is talked of but the gallantry of the transatlantic patriots. Washington is the hero—Franklin the philosopher of the day. Carried away by the general enthusiasm, and glad no doubt of such an opportunity of humbling the pride, and increasing the difficulties of England—although his private correspondence would seem to show otherwise—Louis XVI. took the desperate resolution of supplying the revolted colonies with funds and troops. It was the misfortune of this prince, who possessed many excellent private and public qualities, to do every thing with the best intentions, and to succeed in nothing. "As for the King," says Mr. Carlyle, in his eloquent analytical history of the Revolution, "he, as usual, will go wavering cameleon-like, changing colour and purpose with the colour of his environment—good for no kingly use." This is well observed of Louis. He was as "infirm of purpose" as Macbeth, swayed now by the counsels of the Queen, now by those of the Assembly, and giving in a bold adhesion to neither. In assisting the American insurgents, he took the most suicidal step that it was possible for monarch, situated as he was, to take; for, when his troops returned home—and they constituted the flower of the young *noblesse* and the army—they brought back with them opinions and feelings until then proscribed in France; talked loudly of the duty of resistance to despotic authority; and thus communicated an irreparable shock to the tottering throne of Louis. The final blow however was given by the derangement of the national finances, the annual deficit of which, amounting to above seven millions sterling, compelled the reluctant monarch to summon the States-general, and thus admit the necessity of a radical change in the Government—in other words, to sanction those innovations which could not terminate otherwise than in Revolution.

And now, the work appeared to be complete. The monarchy was abolished, the aristocracy annihilated; religious and moral responsibility was denounced as an empty chimera, and the new system universally proclaimed. But the elements of which it was compounded were discordant, and already, like the armed men produced by the dragon's teeth of Cadmus, they had begun to war on each other. There was hope yet, if the disciples of liberty and equality, who refused to fraternise, had been left to themselves. Nothing could give them strength and permanence but unity; and unity could only come by a pressure from without. In evil hour that pressure was resorted to. The invasion of France by the Duke of Brunswick, and subsequently by the allied armies of Austria and England, under Prince Cobourg, with the avowed objects of conquest and partition, settled the question definitively, and combined all parties in one blended feeling of national patriotism. From that moment the restoration of the monarchy became impossible, and the republic was firmly consolidated. A struggle of twenty years was the consequence of this fatal mistake, from which the exhausted nations have scarcely yet recovered.

The opening portions of M. Thiers' work present an animated picture of the most striking character. We see in the fore-ground, groups of rejoicing, constitutional patriots; Mirabeau is there, with the eloquent leaders of the Gironde, whom Dumouriez has styled, and not without justice, the "Jesuits of the Revolution;" there, too, are Lafayette and Bailly, men in whom a sincere monarch might have had confidence; but grimly scowling in the back-ground—for the Republican pear is not yet ripe—lurk the frightful figures of Robespierre and the Hebertists, biding their time to turn this scene of national exultation into one of tears and blood, despair and raging madness. But enough of prefatory discussion. The eventful drama will sufficiently develop itself in the progress of the history, and requires no lengthened prologue to stimulate expectation.

LONDON,

December 28, 1853.

HISTORY OF THE FRENCH REVOLUTION.

EVERYBODY is acquainted with the revolutions of the French monarchy. It is well known that the Greeks, and afterwards the Romans, introduced their arms and their civilisation among the half savage Gauls; that subsequently the Barbarians established their military hierarchy among them; that this hierarchy, transferred from persons to lands, struck root, as it were, and grew up into the feudal system. Authority was divided between the feudal chief called king, and the secondary chiefs called vassals, who in their turn were kings over their own dependents. In our times, when the necessity for preferring mutual accusations has caused search to be made for reciprocal faults, abundant pains have been taken to teach us that the supreme authority was at first disputed by the vassals, which is always done by those who are nearest to it; that this authority was afterwards divided among them, which constituted feudal anarchy; and that at length it reverted to the throne, where it concentrated itself into despotism under Louis XI., Richelieu, and Louis XIV.

The French population had progressively enfranchised itself by industry, the primary source of wealth and liberty. Though originally agricultural, it soon devoted its attention to commerce and manufactures, and acquired an importance that affected the entire nation. Introduced as a supplicant into the States-general, it appeared there in no other posture than on its knees, in order to be grievously abused. In process of time even Louis XIV. declared that he would nave no more of these cringing assemblies; and this he declared to the parliaments, booted and whip in hand. Thenceforth were seen at the head of the state, a king clothed with a power ill defined in theory, but absolute in practice; grandees who had relinquished their feudal dignity for the favour of the monarch, and who disputed by intrigue what was granted to them out of the substance of the people; beneath them an immense population, having no other relation to the court and the aristocracy than habitual submission and the payment of taxes. Between the court and the people were parliaments invested with the power of administering justice and registering the royal decrees. Authority is always disputed. If not in the legitimate assemblies of the nation, it is contested in the very palace of the prince. It is well known that the parliaments, by refusing to register the royal edicts, rendered them ineffective: this terminated in a "bed of justice" and a concession when the king was weak, but in entire submission when the king was powerful. Louis XIV. had no need to make concessions, for in his reign no parliament durst remonstrate; he drew the nation along in his train, and it glorified him with the prodigies which itself achieved in war and in the arts and sciences. The subjects and the monarch were unanimous, and their actions tended towards one and the same point. But no sooner had Louis XIV. expired, than the Regent afforded the parliaments occasion to revenge themselves for their long nullity. The will of the monarch, so profoundly respected in his lifetime, was violated after his death, and his last testament was cancelled. Authority was then thrown into litigation, and a long struggle commenced between the parliaments, the clergy, and the court, in sight of a nation worn out with long wars and exhausted by supplying the extravagance of its rulers, who gave themselves up alternately to a fondness for pleasure and for arms. Till then it had displayed no skill but for the service and the gratification of the monarch: it now began to apply its intelligence to its own benefit and the examination of its interests.

The human mind is incessantly passing from one object to another. From the theatre and the pulpit, French genius turned to the moral and political sciences: all then became changed. Figure to yourself, during a whole century, the usurpers of all the national rights quarrelling about a worn-out authority; the parliaments persecuting the clergy, the clergy persecuting the parliaments; the latter disputing the authority of the court; the court, careless and calm amid this struggle, squandering the substance of the people in the most profligate debauchery; the nation, enriched and roused, watching these disputes, arming itself with the allegations of one party against the other, deprived of all political action, dogmatizing boldly and ignorantly because it was confined to theories; aspiring, above all, to recover its rank in Europe, and offering in vain its treasure and its blood to regain a place which it had lost through the weakness of its rulers. Such was the eighteenth century.

The scandal had been carried to its height when Louis XVI., an equitable prince, moderate in his propensities, carelessly educated, but naturally of a good disposition, ascended the throne at a very early age. He called to his side an old courtier, and consigned to him the care of his kingdom, and divided his confidence between Maurepas and the Queen, an Austrian princess, young, lively, and amiable, who possessed a complete ascendancy over him. Maurepas and the Queen were not good friends. The King, sometimes giving way to his minister, at others to his consort, began at an early period the long career of his vacillations. Aware of the state of his kingdom, he believed the reports of the philosophers on that subject; but, brought up in the most Christian sentiments, he felt the utmost aversion for them. The public voice, which was loudly expressed, called for Turgot, one of the class of economists, an honest, virtuous man, endowed with firmness of character, a slow genius, but obstinate and profound. Convinced of his probity, delighted with his plans of reform, Louis XVI. frequently repeated: "There are none besides myself and Turgot who are friends of the people." Turgot's reforms were thwarted by the opposition of the highest orders in the state, who were interested in maintaining all kinds of abuses, which the austere minister proposed to suppress. Louis XVI. dismissed him with regret. During his whole life, which was only a long martyrdom, he had the mortification to discern what was right, to wish it sincerely, but to lack the energy requisite for carrying it into execution.

The King, placed between the court, the parliaments, and the people, exposed to intrigues and to suggestions of all sorts, repeatedly changed his ministers. Yielding once more to the public voice, and to the necessity for reform, he summoned to the finance department Necker, a native of Geneva, who had amassed wealth as a banker, a partisan and disciple of Colbert, as Turgot was of Sully; an economical and upright financier, but a vain man, fond of setting himself up for arbitrator in everything—philosophy, religion, liberty; and, misled by the praises of his friends and the public, flattering himself that he could guide and fix the minds of others at that point at which his own had stopped. (*See* Appendix A.)

Necker re-established order in the finances, and found means to defray the heavy expenses of the American war. With a mind more comprehensive, but less flexible, than that of Turgot, possessing more particularly the confidence of capitalists, he found, for the moment, unexpected resources, and revived public credit. But it required something more than financial artifices to put an end to the embarrassments of the exchequer, and he had recourse to reform. He found the higher orders not less adverse to him than they had been to Turgot; the parliaments, apprised of his plans, combined against him and obliged him to retire.

The conviction of the existence of abuses was universal; everybody admitted it; the King knew and was deeply grieved at it. The courtiers, who derived advantage from these abuses, would have been glad to see an end put to the embarrassments of the exchequer, but without its costing them a single sacrifice. They descanted at court on the state of affairs, and there retailed philosophical maxima; 'they deplored, whilst hunting, the oppressions inflicted upon the farmer; nay, they were even seen to applaud the enfranchisement of the Americans, and to receive with honour the young Frenchmen who returned from the New World. The parliaments also talked of the interests of the people, loudly insisted on the sufferings of the poor, and yet opposed the equalisation of the taxes, as well as the abolition of the remains of feudal barbarism. All talked of the public weal, few desired it; and the people, not yet knowing who were its true friends, applauded all those who resisted power, its most obvious enemy.

By the removal of Turgot and Necker the state of affairs was not changed; the distress of the treasury remained the same. Those in power would have been willing to dispense, for a long time to come, with the intervention of the nation, but it was absolutely necessary to subsist—it was absolutely necessary to supply the profusion of the court. The difficulty, removed for a moment by the dismissal of a minister, by a loan, or by the forced imposition of a tax, appeared again in an aggravated form, like every evil injudiciously neglected. The court hesitated, just as a man does who is compelled to take a dreaded but an indispensable step. An intrigue brought forward M. de Calonne, who was not in good odour with the public, because he had contributed to the persecution of La Chalotais. Calonne, clever, brilliant, fertile in resources, relied upon his genius, upon fortune, and upon men, and awaited the future with the most extraordinary apathy. It was his opinion that one ought not to be alarmed beforehand, or to discover an evil till the day before that on which one intends to set about repairing it. He seduced the court by his manners, touched it by his eagerness to grant all that it required, afforded the King and everybody else some happier moments, and dispelled the most gloomy presages by a gleam of prosperity and blind confidence.

That future which had been counted upon now approached; it became necessary at length to adopt decisive measures. It was impossible to burden the people with fresh imposts, and yet the coffers were empty. There was but one remedy which could be applied; that was to reduce the expenses by the suppression of grants; and if this expedient should not suffice, to extend the taxes to a greater number of contributors, that is, to the nobility and clergy. These plans, attempted successively by Turgot and Necker, and resumed by Calonne, appeared to the latter not at all likely to succeed, unless the consent of the privileged classes themselves could be obtained. Calonne, therefore, proposed to collect them together in an assembly, to be called the Assembly of the Notables, in order to lay his plans before them, and to gain their consent either by address or by conviction. The assembly was composed of distinguished members of the nobility, clergy, and magistracy, of a great number of masters of requests, and some magistrates of the provinces. By means of this composition, and still more by the aid of the chief popular gentry and philosophers, whom he had taken care to introduce into this assembly, Calonne flattered himself that he should be able to carry his point.

The too confident minister was mistaken. Public opinion bore him a grudge for occupying the place of Turgot and Necker. Delighted in particular that the minister was obliged to render an account, it supported the resistance of the Notables. Very warm discussions ensued. Calonne did wrong in throwing upon his predecessors, and partly on Necker, the existing state of the exchequer. Necker replied, was exiled, and the opposition became the more obstinate. Calonne met it with presence of mind and composure. He caused M. de Miromel, keeper of the seals, who was conspiring with the parliaments, to be dismissed. But his triumph lasted only two days. The King, who was attached to him, had, in engaging to support him, promised more than he could perform. He was shaken by the representations of the Notables, who promised to sanction the plans of Calonne, but on condition that a minister more moral and more deserving of confidence should be appointed to carry them into execution. The Queen, at the suggestion of the Abbé de Vermont, proposed to the King and prevailed on him to accept a new minister, M. de Brienne, Archbishop of Toulouse, and one of the Notables who had contributed most to the ruin of Calonne, in hopes of succeeding him.

The Archbishop of Toulouse, a man of weak mind and obstinate disposition, had from boyhood set his heart upon becoming minister, and availed himself of all possible means in pursuing this object of his wishes. He relied principally on the influence of women, whom he strove to please, and in which he succeeded. He caused his administration of Languedoc to be everywhere extolled. If, on attaining the post of minister, he did not obtain the favour which Necker had enjoyed, he had at least, in the eyes of the public, the merit of superseding Calonne. At first, he was not prime minister, but he soon became so. Seconded by M. de Lamoignon, keeper of the seals, an inveterate enemy to the parliaments, he commenced his career with considerable advantages.

The Notables, bound by the promises which they had made, readily consented to all that they had at first refused: land-tax, stamp-duty, suppression of the gratuitous services of vassals (*corvées*), provincial assemblies, were all cheerfully granted. It was not these measures themselves, but their author, whom they pretended to have resisted. Public opinion triumphed. Calonne was loaded with execrations; and the Notables, supported by the public suffrage, nevertheless regretted an honour gained at the cost of the greatest sacrifices. Had M. de Brienne known how to profit by the advantages of his position; had he actively proceeded with the execution of the measures assented to by the Notables; had he submitted them all at once and without delay to the parliament, at the instant when the adhesion of the higher orders seemed to be wrung from them; all would probably have been over: the parliament, pressed on all sides, would have consented to everything, and this concession, though partial and forced, would probably have retarded for a long time the struggle which afterwards took place.

Nothing of the kind, however, was done. By imprudent delays occasion was furnished for relapses; the edicts were submitted only one after another; the parliament had time to discuss, to gain courage, and to recover from the sort of surprise by which the Notables had been taken. It registered, after long discussions, the edict enacting the second abolition of the *corvées*, and another permitting the free exportation of corn. Its animosity was particularly directed against the land-tax; but it feared lest by a refusal it should enlighten the public, and show that its opposition was entirely selfish. It hesitated, when it was spared this embarrassment by the simultaneous presentation of the edict on the stamp-duty and the land-tax, and especially by opening the deliberations with the former. The parliament had thus an opportunity of refusing the first without entering into explanations respecting the second; and, in attacking the stamp-duty, which affected the majority of the payers of taxes, it seemed to defend the interest of the public. At a sitting which was attended by the peers, it denounced the abuses, the profligacy, and the prodigality of the court, and demanded statements of expenditure. A councillor, punning upon the *états* (statements) exclaimed, "*Ce ne sont pas des états, mais des états-généraux qu'il nous faut.*" "It is not statements, but States-general that we want." This unexpected demand struck everyone with astonishment. Hitherto people had resisted because they suffered; they had seconded all sorts of opposition, favourable or not to the popular cause, provided they were directed against the court, which was blamed for every evil. At the same time they did not well know what they ought to demand: they had always been so far from possessing any influence over the government, they had been so habituated to confine themselves to complaints, that they complained without conceiving the idea of acting, or of bringing about a revolution. The utterance of a single word presented an unexpected direction to the public mind: it was repeated by every mouth, and States-general were loudly demanded.

D'Espremenil, a young councillor, a vehement orator, an agitator without object, a demagogue in the parliaments, an aristocrat in the States-general, and who was declared insane by a decree of the Constituent Assembly—D'Espremenil showed himself on this occasion one of the most violent parliamentary declaimers. But the opposition was secretly conducted by Dupont, a young man of extraordinary abilities, and of a firm and persevering character, the only one perhaps who, amid these disturbances, had a specific object in view, and was solicitous to lead his company, the court, and the nation, to a very different goal from that of a parliamentary aristocracy.

The parliament was divided into old and young councillors. The first aimed at forming a counterpoise to the royal authority, in order to give consequence to their company. The latter, more ardent and more sincere, were desirous of introducing liberty into the state, yet without overturning the political system under which they were born. The parliament made an important admission: it declared that it had not the power to grant imposts, and that to the States-general alone belonged the right of establishing them; and it required the King to communicate to it statements of the revenues and the expenditure.

This acknowledgment of incompetence and usurpation—for the parliament had till then arrogated to itself the right of sanctioning taxes—could not but excite astonishment. The prelate minister, irritated at this opposition, instantly summoned the parliament to Versailles, and caused the two edicts to be registered in "a bed of justice." The parliament, on its return to Paris, remonstrated, and ordered an inquiry into the prodigalities of Calonne. A decision in council instantly annulled its decrees, and exiled it to Troves.

Such was the state of affairs on the 15th of August, 1787. The King's two brothers, Monsieur and the Count d'Artois, were sent, the one to the Court of Accounts and the other to the Court of Aids, to have the edicts registered there. The former, who had become popular on account of the opinions which he had expressed in the Assembly of the Notables, was hailed with acclamations by an immense multitude, and conducted back to the Luxembourg amidst universal plaudits. The Count d'Artois, who was known to have supported Calonne, was received with murmurs; his attendants were attacked, and it was found necessary to have recourse to the armed force.

The parliaments had around them numerous dependents, composed of lawyers, persons holding situations in the palace, clerks, and students; an active bustling class, ever ready to bestir themselves in their behalf. With these natural allies of the parliaments were united the capitalists, who dreaded a bankruptcy; the enlightened classes, who were devoted to all the opposers of power; and lastly, the multitude, which always sides with agitators. Serious disturbances took place, and the supreme authority had great difficulty to suppress them.

The parliament sitting at Troyes met every day and called causes. Neither advocates nor solicitors appeared, and justice was suspended, as it had been so many times during the preceding century. Meanwhile the magistrates became weary of their exile, and M. de Brienne was without money. He boldly maintained that he did not want any, and tranquilised the court, uneasy on this single point; but, destitute of supplies, and incapable of putting an end to his difficulties by an energetic resolution, he entered into negotiation with some of the members of the parliament. His conditions were a loan of four hundred and forty millions (of livres), payable by instalments, in four years, at the expiration of which the States-general should be convoked. At this rate Brienne was willing to renounce the two imposts, the objects of so much discord. Having made sure of some members, he imagined that he was sure of the whole company, and the parliament was recalled on the 10th of September.

A royal sitting was held on the 20th of the same month. The King went in person to present the edict enacting the creation of the successive loan and the convocation of the States-general in five years. No explanation had been given respecting the nature of this sitting, and it was not known whether it was "a bed of justice" or not. The looks of the members were gloomy, and a profound silence prevailed, when the Duke of Orleans rose with agitated countenance and all the signs of strong emotion; he addressed the King, and asked him if this sitting were "a bed of justice" or a free deliberation. "It is a royal sitting," replied the King. The councillors Freteau, Sabatier, and D'Espremenil spoke after the Duke of Orleans, and declaimed with their usual violence. The registration was immediately enforced: Freteau and Sabatier were exiled to the Hieres Islands, and the Duke of Orleans to Villers-Cotterets. The States-general were postponed for five years.

Such were the principal events of the year 1787. The year 1788 commenced with fresh hostilities. On the 4th of January the parliament passed a decree against *lettres de cachet*, and for the recall of exiled persons. The King cancelled this decree; the parliament confirmed it anew.

Meanwhile the Duke of Orleans, banished to Villers-Cotterets, could not endure his exile. This prince, in quarrelling with the court, had reconciled himself with public opinion, which was at first unfavourable to him. Destitute alike of the dignity of a prince and the firmness of a tribune (*see* Appendix B), he was incapable of enduring so slight a punishment, and, in order to obtain his recall, he descended to solicitations even to the Queen, his personal enemy.

Brienne was exasperated by obstacles, without possessing energy to overcome them. Feeble in Europe against Prussia, to which he sacrificed Holland, feeble in France against the Parliament and the grandees of the state, he had now no supporter but the Queen, and, moreover, was frequently checked in his operations by ill health. He neither knew how to suppress insurrection nor how to enforce the retrenchments decreed by the King; and, notwithstanding the rapidly-approaching exhaustion of the exchequer, he affected an inconceivable security. Meanwhile, amidst all these difficulties, he did not neglect to obtain new benefices for himself, and to heap new dignities upon his family.

Lamoignon, the keeper of the seals, a man of a stronger mind, but possessing less influence than the Archbishop of Toulouse, concerted with him a new plan for accomplishing the principal object, that of destroying the political power of the parliaments. It was of importance to keep it secret. Everything was prepared in silence: private letters were sent to the commandants of the provinces; the office where the edicts were printed was surrounded with guards. It was intended that the plan should not be known till the moment of its communication of the parliaments. That moment approached, and it was rumoured that an important political act was in preparation. D'Espremenil, the councillor, contrived to procure a copy of the edicts, by bribing one of the printer's men; he then repaired to the palace, summoned his colleagues to assemble, and boldly denounced the plan of the minister.

According to this plan, the too extensive authority of the parliament of Paris was to be abridged, by the establishment of six great *baillages* in its jurisdiction. The power of judging without appeal, and of registering the laws and edicts, was to be transferred to a plenary court, composed of peers, prelates, magistrates, and military officers; all appointed by the King. Even the captain of the guard was to have a deliberative voice in it. This plan attacked the judicial authority of the parliament, and utterly annihilated its political power. The company, struck with consternation, knew not what course to pursue. It could not deliberate upon a plan which had not been submitted to it; at the same time it was of importance that it should not suffer itself to be taken by surprise. In this embarrassment it had recourse to an expedient at once firm and adroit,—that of recapitulating and confirming in a decree all that it called constitutional laws of the monarchy, taking care to include in the number its own existence and rights. By this general measure it by no means forestalled the supposed projects of the government, and secured all that it wished to secure.

In consequence, it was declared, on the 5th of May, by the parliament of Paris:—

"That France was a monarchy governed by a king, according to the laws; and that among these laws several, which were fundamental, embraced and consecrated: 1. The right of the reigning house to the throne, from male to male, in the order of primogeniture; 2. The right of the nation to grant subsidies freely through the organ of the States-general, regularly convoked and composed; 3. The customs and capitulations of the provinces; 4. The irremovability of the magistrates; 5. The right of the courts to verify in each province the edicts of the King, and not to order the registration of them, unless they were conformable to the constitutive laws of the province, as well as to the fundamental laws of the state; 6. The right of each citizen not to be tried in any manner by other than his natural judges, who were those appointed by the law; and, 7, the right, without which all the others were useless, of not being arrested by any order whatever, unless to be delivered without delay into the hands of competent judges. The said court protested against all attacks which might be made upon the principles above expressed."

To this energetic resolution the minister replied in the usual way, always injudicious and ineffectual; he adopted violent measures against some of the members of the parliament. D'Espremenil and Goislart de Monsalbert, being apprised that they were threatened, sought refuge amidst the assembled parliament. An officer, Vincent d'Agoult, repaired thither at the head of a company; and, not knowing the persons of the magistrates designated, he called them by their names. The deepest silence at first pervaded the assembly: all the councillors then cried out that they were D'Espremenil. At length the real D'Espremenil declared who he was, and followed the officer ordered to arrest him. The tumult was then at its height; the populace accompanied the magistrates, hailing them with shouts of applause. Three days afterwards, the King, in a bed of justice, caused the edicts to be registered, and the assembled princes and peers exhibited an image of that plenary court which was to succeed the parliaments.

The Chatelet immediately issued a decree against the edicts. The parliament of Rennes declared all who should belong to the plenary court infamous. At Grenoble, the inhabitants defended their magistrates against two regiments. The troops themselves, excited to disobedience by the military noblesse, soon refused to act. When the commandant of Dauphiné assembled his colonels, to inquire if their soldiers were to be relied upon, all of them kept silence. The youngest, who was to speak first, replied that no reliance was to be placed on his, from the colonel downwards. To this resistance the minister opposed decrees of the great council, which cancelled the decisions of the sovereign courts, and he punished eight of them with exile.

The court, annoyed by the higher orders, which made war upon it in espousing the interests of the people and calling for their interference, had recourse, on its part, to the same means. It resolved to summon the *tiers-état* (the third estate) to its aid, as the kings of France had formerly done, to break up the feudal system. It then urged, with all its might, the convocation of the States-general. It ordered investigations respecting the mode of their assembling; it called upon writers and learned bodies to give their opinions; and, whilst the assembled clergy declared on its part that a speedy convocation was desirable, the court, accepting the challenge, suspended at the same time the meeting of the plenary court, and fixed the opening of the States-general for the 1st of

May, 1789. Then followed the retirement of the Archbishop of Toulouse, who, by bold plans feebly executed, had provoked a resistance which he ought either not to have excited or to have overcome. And on quitting office he left the exchequer in distress—the payment of the *rentes* of the Hôtel de Ville suspended—all the authorities in hostility—all the provinces in arms. As for himself, possessing an income of eight hundred thousand francs from benefices, the archbishopric of Sens, and a cardinal's hat, if he did not make the public fortune, he at least made his own. By his last piece of advice he recommended to the King to recall Necker to the ministry of the finances, that he might fortify himself with his popularity against oppositions which had become unconquerable.

It was during the two years 1787 and 1788 that the French were desirous to pass from vain theories to practice. The struggle between the highest authorities excited the wish, and furnished the occasion, to do so. During the whole course of the century, the parliament had attacked the clergy, and exposed its ultramontane predilections. After the clergy, it had attacked the court, condemned its abuses of power, and denounced its extravagance. Threatened with reprisals, and attacked, in its turn, in its existence, it had at length just restored to the nation prerogatives which the court would have wrested from it for the purpose of transferring them to an extraordinary tribunal. After having thus apprised the nation of its rights, it had exerted its energies in exciting and protecting insurrection. On the other hand, the high clergy in delivering their charges, the nobility in fomenting the disobedience of the troops, had joined their efforts to those of the magistracy, and summoned the people to arms in behalf of their privileges.

The court, pressed by these various enemies, had made but a feeble resistance. Aware of the necessity of acting, yet always deferring the moment for doing so, it had at times abolished some abuses, rather for the benefit of the exchequer than of the people, and then sunk again into inactivity. At length, finding itself attacked on all sides, observing that the higher orders were calling the people into the lists, it resolved to introduce them there itself by convoking the States-General. Hostile during the whole of the century to the philosophic spirit, it now appealed to the latter, and submitted the constitutions of the kingdom to its investigation. Thus the first authorities of the state exhibited the singular spectacle of usurpers disputing the possession of an object before the face of the rightful owner, and at last even calling upon him to act as judge between them.

Such was the state of affairs when Necker returned to the ministry. Confidence followed him; credit was instantly restored; the most urgent difficulties were removed. He provided, by means of expedients, for indispensable expenses, till the meeting of the States-general, the remedy that was universally called for.

The great questions relative to their organisation began to be discussed. It was asked what part the *tiers-état* would have to act there; whether it would appear as an equal or a supplicant; whether it would obtain a representation equal in number to that of the two higher orders; whether the discussions would be carried on by individuals or by orders; and whether the *tiers* would not have merely a single voice against the two voices of the nobility and clergy.

The first question discussed was that relative to the number of the deputies. Never had philosophic controversy of the eighteenth century excited such agitation. People's minds became warmed by the positive importance of the question. A keen, concise, energetic writer took, in this discussion, that place which the greatest geniuses of the age had occupied in the philosophical discussions. The Abbé Sieyes, in a book which gave a powerful impulse to the public mind, asked this question: "What is the *tiers-état*?" And he answered: "Nothing." "What ought it to be?" "Everything."

The states of Dauphiné assembled in spite of the court. The two higher orders, more adroit and more popular in that country than anywhere else, decided that the representation of the third estate should be equal to that of the nobility and the clergy. The parliament of

Paris, foreseeing already the consequence of its improvident provocations, perceived plainly that the *tiers-état* was not coming in as auxiliary, but as master; and, in registering the edict of convocation, it enjoined, as an express clause, the maintenance of the forms of 1614, which reduced the third order to a mere cipher. Having already rendered itself unpopular by the difficulties which it had thrown in the way of the edict that restored civil rights to Protestants, it was on that day completely unmasked, and the court fully revenged. It was the first to experience the instability of popular favour; but, if at a later period the nation might appear ungrateful towards chiefs whom it forsook one after another, on this occasion it had good reason to turn its back on the parliament, for that body stopped short before the nation had recovered any of its rights.

The court, not daring to decide these important questions itself, or rather desirous of depriving the two higher orders of their popularity for its own benefit, asked their opinion, with the intention of not adopting it, as it was probable that opinion should be unfavourable to the *tiers-état*. It summoned, therefore, a new Assembly of Notables, in which all the questions relative to the holding of States-general were brought forward. The discussions were warm; on the one hand great stress was laid on ancient traditions; on the other, on natural rights and reason. Even in going back to traditions, the cause of the *tiers-état* still had the advantage; for, in opposition to the forms of 1614 demanded by the higher orders, forms yet more ancient were adduced. Thus, in certain assemblies, and on certain points, the members had voted individually; sometimes they had deliberated by provinces, not by orders; frequently the deputies of the *tiers* had equalled in number the deputies of the nobility and clergy. Why then refer to ancient usages? Had not the powers of the state been in a continual revolution? The royal authority, at first sovereign, then vanquished and despoiled, raising itself again with the aid of the people, and again uniting all the powers in its own hands, exhibited a perpetual conflict and an ever-changing position. The clergy were told that if they were to take ancient times for their standard they would cease to be an order; the nobles, that the possessors of fiefs only were qualified to be elected, and that thus most of them would be excluded from the deputation; the parliaments themselves, that they were but unfaithful officers of royalty; lastly, all were assured that the French constitution had been but one long revolution, during which each power had successively predominated; that everything had been innovation, and that amid this vast conflict it was for reason alone to decide.

The *tiers-état* comprehended nearly the whole nation, all the useful, industrious, enlightened classes. If it possessed but a portion of the lands, at least it wrought them all; and, according to reason, it was not too much to allow to it a number of deputies equal to that of the two other orders.

The Assembly of Notables declared itself against what was called the doubling of the third estate. One of the government officers, that over which Monsieur, the king's brother, presided, voted for this doubling. The court, then, taking, as it said, into consideration the opinion of the minority, the sentiments expressed by several princes of the blood, the wishes of the three orders of Dauphiné, the demand of the provincial assemblies, the example of several countries of the kingdom, *the opinion of various public writers*, and the recommendations contained in a great number of addresses—the court ordained that the total number of the deputies should be at least a thousand; that it should be formed in a ratio composed of the population and the amount of taxes paid by each *baillage*, and that the number of the deputies of the *tiers-état* should be equal to that of the other two orders united.

This declaration excited universal enthusiasm. As it was attributed to Necker, it raised him in the favour of the nation, and gained him the increased enmity of the great. Still it decided nothing as to the vote by individuals or by orders, but it included it by implication; for it was useless to augment the number of votes if they were not to be counted; and it left the *tiers-état* to seize by main force what was refused to it at the moment. It therefore conveyed an idea of the weakness of the court, and of Necker himself. That court included an assemblage of inclinations which rendered any decisive result impossible. The King was moderate, equitable, studious, and too distrustful of his own abilities; loving the people, and readily listening to their complaints. He was nevertheless seized at times with superstitious terrors, and fancied that he beheld anarchy and impiety marching hand in hand with liberty and toleration. The philosophic spirit in its first flights could not but commit extravagances, and a timid and religious king could not help being alarmed at them. Overcome, at every step, by weakness, terror, and uncertainty, the unfortunate Louis XVI. resolved for his own part to make every sacrifice. Not knowing how to impose such conduct on others, the victim of his indulgence for the court, of his condescension to the Queen, he expiated all the faults which he had not committed, but which became his own because he winked at their commission. The Queen, engrossed by pleasure, dazzling all around her by her charms, was desirous that her husband should enjoy tranquillity, that the exchequer should be full, that the court and her subjects should adore her. Sometimes she concurred with the King for the purpose of effecting reforms, when the necessity for them appeared urgent; at others, on the contrary, when she conceived the supreme authority to be threatened, and her court friends despoiled, she stopped the King, removed the popular ministers, and destroyed at once the means and the hopes of improvement. She yielded more especially to the influence of a portion of the nobility who lived around the throne, fattening on favours and abuses. This court nobility was solicitous, no doubt, like the Queen herself, that the King should have wherewithal to supply a lavish profusion; and, from this motive, it was inimical to the parliaments when they refused taxes, but became their ally when they defended its privileges, by refusing, under specious pretexts, the territorial impost. Amidst these contrary influences the King, not daring to face difficulties, to condemn abuses, or to suppress them authoritatively, gave way by turns to the court and to public opinion, without satisfying either.

If, during the course of the eighteenth century, when the philosophers, assembled in an alley of the Tuileries, wished success to Frederick and the Americans, to Turgot and Necker—if, when they did not yet aspire to govern the state, but merely to enlighten princes, and foresaw at most the distant revolutions which the signs of disquiet and the absurdity of existing institutions fully authorised them to expect—if the King had spontaneously established some equality in the official appointments, and given some guarantees, all discontent would have been appeased for a long time, and Louis XVI. would have been as much adored as was Marcus Aurelius. But when all the authorities had been debased by a long struggle, and all the abuses unveiled by an Assembly of Notables; when the nation, called into the quarrel, had conceived the hope and the will to be something, that will became imperative. The States-general was promised to the nation, it demanded that an early time should be fixed for their convocation; when that time was near at hand, it insisted on the preponderance in them: this was refused; but, in the doubling of the representation it was furnished with the means of conquering that preponderance. Thus the government never yielded but partially, and when it could no longer resist; but then the strength of the nation had increased; it was aware of its power, and required all that it conceived itself capable of accomplishing. A continual resistance, irritating its ambition, must soon have the effect of rendering it insatiable. But even then, if a great minister, communicating somewhat of energy to the King, conciliating the Queen, bridling the privileged classes, had anticipated and satisfied at once the national expectations by giving of his own accord a free constitution; if he had gratified the impulse to act which the nation then felt, by summoning it immediately, not to reform the state but to discuss its annual interests in a ready constituted state; perhaps the conflict would not have taken place. But it would have been absolutely necessary to meet the difficulty instead of giving way to it, and, above all, to sacrifice numerous pretensions. It would have required a man of a strong conviction, and possessing a resolution equal to his conviction; and this man, no doubt, bold, energetic, perhaps passionate, would have alarmed the court, which desired no such person. In order to spare at one and the same time the public opinion and the old interests, the King had recourse to half-measures. He selected, as we have seen, a half-philosophic, half-energetic minister, and who possessed immense popularity, because at that time demi-popular intentions in an agent of power surpassed all the hopes and excited the enthusiasm of a people whom the demagogue spirit of its leaders was very soon afterwards incapable of satisfying.

Men's minds were in a universal ferment. Assemblies were formed throughout France, like those of England, and called by the same name, that of clubs. Nothing was discussed in them but the abuses to be abolished, the reforms to be effected, and the constitution to be established. A rigid inquiry into the state of the country produced irritation. Its state, political and economical, was in truth intolerable. There was nothing but privileges belonging to individuals, towns, provinces, and to trades themselves; nothing but shackles upon the industry and genius of man. Civil, ecclesiastical, and military dignities were exclusively reserved for certain classes, and in those classes for certain individuals. A man could not embrace a profession unless upon certain titles and certain pecuniary conditions. The towns possessed their privileges for the apportioning, the assessment, and the levying of taxes, and for the choice of magistrates. The very pensions converted by the survivors into family properties, scarcely allowed the monarch to show any preferences. He had nothing left at his disposal but a few pecuniary gifts, and he had even been obliged to quarrel with the Duke de Coigny about the abolition of a useless place. All was therefore monopolized by a few hands, and the burdens bore upon a single class. The nobility and the clergy possessed nearly two-thirds of the landed property. The other third, belonging to the people, paid taxes to the king, a multitude of feudal dues to the nobility, the tithe to the clergy, and was, moreover, liable to the devastations of noble sportsmen and their game. The taxes on consumption weighed heavily on the great mass, and consequently on the people. The mode in which they were levied was vexatious: the gentry might be in arrear with impunity; the people, on the other hand, ill-treated and imprisoned, were doomed to suffer in body, in default of goods. It subsisted therefore by the sweat of the brow; it defended with its blood the upper classes of society, without being able to subsist itself. The *bourgeoisie*, industrious, enlightened, less miserable certainly than the peasantry, but enriching the kingdom by its industry, reflecting lustre upon it by its talents, obtained none of the advantages to which it had a right. Justice, administered in some of the provinces by the gentry, in the royal jurisdictions by magistrates who purchased their offices, was slow, frequently partial, always ruinous, and particularly atrocious in criminal cases. Individual liberty was violated by *lettres de cachet*, and the liberty of the press by the royal censors. Lastly, the state, ill-defended abroad, betrayed by the mistresses of Louis XV., compromised by the weakness of the ministers of Louis XVI., had recently been dishonoured in Europe by the disgraceful sacrifice of Holland and Poland.

The popular masses began already to put themselves in motion; disturbances had several times broken out during the struggle of the parliaments, and especially on the retirement of the Archbishop of Toulouse. That minister had been burned in effigy; the armed force had been insulted and even attacked; the magistracy had been backward in prosecuting the rioters, who supported their cause. The public mind, agitated by these events, full of the confused idea of a speedy revolution, was in a continual ferment. The parliaments and the higher orders already saw the arms which they had given to the people directed against themselves. In Bretagne, the nobility had opposed the doubling of the third estate, and had refused to elect deputies; the *bourgeoisie*, who had so powerfully served against the court, then turned against them, and sanguinary conflicts ensued. The court conceiving itself not sufficiently revenged on the Breton nobility, refused them its aid, and, on the contrary, imprisoned some of their number who came to Paris for the purpose of remonstrating.

The elements themselves seemed to be let loose. A hailstorm, on the 13th of July, had made havoc among the crops, and was likely to increase the difficulty of supplying Paris, especially amidst the troubles that were preparing. All the activity of commerce was scarcely sufficient to collect the quantity of provisions necessary for that great capital; and it might naturally be expected that it would soon be very difficult to subsist it, when confidence should be shaken and the communications interrupted by political disturbances. Ever since the cruel winter which had succeeded the disasters of Louis XIV., and immortalized the charity of Fénélon, so severe a season had not been known as that of 17881789. The beneficence which was then displayed in the most affecting manner was not sufficient to alleviate the wretchedness of the people. A great number of vagabonds, without profession and without resources, thronged from all parts of France, and paraded their indigence and their nakedness from Versailles to Paris. At the slightest rumour, they eagerly came forward to profit by chances, which are always favourable to those who have everything to gain, even to the subsistence for the passing day.

Thus every thing concurred to produce a revolution. An entire century had contributed to unveil abuses and to carry them to excess; two years to stir up insurrection and to exasperate the popular masses by making them interfere in the quarrel of the privileged orders. In short, natural disasters, and a fortuitous concurrence of various circumstances, brought on the catastrophe, the epoch of which might have been deferred, but which was sure to happen sooner or later.

It was amidst these circumstances that the elections took place. They were tumultuous in some provinces, active everywhere, and very quiet in Paris, where great unanimity prevailed. Lists were distributed, and people strove to promote concord and a good understanding. Tradesmen, lawyers, literary men, astonished to find themselves assembled together for the first time, raised themselves up by degrees to liberty. In Paris, they re-appointed themselves the *bureaux* formed by the King, and without changing the persons, asserted their power by confirming them. The learned Bailly quitted his retreat at Chaillot: a stranger to intrigues, and deeply impressed with his noble mission, he proceeded alone and on foot to the assembly. He paused by the way on the terrace of the Feuillans. A young man, whom he did not know, respectfully accosted him. "You will be returned," said he. "I cannot tell," replied Bailly; "that honour ought neither to be solicited nor refused." The modest academician resumed his walk, repaired to the assembly, and was chosen successively elector and deputy.

The election of the Count de Mirabeau was stormy; rejected by the nobility, supported by the *tiers-état*, he agitated Provence, his native country, and it was not long before he showed himself at Versailles.

The court had no wish to influence the elections. It was not displeased to see a great number of *curés* returned, reckoning upon their opposition to the high ecclesiastical dignitaries, and at the same time upon their respect for the throne. It is true that it did not foresee all that was to happen; and in the deputies of the *tiers* it perceived rather adversaries to the nobility than to itself. The Duke of Orleans was accused of taking active steps to procure the nomination of himself and his partisans. Already numbered among the enemies of the court, the ally of the parliaments, and called for as leader, with or without his consent, by the popular party, he was accused of various underhand practices. A deplorable scene took place in the Fauxbourg St. Antoine, and, as people are fond of giving an author to all events, it was laid to his charge. Reveillon, a manufacturer of stained paper, who had an extensive manufactory, improving our industry and furnishing employment to three hundred workmen, was accused of an intention to reduce their wages to one-half. The populace threatened to burn his house. Means were found to disperse them, but they returned on the following day; the house was broken into, set on fire, and destroyed. Notwithstanding the threats held out on the first day by the assailants, notwithstanding the meeting agreed upon for the second, the authorities were very late before they began to act, and then they acted with extreme severity. They waited till the people had made themselves masters of the house, they then attacked them with fury, and were obliged to slaughter a great number of those ferocious and intrepid men, who afterwards showed themselves on all occasions, and received the name of *brigands*.

All the parties which were already formed accused each other; the court was reproached with its at first tardy and afterwards cruel proceedings; it was supposed that it wished to leave the people time to act that it might make an example and exercise its troops.

The money found on the destroyers of Reveillon's house, and the expressions that dropped from some of them, led to the conjecture that they were urged on by a secret hand. The enemies of the popular party accused the Duke of Orleans of a wish to try his revolutionary bands.

That prince had been endowed with excellent qualities. He had inherited immense wealth; but, addicting himself to dissolute habits, he had abused all these gifts of nature and of fortune. Without consistency of character, alternately regardless of public opinion and greedy of popularity, he was bold and ambitious one day, docile and absent on the morrow. Having quarrelled with the Queen, he had become an enemy to the court. When parties began to form themselves, he had suffered his name to be employed, and, it is said, his wealth also. Flattered with the vague prospect before him, he was active enough to draw accusation on himself, though not to ensure success; and his partisans, if they entertained any serious plans, must have been driven to despair by his inconstant ambition.

The moment of the convocation at length arrived. In this common danger, the higher orders, creeping close to the court, had grouped themselves around the princes of the blood and the Queen. They strove by flattery to gain the country gentlemen, and in their absence they ridiculed their clownishness. The clergy endeavoured to gain over the plebeians of its order, and the military noblesse those belonging to the same class with itself. The parliaments, which had expected to play the principal part in the States-general, began to apprehend that their ambition had miscalculated. The deputies of the *tiers-état*, strong in the superiority of their talents, in the energetic eloquence of their speeches, encouraged by continual intercommunication, nay, spurred on by the doubts which many had conceived respecting the success of their efforts, had taken the firm resolution not to yield.

The King alone, who had not enjoyed a moment's repose since the commencement of his reign, regarded the States-general as the termination of his embarrassments. Jealous of his authority, rather for the sake of his children, to whom he deemed it his duty to transmit this patrimony intact, than for his own, he was not displeased to restore a portion of it to the nation, and to throw upon it the difficulties of the government. Accordingly, it was with joy that he made preparations for this grand assemblage. A hall had been hastily got ready; the costumes were determined upon, and an humiliating badge had been imposed on the *tiers-état*. Men are not less jealous of their dignity than of their rights: with a very just pride, the instructions forbade the deputies to condescend to any degrading ceremonial. This new fault of the court originated, like many others, in the desire to preserve at least the symbols when the realities had ceased to exist. It could not but produce a deep irritation at a moment when, before attacking, the parties began to measure one another with their eyes.

On the 4th of May, the day of the opening, a solemn procession took place. The King, the three orders, all the great dignitaries of the state, repaired to the church of Notre-Dame. The court had displayed extraordinary magnificence. The two higher orders were splendidly dressed. Princes, dukes and peers, gentlemen, prelates, were clad in purple, and wore hats with plumes of feathers. The deputies of the *tiers-état*, covered with plain black cloaks, came next; and, notwithstanding their modest exterior, they seemed strong in their number and their prospects. It was remarked that the Duke of Orleans, placed in the rear of the nobility, chose rather to lag behind, and to mingle with the foremost deputies of the third estate.

This national, military, and religious pomp—those pious chants—those martial instruments—and, above all, the importance of the event—deeply moved all hearts. The discourse delivered by the Bishop of Nanci, full of generous sentiments, was enthusiastically applauded, notwithstanding the sacredness of the place and the presence of the King. Great assemblages elevate us. They detach us from ourselves and attach us to others. A general intoxication was diffused, and all at once many a heart felt its animosities subside, and became filled for a moment with humanity and patriotism. (*See* Appendix C.)

The opening of the States-general took place on the following day, May 5, 1789. The King was seated on an elevated throne, the Queen beside him, the court in stalls, the two higher orders on both sides, the *tiers-état* at the farther end of the hall, and on lower seats. A movement arose at the sight of the Count de Mirabeau; but his look, his step, awed the assembly. The *tiers-état* remained covered like the other orders, notwithstanding the established custom. The King delivered an address, in which he recommended disinterestedness to some, prudence to others, and professed to all his love for his people. Barentin, the keeper of the seals, then spoke, and was followed by Necker, who read a memorial on the state of the kingdom, in which he treated at great length of the finances, admitted a deficit of fifty-sis: millions, and wearied by his prolixity those whom he did not offend by his lessons.

On the next day, the deputies of each order were directed to the place allotted to them. Besides the common hall, which was sufficiently spacious to hold the three orders united, two other halls had been erected for the nobility and the clergy. The common hall was assigned to the *tiers*; and it thus had the advantage, whilst in its own place of meeting, of being in that of the States. The first business was the verification of the powers of the members. It became a question whether this should take place in common or by separate orders. The deputies of the *tiers*, alleging that it was of importance to each portion of the States-general to satisfy itself of the legitimacy of the two others, insisted on the verification in common. The nobility and the clergy, desirous of keeping up the division of orders, maintained that each ought to constitute itself apart. This question had nothing to do with that of individual votes, for they might verify their powers in common and afterwards vote separately, but it nearly resembled it; and on the very first day it produced a division, which it was easy to foresee, and which might have been as easily prevented by putting an end to the dispute beforehand. But the court never had the courage either to deny or to grant what was just, and, besides, it hoped to reign by dividing.

The deputies of the *tiers-état* remained assembled in the general hall, abstaining from taking any measure, and waiting, as they said, to be joined by their colleagues. The nobility and the clergy, retiring to their respective halls, proceeded to deliberate on the verification. The clergy voted the separate verification by a majority of 133 to 114, and the nobility by a majority of 188 to 114. The *tiers-état*, persisting in its inaction, pursued, on the morrow, the same course as on the preceding day. It made a point of avoiding any measure which could cause it to be considered as constituting a separate order. For this reason, in sending a deputation of its members to the other two chambers, it abstained from giving them any express mission. These members were sent to the nobility and clergy to inform them that the *tiers-état* was waiting for them in the common hall. The nobility were not sitting at the moment; the clergy were assembled, and offered to appoint commissioners to settle the differences that had arisen. They actually appointed them, and invited the nobility to do the same. In this contest the clergy manifested a very different spirit from the nobility. Among all the privileged classes it had suffered most from the attacks of the eighteenth century. Its political existence had been disputed; it was divided, owing to the great number of its *curés*; besides, its professional character was that of moderation and the spirit of peace. Accordingly, as we have just seen, it offered a sort of mediation.

The nobility, on the contrary, declined it, by refusing to appoint commissioners. Less prudent than the clergy, more confident in its rights, conceiving itself not bound to moderation but to valour, it vented itself in refusals and threats. These men, who never excused any passion in others, gave the reins to all their own passions, and, like all assemblies, they yielded to the domination of the most violent spirits. Casalés and d'Espréménil, recently ennobled, made the most indiscreet motions, and, after preparing them in a private meeting, procured their adoption in general assembly. In vain did a minority, composed of men more prudent or more prudently ambitious, strive to enlighten these nobles. They would not listen to any thing. They talked of fighting and dying, and they added, for the laws and justice. The *tiers-état*, immoveable, endured with patience every insult. Though irritated, it was silent, conducted itself with the prudence and firmness of all powers which are commencing their career, and received the applause of the tribunes, originally destined for the court, but soon taken possession of by the public.

Several days had already elapsed: the clergy had laid snares for the *tiers-état* by inciting it to certain acts which would have given it the character of a constituted order. It had, however, constantly refused to comply; and, taking only indispensable measures of internal police, it had confined itself to the election of a dean and assistants for the purpose of collecting opinions. It refused to open the letters addressed to it, and it declared that it formed not an order, but *a meeting of citizens assembled by a legitimate authority to wait for other citizens.*

The nobility, after refusing to appoint conciliatory commissioners, at length consented to send deputies to arrange matters with the other orders. But their mission was rendered useless, since it charged them at the same time to declare that it persisted in its decision of the 6th of May, which enjoined the separate verification. The clergy, on the contrary, adhering to its part, had suspended the verification which it had at first commenced in its own chamber, and declared itself not constituted, awaiting the conferences of the conciliatory commissioners. The conferences were opened: the clergy was silent; the deputies of the commons argued their point with calmness, those of the nobility with warmth. Both parties returned soured by the dispute; and the *tiers-état*, determined not to give way, was doubtless not displeased to learn that all compromise was impossible. The nobility was assured every day by its commissioners that they had the advantage, and this served to heighten its exaltation. By a transient gleam of prudence, the first two orders declared that they renounced their pecuniary privileges. The *tiers-état* accepted the concession, but persisted in its refusal to proceed to business, still requiring the common verification.

The conferences yet continued, when it was at length proposed, by way of accommodating the matter, that the powers should be verified by commissioners chosen from the three orders. The deputies of the nobility declared in its name its dissent from this arrangement, and retired without appointing any new conference. Thus the negociation was broken off. The same day the nobility passed a resolution by which it declared anew that for this session the verification should take place separately, and that it should be left for the States to determine upon some other mode in future.

This resolution was communicated to the commons on the 27th of May. They had been assembled ever since the 5th; twenty-two days had consequently elapsed, during which nothing had been done. It was high time to come to a determination. Mirabeau, who gave the impulse to the popular party (*See* Appendix D), observed that it was time to decide upon something, and to commence their labours for the public welfare, which had been too long delayed. He proposed, therefore, in consequence of the resolution passed by the nobility, to send a message to the clergy, in order to obtain an immediate explanation from it, and to ascertain whether it would or would not meet the commons. The proposal was immediately adopted. Target, the deputy, proceeded at the head of a numerous deputation, to the hall of the clergy. "The gentlemen of the commons," said he, "invite the gentlemen of the clergy, IN THE NAME OR THE GOD OF PEACE, and for the national interest, to meet them in the hall of the assembly, to consult upon the means of effecting the concord so necessary at this moment for the public welfare." The clergy was struck with these solemn words. A great number of its members answered them with acclamations, and would have instantly complied with this invitation, had they not been prevented; and the reply given to the deputies of the commons was, that it would deliberate on the subject. On the return of the deputation, the inexorable *tiers-état* determined to await, without breaking up, the answer of the clergy. As this answer did not arrive, a message was sent that the commons were waiting for it. The clergy complained of being hurried, and requested to be allowed the necessary time. The *tiers-état* replied with moderation that the clergy might take its own time, and that the commons would wait, if requisite, the whole day and the whole night.

The situation was difficult. The clergy knew that after its answer the commons would fall to work, and adopt a decisive course. It wished to temporise, in order to concert with the court. It required time till the following day, which was granted with regret. Next day, the King resolved, in accordance with the wishes of the higher orders, to interfere. At this moment, all the animosities between the court and the higher orders began to be forgotten, at the sight of that popular power which rose with such rapidity. The King at length appeared, and invited the three orders to resume their conferences, in the presence of his keeper of the seals. The *tiers-état*, notwithstanding all that has been said of its projects, upon judgments formed after the events, did not extend its wishes beyond moderate monarchy. Knowing the intentions of Louis XVI., it was full of respect for him: and, unwilling to injure its cause by any wrong step, it replied that, out of deference to the King, it consented to renew the conferences, though, in consequence of the declaration of the nobility, it could not but consider them as useless. To this reply it annexed an address, which it charged its dean to deliver to the prince. This dean was Bailly, a simple and virtuous man, an illustrious and modest cultivator of the sciences, who had been suddenly transported from the quiet studies of his closet into the midst of civil broils. Elected to the presidency over a great assembly, he had been alarmed at his new office, had deemed himself unworthy to fill it, and undertaken it solely from a sense of duty. But, raised all at once to liberty, he found within him an unexpected presence of mind and firmness. Amid so many conflicts, he caused the majesty of the assembly to be respected, and represented it with all the dignity of virtue and of reason.

Bailly had the greatest difficulty to penetrate to the King. As he insisted on being introduced, the courtiers reported that he had not even paid respect to the grief of the monarch, afflicted by the death of the dauphin. He was at length presented, contrived to avoid every humiliating ceremonial, and displayed equal firmness and respect. The King received him graciously, but without entering into any explanation of his intentions.

The government, having decided on making some sacrifices to obtain money, designed, by opposing the orders, to become their umpire, to wrest from the nobility its pecuniary privileges with the assistance of the *tiers-état*, and to check the ambition of the latter by means of the nobility. As for the nobility, having no need to concern itself about the embarrassments of the administration, caring only for the sacrifices which were likely to be wrung from it, it hoped to bring about a dissolution of the States-general, and thus to frustrate the object of their convocation. The commons, whom the court and the higher orders would not recognise by that title, were incessantly acquiring fresh strength, and, being resolved to brave all dangers, were anxious not to let slip an opportunity which might never occur.

The conferences demanded by the King took place. The commissioners of the nobility raised all sorts of difficulties about the title of commons which the *tiers-état* had assumed, and about the form and signature of the minutes (*procès-verbal*). At length they entered upon discussion, and they were almost reduced to silence by the reasons urged against them, when Necker, in the name of the King, proposed a new mode of conciliation. Each order was to examine the powers separately, and to communicate them to the others. In case difficulties should arise, commissioners should report upon them to each chamber, and if the decision of the different orders disagreed, the King was to judge definitively. Thus the court would settle the dispute to its own advantage. The conferences were immediately suspended to obtain the adhesion of the orders. The clergy accepted the plan purely and simply. The nobility at first received it favourably; but, urged by its usual instigators, it rejected the advice of its most discreet members, and modified the project of conciliation. From that day must be dated all its disasters.

The commons, apprised of this resolution, waited till it should be communicated to them in order to explain themselves in their turn; but the clergy, with its ordinary cunning, desirous of bringing them into bad odour with the nation, sent them a deputation to invite them to take into consideration, along with it, the distress of the people which was daily increasing, that they might lose no time in providing together against the dearth and high price of provisions. The commons, who would have exposed themselves he popular odium if they had appeared indifferent to such a proposal, opposed craft with craft, and replied that, deeply impressed with the same duties, they awaited the clergy in the great hall, in order to deliberate with it on this important subject. The nobility then arrived, and solemnly communicated its resolution to the commons. It adopted, it said, the plan of conciliation, persisting, however, in the separate verification, and referring to the united orders and to the supreme jurisdiction of the King such difficulties only as might arise respecting the entire deputations of a whole province.

This resolution put an end to all the embarrassments of the commons. Obliged either to yield or to declare war single-handed against the higher orders and the throne, if the plan of conciliation had been adopted, they were relieved from the necessity of explanation, as the plan had been accepted only with important alterations. The moment was decisive. To give way on the separate verification was not, indeed, giving way on the vote by order; but to betray weakness once was to be weak for ever. They must submit to act nearly the part of a cipher, give money to power, be content with the abolition of a few abuses, when they saw the possibility of regenerating the state, or take a strong resolution and seize by force a portion of the legislative power. This was the first revolutionary act, but the assembly did not hesitate.

In consequence, all the minutes (*procès-verbaux*) being signed and the conferences finished, Mirabeau rose: "Any plan of conciliation rejected by one party," said he, "can no longer be examined by the other. A month is past; it is time to take a decisive step: a deputy of Paris has an important motion to make—let us hear him." Mirabeau, having opened the deliberation by his audacity, introduced to the tribune Sieyes, a man of a comprehensive mind, systematic and rigorous in his deductions. Sieyes in a few words recapitulated and explained the motives of the conduct of the commons. They had waited, and had acceded to all the conciliations proposed; their long condescension was unavailing; they could delay no longer without failing in their duty; they ought consequently to send a last invitation to the other two orders, to join them for the purpose of commencing the verification. This proposition, based on sufficient motives (*See* Appendix E), was received with enthusiasm; it was even in contemplation to summon the two orders to meet within an hour. The period, however, was prorogued. The following day, Thursday, being devoted to religious solemnities, it was postponed till Friday. On Friday, the last invitation was communicated. The two orders replied that they would consider of it, and the King that he would make known his intentions. The call of the *baillages* began: on the first day, three *curés* attended and were hailed with applause; on the second, six arrived; and on the third and fourth ten, among whom was the abbé Gregoire.

During the call of the *baillages* and the verification of the powers, a serious dispute arose concerning the title which the assembly was to assume. Mirabeau proposed that of Representatives of the *French People*; Mounier that of *Deliberative Majority in the absence of the Minority*; Legrand that of *National Assembly*. This last was adopted, after a very long discussion, which lasted till the night of the 16th of June. It was one o'clock in the morning, and it became a question whether the assembly should constitute itself before it broke up, or should defer that business till the following day. One portion of the deputies wished that not a moment should be lost, that they might acquire a legal character which should command the respect of the court. A small number, wishing to impede the operations of the assembly, became extremely violent, and uttered furious cries. The two parties, ranged on the two sides a long table, reciprocally threatened each other. Bailly, placed at the centre, was called upon by the one to adjourn the assembly, by the other to put the motion for constituting themselves to the vote. Unshaken amidst shouts and abuse, he continued for more than an hour motionless and silent. The weather was tempestuous; the wind blew with violence into the hall, and added to the tumult. At length the brawlers withdrew. Bailly, then addressing the assembly, which had recovered its tranquillity on the retirement of those by whom it had been disturbed, recommended it to defer till daylight the important act which was proposed. His advice was adopted, and the assembly broke up applauding his firmness and prudence.

Accordingly, on the 17th, the proposition was taken into consideration, and, by a majority of 491 votes against 90, the commons constituted themselves the National Assembly. Sieyes, again charged to report the motives of this determination, did it with his accustomed precision.

"The assembly, deliberating after the verification of the powers, ascertains that it is already composed of representatives sent directly by ninety-six hundredths, at least, of the nation. Such a mass of deputation could not remain inactive on account of the deputies of certain *baillages* or of certain classes of citizens; for the absent, *who have been called*, cannot prevent the present from exercising the plenitude of their rights, especially when the exercise of those rights is an urgent, an imperative duty.

"Moreover, as it belongs only to the verified representatives to concur in the national will, and as all the verified representatives are to be admitted into this assembly, it is further indispensable to conclude that it belongs to it, and to it alone, to interpret and to represent the general will of the nation.

"There cannot exist any veto, any negative power, between the throne and the assembly.

"The assembly, therefore, declares that the general labour of the national restoration can and ought to be begun by the deputies present, and that they ought to prosecute it without interruption and without impediment.

"The denomination of National Assembly is the only one suitable to the assembly in the present state of things, as well because the members who compose it are the only representatives legitimately and publicly known and verified, as because they are sent by nearly the whole of the nation; and, lastly, because, the representation being one and indivisible, none of the deputies, for whatever order or class he has been elected, has a right to exercise those functions separately from this assembly.

"The assembly will never relinquish the hope of collecting in its bosom all the deputies that are now absent; it will not cease to call them to fulfil the obligation imposed upon them to concur in the holding of the States-general. At whatever moment the absent deputies present themselves during the session that is about to be opened, it declares beforehand, that it will be ready to receive them and to share with them, after the verification of their powers, the series of important labours which are to accomplish the regeneration of France."

Immediately after passing this resolution (*arrêté*), the assembly, desiring at once to perform an act of its power and to prove that it had no intention to impede the course of the administration, legalised the levy of the taxes, though imposed without the national consent. With a presentiment of its separation, it added that they should cease to be levied from the day on which it should be broken up: foreseeing, moreover, a bankruptcy, the expedient left to power for putting an end to the financial embarrassments, and, dispensing with the national concurrence, it satisfied prudence and honour by placing the creditors of the state under the safeguard of French integrity. Lastly, it announced that it should immediately direct its attention to the causes of the dearth and of the public distress.

These measures, which displayed equal courage and ability, produced a deep impression. The court and the higher orders were alarmed at such courage and energy. Meanwhile, the clergy was tumultuously deliberating whether it should join the commons. The multitude awaited outside the hall the result of its deliberation; the *curés* at length carried the point, and it was learnt that the union had been voted by a majority of 149 votes to 115. Those who had voted for the junction were received with transports of applause; the others were abused and insulted by the populace.

This moment was destined to bring about a reconciliation between the court and the aristocracy. The danger was equal for both. The last revolution was as prejudicial to the King; as to the two higher orders themselves, whom the commons declared that they could dispense with. The aristocracy immediately threw itself at the feet of the King. The Duke of Luxembourg, the Cardinal de la Rochefoucauld, the Archbishop of Paris, implored him to repress the audacity of the *tiers-état*, and to support their rights, which were attacked. The Parliament proposed to him to do without the States, promising to assent to all the taxes. The King was surrounded by the princes and the Queen; this was more than was requisite for his weakness: they hurried him off to Marty in order to extort from him a vigorous measure.

Necker, the minister, attached to the popular cause, confined himself to useless remonstrances, which the King thought just when his mind was left free, but the effect of which the court soon took care to destroy. As soon as he perceived the necessity for the interference of the royal authority, he formed a plan which, to his courage, appeared very bold. He proposed that the monarch, in a royal sitting, should command the union of the orders, but only for measures of general interest; that he should assume to himself the sanction of all resolutions adopted by the States-general; that he should condemn beforehand every institution hostile to moderate monarchy, such as that of a single assembly; lastly, that he should, promise the abolition of privileges, the equal admission of all Frenchmen to civil and military appointments, &c. As Necker had not had the energy to outstrip time for such a plan, so likewise he had not sufficient to ensure its execution.

The council had followed the King to Marly. There Necker's plan, at first approved, was subjected to discussion; all at once a note was delivered to the King; the council was suspended, resumed, and adjourned till the following day, in spite of the necessity for the utmost dispatch. On the morrow, fresh members were added to the council; the King's brothers were of the number. Necker's plan was modified; he resisted, made some concessions, but finding himself vanquished, returned to Versailles. A page came three times bringing him notes containing new modifications; his plan was wholly disfigured, and the royal sitting was fixed for the 22nd of June.

It was as yet but the 20th, and already the hall of the States was shut up, under the pretext that preparations were requisite for the presence of the King. These preparations might have been made in half a day; but the clergy had deliberated the day before upon joining the commons, and it was desirable to prevent this junction. An order from the King instantly adjourned the sittings till the 22nd. Bailly, conceiving that he was bound to obey the assembly, which, on Friday, the 19th, had adjourned to the next day, Saturday, repaired to the door of the hall. It was surrounded by soldiers of the French guard, who had orders to refuse admittance to every one. The officer on duty received Bailly with respect, and allowed him access to a court for the purpose of drawing up a protest. Some young hotheaded deputies would have forced their way through the sentries; Bailly hastened to the spot, appeased them, and took them with him, that the generous officer, who executed the orders of authority with such moderation, might not be compromised. The deputies collected tumultuously; they persisted in assembling; some proposed to hold a sitting under the very windows of the King, others proposed the Tennis-Court. To the latter they instantly repaired; the master cheerfully gave it up to them.

The hall was spacious, but the walls were dark and bare. There were no seats. An arm-chair was offered to the president, who refused it, and chose rather to stand with the assembly; a bench served for a desk; two deputies were stationed at the door as door-keepers, and were soon relieved by the keeper of the place, who came and offered his services. The populace thronged around, and the deliberation commenced. Complaints were raised on all sides against this suspension of the sittings, and various expedients were proposed to prevent it in future. The agitation increased, and the extreme parties began to work upon the imaginations of their hearers. It was proposed to repair to Paris; this motion, hailed with enthusiasm, was warmly supported: and they began to talk of proceeding thither in a body and on foot. Bailly was apprehensive that violence might be offered to the assembly by the way; dreading, moreover, a rupture, he opposed the scheme. Mounier then proposed to the deputies to bind themselves by oath not to separate before the establishment of a constitution. This proposal was received with transport; the form of the oath was soon agreed upon. Bailly claimed the honour of being the first to take it, and read the form, which was as follows: "You take a solemn oath never to separate, and to assemble wherever circumstances shall require, till the constitution of the kingdom is established and founded on a solid basis." This form, pronounced in a loud and intelligible voice, was heard outside the building. All lips instantly repeated the oath; all hands were outstretched towards Bailly, who, standing and motionless, received this solemn engagement to ensure by laws the exercise of the national rights. The crowd instantly raised loud shouts of *Vive l'Assemblée! vive le Roi!* as if to prove that, without any feeling of anger or animosity, but from duty, it reclaimed what was its due. The deputies then proceeded to sign the declaration which they had just made. One only, Martin d'Auch, added to his name the word opposer. A great tumult took place around him. Bailly, in order to be heard, mounted upon a table, addressed the deputy with moderation, and represented to him that he had a right to refuse his signature, but not to form an opposition. The deputy persisted; and the assembly, out of respect for its liberty, allowed the word to stand and to be inserted in the minutes.

This new act of energy excited the apprehensions of the nobility, who went on the following day to lay their lamentations at the King's feet, to excuse themselves in some measure for the restrictions which they had introduced into the plan of conciliation, and to solicit his assistance. The noble minority protested against this step, maintaining with reason that it was no longer time to solicit the royal interference, after having so unseasonably refused it. This minority, too little attended to, was composed of forty-seven members, among whom were enlightened military officers and magistrates—the Duke de Liancourt, a generous friend to his King and to liberty; the Duke de la Rochefoucauld, distinguished for inflexible virtue and great abilities; Lally-Tollendal, already celebrated for his father's misfortunes and his eloquent reclamations; Clermont-Tonnerre, remarkable for his eloquence; the brothers Lameth, young colonels, known for their intelligence and their bravery; Duport, already noticed for his extraordinary capacity and firmness of character; and lastly, the Marquis de la Fayette, the defender of American freedom, and combining with French vivacity the perseverance and the simplicity of Washington.

Intrigues retarded all the operations of the court. The sitting, at first fixed for Monday the 22nd, was postponed till the 23rd. A note written very late to Bailly, and at the termination of the great council, acquainted him with this postponement, and proved the agitation which pervaded all minds. Necker had resolved not to attend the sitting, that he might not sanction by his presence plans which he disapproved.

Petty means, the ordinary resource of a feeble authority, were employed to prevent the meeting of Monday the 22nd. The princes hired the Tennis-Court for the purpose of playing on that day. The assembly repaired to the church of St. Louis, where it received the majority of the clergy, with the Archbishop of Vienne at its head. This junction, marked by the utmost dignity, excited the greatest joy. The clergy came, it was said, to submit to the common verification.

The following day, the 23rd, was that fixed for the royal sitting. The deputies of the commons were to enter by a side-door, a different one from that reserved for the nobility and clergy. If violence could not be employed, they were not spared humiliations. They waited a long time exposed to the rain: the president was obliged to knock at the door; it was not opened. He knocked repeatedly, and was told that it was not yet time. The deputies were about to retire, when Bailly again knocked. The door was at length opened; the deputies entered, and found the two higher orders in possession of their seats, which they had been desirous to secure by occupying them beforehand. The sitting was not, like that of the 5th of May, at once majestic and touching from a certain effusion of sentiments and hopes. A numerous soldiery, a sullen silence, distinguished it from the former solemnity. The deputies of the commons had resolved to keep the most profound silence. The King addressed the assembly, and betrayed his weakness by using expressions far too energetic for his character. He was made to launch reproaches, and to issue commands. He enjoined the separation into orders; annulled the preceding resolutions (*arrêtés*) of the *tiers-état*, promising to sanction the abdication of the pecuniary privileges when they should be relinquished by the holders. He maintained all the feudal rights, both useful and honorary, as inviolable property. He did not order the meeting of the three estates on matters of general interest, but held out hopes of it from the moderation of the higher orders. Thus he enforced the obedience of the commons, and contented himself with presuming that of the aristocracy. He left the nobility and clergy judges of what specially concerned them, and concluded with saying, that if he met with fresh obstacles he would singly establish the welfare of his people, and that he considered himself as its sole representative. This tone, this language, deeply incensed the minds of the commons, not against the King who had feebly represented passions not his own, but against the aristocracy whose instrument he was.

As soon as he had finished this address, he ordered the assembly to separate immediately. The nobility followed him, together with part of the clergy. The majority of the ecclesiastical deputies remained; the deputies of the commons, without moving, preserved profound silence. Mirabeau, who put himself forward on all occasions, then rose. "Gentlemen," said he, "I admit that what you have must heard might be the salvation of the country, if the gifts of despotism were not always dangerous. . . . The ostentatious display of arms, the violation of the national temple. . . to command you to be happy! . . . Where are the enemies of the nation? Is Catiline at our doors? I demand that, covering yourselves with your dignity, your legislative power, you adhere religiously to your oath: it forbids you to separate before you have framed the constitution."

The Marquis de Brézé, grand-master of the ceremonies, then returned. "You have heard the orders of the King," said he, addressing Bailly. Bailly replied, "I am going to take those of the assembly." Mirabeau stepped forward. "Yes, sir," he exclaimed; "we have heard the intentions that have been suggested to the King; but you have neither voice, nor place, nor right to speak here. However, to avoid all delay, go and tell your master that we are here by the power of the people, and that nothing but the power of bayonets shall drive us away." M. de Brézé retired. Sieyes then said: "We are to-day what we were yesterday; let us deliberate." The assembly collected itself to deliberate on the maintenance of its preceding resolutions (arrêtés). "The first of these resolutions," said Barnave, "has declared what you are; the second relates to the taxes, which you alone have a right to grant; the third is the oath to do your duty. None of these measures needs the royal sanction. The King cannot prevent that to which his assent is not required." At this moment workmen arrived to take away the benches; armed soldiers crossed the hall; others surrounded the outside; the life-guard advanced to the very door. The assembly continued its proceedings without interruption: the members kept their seats, and the votes were collected. They were unanimous for upholding the preceding resolutions. That was not all: amidst the royal town, surrounded by the servants of the court, without the aid of that populace since so formidable, the assembly was liable to be threatened. Mirabeau repaired to the tribune, and proposed to decree the inviolability of every deputy. The assembly, opposing to force but one majestic will, immediately declared each of its members inviolable, and proclaimed every one who should offer them violence a traitor, infamous, and guilty of a capital crime.

Meanwhile the nobility, who looked upon the state as saved by this "bed of justice," presented its congratulations to the prince who had furnished the idea of it, and carried them from the prince to the Queen. The Queen, holding her son in her arms, and showing him to these devoted servants, received their oaths, and unfortunately abandoned herself to a blind confidence. At this very moment shouts were heard; every one ran to inquire the meaning of them, and learned that the people, assembling in crowds, were applauding Necker, because he had not attended the royal sitting. Alarm instantly took the place of joy; the King and Queen sent for Necker, and those august personages were obliged to entreat him to retain his portfolio. The minister complied, and transferred to the court a part of that popularity which he had acquired by absenting himself from that fatal sitting.

Thus was effected the first Revolution. The *tiers-état* had recovered the legislative power, and its adversaries had lost it by attempting to keep it entirely to themselves. In a few days this legislative revolution was completely consummated. Recourse was still had to petty annoyances, such as interrupting the internal communications in the halls of the States; but they were unsuccessful. On the 24th, the majority of the clergy proceeded to the assembly, and demanded the verification in common, in order to deliberate afterwards on the proposals made by the King in the sitting of the 23rd of June. The minority of the clergy continued to deliberate in its own chamber. Juigné, Archbishop of Paris, a virtuous prelate and a benefactor of the people, but a stickler for privileges, was pursued, and forced to promise to join the assembly. He accordingly repaired to the National Assembly, accompanied by the Archbishop of Bordeaux, a popular prelate, who was afterwards minister.

The nobility was in a state of the greatest agitation. Its ordinary instigators inflamed its passions: D'Espréménil proposed to prosecute the *tiers-état*, and to direct proceedings to be instituted against it by the attorney-general: the minority proposed the reunion. This motion was rejected amidst tumult. The Duke of Orleans supported the motion, after having, on the preceding day, given a promise to the contrary to the Polignacs. Forty-seven members having determined to join the general assembly, in spite of the decision of the majority, repaired to it in a body, and were received with demonstrations of public joy. But, notwithstanding the rejoicing caused by their presence, their looks were sad. "We yield to our conscience," said Clermont-Tonnerre, "but it is with pain that we separate ourselves from our colleagues. We have come to concur in the public regeneration; each of us will let you know the degree of activity which his mission allows him."

Every day brought fresh accessions, and the assembly saw the number of its members increase. Addresses poured in from all parts, expressing the good wishes and the approbation of the towns and provinces. Mounier prompted those of Dauphiné; Paris sent one, and even the Palais Royal dispatched a deputation, which the assembly, as yet encompassed with dangers, received, that it might not alienate the multitude. At that time it did not foresee the excesses of the populace; it had need, on the contrary, to presume its energy, and to hope for its support: many, however, doubted the courage of the people, which was as yet but a pleasing dream. Thus the plaudits of the tribunes, frequently annoying to the assembly, had nevertheless supported it, and the assembly durst not prevent them. Bailly would have complained, but his voice and his motion were drowned by thundering applause.

The majority of the nobility continued its sittings, amidst tumult and the most violent animosities. Terror seized those who directed it, and the signal for reunion was made by those very persons who had previously preached resistance. But its passions, already too much excited, were not easily guided. The King was obliged to write a letter; the court, the grandees, were humbled to entreaties. "The junction will be transient," it was said to the most obstinate; "troops are approaching; give way to save the King." Consent was extorted amidst uproar, and the majority of the nobility, accompanied by the minority of the clergy, proceeded, on the 27th of June, to the general assembly. The Duke of Luxembourg, speaking in the name of all, said that they were come to pay a mark of respect to the King, and to give a proof of patriotism to the nation. "The family is complete," replied Bailly. Supposing that the assemblage was entire, and that the question was not to verify but to deliberate in common, he added: "We can now attend without intermission and without distraction to the regeneration of the kingdom and of the public weal."

Many petty artifices were still employed to avoid the appearance of having done what necessity imperatively required. The new-comers always entered after the opening of the sittings, all in a body, so as to give themselves the look of an order. They affected to stand behind the president, or, at least, not to appear to sit. Bailly, with great moderation and firmness, at length overcame all resistance, and prevailed on them to be seated. Attempts were also made to displace him from the presidency, not by main force, but sometimes by secret negotiation, at others by stratagem. Bailly retained it, not out of ambition, but out of duty; and a plain citizen, known only by his virtues and his talents, was seen presiding over all the grandees of the kingdom and the church.

It was too evident that the legislative revolution was accomplished. Though the subject of the first dispute was solely the mode of verification, and not the manner of voting; though some had declared that they joined merely for the common verification, and others in obedience to the royal intentions as expressed on the 23rd of June; it was certain that the voting by individuals had become inevitable: all remonstrance therefore was useless and impolitic. The Cardinal de la Rochefoucauld, nevertheless, protested, in the name of the minority, and declared that he had joined solely to deliberate on general subjects, still retaining the right to form an order. The Archbishop of Vienne replied with warmth that the minority had not had the power to decide anything in the absence of the majority of the clergy, and that it had no right to speak in the name of the order. Mirabeau inveighed strongly against this pretension, observing that it was strange any one should protest in the assembly against the assembly.

"You must," said he, "either recognise its sovereignty or retire."

The question of imperative instructions was next Drought forward. Most of the instructions expressed the wishes of the electors respecting the reforms to be effected, and rendered these wishes obligatory on the deputies. Before they stirred, it was necessary to ascertain to what point they could go: this question, therefore, could not but he the first. It was taken up and resumed several times. Some were for returning to their constituents; others were of opinion that they could not receive from the constituents any other mission than that of voting for them after the subjects should have been discussed by the representatives of the whole nation, but they were not of opinion that deputies could receive instructions ready made beforehand. If we assume, in fact, that we have no power to make laws but in a general council, either because we meet with more intelligence the higher we rise, or because we cannot come to any decision but when all the parts of the nation have reciprocally understood one another, then, indeed, it is true that the deputies ought to be free and unshackled by obligatory instructions. Mirabeau, sharpening reason by irony, observed "that those who considered the instructions as imperative had done wrong to come; they had but to leave instructions on their benches, and those papers would fill the seats as well as they." Sieyes, with his usual sagacity, foreseeing that, notwithstanding the perfectly just decision of the assembly, a great number of members would fall back upon their oaths, and that by taking refuge in their consciences they would render themselves unassailable, moved the order of the day, upon the ground that each was the best judge of the validity of the oath which he had taken.

"Those," said he, "who deem themselves bound by their instructions shall be considered as absent, just the same as those who refused to verify their powers in general assembly." This judicious opinion was adopted. The assembly, by having recourse to constraint, would have furnished the opposers with pretexts; whereas, by leaving them free, it was sure to bring them over to its own way of thinking; for thenceforth its victory was certain.

The object of the new convocation was the reform of the state, that is, the establishment of a constitution, which France as yet had not, whatever may be said to the contrary. If any kind of relations between the governed and the government are to be so called, then indeed France possessed a constitution; a king had commanded and subjects obeyed; ministers had arbitrarily imprisoned; contractors had wrung the last *dénier* from the people; parliaments had sentenced unfortunate wretches to the wheel. The most barbarous nations have such kinds of constitutions. There had been States-general in France, but without precise powers, without fixed times for meeting again, and always without results. There had been a royal authority, alternately null or absolute. There had been sovereign tribunals or courts, which frequently combined the legislative with the judicial power. But there was no law to ensure the responsibility of the agents of power, the liberty of the press, individual liberty; in short, all the guarantees which in the social state make amends for the fiction of natural liberty. (*See* Appendix F.)

The want of a constitution was acknowledged and generally felt; all the instructions had energetically expressed it, and entered into a formal explanation of the fundamental principles of that constitution. They had unanimously prescribed the monarchical government, hereditary succession from male to male, the exclusive attribution of the executive power to the King, the responsibility of all agents, the concurrence of the nation and the King in making the laws, the voting of the taxes, and individual liberty. But they were divided on the creation of one or two legislative chambers, on the permanence, the periods for the meeting, and the dissolution of the legislative body; on the political existence of the clergy and the parliaments; on the extent of the liberty of the press. All these questions, either solved or proposed in the instructions, plainly show to what a degree the public mind was at that time awakened in all parts of the kingdom, and how generally and decisively the wish for liberty was expressed in France. (*See* Appendix G.) But the founding of an entire constitution, amid the rubbish of an ancient legislation in spite of all opposition and the wild flights of many minds, was a great and difficult work. Besides the disagreements which diversity of interests could not fail to produce, the natural divergence of opinions was also to be dreaded. An entire legislation, to be given to a great people, excites their minds so powerfully, inspires them with plans so vast and hopes so chimerical, that measures either vague or exaggerated, and frequently hostile, are naturally to be expected from them. In order to give regularity to the proceedings, a committee was appointed to measure their extent, and to arrange their distribution. This committee was composed of the most moderate members of the Assembly. Mounier, a cool-headed, but obstinate man, was its most laborious and influential member; it was he who drew up the order of the proceedings.

This difficulty of giving a constitution was not the only one that the Assembly had to surmount. Between an ill-disposed government and a starving populace which required speedy relief it was difficult for it to avoid interfering in the administration. Distrusting the supreme authority, and urged to assist the people, it could not help, even without ambition, encroaching by degrees on the executive power. The clergy had already set it the example, by making to the *tiers-état* the insidious proposal to direct its immediate attention to the subject of the public subsistence. The Assembly, as soon as it was formed, appointed a committee of subsistence, applied to the ministry for information on the subject, proposed to favour the circulation of provisions from province to province, to convey them officially to the places where they were needed, and to defray the expense by loans and charitable contributions. The ministry communicated the efficacious measures which it had taken, and which Louis XVI., a careful administrator, had favoured to the utmost of his power. Lally-Tollendal proposed to issue decrees relative to free circulation; upon which Mounier objected that such decrees would require the royal sanction, and this sanction being not yet regulated, would be attended with serious difficulties. Thus all sorts of obstacles combined together. It was requisite to make laws though the legislative forms were not fixed; to superintend the administration without encroaching on the executive authority; and to provide against so many difficulties, in spite of the ill-will of power, the opposition of interests, the jarring of opinions, and the urgency of a populace recently awakened and rousing itself, a few leagues from the Assembly, in the bosom of an immense capital.

A very small distance separates Paris from Versailles, and a person may traverse it several times in one day. All the disturbances in Paris were therefore immediately known at Versailles, both, to the court and to the Assembly. Paris then exhibited a new and extraordinary spectacle. The electors, assembled in sixty districts, refused to separate after the elections, and they remained assembled either to give instructions to their deputies, or from that fondness for agitation which is always to be found in the human heart, and which bursts forth with the greater violence the longer it has been repressed. They had fared just the same as the National Assembly: being shut out of their place of meeting, they had repaired to another; they had finally obtained admittance into the Hôtel de Ville, and there they continued to assemble and to correspond with their deputies. There were yet no public prints that gave an account of the sittings of the National Assembly; people, therefore, felt it necessary to meet for the purpose of learning and conversing upon events. The garden of the Palais Royal was the theatre of the most numerous assemblages. This magnificent garden, surrounded by the richest shops in Europe, and forming an appurtenance to the palace of the Duke of Orleans, was the rendezvous of foreigners, of debauchees, of loungers, and, above all, of the most vehement agitators. The boldest harangues were delivered in the coffee-houses, or in the garden itself. There might be seen an orator mounted upon a table, collecting a crowd around him, and exciting them by the most furious language—language always unpunished—for there the mob reigned as sovereign. Here men, supposed to be the tools of the Duke of Orleans, displayed the greatest violence. The wealth of that prince, his well-known prodigality, the enormous sums which he borrowed, his residence on the spot, his ambition, though vague, all served to point accusation against him. History, without mentioning any name, is authorised at least to declare that money was profusely distributed. If the sound part of the nation was ardently desirous of liberty, if the restless and suffering multitude resorted to agitation for the purpose of bettering its condition, there were instigators who sometimes excited that multitude, and perhaps directed some of its blows. In other respects, this influence is not to be reckoned among the causes of the revolution, for it is not with a little money and with secret manœuvres that you can convulse a nation of twenty-five millions of souls.

An occasion for disturbance soon occurred. The French guards, picked men, destined to compose the King's guard, were at Paris; four companies were detached by turns to do duty at Versailles. Besides the barbarity of the new discipline, these troops had reason to complain also of that of their new colonel. At the pillage of Reveillon's house they had certainly shown some animosity against the populace; but they had subsequently been sorry for it, and, mingling daily with the mob they had yielded to its seductions. Moreover, both privates and subalterns were aware that the door to promotion was closed against them: they were mortified to see their young officers do scarcely any duty, showing themselves only parade-days, and after reviews not even accompanying the regiment to the barracks. Here, as elsewhere, there had been a *tiers-état* which had to do all the work without receiving any share of the profit. Symptoms of insubordination manifested themselves, and some of the privates were confined in the Abbaye!

The men assembled at the Palais Royal, shouting "To the Abbaye!" the mob instantly ran thither. The doors were broken open, and the soldiers brought out, and carried away in triumph. Whilst the populace guarded them at the Palais Royal, a letter was written to the Assembly, demanding their liberation. Placed between the people on the one hand and the government on the other, which was suspected, since it was about to act in its own behalf, the Assembly could not help interfering and committing an encroachment, by meddling with the public police. Taking a resolution at once prudent and adroit, it assured the Parisians of its desire for the maintenance of good order, exhorted them not to disturb it, and at the same time sent a deputation to the King to implore his clemency, as an infallible mode of restoring peace and concord. The King, touched by its moderation, promised his clemency when order should be re-established. The French guards were immediately sent back to prison, from which they were as immediately released by a pardon from the King.

So far all was well; but the nobility, in joining the other two orders, had yielded with regret, and only upon a promise that its union with them should be of short duration. It still continued to assemble every day, and protested against the proceedings of the National Assembly; its meetings gradually became less numerous: on the 3rd of July 138 members attended; on the 10th 93, and on the 11th but 80. The most obstinate, however, had persisted, and on the 11th they determined upon a protest, which succeeding events prevented them from drawing up. The court, on its part, had not yielded without regret and without plan. On recovering from its alarm, after the sitting of the 23rd, it had approved the general union of the three estates, in order to impede the march of the Assembly by means of the nobles, and in the hope of soon dissolving it by main force. Necker had been retained merely to mask by his presence the secret plots that were hatching. Excepting a certain agitation and a degree of reserve that was employed towards him, he had no reason to suspect any grand machination. The King himself was not apprised of all, and there were persons who proposed, no doubt, to go further than he wished. Necker, who conceived that the whole activity of a statesman ought to confine itself to reasoning, and who possessed just so much energy as was necessary to remonstrate, did so without effect. Conjointly with Mounier, Lally-Tollendal, and Clermont-Tonnerre, he meditated the establishment of the English constitution. The court was meanwhile carrying on its secret preparations. The noble deputies having manifested an intention to withdraw, they were detained by hints thrown out to them of an event that would speedily happen.

Troops were approaching: old Marshal de Broglie had been appointed to the chief command of them, and the Baron de Besenval to the particular command of those which were around Paris. Fifteen regiments, mostly foreign, were in the environs of the capital. The exultation of the courtiers revealed the danger; and these conspirators, too prompt to threaten, thus compromised their projects. The popular deputies apprised, not of all the particulars of a plan which is not yet entirely known, with which the King himself was but partially acquainted, but which certainly tended to employ violence, were irritated, and turned their attention to the means of resistance. We are ignorant, and shall probably ever remain so, of the share which secret means had in the insurrection of the 14th of July, but this is of no consequence. The aristocracy was conspiring; the popular party could conspire too. The means employed were equal, setting aside the justice of the cause, and justice was not on their side who would fain have broken up the union of the three orders, dissolved the national representation, and wreaked their vengeance upon its most courageous deputies.

Mirabeau was of opinion that the surest way of intimidating power was to force it to discuss publicly the measures which it was seen to take. To this end it was necessary to denounce it openly. If it hesitated to reply, if it had recourse to evasion, it would be condemned; the nation would be warned and roused.

On the motion of Mirabeau, the discussion of the constitution was suspended, and he proposed to solicit the King to remove the troops. In his language he combined respect for the monarch with the severest reproaches of the government. He stated that fresh troops were daily advancing; that all the communications were intercepted; that the bridges, the promenades, were converted into military posts; that circumstances public and secret, hasty orders and counter-orders, met all eyes, and were the heralds of war: to these facts he added bitter reproaches. "More threatening soldiers," said he, "are shown to the nation, than hostile invaders would perhaps find to encounter, and thousand times more, at least, than could be brought together to succour friends, the martyrs of their fidelity, and above all to preserve that alliance of the Dutch, so valuable, so dearly bought, and so disgracefully lost."

His speech was received with applause; and the address which he proposed was adopted, with the exception of one article, in which, while invoking the removal of the troops, he demanded that they should he replaced by the civic guard: this article was suppressed. The address was voted, with only four dissentient voices. In this celebrated address, which, as it is said, was not written by Mirabeau, but all the ideas of which he had communicated to one of his friends, he foreboded almost everything that was about to happen: the explosion of the multitude, and the defection of the troops from their intermingling with the citizens. Not less acute than hold, he ventured to assure the King that his promises should not be vain. "You have summoned us," said he, "to regenerate the kingdom; your wishes shall he accomplished, in spite of snares, difficulties, dangers, &c."

The address was presented by a deputation of twenty-four members. The King, having resolved not to enter into explanations, replied that the assemblage of troops was for no other purpose than the maintenance of the public tranquillity, and the protection due to the Assembly; that, moreover, if the latter still felt any apprehensions, he would remove it to Soissons or Noyon, and that he would himself repair to Compiègne.

The Assembly could not be satisfied with such an answer, and especially with the proposal to withdraw from the capital, and to place itself between two camps. The Count de Crillon proposed that they should trust to the word of a King who was an honest man. "The word of a King who is an honest man," replied Mirabeau, "is a bad security for the conduct of his ministers; our blind confidence in our kings has undone us: we demanded the withdrawal of the troops, and not permission to flee before them. We must insist again and again."

This opinion was not supported. Mirabeau insisted so strongly upon open means, that he may be forgiven any secret machinations, if it be true that he actually resorted to them.

The 11th of July had now arrived. Necker had several times told the King that, if his services were not acceptable, he would retire with submission. "I take you at your word," replied the King. On the 11th, in the evening, Necker received a note in which Louis XVI. required him to keep his word, and urged him to set out, adding that he had sufficient confidence in him to hope that he would keep his departure a profound secret. Necker, justifying the honourable confidence of the monarch, set out without apprising his friends or even his daughter, and in a few hours was at a considerable distance from Versailles. The following day, July 12th, was Sunday. A report was now circulated at Paris that Necker had been dismissed, as well as Messrs. De Montmorin, De la Luzerne, De Puisegur, and De St. Priest. As their successors, Messrs. De Breteuil, De la Vauguyon, De Broglie, Foulon, and Damécourt were mentioned, almost all known for their opposition to the popular cause. The alarm spread throughout Paris. The people hurried to the Palais Royal. A young man, since celebrated for his republican enthusiasm, endowed with a tender heart but an impetuous spirit, mounted a table, held up a pair of pistols, and shouting "To arms!" plucked a leaf from a tree, of which he made a cockade, and exhorted the crowd to follow his example. The trees were instantly stripped. The people then repaired to a museum containing busts in wax. They seized those of Necker and the Duke of Orleans, who was threatened, it was said, with exile, and then spread themselves in the various quarters of Paris. This mob was passing through the Rue St. Honoré, when it was met, near the Place Vendome, by a detachment of the Royal German regiment, which rushed upon it and wounded several persons, among whom was a soldier of the French guards. The latter, predisposed in favour of the people and against the Royal Germans, with whom they had a few days before had a quarrel, were in barracks near the Place Louis XV. They fired upon the Royal Germans. The Prince de Lambese, who commanded this regiment, instantly fell back upon the garden of the Tuileries, charged the people who were quietly walking there, killed an old man amidst the confusion, and cleared the garden. Meanwhile, the troops surrounding Paris formed in the Champ de Mars and the Place Louis XV. Terror, before unbounded, now changed into fury. People ran into the city, shouting "To arms! "The mob hurried to the Hôtel de Ville to demand weapons. The electors composing the General Assembly were there met. They delivered out the arms, which they could no longer refuse, and which, at the instant when they determined to grant them, the people had already begun to seize. These electors composed at the moment the only established authority. Deprived of all active powers, they assumed such as the occasion required, and ordered the districts to be convoked. All the citizens instantly assembled, to consult upon the means of protecting themselves at one and the same time against the rabble and the attack of the royal troops. During the night, the populace, always ready for excitement, forced and burned the barriers, dispersed the gate-keepers, and afforded free access by all the avenues to the city. The gunsmiths' shops were plundered. Those brigands who had already signalised themselves at Reveillon's, and who on all occasions are seen springing up, as it were, out of the ground, again appeared armed with pikes and bludgeons, spreading consternation. These events took place on Sunday, the 12th of July, and in the night between Sunday and Monday, the 13th. On Monday morning, the electors, still assembled at the Hôtel de Ville, thought it incumbent on them to give a more legal form to their authority: they accordingly summoned the attendance of the provost of the trades (*prévôt des marchands*), the ordinary administrator of the city. The latter refused to comply unless upon a formal requisition. A requisition was in consequence issued; a certain number of electors were appointed as his assistants, and thus was composed a municipality invested with all necessary powers. This municipality sent for the lieutenant of police, and drew up in a few hours a plan for arming the civic militia.

This militia was to consist of forty-eight thousand men, furnished by the districts. The distinctive sign was to be the Parisian cockade, red and blue, instead of the green cockade. Every man found in arms and wearing this cockade, without having been enrolled by his district in the civic guard, was to be apprehended, disarmed, and punished. Such was the primary origin of the national guards. This plan was adopted by all the districts, which hastened to carry it into execution. In the course of the same morning, the people had plundered the house of St. Lazare in search of grain; they had forced the armoury to obtain arms, and had rummaged out the ancient armour and put it on. The rabble, wearing helmets and carrying pikes, were seen inundating the city. The populace now showed itself hostile to pillage; with its usual fickleness, it affected to be disinterested; it spared money, took nothing but arms, and itself apprehended the brigands. The French guards and the night-watch had offered their services, and they had been enrolled in the civic guard.

Arms were still demanded with loud shouts. Flesselles, the provost, who had at first resisted his fellow-citizens, now manifested great zeal, and promised twelve thousand muskets on that very day, and more on the following days. He pretended that he had made a contract with an unknown gunsmith. The thing appeared difficult, considering the short time that had elapsed. Meanwhile, evening drew on; the chests of arms announced by Flesselles were carried to the Hôtel de Ville; they were opened, and found to be full of old linen. At this sight the multitude was fired with indignation against the provost, who declared that he had been deceived. To appease them, he directed them to go to the Carthusians, with the assurance that arms would there be found. The astonished Carthusians admitted the furious mob, conducted them into their retreat, and finally convinced them that they possessed nothing of the sort mentioned by the provost.

The rabble, more exasperated than ever, returned with shouts of "Treachery!" To satisfy them, orders were issued for the manufacture of fifty thousand pikes. Vessels with gunpowder were descending the Seine, on their way to Versailles; these were stopped, and an elector distributed the powder amidst the most imminent danger.

A tremendous confusion now prevailed at the Hôtel de Ville, the seat of the authorities, the head-quarters of the militia, and the centre of all operations. It was necessary to provide at once for the safety of the town, which was threatened by the court, and its internal safety endangered by the brigands; it was requisite every moment to allay the suspicions of the people, who believed that they were betrayed, and to save from their fury those who excited their distrust. About this place were to be seen carriages stopped, waggons intercepted, travellers awaiting permission to proceed on their journey. During the night, the Hôtel de Ville was once more menaced by the brigands. An elector, the courageous Moreau de St. Mery, to whose care it had been committed, caused barrels of powder to be brought, and threatened to blow it up. At this sight the brigands retired. Meanwhile the citizens, who had gone to their homes, held themselves in readiness for every kind of attack: they had unpaved the streets, opened the trenches, and taken all possible measures for resisting a siege.

During these disturbances in the capital, consternation pervaded the Assembly. It had met on the morning of the 13th, alarmed by the events that were in preparation, and still ignorant of what was passing in Paris. Mounier, the deputy, first rose and censured the dismissal of the ministers. Lally-Tollendal, who took his place in the tribune, pronounced a splendid panegyric on Necker, and both joined in proposing an address, for the purpose of soliciting the King to recal his disgraced ministers. M. De Virieu, a deputy of the nobility, even proposed to confirm the resolutions of the 17th of June by a new oath. M. De Clermont-Tonnerre opposed this motion as useless; and, referring to the engagements by which the Assembly had already bound itself, he exclaimed, "The constitution shall be, or we will perish!" The discussion had lasted some time, when news arrived of the disturbances in Paris during the morning of the 13th, and the calamities with which the capital was threatened, between undisciplined Frenchmen, who, according to the expression of the Duke de la Rochefoucauld, were not in anyone's hand, and disciplined foreigners, who were in the hand of despotism. It was instantly resolved to send a deputation to the King, for the purpose of submitting to him a picture of the desolation of the capital, and beseeching him to order the removal of the troops, and the establishment of the civic guards. The King returned a cold, dry answer, which was far from according with his disposition, and alleged that Paris was not capable of guarding itself. The Assembly, then, exalting itself to the noblest courage, passed a memorable resolution, in which it insisted on the removal of the troops and the establishment of civic guards; declared the ministers and all the agents of power responsible; threw upon the counsellors of the King, *of whatever rank* they might be, the responsibility of the calamities that were impending, consolidated the public debt, forbade the mention of the infamous term bankruptcy, persisted in its preceding resolutions, and directed the president to express its regret to M. Necker and to the other ministers. After these measures, fraught alike with energy and prudence, the Assembly, in order to preserve its members from all personal violence, declared itself permanent, and appointed M. De Lafayette vice-president, to relieve the worthy Archbishop of Vienne, whose age did not permit him to sit day and night.

Thus passed the night between the 13th and 14th in agitation and alarm. Fearful tidings were every moment brought and contradicted. All the plans of the court were not known; but it was ascertained that several deputies were threatened, and that violence was to be employed against Paris and the most distinguished members of the Assembly. Having adjourned for a short time, the Assembly again met, at five in the morning of the 14th of July: with imposing calmness it resumed the consideration of the constitution, and discussed with great propriety the means of accelerating its execution, and of conducting it with prudence. A committee was appointed to prepare the questions; it was composed of the Bishop of Autun, the Archbishop of Bordeaux, Messrs. Lally, Clermont-Tonnerre, Mounier, Sieyes, Chapelier, and Bergasse. The morning passed away. Intelligence more and more alarming continued to arrive. The King, it was said, was to set off in the night, and the Assembly would be left exposed to several foreign regiments. At this moment the princes, the Duchess de Polignac, and the Queen were seen walking in the orangery, flattering the officers and the soldiers, and causing refreshments to be distributed among them. It appears that a grand plan had been devised for the night between the 14th and 15th; that Paris was to be attacked on seven points, the Palais Royal surrounded, the Assembly dissolved, the declaration of the 23rd of June submitted to the parliament, and finally, that the wants of the exchequer were to be supplied by bankruptcy and paper-money. So much is certain, that the commandants of the troops had received orders to advance in the night between the 14th and 15th, that the paper-money had been prepared, that the barracks of the Swiss were full of ammunition, and that the governor of the Bastille had disfurnished the fortress, with the exception of some indispensable articles. In the afternoon, the terrors of the Assembly redoubled. The Prince de Lambesc was seen passing at full gallop. The report of cannon was heard, and people clapped their ears to the ground to catch the slightest sounds. Mirabeau then proposed to suspend the discussions, and to send another deputation to the King The deputation set out immediately, to make fresh remonstrances. At this moment, two members of the Assembly, who had come from Paris in the utmost haste, declared that the people there were slaughtering one another;

one of them affirmed that ha had seen the headless body of a man dressed in black. It began to grow dark. The arrival of two electors was announced. The most profound silence pervaded the hall; the sound of their footfalls was heard amid the darkness; and the Assembly learned from their lips that the Bastille was attacked, that cannon had been fired, that blood had been spilt, and that the city was threatened with the direst calamities. A fresh deputation was instantly despatched before the return of the preceding one. Just as it was about to depart, the first arrived, and brought the answer of the King. It reported that the King had ordered the troops encamped in the Champ de Mars to be withdrawn, and, having been apprised of the formation of the civic guard, had appointed officers to command it.

On the arrival of the second deputation, the King, more agitated than ever, said, "Gentlemen, you rend my heart more and more by the account you give me of the calamaties of Paris. It is not possible that the orders given to the troops can be the cause of them." Nothing had yet been obtained but the removal of the army. It was now two in the morning. The answer returned to the city of Paris was, "that two deputations had been sent, and that the applications should be renewed that day, until they had obtained the success which might justly be expected from the heart of the King, when extraneous impressions did not counteract its impulses." The sitting was suspended for a short time, and in the evening intelligence of the events of the 14th arrived.

The populace, ever since the night of the 13th, had thronged about the Bastille. Some musket-shots had been fired, and it appears that ringleaders had repeatedly shouted "To the Bastille!" The wish for its destruction had been expressed in the instructions given to some of the deputies, thus the ideas of the public had beforehand taken that direction. A cry for arms was still kept up. A report was spread that the Hôtel des Invalides contained a considerable quantity. The mob instantly repaired thither. M. De Sombreuil, the governor, ordered admittance to be denied, saying, that he must send for orders to Versailles. The populace, turning a deaf ear to all expostulation, rushed into the hotel, and carried off the cannon, and a great quantity of muskets. A large concourse of people were already besieging the Bastille. They declared that the guns of the fortress were pointed at the city, and that they must take care to prevent their firing upon them. The deputy of a district solicited admission into the place, and obtained it of the commandant. In going over it, he found thirty-two Swiss and eighty-two invalids, and received a promise from the garrison not to fire unless it should be attacked. During this parley, the people, not seeing the deputy return, began to be exasperated, and the latter was obliged to show himself in order to appease the multitude. At length he retired, about eleven o'clock in the forenoon. Half an hour had scarcely elapsed before a fresh mob arrived with arms, shouting, "Let us storm the Bastille!" The garrison summoned the assailants to retire, but they persisted. Two men, with great intrepidity mounted the roof of the guardhouse, and broke with axes the chains of the bridge, which fell down. The rabble rushed upon it, and ran to a second bridge, purposing to pass it in like manner. At this moment a discharge of musketry brought it to a stand; it fell back, but firing at the same time. The conflict lasted for a few moments. The electors, assembled at the Hôtel de Ville, hearing the report of musketry, became more and more alarmed, and sent two deputations, one on the heels of the other, to require the commandant to admit into the fortress a detachment of the Paris militia, on the ground that all the military force in the capital ought to be at the disposal of the city authorities. These two deputations arrived in succession. Amidst this siege by the populace, it was with great difficulty that they could make themselves heard. The sound of the drum, the sight of a flag, for a time suspended the firing. The deputies advanced; the garrison awaited them, but it was difficult to understand each other.

Musket-shots were fired, from some unknown quarter. The mob, persuaded that it was betrayed, then rushed forward to set fire to the building; on this the garrison fired with grape. The French guards thereupon came up with cannon, and commenced an attack in form (*See* Appendix H.)

During these proceedings, a note addressed by the Baron De Besenval to De Launay, governor of the Bastille, was intercepted and read at the Hôtel de Ville. Besenval exhorted De Launay to resist, assuring him that he should soon receive succour. It was in fact in the evening of that day that the plans of the court were to be carried into execution. Meanwhile De Launay, seeing the desperation of the mob, and no succours having arrived, seized a lighted match with the intention of blowing up the fortress. The garrison opposed it, and obliged him to surrender: the signals were made and a bridge lowered. The besiegers approached, promising not to do any mischief. The crowd, however, rushed in, and took possession of all the courts. The Swiss found means to escape. The invalids, attacked by the populace, were saved from their fury solely by the zealous interference of the French guards. At this moment, a female, beautiful, young, and trembling, came forward; she was supposed to be the daughter of De Launay; she was seized and about to be burned, when a brave soldier rushed to the spot, wrested her from the hands of the enraged rabble, conducted her to a place of safety, and hurried back to the affray.

It was now half-past five o'clock. The electors were in the most painful anxiety, when they heard a dull and continuous murmur. A crowd approached, shouting "Victory!" They poured into the hall: a French guardsman covered with wounds and crowned with laurels, was borne in triumph by the mob. The regulations and the keys of the Bastille were carried on the point of a bayonet: a bloody hand raised above the mob exhibited a bunch of hair; it was the queue of De Launay, the governor, whose head had just been stricken off. Two French guards, Elie and Hullin, had defended him to the last extremity. Other victims had fallen, though heroically defended against the ferocity of the mob. A strong animosity began to be expressed against Flesselles, the provost of the trades; he was accused of treason. It was alleged that he had deceived the people by repeatedly promising them arms which he never meant to give them. The hall was soon full of men heated with a long combat, and backed by a hundred thousand more outside the hotel, all eager to enter in their turn. The electors strove to justify Flesselles to the mob. His assurance began to forsake him, and, already quite pale, he exclaimed, "Since I am suspected I will retire." "No," was the reply made to him, "come to the Palais Royal, to be tried." Accordingly, he descended to repair thither. The agitated multitude surrounded and pressed upon him. On reaching the Quai Pelletier, he was struck to the ground by a pistol-shot, fired by a person unknown. It is asserted that a letter had been found upon De Launay, in which Flesselles thus wrote to him: "Hold out, while I amuse the Parisians with cockades."

Such were the disastrous events of that day. A feeling of terror speedily followed the intoxication of victory. The conquerors of the Bastille, astonished at their audacity, and expecting to find the hand of authority formidable on the following day, durst not make themselves known. Every moment rumours were spread that the troops were approaching to storm Paris. Moreau de St. Mery, the same person who on the preceding day had threatened the brigands to blow up the Hôtel de Ville, remained unshaken, and issued upwards of three thousand orders in a few hours. As soon as the capture of the Bastille was known at the Hôtel de Ville, the electors had sent the intelligence to the Assembly, which received it about midnight. The sitting was suspended, and the tidings spread with rapidity. The court, up to this moment, conceiving no notion of the energy of the people, laughing at the efforts of a blind rabble to take a fortress which the great Condé had besieged in vain, was calmly cracking its jokes on the subject. The King, nevertheless, began to be uneasy; his last answers had betrayed his grief. He had retired to bed. The Duke de Liancourt, so well known for his generous sentiments, was the particular friend of Louis XVI., and by virtue of his office of grand-master of the wardrobe, he always had access to the King. On learning the occurrences in Paris, he repaired in all haste to the apartment of the monarch, awoke him in spite of the ministers, and informed him of what had happened. "What rebellion!" exclaimed the prince. "Sire," replied the duke, "rather say revolution." The King, enlightened by his representations, consented to go the next morning to the Assembly. The court yielded also, and this act of confidence was resolved upon. During this interval, the Assembly had resumed its sitting. Unacquainted with the new dispositions imparted to the King, it determined to send a last deputation, to try to move him, and to obtain from him what he had not yet been prevailed upon to grant. This deputation was the fifth since the commencement of those calamitous events. It was composed of twenty-four members, and was just setting out when Mirabeau, more vehement than ever, stopped it. "Tell the King," cried he, "be sure to tell him, that the foreign hordes by which we are invested were yesterday invited by the princes, the princesses, the he-favourites, and the she-favourites, and received their caresses, and their exhortations, and their presents. Tell him that the live-long night these foreign satellites, gorged with money and with wine, have been predicting, in their impious songs, the subjugation of France, and that their brutal wishes invoked the destruction of the National Assembly. Tell him that, in his very palace, the courtiers mingled with their dances the sound of that barbarous music, and that such was the prelude to the massacre of St. Bartholomew. Tell him that that Henry, whose memory the whole world blesses, that one of his ancestors whom he meant to take for his pattern, allowed provisions to be conveyed into rebellious Paris, which he was besieging in person; whereas his ferocious counsellors are turning back the flour that commerce is sending to faithful and famished Paris."

The deputation was just about to proceed to the King, when news arrived that he was coming, of his own accord, without guards and without escort. The hall rang with applause. "Wait," cried Mirabeau, gravely, "till the King has made us acquainted with his good dispositions. Let a sullen respect be the first welcome paid to the monarch in this moment of grief. The silence of nations is a lesson for kings."

Louis XVI. then entered, accompanied by his two brothers. His simple and touching address excited the warmest enthusiasm. He spoke cheeringly to the Assembly, which he called for the first time the National Assembly. He mildly complained of the suspicions that had been conceived of him. "You have been afraid of me," said he; "now, for my part, I put my trust in you." These words were hailed with applause. The deputies immediately rose, surrounded the monarch, and escorted him back on foot to the palace. The throng pressed around him; tears started from every eye; and he could scarcely open himself a passage through this numerous retinue. The Queen, stationed at that moment with the court in a balcony, contemplated from a distance this affecting scene. Her son was in her arms; her daughter, standing beside her, was sportively playing with her brother's hair. The princess, deeply moved, appeared to be delighted by this expression of the love of the French. Ah! how often has a reciprocal emotion reconciled hearts during these fatal dissensions! For a moment all seemed to be forgotten; but on the morrow, nay, perhaps the very same day, the court had resumed its pride, the people their distrust, and implacable hatred recommenced its course.

Peace was made with the Assembly, but it had yet to be made with Paris. The Assembly first sent a deputation to the Hôtel de Ville to convey the tidings of the happy reconciliation brought about with the King. Bailly, Lafayette, and Lally-Tollendal were among its members. Their presence diffused the liveliest joy. The speech of Lally excited such transport that he was carried in triumph to a window of the Hôtel de Ville to be shown to the people. A wreath of flowers was placed on his head, and these honours were paid him facing the very spot where his father expired with a gag in his mouth. The death of the unfortunate Flesselles, the head of the municipality, and the refusal of the Duke d'Aumont to accept the command of the civic militia, left the appointments of provost and commandant-general to be filled up. Bailly was proposed, and amidst the loudest acclamations he was nominated successor to Flesselles, with the title of mayor of Paris. The wreath which had been placed on the head of Lally was transferred to that of the new mayor; he would have taken it off, but the Archbishop of Paris held it where it was in opposition to his wishes. The virtuous old man could not repress his tears, and he resigned himself to his new functions. A worthy representative of a great assembly, in presence of the majesty of a throne, he was less capable of withstanding the storms of a commonalty, where the multitude struggled tumultuously against its magistrates. With exemplary self-denial, however, he prepared to undertake the difficult task of providing subsistence and feeding a populace who repaid him in the sequel with such base ingratitude. A commandant of the militia yet remained to be appointed. There was in the hall a bust sent by enfranchised America to the city of Paris: Moreau de St. Mery pointed to it with his finger; all eyes were directed towards it. It was the bust of the Marquis de Lafayette. A general cry proclaimed him commandant. A *Te Deum* was instantly voted, and the Assembly proceeded in a body to Notre Dame. The new magistrates, the Archbishop of Paris, the electors, mingled with French guards and soldiers of the militia, walking arm-in-arm, repaired to the ancient cathedral, in a species of intoxication. By the way, the Foundlings threw themselves at the feet of Bailly, who had laboured zealously in behalf of the hospitals, and called him their father. Bailly clasped them in his arms, and called them his children. On reaching the church, the ceremony was performed, and the congregation then dispersed in the city, where a delirious joy had succeeded the terrors of the preceding day. At this moment the people were flocking to see the den so long dreaded, to which there was now free access. They visited the Bastille with an eager curiosity, and with a sort of terror. They sought for the instruments of torture, for the deep dungeons. They went thither more particularly to see an enormous stone placed in the middle of a dark and damp prison, to the centre of which was fixed a ponderous chain.

The court, as blind in its apprehensions as it had been in its confidence, felt such a dread of the populace, that it imagined every moment that a Parisian army was marching to Versailles. The Count d'Artois, and the Polignac family, so dear to the Queen, quitted France at that time, and were the first emigrants. Bailly came to cheer the King, and persuaded him to return to Paris, which he resolved to do, in spite of the resistance of the Queen and the court.

The King prepared to set out. Two hundred deputies were directed to accompany him. The Queen took leave of him with profound grief. The body-guard escorted him to Sèvres, where they stopped to await his return. Bailly, at the head of the municipality, received him at the gates of Paris, and presented to him the keys formerly offered to Henry IV. "That good King," said Bailly to him, "had conquered his people; at present it is the people who have reconquered their King." The nation, legislating at Versailles, was armed at Paris. Louis XVI., on entering, found himself surrounded by a silent multitude, arrayed in military order. He arrived at the Hôtel de Ville, passing under an arch of swords crossed over his head as a mark of honour. His address was simple and touching. The people, unable to contain themselves, at length burst forth and lavished upon the King their accustomed applause. These acclamations somewhat soothed the heart of the prince; nevertheless, he could not disguise a feeling of joy on perceiving the body-guard stationed on the heights of Sèvres; and at his return, the Queen, throwing herself into his arms, embraced him as though she had been afraid that she should never see him again.

Louis XVI., in order to satisfy completely the public wish, ordered the dismissal of the new ministers, and the reinstatement of Necker. M. De Liancourt, the friend of the King, and his most useful adviser, was elected president by the Assembly. The noble deputies, who, though they attended the deliberations, still refused to take any part in them, at length yielded and gave their votes. Thus was consummated the amalgamation of the orders. From that moment the Revolution might be looked upon as accomplished. The nation, possessed of the legislative power through the Assembly and of the public force through itself, could henceforward carry into effect whatever was beneficial to its interest. It was by refusing the equality of imposts that the government had rendered the States-general necessary; it was by refusing a just division of authority among those states that it had lost all influence over them; finally, it was in attempting to recover that influence that it had driven Paris to insurrection, and provoked the whole nation to appropriate to itself the public force.

At this moment all was agitation in that immense capital, where a new authority had just been established. The same movement which had impelled the electors to set themselves in action, urged all classes to do the same. The Assembly had been imitated by the Hôtel de Ville, the Hôtel de Ville by the districts, and the districts by all the corporations. Tailors, shoemakers, bakers, domestic servants, meeting at the Louvre, in the place Louis XV., in the Champs Elysées, deliberated in form, notwithstanding the repeated prohibitions of the municipality. Amidst these contrary movements, the Hôtel de Ville, opposed by the districts, and annoyed by the Palais Royal, was encompassed with obstacles, and was scarcely adequate to the duties of its immense administration. It combined in itself alone the civil, judicial, and military authority. The head-quarters of the militia were established there. The judges, at first uncertain respecting their powers, sent thither accused persons. It possessed even the legislative power, for it was charged to form a constitution for itself. For this purpose Bailly had demanded two commissioners for each district, who, by the name of representatives of the commune, were to draw up its constitution. The electors, in order that they might be able to attend to all these duties, had divided themselves into several committees. One, called the committee of research, superintended the police; another, called the committee of subsistence, directed its attention to the supply of provisions—the most difficult and dangerous task of all. It was in the latter that Bailly was obliged himself to labour night and day. It was necessary to make continual purchases of corn, then to get it ground, and afterwards carry it to Paris through the famished country. The convoys were frequently stopped, and it required numerous detachments to prevent pillage by the way and in the markets. Though the state sold corn at a loss, that the bakers might keep down the price of bread, the multitude was not satisfied: it was found expedient to reduce the price still more, and the dearth at Paris was increased by this very diminution, because the country people flocked thither to supply themselves. Pears for the morrow caused all who could to lay in an abundant stock, and thus what was accumulated in some hands left nothing for others. It is confidence that accelerates the operations of commerce, that produces an abundant supply of articles of consumption, and that renders their distribution equal and easy. But when confidence disappears, commercial activity ceases; articles of consumption no longer arriving in sufficient quantity to meet the wants, those wants become importunate, add confusion to dearth, and prevent the proper distribution of the little that is left. The supply of subsistence was therefore the most arduous duty of all. Bailly and the committee were a prey to painful anxieties. The whole labour of the day scarcely sufficed for the wants of the day, and they had to begin again on the morrow with the same perplexities.

Lafayette, commandant of the civic militia, had as many troubles to encounter as Bailly. He had incorporated into this militia the French guards, devoted to the cause of the revolution, a certain number of Swiss, and a great quantity of soldiers who had deserted from their regiments in the hope of higher pay. The King had himself authorised this proceeding. These troops, collectively, formed what were called the companies of the centre. The militia assumed the name of the national guard, adopted a uniform, and added to the two colours of the Parisian cockade, red and blue, the white colour which was that of the King. This was the tricoloured cockade, whose destinies Lafayette predicted, when he declared that it would make the tour ot the world.

It was at the head of these troops that Lafayette strove for two consecutive years to maintain the public tranquillity, and to enforce the execution of the laws which the Assembly daily enacted. Lafayette, the offspring of an ancient family which had remained uncontaminated amidst the corruption of the great, endowed with a firm and upright mind, and fond of true glory, had become weary of the frivolities of the court, and of the pedantic discipline of our armies. As his own country offered nothing noble to be attempted, he decided in favour of the most generous enterprise of the age, and embarked for America, the day after that on which a report reached Europe that it was subdued. He there fought by the side of Washington, and decided the enfranchisement of the New World by the alliance of France. Returning to his own country with a European renown, welcomed at court as a novelty, he showed himself there, simple and free as an American. When philosophy, which had been but a pastime for noble idlers, required sacrifices from them, Lafayette persisted almost alone in his opinions, demanded the States-general, contributed powerfully to the junction of the Orders, and, by way of recompense, was appointed commandant-general of the national guard. Lafayette had not the passions and the genius which frequently lead to the abuse of power: with an equable mind, a sound understanding, and a system, of invariable disinterestedness, he was peculiarly fitted for the part which circumstances had allotted to him—that of superintending the execution of the laws. Adored by his troops, though he had not captivated them by victory, ever calm and full of resources, amidst the ebullitions of the multitude, he preserved order with indefatigable vigilance. The parties which had found him incorruptible depreciated his abilities, because they could not attack his character. He formed, however, no false estimate of men and events, appreciated the court and the party-leaders at no more than their real value, and protected them at the peril of his life without esteeming them; struggled, frequently without hope, against the factions, but with the perseverance of a man who is determined never to forsake the public weal, even when he deems it hopeless.

Lafayette, notwithstanding his indefatigable vigilance, was not always successful in his endeavours to check the popular fury. For, let a force be ever so active, it cannot show itself everywhere against a populace that is everywhere in agitation, and looks upon every man as an enemy. Every moment, the most absurd reports were circulated and credited. Sometimes it was said that the soldiers of the French guards had been poisoned; at others, that the flour had been wilfully adulterated, or that its arrival had been prevented; and those who took the greatest pains to bring it to the capital were obliged to appear before an ignorant mob, who overwhelmed them with abuse or covered them with applause, according to the humour of the moment. Whether it was, however, that men were paid for aggravating the disturbances by instigating the rabble, or that they had still more detestable motives, so much is certain, that they directed the fury of the people, who knew not either how to select or to seek long for their victims. Foulon and Berthier were pursued and apprehended at a distance from Paris. This was done with evident design. There was nothing spontaneous in the proceedings, except the fury of the mob by whom they were murdered. Foulon, formerly an intendant, a harsh and rapacious man, had committed horrible extortions, and had been one of the ministers appointed to succeed Necker and his colleagues. He was apprehended at Virey, though he had spread a report of his death. He was conveyed to Paris, and reproached by the way with having said that the people ought to be made to eat hay. A collar of nettles was put round his neck, a bunch of thistles in his hand, and a truss of hay at his back. In this state he was dragged to the Hôtel de Ville. At the same instant, his son-in-law, Berthier de Sauvigny, was apprehended at Compiègne, by an order, as it was alleged, of the commune of Paris, which had never issued any such order. The commune instantly wrote directing that he should be released; but this injunction was not executed. He was brought to Paris at the very moment that Foulon was exposed at the Hôtel de Ville to the rage of the furious rabble. They were for putting him to death. The remonstrance of Lafayette had pacified them for a moment, and they consented that Foulon should be tried; but they insisted that sentence should be passed forthwith, that they might be gratified by its immediate execution. Some electors had been chosen to act as judges; but they had on various pretexts refused the terrible office. At length, Bailly and Lafayette were designated for it; and they were already reduced to the cruel extremity of devoting themselves to the rage of the populace or sacrificing a victim. Lafayette, however, continued to temporise with great art and firmness: he had several times addressed the crowd with success. The unfortunate Foulon, placed on a seat by his side, had the imprudence to applaud his concluding words. "Look you," said a bystander, "how they play into each other's hands." At this expression the crowd became agitated, and rushed upon Foulon. Lafayette made incredible efforts to save him from the murderers; again the unfortunate old man was dragged from him, and hanged to a lamp. His head was cut off, stuck on a pike, and paraded through Paris. At this moment Berthier arrived in a cabriolet, escorted by guards, and followed by the multitude. The bleeding head was shown to him, without his suspecting that it was the head of his father-in-law. He was conducted to the Hôtel de Ville, where he uttered a few words full of courage and indignation. Seized anew by the mob, he disengaged himself for a moment, snatched a weapon, made a desperate defence, and soon perished like the unhappy Foulon. These murders had been conducted by enemies either to Foulon or the public welfare; for the apprehension of the victims was the result of contrivance, though the fury of the rabble at sight of them had been spontaneous, like most of its movements. Lafayette, full of grief and indignation, resolved to resign. Bailly and the municipality, alarmed at this intention, were anxious to divert him from it. It was then agreed that he should announce his resignation, to show his dissatisfaction with the people, but that he should suffer himself to be persuaded to retain his command by the entreaties that would not fail to be addressed to him. The people and the militia did actually throng around him and promised the utmost obedience in future. On this condition he resumed the command; and, subsequently, he had the satisfaction of preventing many disturbances by his own energy and the zeal of his troops.

Meanwhile Necker had received at Basle the commands of the King and the solicitations of the Assembly. It was the Polignacs, whom he had left triumphant at Versailles, and whom he encountered as fugitives at Basle, that first apprised him of the misfortunes of the throne, and the sudden return to favour that awaited him. He set out and traversed France, drawn in triumph by the people, to whom, according to his custom, he recommended peace and good order. Though an enemy of the Baron de Besenval, he went to his succour, and promised to demand his pardon from the Parisians. The King received him with embarrassment, the Assembly with enthusiasm; and he resolved to proceed to Paris, where he too might expect to have his day of triumph. Necker's intention was to solicit of the electors the pardon and liberation of the Baron de Besenval. In vain did Bailly, not less an enemy than himself to rigorous measures, but a more just appreciator of circumstances, represent to him the danger of such a step, and observe that this favour, obtained in a moment of excitement, would be revoked next day as illegal, because an administrative body could neither condemn nor pardon; Necker persisted, and made a trial of his influence over the capital. He repaired to the Hôtel de Ville on the 29th of July. His hopes were surpassed, and he could not help believing himself omnipotent on beholding the transports of the multitude. Deeply affected, his eyes filled with tears, he demanded a general amnesty, which was instantly granted by acclamation. The two assemblies of the electors and representatives manifested equal enthusiasm: the electors decreed a general amnesty; the representatives of the commune ordered the liberation of Besenval. Necker retired intoxicated, taking to himself the plaudits that were addressed to his dismissal from office. But that very day he was destined to be undeceived. Mirabeau prepared for him a cruel reverse. In the Assembly, in the districts, a general outcry was raised against the sensibility of the minister, very excusable, it was said, but mistaken. The district of the Oratoire, instigated, as we are assured, by Mirabeau, was the first to find fault. It was maintained on all sides that an administrative body could neither condemn nor absolve. The illegal measure of the Hôtel de Ville was annulled, and the detention of the Baron de Besenval confirmed. So soon was verified the opinion of the sagacious Bailly, which Necker could not be persuaded to follow.

At this moment parties began to speak out more decidedly. The parliaments, the nobility, the clergy, the court, all threatened with the same ruin, had united their interests, and acted in concert. Neither the Count d'Artois nor the Polignacs were any longer at the court. Consternation, mingled with despair, pervaded the aristocracy. Having been unable to prevent what it termed the evil, it was now desirous that the people should commit as much evil as possible, in order to bring about good by the very excess of that evil. This system, compounded of spite and perfidy, which is called "political pessimism," begins among parties as soon as they have suffered sufficient losses to make them renounce what they have left in the hope of regaining the whole. The aristocracy began from this time to adopt this system, and it was frequently seen voting with the most violent members of the popular party.

Circumstances draw forth men. The danger which threatened the nobility produced a champion for it. Young Cazalès, captain in the Queen's Dragoons, had found in himself an unlooked-for energy of mind and facility of expression. Precise and simple, he said promptly and suitably what he had to say; and it is to be regretted that his upright mind was devoted to a cause which had no valid reasons to urge till it had been persecuted. The clergy had found its defender in the Abbé Maury. That abbé, a practised and inexhaustible sophist, had many happy sallies and great coolness: he could courageously withstand tumult, and audaciously oppose evidence. Such were the means and the dispositions of the aristocracy.

The ministry was without views and without plans. Necker, hated by the court, which endured him from compulsion—Necker alone had, not a plan, but a wish. He had always a longing after the English constitution—the best, no doubt, that can be adopted—as an accommodation between the throne, the aristocracy, and the people; but this constitution, proposed by the Bishop of Langres before the establishment of a single assembly, and refused by the first orders, had become impracticable. The high nobility would not admit of two chambers, because that would be a compromise; the inferior nobility, because it could not have access to the upper chamber; the popular party, because, still filled with apprehensions of the aristocracy, it was unwilling to leave any influence to the latter. A few deputies only, some from moderation, others because that idea was their own, wished for English institutions, and formed the whole party of the minister—a weak party, because it held forth only conciliatory views to exasperated passions, and opposed to its adversaries arguments alone, without any means of action.

The popular party began to disagree, because it began to conquer. Lally-Tollendal, Mounier, Malouet, and other partisans of Necker, approved of all that had been done thus far, because all that had been done had brought over the government to their ideas, that is to say, to the English constitution. They now judged that this was sufficient: reconciled with power, they wished to stop there. The popular party, on the contrary, conceived that it was not yet time to stop. It was in the Breton club that the question was discussed with the greatest vehemence. A sincere conviction was the motive of the majority; personal pretensions began nevertheless to manifest themselves, and the movements of private interest to succeed the first flights of patriotism. Barnave, a young advocate of Grenoble, endowed with a clear and ready mind, and possessing, in the highest degree, the talents requisite for a good speaker, formed with the two Lameths a triumvirate which interested by its youth, and soon influenced by its activity and its abilities. Duport, the young councillor to the parliament, whom we have already seen distinguishing himself, belonged to their association. It was said at the time that Duport conceived all that ought to be done, that Barnave expressed it, and that the Lameths executed it. However, these young deputies were the friends of one another, without being yet declared enemies to any one.

The most courageous of the popular leaders, he who, ever in the van, opened the boldest discussions, was Mirabeau. The absurd institutions of the old monarchy had shocked just minds, and excited the indignation of upright hearts; but it was impossible that they should not have galled some ardent spirit and inflamed strong passions. This spirit was that of Mirabeau, who, encountering from his birth every kind of tyranny—that of his father, of the government, and of the tribunals—spent his youth in combating and in hating them. He was born beneath the sun of Provence, the offspring of a noble family. He had early made himself notorious by his dissolute manners, his quarrels, and an impetuous eloquence. His travels, observation, and immense reading, had taught him much, and his memory had retained it all. But extravagant, eccentric, nay even a sophist, without the aid of passion, he became by its aid quite a different man. No sooner was he excited by the tribune and the presence of his opponents than his mind took fire: his first ideas were confused, his words incoherent, his whole frame agitated, but presently the light burst forth. His mind then performed in a moment the labour of years; and in the very tribune all was to him new discovery, sudden and energetic expression. If again crossed, he returned still more forcible and more clear, and presented the truth in images either striking or terrible. Were the circumstances difficult, were minds fatigued by a long discussion, or intimidated by danger, an ejaculation, a decisive word dropped from his lips, his countenance looking terrific with ugliness and genius, and the assembly, enlightened or encouraged, enacted laws or passed magnanimous resolutions.

Proud of his high qualities, jesting over his vices, by turns haughty or supple, he won some by his flattery, awed others by his sarcasms, and led all in his train by the extraordinary influence which he possessed. His party was everywhere; among the people in the Assembly, in the very court, with all those, in short, to whom he was at the moment addressing himself. Mingling familiarly with men, just when it was requisite to do so, he had applauded the rising talent of

Barnave, though he disliked his young friends; he appreciated the profound understanding of Sieyes, and humoured his wild disposition; he dreaded too pure a life in Lafayette; in Necker he detested an extreme rigour, the pride of reason, and the pretension of directing a revolution which he knew to be attributable to him. He was not friendly to the Duke of Orleans and his unsteady ambition, and, as we shall soon see, he never had any interest in common with him. Thus, unaided except by his genius, he attacked despotism, which he had sworn to destroy. If, however, he was a foe to the vanities of monarchy, he was still more adverse to the ostracism of republics; but not being sufficiently revenged on the great and on power, he still continued to destroy. Harassed, moreover, by straitened circumstances, dissatisfied with the present, he was advancing towards an unknown future: by his talents, his ambition, his vices, his pecuniary embarrassments, he gave rise to all sorts of conjectures; and, by his cynical language, he authorised all suspicions and calumnies.

Thus were France and the parties divided. The first differences between the popular deputies arose on occasion of the excesses committed by the multitude. Mounier and Lally-Tollendal proposed a solemn proclamation to the people, to reprobate their outrages. The Assembly, sensible of the uselessness of this measure, and the necessity for preserving the good-will of the populace who had supported it, at first rejected this proposal, but afterwards, yielding to the solicitations of some of its members, it at length issued a proclamation, which proved, as it had been foreseen, utterly useless, for it is not by words that an excited populace can be pacified.

The agitation was general. A sudden terror had spread itself everywhere. The name of those brigands who had been seen starting up in the different commotions was in all mouths, and their image in all minds. The court threw the blame of their outrages on the popular party, and the popular party on the court. All at once, couriers, traversing France in all directions, brought tidings that the brigands were coming, and that they were cutting the corn before it was ripe.

People assembled from all quarters, and in a few days all France was in arms, awaiting the brigands, who never made their appearance. This stratagem, which extended the revolution of the 14th of July to every part of the kingdom, by causing the whole nation to take up arms, was attributed to all the parties, and has since been imputed to the popular party, which benefited by its results. It is surprising that a stratagem, more ingenious than culpable, should be bandied about from one to the other. It has been ascribed to Mirabeau, who boasted of being its author, and who nevertheless has disavowed it. It was not unlike a contrivance by Sieyes, and some have imagined that it was he who suggested it to the Duke of Orleans. Lastly, it was imputed by others to the court. Such persons argue that those couriers would have been apprehended at every step had they not been authorized by the government; that the court, never having supposed the revolution to be general, and looking upon it as a mere riot of the Parisians, wished to arm the provinces for the purpose of opposing them to the capital. Be this as it may, the expedient proved beneficial to the nation, by arming and enabling it to protect itself and its rights.

The people of the towns had shaken off their fetters; the country people also determined to shake off theirs. They refused to pay the feudal dues; they attacked such of the landholders as had oppressed them; they set fire to their mansions, burned their title-deeds, and in some parts of the country committed atrocious acts of revenge. A deplorable accident had greatly contributed to excite this universal effervescence. A sieur de Mesmai, *seigneur* of Quincey, gave an entertainment in the grounds about his mansion. All the country people were assembled there, and indulging in various amusements, when a barrel of gunpowder, suddenly taking fire, produced a murderous explosion. This accident, since ascertained to have been the effect of imprudence and not of design, was imputed as a crime to the sieur de Mesmai. The report of it soon spread, and every where provoked the barbarity of those peasants, hardened by misery, and rendered cruel by long sufferings. The ministers came in a body to submit to the Assembly a picture of the deplorable state of France, and to demand from it the means of restoring order. These disasters of all kinds had occurred since the 14th of July. The month of August was beginning, and it became indispensable to re-establish the action of the government and of the laws. But, to attempt this with success, it was necessary to commence the regeneration of the state with the reform of the institutions which were most obnoxious to the people, and had the greatest tendency to excite them to insurrection. One part of the nation, subject to the other, was burdened with a number of what were termed feudal dues. Some, called useful, compelled the peasants to make ruinous advances; others, named honorary, required them to pay humiliating marks of respect and services to their lords. These were relics of the feudal barbarism, the abolition of which was due to humanity. These privileges, considered as property, and even called so by the King in the declaration of the 23rd of June, could not be abolished by a discussion. It was requisite, by a sudden movement, to excite the possessors to resign them of their own accord.

The Assembly was then discussing the famous declaration of the rights of man. It had at first been debated whether there should be such a declaration or not, and it had been decided, on the morning of the 4th of August, that it should be made and placed at the head of the constitution. In the evening of the same day, the committee made its report on the disturbances and the means of putting an end to them. The Viscount de Noailles and the Duke d'Aiguillon, both members of the nobility, then ascended the tribune, and represented that it would be silly to employ force to quiet the people; that the right way would be to destroy the cause of their sufferings, and then the agitation which was the effect of them would instantly cease. Explaining themselves more fully, they proposed to abolish all the vexatious rights, which by the name of feudal rights, oppressed the country people. M. Leguen de Kerengal, a landholder of Bretagne, appeared in the tribune in the dress of a farmer, and drew a frightful picture of the feudal system. Presently, the generosity of some was excited and the pride of others wrought upon to such a degree as to produce a sudden paroxysm of disinterestedness; every one hurried to the tribune to renounce his privileges. The nobility set the first example, which was as cheerfully followed by the clergy. A sort of intoxication seized the Assembly. Setting aside a superfluous discussion, and which certainly was not required to demonstrate the justice of such sacrifices, all orders, all classes, all the possessors of prerogatives of every kind, hastened to renounce them. After the deputies of the first orders, those of the commons came also to offer their sacrifices. Having no personal privileges to give up, they relinquished those of the provinces and the towns. The equality of rights, established between individuals, was thus established also between all the parts of the French territory. Some offered pensions, and a member of the parliament, having nothing else to give, promised his zeal in behalf of the public welfare. The steps of the office were covered with deputies who came to deliver the acts of their renunciation. They were content for the moment to enumerate the sacrifices, and deferred till the following day the drawing up of the articles. The impulse was general, but, amidst this enthusiasm, it was easy to perceive that certain of the privileged persons, so far from being sincere, were desirous of making matters worse. Every thing was to be feared from the effect of that night, and the impulse given, when Lally-Tollendal, perceiving the danger, caused a note to this effect to be handed to the president: "Every thing is to be apprehended from the enthusiasm of the Assembly; break up the sitting." At the same instant, a deputy ran up to him, and grasping his hand with emotion, said to him, "Procure us the royal sanction, and we are friends." Lally-Tollendal, sensible of the necessity of attaching the revolution to the King, then proposed to proclaim him the restorer of French liberty. The motion was hailed with enthusiasm; it was resolved that *Te Deum* should be performed, and the Assembly at length broke up about midnight.

During this memorable night the Assembly had decreed:

The abolition of the quality of serf;

The right of compounding for the seignorial dues;

The abolition of the seignorial jurisdictions;

The suppression of exclusive rights to hunt, to keep dovecotes, warrens, &c.;

The redemption of tithes;

The equality of taxes;

The admission of all the citizens to civil and military employments;

The abolition of the sale of offices;

The suppression of all the privileges of towns and provinces;

The reformation of the *jurandes*;

And the suppression of pensions obtained without claims.

These resolutions had been passed in a general form, and they still remained to be embodied in decrees; and then, the first fervour of generosity having subsided, some strove to extend, others to contract, the concessions obtained. The discussion grew warm, and a late and injudicious resistance did away with all claim to gratitude.

The abolition of feudal rights, had been agreed upon; but it was necessary to make a distinction between such of these rights as were to be abolished and those that were to be redeemed. The conquerors, the first creators of the nobility, when of old they subdued the country, imposed services upon the inhabitants, and a tribute upon the land. They had even seized part of the latter, and had gradually restored it to the cultivators only on condition of being paid perpetual rents. A long possession, followed by numerous transfers, constituting property, all the charges imposed upon the inhabitants and the lands had acquired the same character. The Constituent Assembly was therefore compelled to attack property. In this situation, it was not as more or less acquired, but as being more or less burdensome to society, that the Assembly had to deal with it. It abolished personal services; and, several of these services having been changed into quit-rents, it abolished these quit-rents. Among the tributes imposed upon land, it abolished those which were evidently the relics of servitude, as the fines imposed upon transfer; and it declared redeemable all the perpetual rents, that were the price for which the nobility had formerly ceded part of the lands to the cultivators. Nothing, therefore, is more absurd than to accuse the Constituent Assembly of having violated property, since every thing had become such; and it is strange that the nobility, having so long violated it, either by imposing tributes or by not paying taxes, should become all at once so tenacious of principles, when its own prerogatives were at stake. The seignorial courts were also called property, because they had for ages been transmitted from heir to heir: but the Assembly, disregarding this plea, abolished them; directing, however, that they should be kept up till a substitute should be provided for them.

The exclusive right of the chase was also a subject of warm discussion. Notwithstanding the vain objection that the whole population would soon be in arms if the right of sporting were made general, it was conferred on every one within the limits of his own lands. The privileged dovecotes were in like manner defended. The Assembly decided that every body might keep them, but that in harvest-time pigeons might be killed like ordinary game, upon the lands which they might be visiting. All the captainships were abolished, but it was added that provision should be made for the private pleasures of the King by means compatible with liberty and property.

One article gave rise to discussions of peculiar violence, on account of the more important questions to which it was the prelude, and the interests which it attacked—this was an article relative to tithes. On the night of the 4th of August, the Assembly had declared that tithes might be redeemed. At the moment of drawing up the decree, it determined to abolish them without redemption, taking care to add that the state should provide for the maintenance of the clergy. There was no doubt an informality in this decision, because it interfered with a resolution already adopted. But to this objection Garat answered that this would be a *boná-fide* redemption, since the state actually redeemed the tithes to the relief of the contributor, by undertaking to make a provision for the clergy. The Abbé Sieyes, who was seen with surprise among the defenders of the tithes, and who was not supposed to be a disinterested defender of that impost, admitted in fact that the state really redeemed the tithes, but that it committed a robbery on the mass of the nation by throwing upon its shoulders a debt which ought to be borne by the landed proprietors alone. This objection, urged in a striking manner, was accompanied with this keen and since frequently repeated expression: "You want to be free and you know not how to be just." Though Sieyes thought this objection unanswerable, the answer to it was easy. The debt incurred for the support of religion is the debt of all; whether it should be paid by the landed proprietors rather than by the whole of the tenants, is a point for the state to decide. It robs nobody by dividing the burden in such a manner as it deems most proper. Tithes, by oppressing the little proprietors, destroyed agriculture; the state had therefore a right to provide a substitute for that impost; and this Mirabeau proved to demonstration. The clergy, which preferred tithes, because it foresaw that the salary adjudged by the state would be measured according to its real necessities, claimed a property in tithes by immemorial concessions; it renewed that oft-repeated argument of long possession, which proves nothing; otherwise every thing, not excepting tyranny itself, would be rendered legitimate by possession. It was answered that tithe was only a life-interest, that it was not transferable, and had not the principal characters of property; that it was evidently a tax imposed in favour of the clergy; and that the state undertook to change this tax into another. The pride of the clergy revolted at the idea of its receiving a salary; on this subject it combined with vehemence; and Mirabeau, who was particularly dexterous in launching the shafts of reason and irony, replied to the complainants that he knew of but three ways of existing in society—by robbing, begging, or being paid a salary. The clergy felt that it behoved it to give up what it was no longer able to defend. The *curés* in particular, knowing that they had everything to gain from the spirit of justice which pervaded the Assembly, and that it was the opulence of the prelates which was the especial object of attack, were the first to desist. The entire abolition of tithes was therefore decreed; it was added that the state would take upon itself the expense of providing for the ministers of religion, and that meanwhile the tithe should continue to be levied. This latter clause, fraught with respect, proved indeed useless. The people would no longer pay, but that they would not do even before the passing of the decree; and, when the Assembly abolished the feudal system, it was already in fact overthrown. On the 11th, all the articles were presented to the monarch, who accepted the title of the restorer of French liberty, and was present at the *Te Deum*, having the president at his right hand and all the deputies in his train.

Thus was consummated the most important reform of the revolution. The Assembly had manifested equal energy and moderation. Unfortunately, a nation never knows how to resume with moderation the exercise of its rights. Atrocious outrages were committed throughout the whole kingdom. The mansions of the gentry continued to be set on fire, and the country was inundated by sportsmen eager to avail themselves of their newly acquired rights. They spread over the lands formerly reserved for the exclusive pleasure of their oppressors, and committed frightful devastations. Every usurpation meets with a cruel retribution, and he who usurps ought at least to consider his children, who almost always have to pay the penalty. Numerous accidents occurred. So early as the 7th of August, the ministers again attended the Assembly for the purpose of laying before it a report on the state of the kingdom. The keeper of the seals announced the alarming disturbances which had taken place; Necker revealed the deplorable state of the finances. The Assembly received this two-fold message with sorrow, but without discouragement. On the 10th, it passed a decree relative to the public tranquillity, by which the municipalities were directed to provide for the preservation of order by dispersing all seditious assemblages. They were to deliver up mere rioters to the tribunals; but those who had excited alarms, circulated false orders, or instigated to outrages, were to be imprisoned, and the proceedings addressed to the National Assembly, that it might be enabled to ascertain the cause of these disturbances. The national militia and the regular troops were placed at the disposal of the municipalities, and they were to take an oath to be faithful to the nation, the King, and the law. This oath was afterwards called the civic oath.

The report of Necker on the finances was extremely alarming. It was the want of subsidies that had caused recourse to be had to a National Assembly; no sooner had this Assembly met, than it had commenced a struggle with power; and, directing its whole attention to the urgent necessity of establishing guarantees, it had neglected that of securing the revenues of the state. On Necker alone rested the whole care of the finances. While Bailly, charged with provisioning the capital, was in the most painful anxiety, Necker, harassed by less urgent but far more extensive wants—Necker, absorbed in laborious calculations, tormented by a thousand troubles, strove to supply the public necessities: and, while he was thinking only of financial questions, he was not aware that the Assembly was thinking exclusively of political questions. Necker and the Assembly, each engrossed by their own object, perceived no other. If, however, the alarm of Necker was justified by the actual distress, so was the confidence of the Assembly by the elevation of its views That Assembly, embracing France and its future fortunes, could not believe that this fine kingdom, though involved for the moment in embarrassments, was for ever plunged into indigence.

Necker, when he entered upon office in August, 1788, had found but four hundred thousand francs in the exchequer. He had, by dint of assiduity, provided for the most urgent wants; and circumstances had since increased those wants by diminishing the resources. It had been found necessary to purchase corn and to sell it again for less than the cost price; to give away considerable sums in alms; to undertake public works, in order to furnish employment to the workmen. For this latter purpose so much as twelve thousand francs per day had been issued by the exchequer. While the expenses had increased, the receipts had diminished. The reduction of the price of salt, the delay of payments, and in many cases the absolute refusal to pay the taxes, the smuggling carried on by armed force, the destruction of the barriers, nay, the plunder of the registers and the murder of the clerks, had annihilated part of the public revenue. Necker, in consequence, demanded a loan of thirty millions. The first impression was so strong, that the Assembly was about to vote the loan by acclamation; but this first impression soon subsided. A dislike was expressed for new loans; a kind of contradiction was committed by appealing to the instructions, which had already been renounced, and which forbade the granting of imposts till the constitution had been framed: members even went so far as to enter into a calculation of the sums received since the preceding year, as if they distrusted the minister. However, the absolute necessity of providing for the wants of the state caused the loan to be carried; but the minister's plan was changed, and the interest reduced to four-and-a-half per cent., in false reliance upon a patriotism which was in the nation, but which could not exist in money-lenders by profession, the only persons who in general enter into financial speculations of this kind. This first blunder was one of those which assemblies usually commit, because they supersede the immediate views of the minister who acts by the general views of twelve hundred minds which speculate. It was easy to perceive, therefore, that the spirit of the nation began already not to harmonise with the timidity of the minister.

Having bestowed this indispensable care on the public tranquillity and the finances, the Assembly directed its attention to the declaration of rights. The first idea of it had been furnished by Lafayette, who had himself borrowed it from the Americans. This discussion, interrupted by the revolution of the 14th of July, renewed on the 1st of August, a second time interrupted by the abolition of the feudal system, was anew and definitively resumed on the 12th of August. This idea had something important which struck the Assembly. The enthusiasm pervading the minds of the members disposed them to everything that was grand; this enthusiasm produced their sincerity, their courage, their good and their bad resolutions. Accordingly they caught at this idea, and resolved to carry it into execution. Had they meant only to proclaim certain principles, particularly obnoxious to the authority whose yoke they had just shaken off, such as the voting of taxes, religious liberty, the liberty of the press, and ministerial responsibility, nothing would have been more easy. This was what America and England had formerly done. France might have compressed into a few pithy and positive maxims the new principles which she imposed upon her government; but, desiring to go back to a state of nature, she aspired to give a complete declaration of all the rights of the man and of the citizen. At first the necessity and the danger of such a declaration were discussed. Much was said and to no purpose on this subject, for there was neither utility nor danger in issuing a declaration composed of formulas that were above the comprehension of the people. It was something only for a certain number of philosophic minds, which never take any great part in popular seditions. It was resolved that it should be made and placed at the head of the constitutional acts. But it was necessary to draw it up, and that was the most difficult point. "What is a right?—that which is due to men. Now all the good that can be done to them is their due; every wise measure of government is therefore a right. Thus all the proposed plans contained a definition of the law, the manner in which it was to be made, the principle of the sovereignty, &c. It was objected that these were not rights but general maxims. It was nevertheless of importance to express those maxims. Mirabeau, becoming impatient, at length exclaimed, "Omit the word rights, and say 'For the interest of all it has been declared.' " The more imposing title of declaration of rights was nevertheless preferred, and under it were blended maxims, principles, and declarations. Out of the whole was composed the celebrated declaration placed at the head of the constitution of 1791. In other respects, there was no great harm done in wasting a few sittings on a philosophic commonplace. But who can censure men for becoming intoxicated with an object by which they were so much engrossed?

It was at length time to turn to the consideration of the constitution. The fatigue occasioned by the preliminaries was general, and the fundamental questions began already to be discussed out of the

Assembly. The English constitution was the model that naturally presented itself to many minds, since it was the compact made in England in consequence of a similar struggle between the King, the aristocracy, and the people. This constitution resided essentially in the establishment of two chambers and in the royal sanction. Minds in their first flight go to the simplest ideas: a people declaring its will, and a king who executes it, appeared to them the only legitimate form of government. To give to the aristocracy a share equal to that of the nation, by means of an upper chamber; to give to the King the right of annulling the national will, seemed to them an absurdity. *The nation wills, the king executes*: they could not get beyond these simple elements, and they imagined that they wished for a monarchy, because they left a king as the executor of the national resolutions. Real monarchy, as it exists even in states reputed free, is the rule of one, to which limits are set by means of the national concurrence. There the will of the prince in reality does almost everything, and that of the nation is confined to the prevention of evil, either by disputing the taxes, or by concurring in the law. But the moment that the nation can order what it pleases, without the king's having the power to oppose it by a veto, the king is no more than a magistrate. It is then a republic, with one consul instead of several. The government of Poland, though it had a king, was never called a monarchy, but a republic; there was a king also at Lacadæmon.

Monarchy, properly understood, requires therefore great concessions from opinion. But it is not after a long nullity, and in their first enthusiasm, that they are disposed to make them. Thus the republic existed in men's opinions, without being mentioned, and they were republicans without being aware of it.

In the discussion, the members did not explain themselves with precision: accordingly, notwithstanding the genius and knowledge to be found by the Assembly, the question was superficially treated and imperfectly understood. The partisans of the English constitution, Necker, Mounier, and Lally, could not see in what the monarchy ought to consist; and if they had seen it, they durst not have told the Assembly plainly that the national will ought not to be omnipotent, and that it ought to confine itself to prevention rather than take upon itself the executive. All they had to urge was, that it was necessary that the King should possess the power of checking the encroachments of an assembly; that, in order to his duly executing the law, and executing it cheerfully, it was requisite that he should have co-operated in it; and finally that there ought to exist a connection between the executive and legislative powers. These reasons were bad, or at any rate weak. It was ridiculous, in fact, whilst recognising the national sovereignty, to pretend to oppose to it the sole will of the King.

They defended the two chambers more successfully, because there are, in fact, even in a republic, higher classes which must oppose the too rapid movements of the classes that are raising themselves, by defending the ancient institutions against the new institutions. But that upper chamber, more indispensable than the royal prerogative, since there is no instance of a republic without a senate, was more scouted than the sanction, because people were more exasperated against the aristocracy than against royalty. It was impractable then to form an upper chamber, because nobody wished for it: the inferior nobility opposed it, because they could not obtain admission into it; the privileged persons themselves, who were desperate, because they desired the worst; the popular party, because it would not leave the aristocracy a post whence it might command the national will. Mounier, Lally, and Necker, were almost the only members who wished for this upper chamber. Sieyes, by an absolute error in judgment, would not admit either of the two chambers or of the royal sanction. He conceived society to be completely uniform; according to him, the mass, without distinction of classes, ought to be charged to will, and the king, as the sole magistrate, to De charged to execute. He was, therefore, quite sincere when he said that, whether monarchy or republic, it was the same thing, since the difference consisted, in his opinion, only in the number of the magistrates charged with the execution. The characteristic of the mind of Sieyes was concatenation; that is to say, the strict connection of his own ideas. He was in the best understanding with himself, but he harmonised neither with the nature of things nor with minds different from his own. He subdued them by the empire of his absolute maxims, but rarely persuaded them: therefore, as he could neither break his systems into parts nor cause them to be adopted entire, he naturally began soon to be in an ill humour. Mirabeau, a man of straightforward, prompt, supple mind, was not further advanced, in point of political science, than the Assembly itself; he was adverse to the two chambers, not from conviction, but from the knowledge of their then impracticability, and from hatred of the aristocracy. He defended the royal sanction from a monarchical predilection, and he had pledged himself to it at the opening of the states, when he said, that without the sanction he would rather live at Constantinople than in Paris. Barnave, Duport, and Lameth could not agree in these sentiments of Mirabeau. They were for not admitting either of the upper chamber or of the royal sanction; but they were not so obstinate as Sieyes, and consented to modify their opinion by allowing the King and the upper chamber a merely suspensive veto, that is to say, the power of temporarily opposing the national will, expressed in the lower chamber.

The first discussions took place on the 28th and 29th of August. The friends of Barnave were desirous of treating with Mounier, whose obstinacy had made him leader of the party in favour of the English constitution. It behoved them to gain over the most inflexible, and to him therefore they addressed themselves. Conferences were held; when it was found to be impossible to change an opinion that had been long cherished by him; they assented to those English forms to which he was so wedded; but on condition that, in opposing to the popular chamber an upper chamber and the King, only one suspensive veto should be given to the two, and that, moreover, the King should not have authority to dissolve the Assembly. Mounier replied, like a man whose mind is thoroughly convinced, that truth was not his property, and that he could not sacrifice one part to save the other. Thus did he wreck both institutions by refusing to modify them. And if it were true, which it was not, as we shall presently see, that the constitution of 1791 overturned the throne by the suppression of the upper chamber, Mounier would have occasion to reproach himself severely. Mounier was not passionate but obstinate; he was as absolute in his system as Sieyes was in his, and preferred losing all to giving up anything. The negotiations were broken off in anger. Mounier had been threatened with the public opinion of Paris, and his adversaries set out, he said, to exercise that influence with which he had been menaced. (*See* Appendix I.)

These questions divided the people as well as the representatives, and if they did not comprehend them, they attacked or defended them with not the less warmth. They summed them all up in the short and expeditious term *veto*. They approved or disapproved the veto, and this signified that they wished or did not wish for tyranny. The populace, without even understanding this, took the veto for a tax winch ought to be abolished, or an enemy that ought to be hung, and were eager to consign him to the lamppost.

The Palais Royal, in particular, was in the greatest fermentation. Men of ardent minds assembled there, who, spurning even the forms imposed in the districts, mounted a chair, began their uncalled-for harangues, and were hissed or borne in triumph by an immense crowd, which hastened to execute what they proposed. There, Camille Desmoulins, already mentioned in this history, distinguished himself by the energy, originality, and cynical turn of his mind; and without being cruel himself he demanded cruelties. There, too, was seen St. Hurugue, an ancient marquis, long imprisoned in the Bastille on account of family quarrels, and incensed to madness against the supreme authority. There it was every day repeated that they ought all to go to Versailles, to call the King and the Assembly to account for their hesitation to secure the welfare of the people. Lafayette had the greatest difficulty to keep them within bounds by continual patroles. The national guard was already accused of aristocracy. "There was no patrole at the

Ceramieus," observed Desmoulins. The name of Cromwell had already been pronounced along with that of Lafayette. One day—it was Sunday, the 30th of August—a motion was made at the Palais Royal; Mounier was accused, Mirabeau represented to be in danger, and it was proposed to proceed to Versailles, to ensure the personal safety of the latter. Mirabeau, nevertheless, defended the sanction, but without relinquishing his office as a popular tribune, and without appearing less such in the eyes of the multitude. St. Hurugue, followed by a few hot-headed persons, took the road to Versailles. They intended, they said, to prevail upon the Assembly to expel its unfaithful representatives, that others might be elected, and to entreat the King and the dauphin to remove to Paris, and to place themselves in safety amidst the people. Lafayette hastened after them, stopped them, and obliged them to turn back. On the following day, Monday, the 31st, they again met. They drew up an address to the commune, in which they demanded the convocation of the districts, in order to condemn the veto, to censure the deputies who supported it, to cashier them, and to nominate others in their stead. The commune repulsed them twice with the greatest firmness.

Agitation meanwhile pervaded the Assembly. Letters full of threats and invectives had been sent to the principal deputies; one of these was signed with the name of St. Hurugue. On Monday, the 31st, at the opening of the sitting, Lally denounced a deputation which he had received from the Palais Royal. This deputation had exhorted him to separate himself from the bad citizens who defended the veto, and added, that an army of twenty thousand men was ready to march. Mounier also read letters which he had received, proposed that search should be made for the secret authors of these machinations, and urged the Assembly to offer five hundred thousand francs to any one who should denounce them. The discussion was tumultuous. Duport maintained that it was beneath the dignity of the Assembly to direct its attention to such matters. Mirabeau, too, read letters addressed to him, in which the enemies of the popular cause treated him no better than they had treated Mounier. The Assembly passed to the order of the day, and St. Hurugue, having signed one of the denounced letters, was imprisoned by order of the commune.

The three questions, concerning the permanence of the Assemblies, the two chambers, and the veto, were discussed at once. The permanence of the Assembly was voted almost unanimously. The people had suffered too much from the long interruption of the national Assemblies, not to render them permanent. The great question of the unity of the legislative body was then taken up. The tribunes were occupied by a numerous and noisy multitude. Many of the deputies withdrew. The president, then the Bishop of Langres, strove in vain to stop them; they went away in great numbers. Loud cries from all quarters required that the question should be put to the vote. Lally claimed permission to speak again; it was refused, and the president was accused of having sent him to the tribune. One member even went so far as to ask the president if he was not tired of annoying the Assembly. Offended at this expression, the president left the chair, and the discussion was again adjourned. On the following day, the 10th of September, an address was read from the city of Rennes, declaring the veto to be inadmissible, and those who should vote for it, traitors to the country. Mounier and his partisans were exasperated, and proposed to reprove the municipality. Mirabeau replied that it was not the province of the Assembly to lecture municipal officers, and that it would be right to pass to the order of the day. This question of the two chambers was finally put to the vote, and the unity of the Assembly was decreed amidst tumultuous applause. Four hundred and ninety-eight votes were in favour of one chamber, ninety-nine in favour of two, and one hundred and twenty-two votes were lost, owing to the apprehensions excited in many of the deputies.

The question of the veto at length came on. A middle term had been found in the suspensive veto, which should suspend the law, but only for a time during one or more sessions. This was considered as an appeal to the people, because the King, recurring to new assemblies, and yielding to them if they persisted, seemed in reality to appeal from them to the national authority. Mounier and his party opposed this: they were right with reference to the system of the English monarchy, where the King consults the national representation, and never obeys it; but they were wrong in the situation in which they were placed. Their only object had been, they said, to prevent a too hasty resolution. Now the suspensive veto produced this effect quite as effectually as the absolute veto. If the representation should persist, the national will would be made manifest, and whilst admitting its sovereignty it was ridiculous to resist it indefinitely.

The ministry actually felt that the suspensive veto produced materially the effect of the absolute veto, and Necker advised the King to secure to himself the advantages of a voluntary sacrifice, by addressing a memorial to the Assembly, desiring the suspensive veto. A rumour of this got abroad, and the object and spirit of the memorial were known beforehand. It was presented on the 11th; everybody was acquainted with its purport. It would appear that Mounier, supporting the interests of the throne, ought not to have had any other views than the throne itself; but parties very soon have an interest distinct from those whom they serve. Mounier was for rejecting this communication, alleging that, if the King renounced a prerogative beneficial to the nation, it ought to be given to him in spite of himself, and for the public interest. The parts were now reversed, and the adversaries of the King maintained on this occasion his right of interference. Fresh explanations were entered into respecting the word sanction: the question, whether it should be necessary for the constitution, was discussed. After specifying that the constituting power was superior to the constituted powers, it was determined that the sanction could be exercised only upon legislative acts, but by no means upon constitutive acts, and that the latter should only be promulgated. Six hundred and seventy-three votes were in favour of the suspensive veto, three hundred and fifty-five for the absolute veto. Thus the fundamental articles of the new constitution were determined upon. Mounier and

Lally-Tollendal immediately resigned their places as members of the committee of constitution.

Up to this time a great number of decrees had been passed, without being submitted to the royal acceptance. It was resolved to present to the King the articles of the 4th of August. The question to be decided was whether they should apply for the sanction or the mere promulgation, considering them as legislative or constitutive acts. Maury and even Lally-Tollendal were indiscreet enough to maintain that they were legislative, and to require the sanction, as if they had expected some obstacle from the royal power. Mirabeau, with rare justice, asserted that some abolished the feudal system and were eminently constitutive; and others were a pure munificence on the part of the nobility and clergy, and that, undoubtedly, the clergy and the nobility did not wish the King to revoke their liberality. Chapelier added that there was not even any occasion to suppose the consent of the King to be necessary, as he had already approved them by accepting the title of restorer of French liberty and attending the *Te Deum*. The King was in consequence solicited to make a mere promulgation.

A member all at once proposed the hereditary transmission of the crown and the inviolability of the royal person. The Assembly, which sincerely wished for the King as its hereditary first magistrate, voted these two articles by acclamation. The inviolability of the heir presumptive was proposed; but the Duke de Mortemart instantly remarked that sons had sometimes endeavoured to dethrone their lathers, and that they ought to reserve to themselves the means of punishing them. On this ground the proposal was rejected. With respect to the article on the hereditary descent from male to male and from branch to branch, Arnoult proposed to confirm the renunciations of the Spanish branch made in the treaty of Utrecht. It was urged that there was no occasion to discuss this point, because they ought not to alienate a faithful ally. Mirabeau supported this opinion, and the Assembly passed to the order of the day. All at once Mirabeau, for the purpose of making an experiment that was ill judged, attempted to bring forward the very question which he had himself contributed to silence. The house of Orleans would become a competitor with the Spanish house, in case of the extinction of the reigning branch. Mirabeau had observed an extraordinary eagerness to pass to the order of the day. A stranger to the Duke of Orleans, though familiar with him, as he could be with everybody, he nevertheless wished to ascertain the state of parties, and to discover who were the friends and the enemies of the duke. The question of a regency came forward. In case of minority, the King's brothers could not be guardians of their nephew, as heirs to the royal ward, and not being interested in his preservation. The regency, therefore, would belong to the nearest relatives; this was either the Queen, or the Duke of Orleans, or the Spanish family. Mirabeau then proposed that the regency should not be given to any but a man born in France. "My acquaintance," said he, "with the geography of the Assembly, the point whence proceeded those cries for the order of the day, prove to me that the question here is nothing less than that of a foreign domination, and that the proposition not to deliberate, apparently Spanish, is perhaps an Austrian proposition."

Loud cries succeeded these words; the discussion recommenced with extraordinary violence; all the opposers again called for the order of the day. To no purpose did Mirabeau every moment repeat that they could have but one motive, that of bringing a foreign domination into France; they made no reply, because, in fact, they would have preferred a foreigner to the Duke of Orleans. At length, after a debate of two days, it was again decided that there was no occasion to deliberate. But Mirabeau had attained his object, in making the parties declare themselves. This experiment could not fail to draw down accusations upon him, and he passed thenceforward for an agent of the Orleans party. (*See* Appendix J.)

While yet strongly agitated by this discussion, the Assembly received the King's answer to the articles of the 4th of August. The King approved of their spirit, but gave only a conditional adhesion to some of them, in the hope that they would be modified on being carried into execution; he renewed, with regard to most, the objections made in the discussion and set aside by the Assembly. Mirabeau again appeared at the tribune. "We have not," said he, "yet examined the superiority of the constituent power over the executive power: we have, in some measure, thrown a veil over these questions [the Assembly had, in fact, explained for itself the mariner in which they were to be understood, without passing any resolution on the subject]; but, if our constituent power were to be contested, we should be obliged to declare it. Let us act in this case frankly and with good faith. We admit that there would be difficulties in the execution, but we do not insist upon it. Thus we demand the abolition of offices, but assign for the future a compensation, and a pledge for the compensation: we declare the impost which supplies the salaries of the clergy destructive of agriculture, but, till a substitute is provided, we direct the collection of tithes; we abolish seignorial courts, but allow them to exist till other tribunals are established. The same is the case with other articles: all of them involve only such principles as it is necessary to render irrevocable by promulgating them. Let us ingenuously repeat to the King, what the fool of Philip II. said to that most absolute prince: 'What would become of thee, Philip, if all the world were to say yes, when thou sayest no?'"

The Assembly again directed the president to wait upon the King to solicit of him his promulgation. The King granted it. The Assembly, on its part, deliberating on the duration of the suspensive veto, extended it to two sessions. But it was wrong to let it be seen that this was, in some sort, a recompense given to Louis XVI. for the concessions that he had just made to the public opinion.

While the Assembly pursued its course amidst obstacles raised by the ill-will of the privileged orders and by the popular commotions, other embarrassments thronged to meet it, and its enemies exulted over them. They hoped that it would be stopped short by the wretched state of the finances, as the court itself had been. The first loan of thirty millions had not succeeded; a second of eighty, ordered agreeably to a new plan of Necker, had not been attended with happier results. "Go on discussing," said M. Degouy d'Arcy one day, "throw in delays, and at the expiration of those delays we shall no longer be. . . . . I have just heard fearful truths."—"Order! order!" exclaimed some. "No, no, speak!" rejoined others. A deputy rose. "Proceed," said he to M. Degouy; "spread around alarm and terror. What will be the consequence? We shall give part of our fortune, and all will be over." M. Degouy continued: "The loans which you have voted have produced nothing; there are not ten millions in the exchequer." At these words, he was again surrounded, censured, and reduced to silence. The Duke d'Aiguillon, president of the committee of the finances, contradicted him, and proved that there must be twenty-two millions in the coffers of the state. It was, nevertheless, resolved that Fridays and Saturdays should be specially devoted to the finances.

Necker at length arrived. Ill with his incessant efforts, he renewed his everlasting complaints: he reproached the Assembly with having done nothing for the finances after a session of five months. The two loans had failed, because disturbances had destroyed public credit. Large sums of money were concealed; the capital of foreigners had been withheld from the proposed loans. Emigration and absence of travellers had also served to decrease the circulating medium, so that there was actually not enough left for the daily wants. The King and Queen had been obliged to send their plate to the mint. Necker, in consequence, demanded an instalment of one-fourth of the revenue, declaring that these means appeared to him to be sufficient. A committee took three days to examine this plan and entirely approved of it. Mirabeau, a known enemy to the minister, was the first to speak, for the purpose of exhorting the Assembly to agree to this plan without discussion. "Not having time," said he, "to investigate it, the Assembly ought not to take upon itself the responsibility of the event, by approving or disapproving the proposed expedients." On this ground he advised that it should be voted immediately and with confidence. The Assembly, hurried away by his arguments, adopted this proposal, and directed Mirabeau to retire and draw up the decree. Meanwhile, the enthusiasm began to subside;

the minister's enemies pretended to discover resources where he could find none. His friends, on the contrary, attacked Mirabeau, and complained that he wanted to crush him under the responsibility which events might throw upon him. Mirabeau returned and read his decree. "You murder the minister's plan," exclaimed M. De Virieu. Mirabeau, who was not in the habit of receding without a reply, frankly avowed his motive, and admitted that those had guessed it who alleged that he wished to throw on M. Necker alone the responsibility; he said that he had not the honour to be his friend, but that, were he his most affectionate friend, he, a citizen above all things, would not hesitate to compromise him rather than the Assembly: that he did not believe the kingdom to be in danger, though M. Necker should prove to be mistaken; and that, on the other hand, the public welfare would be deeply compromised, if the Assembly had lost its credit and failed in a decisive operation. He immediately proposed an address to rouse the national patriotism and to support the plan of the minister.

He was applauded, but the discussion was continued. A thousand propositions were made, and time was wasted in vain subtilties. Weary of so many contradictions, impressed with the urgency of the public wants, he ascended the tribune for the last time, took possession of it, again expounded the question with admirable precision, and showed the impossibility of retreating from the necessity of the moment. His imagination warming as he proceeded, he painted the horrors of bankruptcy; he exhibited it as a ruinous tax, which, instead of pressing lightly upon all, falls only upon some whom it crushes by its weight; he then described it as a gulf into which living victims are thrown, and which does not close again even after devouring them; for we owe none the less even after we have refused to pay. As he concluded, he thrilled the Assembly with terror. "The other day," said he, "when a ridiculous motion was made at the Palais Royal, some one exclaimed 'Catiline is at the gates of Rome, and you deliberate!' but most assuredly there was neither Catiline, nor danger, nor Rome; and to-day hideous bankruptcy is here, threatening to consume you, your honour, your fortunes—and you deliberate!"

At these words the transported Assembly rose with shouts of enthusiasm. A deputy prepared to reply; he advanced, but, affrighted at the task, he stood motionless and speechless. The Assembly then declared that, having heard the report of the committee, it adopted in confidence the plan of the minister of the finances. This was a happy stroke of eloquence; but he alone would be capable of it, who should possess the reason as well as the passions of Mirabeau.

While the Assembly thus laid hands upon all parts of the edifice, important events were arising. By the union of the orders, the nation had recovered the legislative omnipotence. By the 14th of July it had taken arms in support of its representatives. Thus the King and the aristocracy remained separated and disarmed, with the mere opinion of their rights in which no one participated, and in presence of a nation ready to conceive everything, and to execute everything. The court, however, secluded in a small town, peopled entirely by its servants, was in some respect beyond the popular influence, and could even attempt a coup de main against the Assembly. It was natural that Paris, but a few leagues distant from Versailles—Paris, the capital of the kingdom—should wish to draw the King back to its bosom, in order to remove him from all aristocratic influence, and to recover the advantages which a city derives from the presence of the court and of the government. After curtailing the authority of the King, all that it had left to do was to make sure of his person. The course of events favoured this wish, and from all quarters was heard the cry of "The King to Paris!" The aristocracy ceased to think of defending itself against fresh losses. It felt too much disdain for what was left it to care about preserving that; it was therefore desirous of a violent change, just like the popular party. A revolution is infallible, when two parties join in desiring it. Both contribute to the event, and the stronger profits by the result. While the patriots wished to bring the King to Paris, the court had it in contemplation to carry him to Metz. There, in a fortress, it might order all that it pleased, or, to speak more correctly, all that others should please for it. The courtiers formed plans, circulated projects, strove to enlist partisans; and, indulging vain hopes, betrayed themselves by imprudent threats. D'Estaing, formerly so renowned at the head of our fleets, commanded the national guard of Versailles. He desired to be faithful both to the nation and to the court; a difficult part, which is always exposed to calumny, and which great firmness alone can render honourable. He learned the machinations of the courtiers. The highest personages were involved in them; witnesses most worthy of belief had been mentioned to him, and he addressed to the Queen his celebrated letter, in which he expatiated with respectful firmness on the impropriety and danger of such intrigues. He disguised nothing, and mentioned every person by name. (*See* Appendix K.) The letter had no effect. In venturing upon such enterprises, the Queen must have expected remonstrances, and could not have been surprised at them.

About the same period, a great number of new faces appeared at Versailles; nay, even strange uniforms were seen there. The company of the life-guards, whose term of duty had just expired, was retained; some dragoons and chasseurs of the Trois-Evêchés were sent for. The French guards, who had quitted the King's duty, irritated at its being assigned to others, talked of going to Versailles to resume it. Assuredly they had no reason whatever to complain, since they had of themselves relinquished that duty. But they were instigated, it is said, to this purpose. It was asserted at the time that the court wished by this contrivance to alarm the King, and to prevail on him to remove to Metz One fact affords sufficient proof of this intention: ever since the commotions at the Palais Royal, Lafayette had placed a post at Sèvres to defend the passage between Paris and Versailles. Lafayette found means to stop the French guards, and to divert them from their purpose. He wrote confidentially to St. Priest, the minister, to inform him of what had passed, and to allay all apprehensions. St. Priest, abusing the confidence of Lafayette, showed the letter to d'Estaing, who communicated it to the officers of the national guard of Versailles and the municipality, in order to apprise them of the dangers which threatened and might still threaten that town. It was proposed to send for the Flanders regiment; a great number of battalions of the Versailles guard were adverse to this measure; the municipality nevertheless presented its requisition, and the regiment was sent for. One regiment against the Assembly was no great matter, but it would be enough to carry off the King, and to protect his flight, D'Estaing informed the National Assembly of the measures that had been adopted, and obtained its approbation. The regiment arrived: the military train that followed it, though inconsiderable, did not fail to excite murmurs. The lifeguards and the courtiers sought the society of the officers, loaded them with attentions, and they appeared, as previously to the 14th of July, to coalesce, to harmonise, and to conceive great hopes.

The confidence of the court increased the distrust of Paris; and entertainments soon exasperated the sufferings of the populace. On the 2nd of October, the life-guards gave a dinner to the officers of the garrison. It was held in the theatre. The boxes were filled with spectators belonging to the court. The officers of the national guard were among the guests. Much gaiety prevailed during the repast, and the wine soon raised it to exaltation. The soldiers of the regiments were then introduced. The company, with drawn swords, drank the health of the royal family; the toast of the nation was refused—or, at least, omitted; the trumpets sounded a charge; the boxes were scaled with loud shouts; the expressive and celebrated song, "Oh Richard! ô mon roi! l'univers t'abandonne," was sung; they vowed to die for the King, as if he had been in the most imminent danger: in short, the delirium had no bounds. Cockades, white or black, but all of a single colour, were distributed. The young, women, as well as the young men, were animated with chivalrous recollections. At this moment, it is said, the national cockade was trodden under foot. This fact has since been denied; but does not wine render everything credible—everything excusable? Besides, of what use were these meetings, which produce on the one side but an' illusory zeal, and excite on the other a real and terrible irritation? At this juncture some one ran to the Queen; she consented to come to the entertainment. A number of persons surrounded the King, who was just returning from hunting, and he too was drawn thither: the company threw themselves at the feet of both, and escorted them, as in triumph, to their apartments. It is soothing, no doubt, to those who regard themselves as stripped of their authority and threatened, to meet with friends; but why should they thus deceive themselves in regard to their' rights, their strength, or their means? The report of this entertainment soon spread, and no doubt the popular imagination, in relating the circumstances, added its own exaggerations to those which the event itself had produced. The promises made to the King were construed as threats held out to the nation: this prodigality was considered as an insult to the public distress, and the shouts of "To Versailles!" were renewed with more vehemence than ever. Thus petty causes concurred to strengthen the effect of general causes. Young men appeared in Paris with black cockades; they were pursued: one of them was dragged away by the people, and the commune was obliged to prohibit cockades of a single colour.

The day after this unfortunate dinner, a nearly similar scene took place at a breakfast given by the life-guards. The company presented themselves, as on the former occasion, before the Queen, who said that she had been quite delighted with the dinner of Thursday. She was eagerly listened to; because less reserved than the King, the avowal of the sentiments of the court was expected from her lips. Every word she uttered was repeated. Irritation was at its height, and the most calamitous events might be anticipated. A commotion was convenient to the people and to the court: to the people, in order that they might seize the person of the King; to the court, that terror might drive him to Metz. It was also convenient to the Duke of Orleans, who hoped to obtain the lieutenancy of the kingdom, if the King should withdraw; nay, it has been said that this prince went so far as to hope for the crown, which is scarcely credible, for he had not a spirit bold enough for so high an ambition. The advantages which he had reason to expect from this new insurrection have brought upon him the charge of having had a hand in it; but this is unfounded. He cannot have communicated the impulse, for it resulted from the force of circumstances: he appeared at most to have seconded it; and even on this point an immense body of evidence, and time, which explains everything, have brought to light no trace of a concerted plan. No doubt, on this occasion, as during the whole revolution, the Duke of Orleans was merely following in the train of the popular movement, scattering, perhaps, a little money, giving rise to rumours, and having himself but vague hopes.

The populace, agitated by the discussions on the veto, irritated by the black cockades, annoyed by the continual patroles, and suffering from hunger, was in commotion. Bailly and Necker had neglected no means of procuring an abundant supply of provisions: but, either from the difficulty of conveyance or the pillage which took place by the way, and, above all, from the impossibility of making amends for the spontaneous movement of commerce, there was still a scarcity of flour. On the 4th of October, the agitation was greater than ever. People talked of the departure of the King for Metz, and the necessity of going to fetch him from Versailles; they kept an eager look-out for black cockades, and vociferously demanded bread! Numerous patroles succeeded in preventing tumult. The night passed off quietly. In the morning of the following day crowds began again to assemble. The women went to the bakers' shops; there was a want of bread, and they ran to the Square in which the Hôtel de Ville is situated, to complain of it to the representatives of the commune. The latter had not yet met, and a battalion of the national guard was drawn up in the *place* of the Hôtel de Ville. A number of men joined these women, but they refused their assistance, saying, that men were unfit to act. They then rushed upon the battalion, and drove it back by a volley of stones. At this moment a door was forced open; the women poured into the Hôtel de Ville; brigands, with pikes, hurried in along with them, and would have set fire to the building. They were kept back, but they succeeded in taking possession of the door leading to the great bell, and sounded the tocsin. The fauxbourgs were instantly in motion. A citizen, named Maillard, one of those who had signalised themselves at the capture of the Bastille, consulted the officer commanding the battalion of the national guard upon the means of clearing the Hôtel de Ville of these furious women. The officer durst not approve the expedient which he proposed; it was to collect them together, under the pretext of going to Versailles, but without leading them thither. Maillard, nevertheless, determined to adopt it, took a drum and soon drew them off after him. They were armed with bludgeons, broomsticks, muskets, and cutlasses. "With this singular army he proceeded along the quay, crossed the Louvre, was forced, in spite of his teeth, to lead them through the Tuileries, and arrived at the Champs Elysées. Here he succeeded in disarming them, by representing to them that it would be better to appear before the Assembly as petitioners than as furies with weapons. They assented, and Maillard was obliged to conduct them to Versailles, for it was now impossible to dissuade them from proceeding thither. To that point all were at this moment directing their course. Some hordes set out dragging with them pieces of cannon, others surrounded the national guard, which itself surrounded its commander, to prevail on him to go to Versailles, the goal of all wishes.

Meanwhile the court remained tranquil, but the Assembly had received a message from the King which occasioned much tumult. It had presented for his acceptance the constitutional articles and the declaration of rights. The answer was to be a mere simple acceptance, with a promise to promulgate. For the second time, the King, without clearly explaining himself, addressed observations to the Assembly; he signified his accession to the constitutional articles, without however approving of them; he found excellent maxims in the declaration of rights, but they needed explanation; in short, he said, a proper judgment could not he formed of the whole till the constitution should be entirely completed. This was certainly a tenable opinion; it was held by many political writers, as well as the King, but was it prudent to express it at this particular moment? No sooner was this declaration read than complaints arose. (*See* Appendix L.) Robespierre said that it was not for the King to criticise the Assembly; and Duport, that this answer ought to be countersigned by a responsible minister. (*See* Appendix M.). Petion took occasion to refer to the dinner of the life-guards, and denounced the imprecations uttered against the Assembly. Gregoire adverted to the dearth, and inquired why a letter had been sent to a miller with a promise of two hundred livres a week if he would give up grinding. The letter proved nothing, for any of the parties might have written it; still it excited a great tumult, and M. de Monspey proposed that Petion should sign its denunciation. Mirabeau, who had disapproved in the tribune itself of the course adopted by Petion and Gregoire, then came forward to reply to M. de Monspey. "I have been the very first," said he, "to disapprove of these impolitic denunciations; but, since they are insisted upon, I will myself denounce, and I will sign when it has been declared that there is nothing inviolable in France but the King." Silence succeeded to this terrible apostrophe; and the Assembly returned to the consideration of the King's answer. It was eleven in the forenoon; tidings of the movements in Paris arrived. Mirabeau went up to Mounier, the president, who, recently elected in spite of the Palais Royal, and threatened with a glorious fall, exhibited on this melancholy day unconquerable firmness. Mirabeau approached him. "Paris," said he, "is marching upon us; would it be amiss to go to the palace to tell the King to accept purely and simply?"—"Paris is marching!" replied Mounier; "so much the better; let them kill us all—yes, all! the state will be a gainer by it."—"A very pretty sentiment indeed!" rejoined Mirabeau; and he returned to his seat. The discussion continued till three o'clock, and it was decided that the president should go to the King to demand his bare and simple acceptance. At the moment when Mounier was setting out for the palace, a deputation was announced: it was Maillard and the women who had followed him. Maillard desired to be admitted and heard. He was introduced; the women rushed in after him, and penetrated into the hall. He then represented what had happened, the scarcity of bread, and the distress of the people. He mentioned the letter addressed to the miller, and said that a person whom they met by the way had told them that a clergyman was charged to denounce it. This clergyman was Gregoire, and, as we have just seen, it had actually been denounced by him. A voice then accused Juigne, bishop of Paris, of being the writer of the letter. Cries of indignation arose to repel the imputation cast on the virtuous prelate. Maillard and his deputation were called to order. He was told that means had been adopted to supply Paris with provisions; that the King had neglected nothing; that the Assembly was going to petition him to take fresh measures; that he and his followers must retire; and that disturbance was not the way to put an end to the dearth. Mounier then retired to proceed to the palace; but the women surrounded and insisted on accompanying him. He at first declined, but was obliged to allow six to go with him. He passed through the mob which had come from Paris, and which was armed with pikes, hatchets, and sticks pointed with iron. A heavy rain was falling. A detachment of the life-guards fell upon the crowd which surrounded the president and dispersed it; but the women soon overtook Mounier, and he reached the palace, where the Flanders regiment, the dragoons, the Swiss, and the national militia of Versailles were drawn up in order of battle. Instead of six women, he was obliged to introduce twelve. The King received them graciously, and deplored their distress. They were affected. One of them, young and handsome, overawed at the sight of the monarch, could scarcely give utterance to the word *Bread!* The King, deeply moved, embraced her, and the women returned softened by this reception. Their companions received them at the gate of the palace; they would not believe their report, declared that they had suffered themselves to be tampered with, and prepared to tear them in pieces. The life-guards, commanded by the Count de Guiche, hastened to release them; musket-shots were fired from various quarters; two of the guards fell, and several of the women were wounded. Not far from the spot, one of the mob, at the head of a party of women, forced his way through the ranks of the battalions and advanced to the iron-gate of the palace. M. de Savonnières pursued him, but he received a ball which broke his arm. These skirmishes produced the greatest irritation on both sides. The King, apprised of the danger, sent orders to his guards not to fire, and to retire to their hotel. While they were retiring, a few shots were exchanged between them and the national guard of Versailles, and it never could be ascertained from which side the first were fired.

Meanwhile the King was holding a council, and Mounier impatiently awaited his answer. He sent word repeatedly that his functions required his presence with the Assembly, that the news of the sanction would pacify all minds, that he would retire if an answer were not brought, for he would not longer absent himself from the post to which his duties called him. The question discussed in the council was, whether the King should leave Versailles. The council lasted from six till ten at night, and the King, it is said, was against leaving the place vacant for the Duke of Orleans. An attempt was made to send off the Queen and the children, but the crowd stopped the carriages the moment they appeared; and, besides, the Queen was firmly resolved not to leave her husband. At length, about 10 o'clock, Mounier received the bare and simple acceptance and returned to the Assembly. The deputies had retired, and the women occupied the hall. He communicated to them the King's acceptance, with which they were highly pleased; and they inquired if they should be the better for it, and especially if they should have bread. Mounier gave them the most favourable answer that he could, and directed all the bread that could be procured to be distributed among them. In the course of this night, the faults of which it is so difficult to charge to the right account, the municipality committed the blunder of neglecting to provide for the wants of this famished mob, which had left Paris owing to the want of bread, and which could not since have found any on the way.

At this moment, intelligence was received of the arrival of Lafayette. For eight hours he had been opposing the national militia of Paris, who were for proceeding to Versailles. "General," said one of his grenadiers to him, "you do not deceive us, but you deceive yourself. Instead of turning our arms against women, let us go to Versailles to fetch the King, and make sure of his good disposition by placing him in the midst of us." Lafayette had hitherto withstood the solicitations of his army and the inundation of the mob. His soldiers were not attached to him by victory, but by opinion; and, abandoned by their opinion, he could no longer control them. He nevertheless contrived to stop them till night; but his voice readied only to a small distance, and beyond that nothing could appease the fury of the multitude. His life had several times been threatened, and still he resisted. He knew, nevertheless, that hordes were continually leaving Paris, and, as the insurrection was transferring itself to Versailles, it became his duty to follow it thither. The commune directed him to go, and at last he set out. By the way, he halted his army, made it swear to be faithful to the King, and arrived at Versailles about midnight. He sent word to Mounier that the army had promised to do its duty, and that nothing should be done contrary to the law. He hastened to the palace: with every demonstration of respect and sorrow he informed the King of the precautions which had been taken, and assured him of his attachment and that of his army. The King appeared tranquilised, and retired to rest. The guard of the palace had been refused to Lafayette, and the outposts alone had been granted to him. The other posts were destined for the Flanders regiment, whose dispositions could not be implicitly relied on, for the Swiss, and for the life-guards. These latter had at first been ordered to retire; they had afterwards been recalled, and, being unable to assemble, there was but a small number of them at their post. Amidst the tumult which prevailed, all the accessible parts had not been defended; an iron-gate had even been left open. Lafayette caused the outer posts intrusted to him to be occupied, and none of them was forced or even attacked.

The Assembly, notwithstanding the uproar, had resumed its sitting, and was engaged, with the most imposing attitude, in a discussion on the penal laws. Mirabeau, wearied out, exclaimed aloud that the Assembly had not to receive the law from any one, and that it should direct the tribunes to be cleared. The people vehemently applauded his apostrophe; but the Assembly deemed it prudent not to make any more resistance. Lafayette having sent word to Mounier that all appeared to him to be quiet, and that he might dismiss the deputies, the Assembly adjourned till eleven the following day, and broke up.

The crowd had dispersed itself here and there, and appeared to be pacified. Lafayette had reason to feel confidence, as well from the attachment of his army, which in fact did not belie his good opinion, as from the tranquillity which seemed everywhere to prevail. He had secured the hotel of the life-guards, and sent out numerous patroles.

At five in the morning he was still up. Conceiving that all was then quiet, he took some refreshment, and threw himself upon a bed, to obtain a little rest, of which he had been deprived for the last twenty-four hours. (*See* Appendix N.)

At this moment the people began to stir, and they were already thronging to the environs of the palace. A quarrel took place with one of the life-guards, who fired from the windows. The brigands immediately rushed on, passed the gate which had been left open, ascended a staircase, where they found no obstruction, and were at length stopped by two life-guardsmen, who heroically defended themselves, falling back only foot by foot, and retiring from door to door. One of these generous servants was Miomandre; he shouted, "Save the Queen! "This cry was heard, and the Queen ran trembling to the King's apartments. "While she was escaping, the brigands pushed forward, found the royal bed forsaken, and would have penetrated farther, but they were again checked by the life-guards, posted in considerable number at that point. At this moment the French guards belonging to Lafayette, stationed near the palace, hearing the uproar, hastened to the spot and dispersed the brigands. They arrived at the door behind which the life-guards were intrenched. "Open the door," they cried: "the French guards have not forgotten that you saved their regiment at Fontenoi." The door was opened, and they rushed into each other's arms.

Tumult reigned without. Lafayette, who had lain down only for a few moments, and had not even fallen . asleep, hearing the noise, leaped upon the first horse he met with, galloped into the thick of the fray, and there found several of the life-guards on the point of being slaughtered. "While he was disengaging them, he ordered his troops to hasten to the palace, and remained alone amidst the brigands. One of them took aim at him. Lafayette coolly commanded the people to bring the man to him. The mob instantly seized the culprit, and, before the face of Lafayette, dashed out his brains against the pavement. After saving the life-guards, Lafayette flew with them to the palace, and there found his grenadiers, who had already repaired thither. They all surrounded him, and vowed to die for the King. At this moment, the life-guards who had been saved from destruction shouted *Lafayette for ever!* The whole court, seeing themselves preserved by him and his troops, acknowledged that to him they were indebted for their lives. These testimonies of gratitude were universal. Madame Adelaide, the King's aunt, ran up to him, and clasped him in her arms, saying, "General, you have saved us."

The populace at this moment insisted with loud cries that the King should go to Paris. (*See* Appendix O.) A council was held. Lafayette, being invited to attend it, refused, that he might not impose any restraint on the freedom of opinion. It was at length decided that the court should comply with the wish of the people. Slips of paper, containing this intimation, were thrown out of the windows. Louis XVI. then showed himself at the balcony, accompanied by the general, and was greeted with shouts of "*Long live the King!*" But the Queen did not fare the same: threatening voices were raised against her. Lafayette accosted her. "Madam," said he, "what will you do?" "Accompany the King," undauntedly replied the Queen. "Come with me then," rejoined the general, and he led her in amaze to the balcony. Some threats were offered by the populace. A fatal shot might be fired; words could not be heard; it was necessary to strike the eye. Stooping and taking the hand of the Queen, the general kissed it respectfully. The mob of Frenchmen was transported at this action, and confirmed the reconciliation by shouts of *Long live the Queen! Long live Lafayette!* Peace was not yet made with the life-guards. "Will you not do something for my guards?" said the King to Lafayette. The latter took one of them, led him to the balcony, clasped him in his arms, and put on him his own shoulder-belt. The populace again cheered, and ratified by its plaudits this new reconciliation.

The Assembly had not deemed it consistent with its dignity to go to the monarch, though he had desired it to do so. It had contented itself with sending to him a deputation of thirty-six members. As soon as it was apprised of his intended departure, it passed a resolution purporting that the Assembly was inseparable from the person of the sovereign, and it nominated one hundred deputies to accompany him to Paris. The King received the resolution, and set out. (*See* Appendix P.)

The principal bands of the mob had already gone. Lafayette had sent after them a detachment of the army, to prevent them from turning back. He also issued orders for disarming the brigands who were carrying the heads of two life-guardsmen on the point of their pikes. These horrible trophies were taken from them, and it is not true that they were borne before the carriage of the King (*See* Appendix Q.)

Louis XVI. at length returned amidst a considerable concourse, and was received by Bailly at the Hôtel de Ville. "I return with *confidence,*" said the King, "into the midst of my people of Paris." Bailly repeated these words to those who could not hear them, but he forgot the word *confidence.* "Add *with confidence,*" said the Queen. "You are happier," replied Bailly, "than if I had said it myself." (*See* Appendix R.)

The royal family repaired to the palace of the Tuileries, which had not been inhabited for a century, and where there had not been time to make the necessary preparations. The guard of it was confided to the Parisian militia, and Lafayette was thus made responsible to the nation for the person of the King, for which all the parties were contending. The nobles were desirous to carry him to some fortress, in order to exercise despotism in his name. The popular party, which had not yet conceived the idea of dispensing with him, wished to keep him, to complete the constitution and to withdraw a chief from civil war. Hence the malignity of the privileged classes called Lafayette a gaoler; and yet his vigilance proved only one thing—the sincere desire to have a King.

From this moment the march of the parties displayed itself in a new manner. The aristocracy, separated from Louis XVI. and incapable of executing any enterprise by his side, dispersed itself abroad, and in the provinces. It was from this time that the emigration began to be considerable. A great number of nobles fled to Turin, to the Count d'Artois, who had found an asylum with his father-in-law. Here their policy consisted in exciting the departments of the south, and in supposing that the King was not free. The Queen, who was an Austrian, and moreover an enemy to the new court formed at Turin, fixed her hopes on Austria. The King, amidst these machinations, saw everything, prevented nothing, and awaited his salvation, come from what quarter it might. From time to time he made the disavowals required by the Assembly, and was not really free, any more than he would have been at Turin or at Coblentz, or than he was under Maurepas; for it is the lot of weakness to be everywhere dependent.

The popular party, thenceforward triumphant, was divided among the Duke of Orleans, Lafayette, Mirabeau, Barnave, and the Lameths. The public voice charged the Duke of Orleans and Mirabeau with being the authors of the late insurrection. Witnesses who were not unworthy of credit, asserted that they had seen the Duke and Mirabeau on the deplorable field of battle on the 6th of October. These statements were afterwards contradicted; at the moment, however, they were believed. The conspirators had intended to remove the King and even to put him to death, said the boldest calumniators. The Duke of Orleans, they added, had aspired to be lieutenant of the kingdom, and Mirabeau minister. As none of these plans had succeeded, Lafayette, appearing to have thwarted them by his presence, was regarded as the saviour of the King, and the conqueror of the Duke of Orleans and Mirabeau. The court, which had not yet had time to become ungrateful, acknowledged

Lafayette to be its preserver, and the power of the general at this moment seemed immense. The hotheaded patriots were incensed at it, and began already to mutter the name of Cromwell. Mirabeau, who, as we shall presently see, had no connexion with the Duke of Orleans, was jealous of Lafayette, and called him Cromwell Grandison. The aristocracy seconded these distrusts, and added to them its own calumnies. Lafayette, however, was determined, in spite of all obstacles, to uphold the King and the constitution. For this purpose he resolved in the first place to remove the Duke of Orleans, whose presence gave occasion to many reports, and might furnish, if not the means, at least a pretext, for disturbances. He had an interview with the prince, intimidated him by his firmness, and obliged him to withdraw. The King, who was in the scheme, feigned, with his usual weakness, to be forced into this measure; and writing to the Duke of Orleans, he told him that it was absolutely necessary for him or M. de Lafayette to retire; that, in the state of opinions, the choice was not doubtful; and that, in consequence, he gave him a commission for England. We have since been informed that M. de Montmorin, minister for foreign affairs, in order to rid himself of the ambition of the Duke of Orleans, directed him towards the Netherlands, then in rebellion against Austria, and that he had held out hopes to him of acquiring the title of Duke of Brabant. His friends, when apprised of this resolution, were indignant at his weakness. More ambitious than he, they would have persuaded him not to comply. They went to Mirabeau, and entreated him to denounce in the tribune the violence which Lafayette was committing against the prince. Mirabeau, already jealous of the general's popularity, sent word to him and to the duke, that he would denounce both of them in the tribune if the departure for England should take place. The Duke of Orleans was shaken: a fresh summons from Lafayette decided him; and Mirabeau, on receiving in the Assembly a note acquainting him with the retreat of the prince, exclaimed in vexation: "He is not worth the trouble that is taken about him." This expression and many others equally inconsiderate have caused him to be frequently accused of being one of the agents of the Duke of Orleans; but this he never was. His straitened circumstances, the imprudence of his language, his familiarity with the Duke of Orleans, though indeed he treated everybody in the same manner, his proposal relative to the Spanish succession, and lastly his opposition to the departure of the duke, could not but excite suspicions; it is nevertheless true that Mirabeau had no party, nay, that he had no other aim but to destroy the aristocracy and arbitrary power.

The authors of these suppositions ought to have known that Mirabeau was at this time under the necessity of borrowing the most trifling sums, which would not have been the case, if he had been the agent of a prince immensely rich, and who is believed to have been almost ruined by his partisans. Mirabeau had already foreboded the speedy dissolution of the state. A conversation with an intimate friend, which lasted a whole night, in the park of Versailles, caused him to decide on adopting an entirely new plan; and he determined for his glory, for the welfare of the state, and lastly for his own fortune—for Mirabeau was the man for attending to all these interests at once—to stand immovable between the disaffected and the throne, and to consolidate the monarchy while making a place in it for himself. The court had tried to gain him, but the affair had been clumsily managed, and without the delicacy requisite towards a man of great pride, and desirous of retaining his popularity, in default of the esteem which he did not yet possess. Malouet, a friend of Necker, and connected with Mirabeau, wished to bring them into communication. Mirabeau had frequently declined this, being certain that he could never agree with the minister. He nevertheless assented. Malouet introduced him, and the incompatibility of the two characters was still more strongly felt after this interview, in which, according to the admission of all present, Mirabeau displayed the superiority which he had in private life, as well as in the tribune. It was reported that he had manifested a wish to be bought, and that, as Necker made no overture, he said on going away: "*The minister shall hear of me.*" This again is an interpretation of the parties, but it is false. Malouet had proposed to Mirabeau, who was known to be satisfied with the liberty required, to come to an understanding with the minister, and nothing more. Besides, it was at this very period that a direct negotiation was opened with the court. A foreign prince, connected with men of all parties, made the first overtures. A friend, who served as intermediate agent, explained that no sacrifice of principles would be obtained from Mirabeau; but that, if the government would adhere to the constitution, it would find in him a staunch supporter; that, as to the conditions, they were dictated by his situation; that it was requisite, even for the interest of those who wished to employ him, that that situation should be rendered honourable and independent—in other words, that his debts should be paid; that, finally, it was necessary to make him attached to the new social order, and without actually giving him the ministry, to hold out hopes of it at some future time. The negotiations were not entirely concluded till two or three months afterwards, that is, in the first months of 1790. Historians unacquainted with these particulars, and misled by the perseverance of Mirabeau in opposing the government, have assigned a later period to this treaty. It was, however, nearly concluded at the commencement of 1790. We shall notice it in its proper place.

The only way in which Barnave and the Lameths could rival Mirabeau was by a far greater patriotic austerity. Apprised of the negotiations which were in progress, they accredited the rumour already circulated, that the ministry in about to be conferred on him, in order that they might thus deprive him of the means of accepting it. An occasion for thwarting his views soon occurred. The ministers had no right to speak in the Assembly. Mirabeau was unwilling, when appointed minister, to lose the right of speaking, which was the chief instrument of his influence; he wished, moreover, to bring Necker into the tribune, that he might crush him there. He proposed, therefore, to give a consultive voice to the ministers. The popular party, in alarm, opposed the motion without any reasonable motive, and appeared to have a dread of ministerial seductions. But its apprehensions were absurd; for it is not by their public communications with the chambers that the ministers usually corrupt the national representation. Mirabeau's motion was negatived, and Lanjuinais, pushing rigour still further, proposed to forbid the existing deputies to accept the ministry. A violent debate ensued. Though the motive of these propositions was known, it was not avowed; and Mirabeau, who was incapable of dissimulation, at length exclaimed that it would be wrong, for the sake of a single individual, to take a measure pernicious to the state; that he supported the motion, on condition that the ministry should be interdicted, not to all the present deputies, but only to M. de Mirabeau, deputy of the seneschalship of Aix. His frankness and boldness were of no avail, and the motion was unanimously adopted.

We have seen how the state was divided between the emigrants, the Queen, the King, and different popular chiefs, such as Lafayette, Mirabeau, Barnave, and Lameth. No decisive event, like that of the 14th of July or the 5th of October, was possible for a long time to come. It was requisite that fresh contrarieties should exasperate the court and the people, and produce a signal rupture.

The Assembly had removed to Paris, after repeated assurances of tranquillity on the part of the commune, and the promise of entire liberty in their votes. Mounier and Lally-Tollendal, indignant at the events of the 5th and 6th of October, had resigned their seats, saying that they would not be either spectators of, or accomplices in, the crimes of the factious. They must have regretted this desertion of the public welfare, especially when they saw Maury and Cazalès, after seceding from the Assembly, soon return to it and courageously support to the end the cause which they had espoused. Mounier, retiring to Dauphiné, assembled the states of the province, but a decree soon caused them to be dissolved, without any resistance. Thus Mounier and Lally, who, at the period of the junction of the orders, and of the oath at the Tennis Court, had been the heroes of the people, were no logger held in any estimation by them. The parliaments had been first outstripped by the popular power; so had Mounier, Lally, and Necker been after them; and so many others were very soon destined to be.

The dearth, the exaggerated but nevertheless real cause of the disturbances, gave occasion also to a crime. A baker, named Francois, was murdered by some brigands. Lafayette succeeded in securing the culprits, and delivered them up to the Chatelet, which was invested with an extraordinary jurisdiction over all offences relative to the Revolution. Here Besenval, and all those who were accused of having a hand in the aristocratic conspiracy foiled on the 14th of July, were under trial. The Chatelet was authorised to try according to new forms. Till the introduction of the trial by jury, which was not yet instituted, the Assembly had ordered publicity, the contradictory defence, and all the measures which operated as safeguards to innocence. The murderers of Francois were condemned, and tranquillity was restored. Upon this occasion, Lafayette and Bailly proposed the adoption of martial law. The motion, though strongly opposed by Robespierre, who thenceforward showed himself a warm partisan of the people and the poor, was nevertheless approved by the majority. By virtue of this law, the municipalities were responsible for the public tranquillity; in case of disturbance, they were directed to require the aid of the regular troops or the militia; and they were enjoined, after three warnings, to employ force against seditious assemblages. A committee of search was established in the commune of Paris and in the National Assembly, to look after the numerous enemies, whose machinations crossed each other in all directions. All these measures were not more than sufficient to control the host of adversaries leagued against the new revolution.

The formation of the constitution was prosecuted with activity. The feudal system had been abolished, but there was still wanting a last measure for destroying those great bodies which had been enemies constituted in the state against the state. The clergy possessed immense property. It had been conferred on them by princes as feudal grants, or by the pious by way of legacy. If the property of individuals, the fruit and object of their labour, ought to be respected, that which had been given to bodies for a certain purpose might have another destination assigned to it by the law. It was for the service of religion, or at least upon this pretext, that it had been bestowed; religion being a public service, the law had a right to pre vide for it in a totally different manner. The Abbé Maury here displayed his imperturbable spirit: he gave the alarm to the landed proprietors, threatened them with speedy spoliation, and declared that the provinces were sacrificed to the stockjobbers of the capital. His sophistry was singular enough to be recorded. It was to pay the public debt that the property of the clergy was disposed of; the creditors were the great capitalists of Paris; the property which was sacrificed to them was in the provinces: hence the bold reasoner concluded that it was sacrificing the country to the capital; as if the country were not, on the contrary, a gainer by the new division of those immense estates hitherto reserved for the luxury of a few indolent churchmen.

All these efforts were useless. The Bishop of Autun, the author of the proposal, and Thouret, the deputy, demolished these vain sophisms. The Assembly was proceeding to resolve that all the possessions of the clergy belonged to the state; the opposition, however, still insisted on the question of property. They were told that, if they were proprietors, the nation had a right to make use of their property, since this kind of property had frequently been employed in cases of emergency for the service of the state. This they did not deny. Taking advantage of their assent, Mirabeau then moved that for the words *belong to*, should be substituted, *are at the disposal of*, the state; and the discussion was instantly terminated by a great majority. The Assembly thus destroyed the formidable power of the clergy and the luxury of the high dignitaries of the order, and secured those immense financial resources which so long upheld the Revolution. At the same time, it provided for the subsistence of the *curés*, by resolving that their salaries should not be less than twelve hundred francs, adding, moreover, the use of a parsonage-house and garden. It declared that it ceased to recognise religious vows, and restored liberty to all the inmates of cloisters, leaving to those who preferred it the right of continuing the monastic life. Their property was withdrawn, and pensions were granted in its stead. Carrying its forecast still farther, it established a difference between the wealthy orders and the mendicant orders, and proportioned the salary of both to their former condition. It pursued the same course in regard to pensions; and when Camus the Jansenist, desirous of returning to the evangelical simplicity, proposed to reduce all pensions to one very low standard, the Assembly, on the recommendation of Mirabeau, reduced them proportionably to their actual value, and suitably to the former state of the receivers. It was impossible to carry attention to previous habits to a greater length, and in this consists the *real respect* for property. In like manner, when the Protestants, expatriated ever since the edict of Nantes, reclaimed their possessions, the Assembly restored such only as had not been sold.

Prudent and delicate in regard to persons, the Assembly treated things without ceremony, and was much bolder in matters relating to the constitution. The prerogatives of the great powers had been fixed: the question now was, the division of the territory of the kingdom. It had always been divided into provinces, successively united with ancient France. These provinces, differing from one another in laws, privileges, and manners, formed a most heterogeneous whole. Sièyes conceived the idea of blending them together by a new division, which should annihilate the ancient demarcations, and introduce the same laws and the same spirit into all parts of the kingdom. This was accomplished by the division into departments. These were divided into districts, and the districts into municipalities. In all these degrees, the principle of representation was admitted. The departmental administration, that of the district, and that of the communes, were assigned to a deliberative council and to an executive council; both were elective. These various authorities depended the one on the other, and they had the same powers throughout their respective jurisdictions. The department made the assessments of the taxes upon the districts, the districts upon the communes, and the commune upon individuals.

The Assembly then fixed the quality of a citizen enjoying political rights. It required the age of twenty-five years, and the payment of contributions to the amount of one silver mark. Every man who combined these conditions had the title of active citizen, and those who did not, styled themselves passive citizens. These extremely simple denominations were turned into ridicule; for it is names that people lay hold of when they want to depreciate things; but they were natural, and aptly expressed their object. The active citizen concurred in elections, either for the formation of the administrations, or for that of the Assembly. The elections of the deputies had two degrees. No specific condition was required to constitute eligibility; for, as it was observed in the Assembly, a man is an elector by his existence in society, and he must be eligible from the mere confidence of the electors.

These operations, interrupted by a thousand incidental discussions, were nevertheless prosecuted with great ardour. The right side (the party of the nobility and clergy), only contributed by its obstinacy to impede them, the moment opportunity offered to contest any portion of influence with the nation. The popular deputies, on the contrary, though forming several parties, acted in concert, or differed without animosity, agreeably to their private opinions. It was easy to perceive that among them conviction predominated over party considerations. Thouret, Mirabeau, Duport, Sieyes, Camus, Chapelier, were seen alternately uniting and dividing, according to their opinion, in each discussion. As for the members of the nobility and clergy, they never appeared but in party discussions. If the parliaments had issued decrees against the Assembly, if deputies or writers had insulted it, they then came forward, ready to support them. They supported also the military commandants against the people, the slave-traders against the negro slaves; they were against the admission of Jews and Protestants to the enjoyment of the common rights. Lastly, when Genoa declared against France, on account of the enfranchisement of Corsica, and the union of that island with the kingdom, they were in favour of Genoa against France. In short, aliens, indifferent to all beneficial discussions, not listening to them, but conversing among themselves, they never rose but when there were rights or liberty to be refused. (*See* Appendix S.)

As we have already observed, it was no longer possible to attempt any great conspiracy in favour of the King, since the aristocracy was put to flight, and the court was encompassed by the Assembly, the people, and the national militia. Partial movements were therefore all that the malcontents could attempt. They fomented the discontent of the officers who adhered to the former order of things; while the soldiers, having everything to gain, inclined to the new. Violent quarrels took place between the army and the populace: the soldiers frequently gave up their officers to the mob, who murdered them; at other times, these mutual jealousies were happily appeased, and all again became quiet, when the commandants of towns could conduct themselves with any address, and had taken the oath of fidelity to the new constitution. The clergy had inundated Britanny with protestations against the alienation of its property. Attempts were made to excite a remnant of religious fanaticism in the provinces, where the ancient superstition still prevailed. The parliaments were also employed, and a last trial was made of their authority. Their vacation had been prorogued by the Assembly, because it did not wish to have any discussion with them during the interval that should elapse before it could dissolve them. The chambers of vacation administered justice in their absence. At Rouen, at Nantes, at Rennes, they passed resolutions, in which they deplored the ruin of the ancient monarchy and the violation of its laws; and, without mentioning the Assembly, they seemed to point to it as the cause of all the prevailing evils. They were called to the bar, and delicately reprimanded. That of Rennes, as the most culpable, was declared incapable of fulfilling its functions. That of Metz had insinuated that the King was not free. Such, as we have already observed, was the policy of the discontented: as they could not make use of the King, they sought to represent him as in a state of restraint, and for this reason they were desirous of annulling all the laws to which he appeared to assent. He seemed himself to second this policy. He would not recall his lifeguards, who were dismissed on the 5th and 6th of October, and caused the duty about his person to be performed by the national militia, among whom he knew that he was safe. His intention was to appear to be a captive. The commune of Paris foiled this too petty artifice, by soliciting the King to recall his guards, which he refused to do upon frivolous pretexts, and through the medium of the Queen.

The year 1790 had just commenced, and a general agitation began to be perceptible. Three tolerably quiet months had passed since the 5th and 6th of October, and the commotion seemed to be breaking out anew. Violent storms are always followed by calms, and these calms by petty gusts, which gradually become more and more vehement. These disturbances were laid to the charge of the clergy, the nobility, the court, and even of England, who directed her ambassador to justify her conduct. The paid companies of the national guard were themselves infected with this general discontent. Some soldiers assembled in the Champs Elysées, and demanded an increase of pay. Lafayette, present everywhere, hastened to the spot, dispersed and punished them, and restored quiet among his troops, who were still faithful, notwithstanding these slight interruptions of discipline.

There were great rumours of a plot against the Assembly and the municipality, the supposed ringleader of which was the Marquis de Favras. (*See* Appendix T.) He was apprehended, with circumstances of public notoriety, and sent to the Chatelet. It was immediately reported that Bailly and Lafayette were to have been assassinated; that twelve hundred horse were ready at Versailles to carry off the King; that an army, composed of Swiss and Piedmontese, was to receive him and to march to Paris. The alarm spread. It was added that Favras was the secret agent of the highest personages. Suspicion was directed to Monsieur, the King's brother. Favras had been in his guards, and moreover had negotiated a loan in his behalf. Monsieur, alarmed at the agitation which prevailed, repaired to the Hôtel de Ville, protested against the insinuations thrown out against him, explained his connexion with Favras, appealed to his popular sentiments formerly manifested in the Assembly of the Notables, and desired that he might be judged, not from public rumours, but from his known and unswerving patriotism. His speech was received with shouts of applause, and the crowd escorted him back to his residence.

The trial of Favras was continued. This Favras had run all over Europe, married a foreign princess, and been devising plans for retrieving his fortunes. He had been engaged in them on the 14th of July, on the 5th and 6th of October, and in the last months of 1789. The witnesses who accused him furnished precise particulars of his last scheme. The murder of Bailly and Lafayette, and the abduction of the King appeared to form part of this scheme; but there was no proof that the twelve hundred horse were in readiness, or that the Swiss and Piedmontese army was in motion. Circumstances were far from favourable to Favras. The Chatelet had just liberated Besenval and the other persons implicated in the plot of the 14th of July: public opinion was dissatisfied. Lafayette nevertheless encouraged the gentlemen of the Chatelet, exhorted them to be just, and assured them that their sentence, be it what it might, should be executed.

This trial revived the suspicions against the court. These new schemes caused it to be deemed incorrigible; for, even in the midst of Paris, it was still seen conspiring. The King was therefore advised to take a decisive step, which should satisfy public opinion.

On the 4th of February, 1790, the Assembly was surprised to perceive some alterations in the arrangement of the hall. The steps of the bureau were covered with a carpet sprinkled with fleurs-de-lis. The arm-chair of the secretaries was lowered; the president was standing beside the seat which he usually occupied. "Here is the King!" suddenly exclaimed the door-keepers; and Louis XVI. instantly entered the hall. The Assembly rose at his appearance, and he was received with applause. A concourse of spectators, quickly collected, filled the tribunes, thronged all parts of the hall, and awaited the royal speech with the utmost impatience. Louis XVI., standing, addressed the seated Assembly: he began by referring to the troubles to which France had fallen a prey, the efforts which he had made to allay them, and to supply the wants of the people; he recapitulated the proceedings of the representatives, observing that he had attempted the same things in the provincial assemblies; lastly, he showed that he had himself formerly the very same wishes which had just been realized. He added, that he deemed it his duty to unite more particularly with the representatives of the nation, at a moment when decrees destined to establish a new organization in the kingdom had been submitted to him. He would promote, he said, with all his power the success of that vast organization; every attempt hostile to it should be held culpable, and opposed with all his means. At these words, the hall rang with plaudits. The King continued; and, referring to his own sacrifices, he exhorted all those who had been losers to take example from his resignation, and to indemnify themselves for their losses by the blessings which the new constitution promised to France. But when, after vowing to defend that constitution, he added, that he would do still more, and that, in concert with the Queen, he would early predispose the mind and heart of his son in favour of the new order of things, and accustom him to seek happiness in the happiness of the French, cries of attachment burst forth from all quarters—all hands were outstretched towards the monarch, all eyes looked for the mother and her son, all voices asked for them: the transport was universal. At length the King concluded his speech, by recommending peace and concord to his *good people, by whom he is assured that he is loved, when those around him wish to cheer him up under his troubles.* (*See* Appendix U.) At these last words all present burst forth into exclamations of gratitude. The president made a short reply, in which he adverted to the disturbed feelings which prevailed in all hearts. The Prince was conducted back to the Tuileries by the multitude. The Assembly voted thanks to him and to the Queen. A new idea was started; Louis XVI. had engaged to uphold the constitution; it was fitting that the deputies should hind themselves to do the same. The civic oath was therefore proposed, and every deputy came forward to swear to be faithful to the nation, to the law, and *to the King; and to uphold with all his power the constitution decreed by the National Assembly, and accepted by the King*. The supplementary members, the deputies of commerce, desired to take the oath in their turn; the tribunes and the galleries followed their example, and on all sides nothing was to be heard but the words, I swear it.

The oath was repeated at the Hôtel de Ville, and by commune after commune throughout France. Rejoicings were ordered, which appeared to be general and sincere. This was certainly a fair occasion for the court to commence a new line of conduct, instead of frustrating this, as all previous advances towards a reconciliation on the part of the people; but, the very same evening, whilst Paris was in a blaze with bonfires kindled to celebrate the happy event, the court had betaken itself again to its ill-humour, and the popular deputies experienced from it a reception wholly different from that which was reserved for the noble deputies. In vain did Lafayette, whose advice was replete with good sense and zeal, repeat to the court that the King could no longer waver, and that he ought to attach himself altogether to the popular party, and strive to win its confidence; that for this purpose it was requisite that his intentions should not only be proclaimed to the Assembly, but that they should be manifested by his minutest actions; that he ought to show displeasure at every expression in the least degree equivocal, used in his presence, and reprove the slightest doubt thrown out as to his real sentiments; that he ought to show neither restraint nor dissatisfaction, nor to leave any secret hope to the aristocrats; and lastly, that the ministers ought to be united, instead of entering into rivalship with the Assembly, and obliging it to have recourse incessantly to the public opinion. In vain did Lafayette repeat these prudent counsels with respectful earnestness: the King received his letters and thought him an honest man; the Queen repulsed them with petulance, and even seemed to be irritated by the respect paid by the general. She gave a much better reception to Mirabeau, who possessed more influence, but was certainly a man of less irreproachable character than Lafayette.

The communications of Mirabeau with the court still continued. He had even kept up an intercourse with Monsieur, whose opinions rendered him more accessible to the popular party, and he had repeated to him what he had never ceased to tell the Queen and M. De Montmorin, that the monarchy could not be saved unless by liberty. Mirabeau at length came to terms with the court by means of an intermediate agent. He declared his principles in a kind of profession of faith; he engaged not to swerve from them, and to support the court so long as it should follow the same Line. A considerable salary was given to him in return. Morality indeed condemns such treaties, and insists that a man ought to do his duty for the sake of duty alone. But was this selling himself? A weak man would no doubt have sold himself by sacrificing his principles; but the mighty Mirabeau, so far from sacrificing his, brought power over to the court, and received from it that aid which his urgent necessities and his licentious passions rendered indispensable to him. Unlike those who give up for a high price mean talents and a cowardly conscience, Mirabeau, inflexible in his principles, combated by turns his own party and the court, as if he had not expected popularity from the former, or the means of existence from the latter. To such a point was this opposition carried, that historians, unable to believe him an ally of the court which he combated, have not fixed the date of his treaty earlier than the year 1791, though it was concluded in the very first months of 1790. Mirabeau saw the Queen, charmed her by his superiority, and experienced from her a reception that flattered him exceedingly. (*See* Appendix V.) That extraordinary man had a keen relish for all pleasures—for those of vanity as well as for those of the passions. It was necessary to take him with his strength and his foibles, and to employ him for the common cause. Besides Lafayette and Mirabeau, the court relied on Bouillé, whom it is time to introduce to the reader. (*See* Appendix W.)

Bouillé, full of courage, integrity, and talent, had all the prejudices of the aristocracy, and was distinguished from it only by less infatuation, and more experience in business. Having retired to Metz, where he commanded a vast extent of frontier and a great part of the army, he strove to foment jealousies between his troops and the national guard, in order that he might keep his soldiers steady to the court. Placed there on the watch, he scared the popular party; he seemed the general of the monarchy, as Lafayette was the general of the constitution. The aristocracy nevertheless displeased him, the weakness of the King disgusted him with the service, and he would have quitted it had he not been pressed by Louis XVI. to continue in it. Bouillé was full of honour. After taking his oath, he thought of nothing but how to serve the King and the constitution. The court, therefore, needed but to unite Lafayette, Mirabeau, and Bouillé; and through them it would have had the national guards, the Assembly and the army, that is to say, the three powers of the day. Some motives, it is true, divided these three personages. Lafayette, full of good-nature, was ready to unite with all who were desirous of serving the King and the constitution; but Mirabeau was jealous of Lafayette's power, dreaded his purity, which was so highly extolled, and seemed to regard it as a reproach. Bouillé hated in Lafayette his enthusiastic character, and perhaps viewed in him; irreproachable enemy; he preferred Mirabeau, whom he deemed more manageable and less rigorous in his political creed. It was for the court to unite these three men by removing their particular motives for keeping aloof from each other. But there was only one bond of union, a free monarchy. The court ought therefore to have frankly resigned itself to its only course, and to have followed it up with all its might. But the court, ever unsteady, received Lafayette coldly, without repulsing him; paid Mirabeau, who lectured it from time to time; kept up Bouillé's dislike of the Revolution; looked to Austria with hope; and suffered the emigrants at Turin to take active measures. Such is the way with weakness. It strives to delude itself with hopes rather than to ensure success, and in this manner it ultimately ruins itself by exciting suspicions which irritate parties as much as decided opposition. It is much better to strike than to threaten them.

In vain Lafayette, who would fain have done what the court neglected to do, wrote to Bouillé, his kinsman, exhorting him to serve the throne jointly with himself, and by the only possible means, those of frankness and liberty. Bouillé, at the evil instigation of the court, replied coldly and evasively, and, without attempting anything against the constitution, he continued to render himself formidable by the secrecy of his intentions and the strength of his army.

The reconciliation of the 4th of February, which might have led to such important results, was therefore useless. The trial of Favras was concluded, and, whether from fear or from a conviction of his guilt, the Chatelet sentenced him to be hanged. Favras displayed in his last moments a firmness more worthy of a martyr than of an intriguer. He protested his innocence, and demanded permission to make a declaration before he died. The scaffold was erected in the Place de Grève. He was conveyed to the Hôtel de Ville, where he remained till night. The populace, eager to see a marquis hanged, impatiently awaited this example of equality in punishments. Favras related that he had held communications with a high dignitary of the state, who had engaged him to dispose the public mind favourably towards the King. As this would have put him to considerable expense, the personage in question had given him one hundred louis, which he had accepted. He affirmed that this was the whole extent of his crime; and he mentioned no name. He asked, however, if the confession of names could save him. Not satisfied with the answer that was returned, "In that case," said he, "I will take my secret with me;" and he walked with great firmness towards the place of execution. It was night: the Place and the gibbet itself were lighted up. The populace enjoyed the sight, delighted to find equality even on the scaffold. It was to them a subject for cruel jests; and they parodied, in various ways, the execution of this unfortunate man. The body of Favras was delivered to his family, and fresh events soon caused his death to be forgotten alike by those who had punished and those who had employed him.

The exasperated clergy continued to excite petty disturbances throughout France. The nobility relied, much upon its influence among the people. So long as the Assembly had proceeded no further than by a decree to place ecclesiastical property at the disposal of the nation, the clergy had hoped that the decree would not be carried into execution; and, in order to render it useless, it proposed a variety of plans for supplying the wants of the exchequer. The Abbé Maury (*See* Appendix X.) had proposed a tax on luxury, and the Abbé Salside had replied, by moving that no ecclesiastic should possess an income exceeding one thousand crowns. The wealthy abbé was silenced by such a proposal. On another occasion, in discussing the debt of the state, Cazalès had proposed to investigate, not the titles of each credit, but the credit itself, its origin, and its motive; which would have been renewing bankruptcy by the odious and worn-out expedient of *chambres ardentes*. The clergy, inimical to the creditors of the state, to whom it deemed itself sacrificed, had supported the proposal, notwithstanding the strictness of its principles in regard to property. Maury had spoken with great warmth, and had even violated the respect due to the Assembly, by saying to some of its members, that they had only the *courage of shame*. The Assembly had taken offence at this expression, and thought of expelling him. But Mirabeau, who had reason to suppose that the attack was aimed at him, represented to his colleagues that each deputy belonged to his constituents, and that they had no right to exclude any individual. This moderation befitted real superiority. It was successful, and Maury was more severely punished by a reprimand, than he would have been by expulsion. All these expedients for putting the creditors of the state in the same condition as themselves were useless to the clergy; and the Assembly decreed the sale of property belonging to the crown and the Church to the amount of four hundred millions.

The clergy, rendered desperate, then circulated writings among the people, and declared that the plan of the revolutionists was to attack the Catholic religion. It was in the southern provinces that it hoped to be most successful. We have seen that the first emigration had directed its course towards Turin. It was with Provence and Languedoc that its principal communications were kept up. Calonne, so celebrated at the time of the Notables (*See* Appendix Y.), was the minister of the fugitive court. The court was split into two parties. The high nobility was solicitous to maintain its empire, and dreaded the interference of the provincial noblesse, and still more that of the *bourgeoisie*. In consequence, it would have recourse to none but foreign aid to re-establish the throne. Besides to employ religion, as the emissaries of the provinces proposed to do, appeared ridiculous to men who had diverted themselves for a century with the pleasantries of Voltaire.

The other party, composed of petty nobles and expatriated citizens, proposed to combat the passion for liberty by a still stronger passion, fanaticism, and to conquer single-handed without laying itself under obligation to foreigners. The former alleged the vindictive nature of civil war as an excuse for foreign interference. The latter maintained that the effusion of blood was inseparable from such war, but that it ought not to be sullied by a treason. These men, more courageous, more patriotic, but more ferocious than the others, could not possibly succeed in a court where Calonne ruled. As, however, this court had need of everybody, the communications between Turin and the southern provinces were continued. It was determined to attack the revolution by foreign as well as by civil war, and to this end an attempt was made to awaken the ancient fanaticism of those countries. (*See* Appendix Z.)

The clergy neglected no means of seconding this plan. The Protestants in those parts excited the envy of the Catholics. The clergy took advantage of these dissensions, especially during the solemnities of Easter. At Montpellier, at Nimes, at Montauban, the old fanaticism was roused in all possible ways.

Charles Lameth complained in the tribune that the festival of Easter had been abused for the purpose of misleading the people, and exciting them against the new laws. At these words the clergy rose, and would have quitted the Assembly. The Bishop of Clermont threatened to do so, and a great number of ecclesiastics were already on their legs, and about to retire, when Charles Lameth was called to order, and the tumult subsided. Meanwhile the sale of the possessions of the clergy was carried into execution. This was warmly resented by them, and they omitted no occasion of manifesting their indignation.

Dom Gerle, a Carthusian, a man perfectly sincere in his religious and patriotic sentiments, one day desired permission to speak, and proposed that the Catholic religion should be declared the only religion of the state. A great number of deputies instantly rose, and were ready to vote the motion by acclamation, saying that the Assembly had now an opportunity to clear itself from the charge preferred against it of attacking the Catholic religion. Still, what was the tendency of such a motion? It either aimed at giving a privilege to the Catholic religion, and no religion ought to have any; or it was the declaration of a fact, namely, that the majority of the French were Catholics—a fact which need not have been declared. Such a motion, therefore, could not be entertained. Accordingly, in spite of the efforts of the nobility and clergy, the debate was adjourned to the following day. An immense crowd collected. Lafayette, apprised that evil-disposed persons intended to excite disturbance, had doubled the guard. The discussion commenced. An ecclesiastic threatened the Assembly with malediction. Maury uttered his usual cries. Menou calmly replied to all the reproaches brought against the Assembly, and said that it could not reasonably be accused of an intention to abolish the Catholic religion, at the very moment when it was making the cost of its worship an item in the public expenditure. He proposed, therefore, to pass to the order of the day. Dom Gerle was persuaded to withdraw his motion, and excused himself for having excited such a tumult. M. de la Rochefoucault submitted a motion differently worded, which succeeded that of Menou.

All at once a member of the right side complained that the Assembly was not free. He called upon Lafayette, and inquired why he had doubled the guard. The motive was not suspected, for it was not the left side that could be afraid of the people, and it was not his own friends that Lafayette sought to protect. This appeal increased the tumult; the discussion nevertheless continued. In the course of the debate Louis XIV. was mentioned. "I am not surprised," exclaimed Mirabeau, "that reference should be made to the reign in which the edict of Nantes was revoked; but consider that, from this tribune whence I address you, I see that fatal window where a king, the murderer of his subjects, mingling worldly interests with those of religion, gave the signal for the massacre of St. Bartholomew!" This terrible apostrophe did not put an end to the discussion. It lasted some time longer, and the motion of the Duke de la Rochefoucault was finally adopted. The Assembly declared that its sentiments were known, but that, out of regard for the liberty of conscience, it neither could nor ought to deliberate on the motion submitted to it.

Scarcely had a few days elapsed before a new expedient was employed to threaten and to dissolve the Assembly. The new organization of the kingdom was completed; the people were about to be convoked to elect their magistrates, and it was conceived that they might as well choose at the same time new deputies instead of those who composed the Assembly then sitting. This plan, proposed and discussed before, had already been rejected. It was again brought forward in April, 1790. Some of the instructions limited the powers to one year; and the deputies had actually been nearly a year assembled. They had met in May, 1789, and it was now near the month of April, 1790. Though the instructions had been annulled, and they had bound themselves not to separate before the completion of the constitution, these men, for whom there was neither decree passed nor oath taken, proposed to have other deputies elected, and to give up their places to them.

Maury, charged to propose this measure, played his part with more assurance than ever, but with more address than usual. He appealed to the sovereignty of the people, and said that they could no longer put themselves in the place of the nation and prolong powers which were but temporary. He asked by what right they had invested themselves with sovereign attributes; he insisted that this distinction between the legislative and constituent power was a chimerical distinction; that a sovereign convention could not exist unless in the absence of all government; and that, if the Assembly were that convention, it had only to depose the King, and to declare the throne vacant. Loud cries interrupted these words and expressed the general indignation. Mirabeau then rose with dignity. "We are asked," said he, "since what time the deputies of the people have become a National Convention. I answer, from the day when, finding the entry to their seats encompassed by soldiers, they went and met in the first place where they could assemble, to swear to perish rather than to betray and abandon the rights of the nation. On that day the nature of our powers, whatever they were, was changed. Be the powers that we have exercised what they may, our efforts, our labours, have legitimated them. The adhesion of the whole nation has sanctified them. All of you recollect the expression of that great man of antiquity, who had neglected the legal forms for saving the country. Galled upon by a factious tribune to say if he had observed the laws, he replied, 'I swear that I have saved the country.' Gentlemen," added Mirabeau, addressing the deputies of the commons, "I swear that you have saved France!"

At this magnificent oath, says Ferrières, the whole Assembly, as if under the influence of a sudden inspiration, closed the discussion, and resolved that the electoral bodies should not proceed to the election of new deputies.

Thus was this new scheme frustrated, and the Assembly enabled to proceed with its labours. Disturbances nevertheless continued throughout France. The commandant De Voisin was murdered by the people. The forts of Marseilles were seized by the National Guard. Commotions originating in a different spirit took place at Nimes and Montauban. Emissaries from Turin had excited the Catholics; they had delivered addresses, in which they declared the monarchy in danger, and insisted that the Catholic religion should be declared the religion of the state. A royal proclamation had in vain replied. They had rejoined. The Protestants had come to blows with the Catholics on the subject; and the latter, waiting in vain for the promised aid from Turin, had been at length repulsed. Several of the National Guards had set themselves in motion to assist the patriots against the insurgents; the combat had thus commenced, and the Count de Mirabeau, the declared adversary of his illustrious brother, announcing the civil war from the tribune, seemed by his motions, his gestures, and his words, to excite it amidst the Assembly.

Thus, while the more moderate deputies strove to allay the revolutionary ardour, an indiscreet opposition excited a fever, which repose might have reduced, and furnished the most vehement popular orators with pretexts. The violence of the clubs increased in consequence. That of the Jacobins, the offspring of the Breton Club, at first established at Versailles, afterwards at Paris, surpassed the others in numbers, talents, and violence. Its sittings were frequented like those of the Assembly itself. Here met the principal popular deputies, and here the most obstinate of them found excitements. Lafayette, with a view to counteract this terrible influence, had combined with Badly and the most enlightened men, to form another club, called the Club of 1789, and subsequently that of the Feuillans. But the remedy was powerless. An assemblage of a hundred cool, well-informed persons could not attract the multitude, like the club of the Jacobins, where all the popular passions were allowed full scope. To shut up the clubs would have been the only course; but the court had too little frankness, and excited too little mistrust, for the popular parts co think of resorting to such an expedient. The Lameth were at the head of the club of the Jacobins. Mirabeau was as often at the one as at the other; and it was evident to every one that his place was between all the parties. An occasion soon occurred on which he assumed a more decided character, and gained a memorable advantage for monarchy.

The French Revolution began to attract the attention of foreign sovereigns; its language was so lofty, so firm, and it had a character of such generality, that foreign princes could not but be alarmed at it. Up to this time it might have been taken for a temporary agitation; but the success of the Assembly, its firmness, its unexpected constancy, and, above all, the prospect which it held forth to France and to all nations, could not fail to draw upon it both respect and hatred, and to engage the notice of cabinets. Europe was then divided between two great hostile leagues—the Anglo-Prussian league on the one hand, and the imperial courts on the other.

Frederick William had succeeded the great Frederick on the throne of Prussia. This prince, fickle and weak, renouncing the politics of his illustrious predecessor, had forsaken the alliance of France for that of England. United with the latter power, he had formed that famous Anglo-Prussian league, which attempted such great things, and executed none of them; which excited Sweden, Poland, and the Porte against Russia and Austria—then abandoned all those whom it had so excited, and even assisted in despoiling them, by the partition of Poland.

The plan of England and Prussia united had been to ruin Russia and Austria, by raising against them Sweden, where reigned the chivalrous Gustavus, Poland groaning under a former partition, and the Porte smarting from Russian invasions. The particular intention of England in this league was, without declaring war against France, to revenge herself for the assistance afforded to the American colonies. She had found the means of doing so in setting the Turks and the Russians at variance. France could not remain neuter between these two nations, without alienating the Turks, who reckoned upon her, and without losing her commercial preponderance in the Levant. On the other hand, by taking part in the war, she should lose the alliance of Russia, with which she had just concluded a most advantageous treaty, which ensured her supplies of timber and of all the article that the North furnishes in abundance for the navy. Thus in either case France must sustain injury. Meanwhile England was equipping her forces, and preparing to employ them according to circumstances. Morover, observing the derangement of the finances under the Notables, and the popular excesses under the Constituent Assembly, she conceived that she should have no occasion for war; and it has been thought that she would have been better pleased to destroy France by means of internal disturbances than by arms. Hence she has always been charged with encouraging our dissensions.

This Anglo-Prussian league had occasioned some battles to be fought, with doubtful success. Gustavus had extricated himself like a hero from a position into which he had brought himself like an adventurer. Holland, which had risen against the Stadtholder, had been again subjected to him by English intrigues and Prussian armies. England had thus skilfully deprived France of a powerful maritime alliance; and the Prussian monarch, who sought triumphs of vanity only, had revenged an outrage committed by the states of Holland against the wife of the Stadtholder, who was his own sister. Poland completed her constitution, and was about to take up arms. Turkey had been beaten by Russia. Meanwhile the death of Joseph II., Emperor of Austria, which happened in January 1794, had changed the aspect of things. He had been succeeded by Leopold, that enlightened and pacific prince, whose happy reign had blessed Tuscany. Leopold, clever as he was wise, wished to put an end to the war; and in order to succeed the better, he employed the resources of seduction, which had such power over the fickle imagination of Frederick William. Representations were made to that prince, picturing the blessings of peace, the evils of war which had so long pressed heavily upon his people, and, lastly, the dangers of the French revolution, which proclaimed such mischievous principles. Ideas of absolute power were awakened within him; he was even led to conceive hopes of chastising the French revolutionists, as he had chastised those of Holland. He suffered himself to be persuaded at the moment when he was about to reap the advantages of that league, so boldly planned by his minister Hertzberg.

It was in July, 1790, that peace was signed at Reichenbach. In August Russia made hers with Sweden, and then had to cope only with Poland, which was far from formidable, and the Turks, who were beaten at all points. We shall notice hereafter these various events. Thus then the attention of the powers was almost exclusively directed to the French revolution. Some time before the conclusion of peace between Prussia and Leopold, when the Anglo-Prussian league threatened the two imperial courts, and secretly injured France, as well as Spain, our constant and faithful ally, some English vessels were seized by the Spaniards in Nootka Sound. Warm remonstrances were made and followed up by a general armament in the English ports. Spain, appealing to treaties, immediately applied to France for assistance, and Louis XVI. ordered the equipment of fifteen sail. England was accused of wishing, on this occasion, to increase our embarrassments. The clubs of London, it is true, had several times complimented the National Assembly, but the cabinet left a few philanthropists to indulge in these philosophic effusions, and was meanwhile paying, it is said, those astonishing agitators who appeared everywhere, and gave so much trouble to the national guards of the kingdom.

The disturbances were still greater at the moment of the general armament, and people could not help perceiving a connexion between the threats of England and the renewal of the commotions. Lafayette, in particular, who never spoke in the Assembly but on subjects which concerned the public tranquillity, denounced from the tribune a secret influence. "I cannot forbear directing the attention of the Assembly," said he, "to that new fermentation which manifests itself from Strasburg to Nimes, and from Brest to Toulon, and which the enemies of the people would in vain attribute to them, since it bears all the characteristics of a secret influence. If we talk of establishing departments, the country is laid waste. If neighbouring powers begin to arm, disturbances immediately break out in our ports and in our arsenals." Several commandants had in fact been murdered, and either through accident or design the best officers in our navy had been sacrificed. The English ambassador had been directed by his court to repel these imputations. But every one knows what confidence is due to such messages. Calonne, too, had written to the King, to justify England, but Calonne's testimony in favour of a foreign country was liable to suspicion. He urged to no purpose that every expense is known in a representative government, that even secret expenses are at least acknowledged as such, and that there was no item of that kind in the English budgets. Experience has proved that even responsible ministers are never without money. The most that can be said is that time, which reveals everything, has revealed nothing on this head, and that Necker, whose situation qualified him to judge, never believed in this secret influence.

The King, as we have just seen, had notified to the Assembly the equipment of fifteen sail of the line, thinking that it would approve of that measure and vote the necessary supplies. The Assembly gave the most favourable reception to the message, but perceived that it involved a constitutional question, which it behoved it to resolve, before it replied to the King. "The measures are taken," said Alexandre Lameth; "our discussion cannot delay them; we must therefore first decide whether the King or the Assembly shall be invested with the right of making peace and war." It was, in fact, almost the last important prerogative to be determined, and one of those which could not but excite the strongest interest. The imaginations of men were filled with the blunders of courts; and they were against leaving to the throne the power of plunging the nation into dangerous wars, or dishonouring it by base compromises. Nevertheless, among all the duties of government, the making of war and peace is that which involves the most action, and over which the executive power ought to exercise the most influence; it is that in which it must be left most liberty, that it may act freely and properly. The opinion of Mirabeau, who was said to have been gained by the court, was known beforehand. The opportunity was favourable for wresting from the orator his much-envied popularity. The Lameths were aware of this, and had charged Barnave to crush Mirabeau. The right side drew back, as it were, and left the field clear for those two rivals.

The discussion was awaited with impatience: it commenced. After several speakers had thrown out merely preliminary ideas, Mirabeau addressed the Assembly, and placed the question in a new light. War, according to him, is almost always unforeseen. Hostilities commence before threats. The King, charged with the public safety, ought to repel them, and thus war is begun before the Assembly has time to interfere. The same is the case with treaties. The King alone can seize the proper moment for negociating, for conferring, for disputing, with other powers; the Assembly can but ratify the conditions obtained. In either predicament, the King alone can act and the Assembly approve or disapprove. Mirabeau therefore thought that the executive power should be held bound to prosecute the hostilities commenced, and that the legislative power should, as the case might be, allow the war to continue or demand peace.

This opinion was applauded, because Mirabeau's opinion always was. Barnave nevertheless rose, and, without noticing the other speakers, merely answered Mirabeau. He admitted that the sword is frequently drawn before the nation can be consulted, but he maintained that hostilities are not war; that the King ought to repel them, and, as speedily as possible to apprize the Assembly, which then, as sovereign, declares its own intentions. Thus the whole difference lay in the words, for Mirabeau gave to the Assembly the right of disapproving the war and requiring peace, Barnave that of alike declaring both; but in either case the decision of the Assembly was to be obligatory, and Barnave allowed it no more right than Mirabeau. Barnave was nevertheless applauded and carried in triumph by the populace, and it was alleged that his adversary was sold. A pamphlet entitled "Great Treason of the Count de Mirabeau" was hawked about the streets with loud cries. The occasion was decisive; every one expected an effort from the terrible champion. He demanded permission to reply, obtained it, ascended the tribune in the presence of an immense multitude assembled to hear him, and declared, as he went up to it, that he would come down again either dead or victorious. "I too," he began, "have been borne in triumph, and yet they are crying to-day, the *great treason of the Count de Mirabeau*. I needed not this example to learn that it is but a step from the Capitol to the Tarpeian rock. Yet these strokes from below shall not stop me in my career." After this impressive exordium, he intimated that he should reply to Barnave only, and he thus proceeded: "Explain yourself," said he to him; "you have in your opinion limited the King to the notification of hostilities, and you have given to the Assembly alone the right of declaring the national will on that point. There I stop you, and recall you to our principles, which share the expression of the national will between the Assembly and the King . . . In attributing it to the Assembly alone, you have transgressed against the constitution. I call you to order . . . . You answer not I shall continue."

No answer could in fact be given. Throughout a long reply, Barnave remained exposed to these thundering apostrophes. Mirabeau answered him article by article, and demonstrated that Barnave had not given to the Assembly any thing more than he had himself given to it; but that, by limiting the King to a mere notification, he had deprived him of his necessary concurrence in the expression of the national will. He concluded by reproaching Barnave with those culpable rivalries between men, who, he said, ought to live like true comrades in arms. Barnave had enumerated the partisans of his opinion. Mirabeau in his turn mentioned his. He pointed out among them those moderate men, the first founders of the constitution, and who talked to the French of liberty, whilst his base calumniators were sucking the milk of courts (alluded to the Lameths, who had received favours from the Queen), "men," added he, "who will boast while they live of their friends and of their enemies."

Mirabeau's speech gained unanimous applause. There was in the Assembly a considerable number of deputies, who belonged neither to the right nor to the left side, but who, without espousing any party, decided upon the impression of the moment. It was they who gave the victory to genius and reason, because they created a majority on which side soever they voted. Barnave would have replied; the Assembly opposed his intention and insisted that the question should be put to the vote. The decree of Mirabeau, ably amended by Chapelier, had the preference, and was finally adopted to the general satisfaction; for these rivalries did not extend beyond the circle in which they originated, and the popular party conceived that it conquered just as well with Mirabeau as with the Lameths.

The decree conferred on the King and the nation the right of making peace and war. To the King was assigned the disposal of the forces. He was to notify the commencement of hostilities; to call together the Assembly if it was not sitting, and to propose the decree of peace or war. The Assembly was to deliberate on his express proposition, and the King was afterwards to sanction its deliberation. It was Chapelier who, by a very judicious amendment, had required the express proposition and the definitive sanction. This decree, comformable with reason, and with the principles already established, excited sincere joy among the constitutionalists, and foolish hopes among the counter-revolutionists, who imagined that the public mind was about to change, and that this victory of Mirabeau's was to become their own. Lafayette, who, on this occasion had joined Mirabeau, wrote on the subject to Bouillé, held out to him hopes of tranquillity and moderation, and strove, as he always did, to reconcile him to the new order of things.

The Assembly continued its financial labours. They consisted in disposing to the best advantage of the property of the clergy, the sale of which, long decreed, could not be prevented, either by protests, or by pastoral charges, or by intrigues. To dispossess a too powerful body of a great portion of the territory of the kingdom—to divide it in the best possible manner, so as to fertilize it by division; to make landed proprietors of a considerable portion of the people who were not such; lastly, to extinguish by the same operation the debts of the state and to restore order in the finances—such were the objects of the Assembly, and it was too sensible of their utility to be deterred by obstacles. The Assembly had already ordered the sale of crown and church property to the amount of four hundred millions, but it was necessary to find means to dispose of these possessions without lowering their value by putting them up to sale all at once. Bailly proposed, in the name of the municipality of Paris, a plan that was ably conceived, namely, to transfer these possessions to the municipalities, which should purchase them in a mass, for the purpose of selling them again by degrees, so that the sales of the whole might not take place at once. The municipalities not having funds to pay immediately, should give bills at a certain date, and the creditors of the state were to be paid with *bons* on communes, which they were required to pay off in succession. These *bons*, which in the discussion were called municipal paper, furnished the first idea of the assignats.

In following up Bailly's plan, the church property was invaded; it was to be divided among the communes, and the creditors were to be brought nearer to their pledge, by acquiring a claim upon the municipalities, instead of having a claim upon the state. The guarantees would therefore be augmented, since the payment was to be brought nearer; it would even depend upon the creditors to effect it themselves, since with these *bons* or assignats they could acquire a proportionable value in property put up to sale. Thus a great deal would have been done for them. But this was not all. They might not choose to convert their *bons* into land, either from scruples or from any other motive. They would then be obliged to keep their *bons*, which, as they could not circulate like money, would be mere unpaid obligations. There remained but one more measure to be taken, which was, to give to these *bons* or obligations the faculty of circulation. They would then become really and truly money, and the creditors, being enabled to pay with them, would be actually reimbursed. Another consideration was decisive. There was a scarcity of specie. This was attributed to the emigration which carried away a great deal of ready money, to the payments that had to be made to foreigners, and lastly to malevolence. The real cause was the want of confidence occasioned by the disturbances. Specie is apparent by the circulation. When confidence prevails, the activity of the exchange is extreme; money moves about rapidly, is seen everywhere, and is believed to be more considerable because it is more serviceable; but when political commotions create alarm, capital languishes, specie moves slowly; it is frequently hoarded, and complaints are unjustly made of its absence.

The desire to provide a substitute for metallic specie, which the Assembly considered scarce, by putting into the hands of the creditors something better than a dead obligation, and the necessity of supplying a multitude of other urgent wants, caused the forced currency of money to be given to these *bons* or assignats. The creditor was thereby paid, since he could oblige others to take the paper which he had received, and thus supply all his wants. If he did not choose to purchase lauds, those who had taken the circulating paper of him would eventually buy them. The assignats which should come in by this method were to be burnt; thus the lands of the clergy would soon be distributed and the paper suppressed. The assignats bore interest at so much per day, and acquired value by remaining in the hands of those who held them.

The clergy, viewing this measure as an instrument of execution against its possessions, strongly opposed it. Its noble and other allies, adverse to every thing that facilitated the progress of the revolution, opposed it also, and cried out against paper-money. The name of Law was brought forward, and the memory of his bankruptcy revived. The comparison, however, was not just, because the value of Law's paper-money depended on the profits to be gained by the India Company, while that of the assignats was founded on a territorial capital, real and easily convertible. Law had committed considerable frauds on the court, and had greatly exceeded the presumed amount of the Company's capital. The Assembly, on the contrary, could not believe that, with the new forms which it had just established, such errors could take place. Lastly, the amount of the assignats created formed but a very small portion of the capital allotted to them. But it was true enough that paper, however safe, is not like money, a reality, or according to Bailly's expression, "a physical actuality." Specie carries its own value along with it. Paper, on the contrary, requires one more operation, a purchase of land, a realization. It must therefore be below specie, and as soon as it is below it, money, which nobody will give for paper, is hoarded and at length disappears. If, moreover, abuses in the administration of the property, and in moderate issues of paper, destroy the proportion between the circulating medium and the capital, confidence vanishes; the nominal value is retained, but the real value ceases; he who gives this conventional money, robs him who receives it, and a great crisis ensues. All this was possible enough, and with more experience would have appeared certain. As a financial measure, the issue of assignats was therefore highly censurable; but it was necessary as a political measure; for it supplied urgent wants, and divided property without the aid of an agrarian law. The Assembly, therefore, had no reason to hesitate; and, in spite of Maury and his partisans, it decreed four hundred millions of forced assignats with interest.

Necker had long since lost the confidence of the King, the former deference of his colleagues and the enthusiasm of the nation. Engrossed by his calculations, he sometimes entered into discussion with the Assembly. His reserve for extraordinary expenses occasioned a demand for the production of the red book, the famous register, containing, it was said, a list of all the secret disbursements. Louis XVI. complied with pain, and caused seals to be put upon the leaves in which were entered the expenses of his predecessor, Louis XV. The Assembly respected his delicacy, and confined itself to the expenditure of the current reign. Nothing personally concerning the King was found. Every prodigality had been for the benefit of courtiers. The Lameths were found down for a gratuity of sixty thousand francs, granted by the Queen for their education. They sent back that sum to the public exchequer. The pensions were reduced according to the twofold proportion of services and the former condition of the persons. The Assembly showed in every point the greatest moderation. It petitioned the King to fix the civil list himself, and it voted by acclamation the twenty-five millions which he demanded.

This Assembly, strong in its number, in its intelligence, in its power, in its resolutions, had conceived the immense plan of regenerating all the departments of the state, and it had just framed the new judicial system. It had distributed the courts in the same manner as the local administrations, by districts and departments. The judges were left to the popular election. This last measure had been strongly opposed. Political metaphysics had been again enlisted on this occasion to prove that the judicial power was dependent on the executive, and that the King ought to appoint the judges. Reasons had been found on both sides; but the only one that should have been given to the Assembly, which was on the point of making a monarchy, was that royalty, successively stripped of its prerogatives, becomes a mere magistracy, and the state a republic. But to say what monarchy was, would have been too bold, requiring concessions which a nation never consents to make in the first moment of its awaking. The fault of nations is to demand either too much or nothing. The Assembly sincerely wished well to the King; it was full of deference for him, and manifested it on every occasion; but it was attached to the person, and without being aware of it, destroyed the thing.

After introducing this uniformity into the law, and the administration, the Assembly had still to regulate the service of religion and to organize it like all the other systems. Thus, when it had established a court of appeal and a superior administration in every department, it was natural to place there a bishopric also. How, indeed, could certain episcopal sees be suffered to comprehend fifteen hundred square leagues, whilst others embraced but twenty;—certain livings to be ten leagues in circumference, whilst others numbered scarcely fifteen houses; and certain *curés* to have at the utmost but seven hundred livres, whilst there were beneficed ecclesiastics, who possessed incomes of ten and fifteen thousand livres?

The Assembly, in reforming abuses, was interfering neither with the doctrines of the Church, nor with the Papal authority, since the circumscriptions had always belonged to the temporal power. It determined, therefore, to form a new division, and to subject, as of old, both *curés* and bishops to the popular election. Here, it was encroaching on the temporal power alone, since it was the King who chose, and the Pope who instituted the ecclesiastical dignitaries. This plan, which was called the civil constitution of the clergy, and which drew upon the Assembly more calumny than anything it had yet done, was, nevertheless, the work of the most pious deputies. It was Camus and other Jansenists, who, desirous of invigorating religion in the state, strove to bring it into harmony with the new laws. It is certain that, justice being everywhere else reestablished, it would have been strange had it not also been introduced into the ecclesiastical administration. With the exception of Camus and some others of his stamp, the members of the Assembly, educated in the school of the philosophers, would have treated Christianity like all the other religions admitted into the state, and would not have bestowed a thought upon it. They entertained sentiments which in our present social state it is usual not to combat, even when we do not share them. They supported, therefore, the religious and sincerely Christian plan of Camus. The clergy opposed it, alleging that it encroached on the spiritual authority of the Pope, and appealed to Rome. The principal bases of the plan were nevertheless adopted, and immediately presented to the King, who asked for time that he might refer to the high Pontiff. The King, whose enlightened religion recognised the wisdom of this plan, wrote to the Pope, with a sincere desire of obtaining his assent, and thus overthrowing all the objections of the clergy. We shall presently see what intrigues prevented the success of his wishes.

The month of July approached. It was nearly a year since the Bastille was taken, since the nation had seized, all power, since it had announced its intentions by the Assembly, and executed them itself, or caused them to be executed under its superintendence. The 14th of July was considered as the day which had commenced a new era, and it was resolved that its anniversary should be celebrated with great festivity. The provinces and the towns had already set the example of confederating, to resist with united strength the enemies of the Revolution. The municipality of Paris proposed for the 14th of July a general federation of all France, which should be celebrated in the heart of the capital by the deputies of all the national guards and of all the corps of the army. This plan was hailed with enthusiasm, and immense preparations were made to render the festival worthy of its object.

Other nations, as we have seen, had long turned their eyes upon France. The sovereigns began to hate and fear, the people to esteem, us. A party of foreign enthusiasts appeared, before the Assembly in the costume of their respective nations. Their spokesman, Anacharsis Clootz, by birth a Prussian, a man of wayward imagination, demanded, in the name of the human race, to be admitted into the Federation. (*See* Appendix A A.) These scenes, which appear ridiculous to those who are not eye-witnesses of them, make a deep impression upon all who are. The Assembly complied with the demand, and the President replied to these foreigners that they should be admitted, in order that they might be able to relate to their countrymen what they had seen, and to make them acquainted with the joys and the blessings of liberty.

The emotion caused by this scene produced another. An equestrian statue of Louis XIV. represented him trampling upon the image of several conquered provinces. "In the days of liberty," exclaimed one of the Lameths, "these monuments of slavery ought not to be endured. It is not fit that the people of Franche-Comté, when they come to Paris, should see their image thus enchained." Maury opposed a measure in itself unimportant, but which it was necessary to concede to the public enthusiasm. At the same moment a member proposed to abolish the titles of count, marquis, baron, &c.; to prohibit liveries; in short, to suppress all hereditary titles. Young Montmorenci seconded the motion.

A noble asked what they would substitute for the words, "Such a one was created count for services rendered to the state."—"Let it merely be said," replied Lafayette, "that on such a day such a person saved the state." The motion was carried, notwithstanding the extraordinary irritation of the nobility, which was more galled by the abolition of its titles than by the more substantial losses which it had sustained since the commencement of the Revolution. The more moderate portion of the Assembly had proposed that, in abolishing titles, those who chose to retain them should be at liberty to do so. Lafayette lost no time in apprising the court before the decree was sanctioned, and advised that it should be sent back to the Assembly, which would consent to amend it; but the King instantly gave his sanction, in which some thought they could discover the disingenuous intention of driving things to extremities.

The object of the Federation was the civic oath. It was discussed whether the Federalists and the Assembly should take the oath to the King, or whether the King, considered as the highest public functionary, should swear with all the others at the altar of the country. The latter course was preferred. Thus did the Assembly put etiquette in complete harmony with the laws, and the King would be no more in the ceremony than he was in the constitution. The court, which was constantly conceiving distrust of Lafayette, was alarmed at a rumour that was circulated, purporting that he was about to be appointed commandant of all the national guards of the kingdom. It was but natural that those who did not know Lafayette should feel this distrust; and his enemies, of all parties, strove to augment it. How, in fact, could it be supposed that a man, possessing such popularity, at the head of a considerable force, would not abuse it? Nothing, however, was further from his intention; he had resolved to be nothing but a citizen, and, whether from virtue or well-judged ambition, the merit is the same. Human pride must be placed somewhere—it is virtue to place it in doing what is right.

Lafayette, in order to remove the alarm of the court, proposed that one and the same person should not command more than the guard of one department. The motion was carried by acclamation, and the disinterestedness of the general was warmly applauded. Lafayette was nevertheless charged with the whole arrangement of the festival, and appointed chief of the Federation in his quality of commandant of the Parisian guard.

The day approached, and the preparations were carried on with great activity. The ceremony was to take place in the Champ de Mars, a spacious area, extending from the Military School to the bank of the Seine. It had been planned to remove the earth from the centre to the sides, so as to form an amphitheatre capable of containing the mass of the spectators. Twelve thousand labourers were kept at work without intermission, and yet it was apprehended that the operations could not be finished by the 14th. The inhabitants then proposed to assist the workmen. In an instant the whole population were transformed into labourers. Churchmen, soldiers, persons of all classes, took up the spade and pickaxe. Elegant females themselves lent a hand. The enthusiasm soon became general. The people repaired to the spot by sections, with banners of different colours, and to the sound of drums. On arriving, they mingled and worked together. At nightfall, on a given signal, each rejoined his company, and returned to his home. This fraternal harmony prevailed till the work was finished. Meanwhile, the federalists kept arriving, and they were received with the greatest kindness and hospitality. The enthusiasm was general, in spite of the alarm which the very small number of persons who remained inaccessible to emotions strove to excite. It was said that the brigands meant to take advantage of the moment when the people should be at the Federation to plunder the city. It was insinuated that the Duke of Orleans, who had returned from London, entertained sinister designs. The national gaiety was nevertheless undiminished, and no faith was put in any of these evil forebodings.

The 14th at length arrived. All the federate deputies of the provinces and the army, ranged under their chiefs and their banners, set out from the Place of the Bastille and proceeded to the Tuileries. The deputies of Béarn, in passing the Place de Feronnerie, where Henry IV. was assassinated, paid him a tribute of respect, which, in this moment of emotion, was expressed by tears. The federalists, on their arrival in the garden of the Tuileries, received into their ranks the municipality of the Assembly. A battalion of boys, armed like their fathers, preceded the Assembly. A body of old men followed it, and thus revived the memory of ancient Sparta. The procession moved forward amidst the shouts and applause of the people. The quays were lined with spectators. The houses were covered with them. A bridge thrown in a few days across the Seine, and strewed with flowers, led from one bank to the other, facing the scene of the Federation. The procession crossed it, and each took his place. A magnificent amphitheatre, formed at the farthest extremity, was destined for the national authorities. The King and the president sat beside one another on similar seats, sprinkled with golden fleurs-de-lis. Behind the King there was an elevated balcony for the Queen and the court. The ministers were at some distance from the King, and the deputies ranged on either side. Four hundred thousand spectators occupied the lateral amphitheatres. Sixty thousand armed federalists performed their evolutions in the intermediate space; and in the centre, upon a base twenty-five feet high, stood the altar of the country. Three hundred priests, in white surplices and tricoloured scarfs, covered the steps, and were to officiate in the mass.

It was three hours before all the federalists had arrived. During this interval the sky was overcast with clouds, and the rain fell in torrents. The sky, whose brightness harmonizes so well with human joys, refused at this moment serenity and light. One of the battalions, as it came up, grounded arms, and conceived the idea of forming a dance. Its example was instantly followed by all the others, and, in a moment, the intermediate space was filled by sixty thousand men, soldiers, and citizens, opposing gaiety of heart to the unfavourable weather. At length the ceremony commenced. The sky happily cleared, and threw its brilliancy over this solemn scene. The Bishop of Autun (*See* Appendix B B) began the mass. The choristers accompanied the voice of the prelate; the cannon mingled with it their solemn peals. Divine service over, Lafayette alighted from his horse, ascended the steps of the throne, and received the orders of the King, who handed to him the form of the oath. Lafayette carried it to the altar. At that moment all the banners waved, every sabre glistened. The general, the army, the president, the deputies, cried, "I swear it." The King, standing with his hand outstretched towards the altar, said: "I, King of the French, swear to employ the power delegated to me by the constitutional act of the state in maintaining the constitution decreed by the National Assembly and accepted by me." At this moment, the Queen, moved by the general emotion, clasped in her arms the august child, the heir to the throne, and, from the balcony where she was stationed, showed him to the assembled nation. At this movement, shouts of joy, attachment, and enthusiasm, were addressed to the mother and the child, and all hearts were hers. At this very same moment all France, assembled in the eighty-three chief towns of the departments, took the same oath to love the King who would love them. In such moments hatred itself is softened, pride gives way, all are happy in the general happiness and proud of the dignity of all. Why, alas! are these pleasures of concord so soon forgotten!

This' august ceremony over, the procession returned, and the people gave themselves up to rejoicing. (*See* Appendix C C.) These rejoicings lasted several days. A general review of the federalists was held. Sixty thousand men were under arms, and exhibited a magnificent sight, at once military and national. At night Paris was the scene of a charming *fête*. The principal places of assemblage were the Champs Elysées and the Bastille. On the site of this ancient prison, now converted into an open square, was set up this inscription: "Place for dancing." Brilliant lamps arranged in festoons made amends for the daylight. Opulence had been forbidden to annoy this quiet fete by the movement of carriages. Each was expected to make himself one of the people, and to feel happy in being so. The Champs Elysées exhibited a touching scene. There every one walked about without noise, without tumult, without rivalry, without animosity. All classes intermingled, enjoyed themselves beneath the mild lamp-light, and seemed delighted to be together. Thus, even in the bosom of ancient civilisation, men seemed to have found anew the times of primitive fraternity.

The federalists, after attending the imposing discussions of the National Assembly, after witnessing the pomp of the court and the magnificence of Paris, after experiencing the kindness of the King, whom they all visited, and by whom they were received with touching expressions of benevolence, returned home in transports of intoxication, full of good feelings and illusions. After so many painful events, and while preparing to describe others still more terrible, the historian dwells with pleasure on these too transient scenes, where all hearts had but one sentiment, love for the public weal. (*See* Appendix D D.)

This touching festival of the Federation was but a fugitive emotion. On the morrow, all hearts still wished what they had wished the day before, and the war had recommenced. Petty quarrels with the ministry again began. Complaints were made that a passage had been granted to the Austrian troops into the country of Liege. St. Priest was charged with having favoured the escape of several accused persons who were suspected of counter-revolutionary machinations. The court, out of revenge, again placed in the order of the day the proceedings commenced at the Chatelet against the authors of the disturbances of the 5th and 6th of October. The Duke of Orleans and Mirabeau were implicated in them. These singular proceedings, several times relinquished and resumed, betrayed the different influences under which they had been carried on. They were full of contradictions, and presented no sufficient charge against the two principal persons accused. The court, in conciliating Mirabeau, had nevertheless no settled plan in regard to him. It approached and withdrew from him by turns, and sought rather to appease him than to follow his advice.

In renewing the proceedings of the 5th and 6th of October, it was not at him that it aimed, but at the Duke of Orleans, who had been much applauded on his return from London, and whom it had harshly repulsed, when he begged to be again taken into favour by the King. Chabroud was to report to the Assembly, that it might judge whether there was ground or not for the accusation. The court was desirous that Mirabeau should keep silence, and that he should abandon the Duke of Orleans, against whom alone it bore a grudge. He nevertheless spoke, and showed how ridiculous were the imputations thrown out against him. He was accused, in fact, of having apprized Mounier that Paris was marching upon Versailles, and of having added this expression: "We want a King, but no matter whether it be Louis XVI. or Louis XVII.;" of having gone through the Flanders regiment, sword in hand, and exclaimed at the moment of the departure of the Duke of Orleans: "This *j . . . f* is not worth the trouble that is taken about him." Nothing could be more frivolous than such allegations. Mirabeau showed their weakness and absurdity, said but a few words respecting the Duke of Orleans, and exclaimed, when concluding: "Yes, the secret of these infernal proceedings is at length laid bare; it is yonder, whole and entire (pointing to the right side); it is to be found in the interest of those whose evidence and whose calumnies have formed their tissue; it is in the resources which they have furnished to the enemies of the Revolution; it is—it is in the hearts of the judges such as it will soon be graven in history by the most just and the most implacable vengeance."

Plaudits accompanied Mirabeau to his seat; the Assembly resolved that there was no ground of accusation against the persons inculpated, and the court incurred the disgrace of a useless attempt.

The Revolution was destined to run its course everywhere, in the army as well as among the people. The army, the last instrument of power, was also the last fear of the popular party. All the military chiefs were enemies of the Revolution, because, being exclusive possessors of promotion and favours, they saw merit admitted to equal privileges with themselves. From the contrary motive, the soldiers inclined to the new order of things; and no doubt the dislike of discipline, and the desire of higher pay, acted as powerfully upon them as the spirit of liberty. A dangerous insubordination manifested itself throughout almost the whole army. The infantry, in particular, perhaps because it mingles more with the people, was in a state of absolute insurrection. Bouillé, who was mortified to see his army slipping out of his hands, employed all possible means to prevent this contagion of the revolutionary spirit. He had received the most extensive powers from Latour du Pin, minister at war; he avaded himself of them to keep shifting his troops about continually, and thus to prevent them from contracting a familiarity with the people by staying in the same place. He forbade them above all things to frequent the clubs, and in short he neglected no means of maintaining military subordination. Bouillé, after a long resistance, had at length taken the oath to the constitution. He was a man of honour, and from that moment he seemed to have formed the resolution to be faithful to the constitution and to the King. His dislike of Lafayette, whose disinterestedness he could not but acknowledge, was overcome, and he was more disposed to be on good terms with him. The national guards of the extensive country under his command had proposed to appoint him their general. He had refused the offer in his first fit of pique, but was sorry for having done so afterwards, when he thought of all the good that he should have had it in his power to do. Nevertheless, in spite of some denunciations of the clubs, he still maintained himself in the popular favour.

Revolt first broke out at Metz. The soldiers confined their officers, seized the colours and the military chests, and wished even to make the municipality contribute. Bouillé exposed himself to the greatest danger, and succeeded in his efforts to suppress the sedition. Soon afterwards, a similar mutiny took place at Nancy. Some Swiss regiments were implicated in it, and there was reason to apprehend that, if this example were followed, the whole kingdom would soon be a prey to the united excesses of the soldiery and the populace. The Assembly itself trembled at this prospect. An officer was charged to carry the decree passed against the rebels. He could not put it into execution, and Bouillé was ordered to march to Nancy, that the law might have the assistance of force. He had but few soldiers on whom he could rely. Luckily the troops which had lately mutinied at Metz, humbled because he durst not trust them, offered to march against the rebels: the national guards made a similar offer, and he advanced upon Nancy with these united forces and a tolerably numerous body of cavalry. His situation was perplexing, for he could not employ his cavalry, and his infantry was not strong enough to attack the rebels seconded by the populace. Nevertheless, he addressed them with the greatest firmness and contrived to overawe them. They were even about to yield and to leave the city agreeably to his orders, when some musket-shots were fired, from some unknown quarter. An action now became inevitable. Bouillé's troops, under the idea of treachery, fought with the greatest ardour; but the engagement was obstinate, and they penetrated only step by step through a destructive fire. Being at length master of the principal squares, Bouillé gained the submission of the revolted regiments and compelled them to leave the city; he liberated the imprisoned officers and the authorities, and caused the principal ringleaders to be picked out, and delivered them up to the National Assembly.

This victory diffused general joy, and allayed the fears which had been excited for the tranquillity of the kingdom. Bouillé received congratulations and commendations from the King and the Assembly. He was subsequently calumniated, and his conduct charged with cruelty. It was nevertheless irreproachable, and at the moment it was applauded as such. The King augmented his command, which became very considerable, extending from Switzerland to the Sambre, and comprehending the greatest part of the frontiers. Bouillé, having more reliance on the cavalry than on the infantry, chose the banks of the Seille, which falls into the Moselle, for his cantonments. He there had plains for manœuvring his cavalry, forage for its support, places of considerable strength for intrenching it, and, above all, a thin population. Bouillé had determined to take no step against the constitution, but he distrusted the patriots, and he took precautions with a view to succour the King, if circumstances should render it necessary.

The Assembly had abolished the parliaments, instituted juries, suppressed *jurandes*, and was about to order a fresh issue of assignats. The property of the clergy offering an immense capital, and the assignats rendering it continually disposable, it was natural that the Assembly should employ it. All the objections already urged were renewed with still greater violence. The Bishop of Autun himself declared against this new issue, and had the sagacity to foresee all the financial results of that measure. (*See* Appendix E E.) Mirabeau, looking chiefly at the political results, obstinately persisted, and with success. Eight hundred millions in assignats were decreed; and this time it was decided that they should not bear interest. It would have been useless, in fact, to add interest to a circulating medium. Let this be done for a paper which cannot circulate but remains idle in the hands of the holder—nothing is more just: but for a value which becomes actual by its forced currency, it is an error which the Assembly did not commit a second time.

Necker opposed this new issue, and sent in a memorial which was not listened to. Times were materially changed for him, and he was no longer the minister whose continuance in office was deemed by the people essential to their welfare a year before. Deprived of the confidence of the King, embroiled with his colleagues, excepting Montmorin, he was neglected by the Assembly, and not treated by it with that attention which he had a right to expect. Necker's error consisted in believing that reason is sufficient for all things, and that, combined with a medley of sentiment and logic, it could not fail to triumph over the infatuation of the aristocrats and the irritation of the patriots. Necker possessed that somewhat vainglorious reason, which sits in judgment on the vagaries of the passions, and condemns them; but he lacked that other sort of reason, more lofty but less proud, which does not confine itself to condemning, but knows how to govern them also. Thus, placed in the midst of parties, he only irritated all, without being a bridle upon any. Left without friends, since the secession of Mounier and Lally, he had retained none but the useless Mallouet. He had offended the Assembly by reminding it continually, and with reproaches, of the most difficult of all duties—that of attending to the finances. He had, moreover, incurred ridicule by the manner in which he spoke of himself. His resignation was accepted with pleasure by all parties. His carriage was stopped as it was quitting the kingdom by the same populace which had before drawn him in triumph; and it was necessary to apply to the Assembly for an order directing that he should be allowed to go to Switzerland. He soon obtained this permission, and retired to Coppet, there to contemplate at a distance a Revolution which he was no longer qualified to observe closely or to guide.

The ministry was now reduced to as complete a cipher as the King, and chiefly busied itself with intrigues, which were either futile or culpable. St. Priest communicated with the emigrants. Latour du Pin lent himself to all the schemes of the military chiefs; Montmorin (*See* Appendix F F.) possessed the esteem of the court but not its confidence, and he was employed in intrigues with the popular leaders, with whom his moderation made him acquainted. The ministers were all denounced on the plea of new plots. "I, too," exclaimed Cazalès, "I too would denounce them, if it were generous to attack such weak men; I would charge the minister of the finances with having kept the Assembly in the dark respecting the real resources of the state, and with not having directed a Revolution Which he had provoked; I would charge the minister at war with having suffered the army to be disorganised; the minister of the interior with not having enforced the observance of the King's orders; all, in short, with their nullity and the cowardly advice given to their master." Inactivity is a crime in the eyes of parties desirous of proceeding to their goal. Accordingly, the right side condemned the ministers, not for what they had done, but for what they had not done. Cazalès and his supporters, though they condemned them, were nevertheless averse to applying to the King for their dismissal, because they regarded such an application as an infringement of the royal prerogative. The motion was not pressed; but the ministers successively resigned, excepting Montmorin, who alone was retained. Duport-du-Tertre, who was merely an advocate, was appointed keeper of the seals. Duportail, recommended to the King by Lafayette, succeeded Latour du Pin in the war department, and showed himself more favourably disposed towards the popular party. One of the measures taken by him was to deprive Bouillé of all the liberty which he assumed in his command, and especially of the power of displacing the troops at his pleasure;—a power which Bouillé employed, as we have seen, to prevent his soldiers from fraternising with the people.

The King had studied the history of the English Revolution with particular attention. He had always been powerfully struck by the fate of Charles I., and he could not help feeling sinister forebodings. He had particularly remarked the motive of Charles's condemnation. That motive was civil war. He had thence contracted an invincible horror of every measure that could produce bloodshed, and invariably opposed all the schemes of flight proposed by the Queen and the court.

During the summer which he passed at St. Cloud in 1790, he had opportunities enough for flight, but he never would listen to the mention of it. The friends of the constitution dreaded like him such a step, which seemed likely to lead to a civil war. The aristocrats alone desired it, because, in becoming masters of the King, by withdrawing him from the Assembly, they flattered themselves with the prospect of governing in his name, and returning with him at the head of foreigners; not yet knowing that in such cases one can never go anywhere but in the rear. With the aristocrats were perhaps united some precocious imaginations, which already began to dream of a republic, which no one else yet thought of, and the name of which had never yet been mentioned, unless by the Queen, in her fits of passion against Lafayette and the Assembly, whom she accused of urging it on with all their might. Lafayette, chief of the constitutional army and of all the sincere friends of liberty, kept incessant watch over the person of the monarch. Those two ideas—the departure of the King and civil war—were so strongly associated in all minds ever since the commencement of the Revolution, that such an event was considered as the greatest calamity that could be apprehended.

Meanwhile the expulsion of the ministry, which, if it had not the confidence of Louis XVI., was at least his choice, indisposed him towards the Assembly, and excited his fears for the total loss of the executive power. The new religious debates, to which the bad faith of the clergy gave rise on occasion of the civil constitution, affrighted his timid conscience, and thenceforward he thought of departure. It was towards the end of 1790 that he wrote on the subject to Bouillé, who at first opposed the scheme, but afterwards gave way, lest he should cause the unfortunate monarch to doubt his zeal. Mirabeau, on his part, had formed a plan for upholding the monarchy. In continual communication with Montmorin, he had hitherto undertaken nothing of consequence; because the court, hesitating between emigration and the National party, was not cordially disposed towards anything, and dreaded, above all other schemes, that which would subject it to a master so sincerely constitutional as Mirabeau. Nevertheless, at this period it cordially agreed with him. Everything was promised him if he succeeded. All possible resources were placed at his disposal. Talon, civil lieutenant to the Chatelet, and Laporte, recently summoned by the King to manage the civil list, had orders to see him, and to aid in the execution of his plans. Mirabeau condemned the new constitution. For a monarchy it was, according to him-, too democratic, and for a republic there was a Icing too much. Observing, above all, the popular violence, which kept continually increasing, he resolved to set bounds to it. At Paris, under the rule of the mob and of an all-powerful Assembly, any attempt of this sort was impossible. He felt that there was but one alternative, to remove the King from Paris, and place him at Lyons. There the King could have explained himself—he could have energetically stated the reasons which caused him to condemn the new constitution, and have given another, which was ready prepared. At the same instant a first session would have been convoked. Mirabeau, in conferring in writing with the most popular members, had had the art to draw from all of them the acknowledgment of their disapprobation of an article in the existing constitution. On comparing these different opinions, it was found that the constitution was altogether condemned by its framers themselves. He proposed to annex them to the manifesto of the King, to ensure its effect, and to cause the necessity for a new constitution to be the more strongly felt. We are not acquainted with all his means of execution; but we know that, through the policy of Talon, civil lieutenant, he had secured pamphleteers and club and mob orators, and that by his immense correspondence he could have made sure of thirty-six departments of the South. No doubt he meant to gain the aid of Bouillé, but he would not place himself at the mercy of that general. While Bouillé should be encamped at Montmedy, he wished the King to stay at Lyons; and he himself was to be at Lyons or Paris, according to circumstances. A foreign prince, a friend of Mirabeau, saw Bouillé on behalf of the King, and communicated to him this plan, but unknown to Mirabeau, who had no thought of Montmedy, for which place the King subsequently set out. Bouillé, struck by the genius of Mirabeau, declared that everything ought to be done to win such a man, and that for his own part he was ready to second him with all his means.

M. de Lafayette was unacquainted with this plan. Though sincerely attached to the person of the King, he had not the confidence of the court; and, besides, he excited the envy of Mirabeau, who was not desirous of having such a companion. M. de Lafayette, moreover, was known to pursue only the direct road; and this plan was too bold—it deviated too much from the legal course to suit him. Be this as it may, Mirabeau wished to be the sole executor of his plan, and in fact he carried it on quite alone during the whiter of 1790-1. It is impossible to tell whether it would have succeeded, but thus much is certain, that, without stemming the revolutionary torrent, it would at least have influenced its direction; and that, though it would undoubtedly not have changed the inevitable result of the Revolution, it would have modified events by its powerful opposition. It is still a question, however, whether, had he even succeeded in quelling the popular party, he could have made himself master of the aristocracy and of the court. One of his friends mentioned to him this last objection. "They have promised me everything," said Mirabeau. "And if they should not keep their word?" "If they do not keep their word, I will soon turn them into a republic."

The principal articles of the civil constitution, such as the new circumscription of the bishoprics and the election of all the ecclesiastical functionaries, had been decreed. The King had referred to the Pope, who, after answering him in a tone half severe and half paternal, had appealed in his turn to the clergy of France. The clergy, availing itself of this occasion, alleged that spiritual interests were compromised by the measures of the Assembly. At the same time it circulated pastoral charges, declared that the displaced bishops would not quit their sees but by compulsion and force; that they would hire houses and continue their ecclesiastical functions; and that all who adhered faithfully to their religion ought to have recourse to them alone. The clergy intrigued, particularly in La Vendée and in some of the southern departments, where it acted in concert with the emigrants. A federative camp had been formed at Jallez, where, under the apparent pretext of federation, the pretended federalists purposed to establish a centre of opposition to the measures of the Assembly. The popular parry was exasperated at these proceedings; and, strong in its power, weary of moderation, it resolved to resort to a decisive expedient. We have already seen what were the motives that had influenced the adoption of the civil constitution. The trainers of that constitution were the most sincere Christians in the Assembly; and these, irritated by an unjust resistance, resolved to overcome it.

The reader knows that a decree obliged all the public functionaries to take an oath to the new constitution. When this civic oath was discussed the clergy endeavoured to make a distinction between the political constitution and the ecclesiastical constitution: but the

Assembly had gone still farther. On this occasion it resolved to require of the ecclesiastics a rigorous oath, which should impose on them the necessity of retiring if they refused to take it, or of faithfully performing their duties if they did take it. It had the precaution to declare that it meant not to do violence to consciences; that it should respect the refusal of those who, considering religion as compromised by the new laws, would not take the oath; but that it was desirous of knowing them, that it might not consign the new bishoprics to their charge. In this course its motives were just and frank. It added to its decree, that those who should refuse to take the oath should be deprived of their functions and salary. Moreover, by way of setting the example, all the ecclesiastics who were deputies were required to take the oath in the Assembly itself, eight days after the sanction of the new decree.

The right side opposed this. Maury gave vent to all his violence, and did all that lay in his power to provoke interruption, that he might have ground for complaint. Alexandre Lameth, who filled the president's chair, maintained order while he spoke, and deprived him of the pleasure of being driven from the tribune. Mirabeau, more eloquent than ever, defended the Assembly. "You," he exclaimed, "the persecutors of religion! you, who have paid it so noble and so touching an homage in the most admirable of your decrees! you, who devote to its worship part of the public revenue, of which your prudence and your justice have rendered you so economical! you, who have summoned religion to assist in the division of the kingdom, and have planted the sign of the cross on all the boundaries of the departments! you, in short, who know that God is as necessary to man as liberty!"

The Assembly decreed the oath. The King referred immediately to Home. The Bishop of Aix, who had at first opposed the civil constitution, feeling the necessity of a pacification, joined the King and some of the more moderate of his colleagues in soliciting the assent of the Pope. The emigrants at Turin, and the opposing bishops of France, wrote also to Rome, but in a directly contrary spirit; and the Pope, upon various pretexts, postponed his answer. The Assembly, irritated at these delays, insisted on having the sanction of the King, who, having made up his mind to comply, resorted to the usual stratagems of weakness. He wished to oblige the Assembly to use constraint towards him, that he might seem not to act freely. In fact, he expected a commotion, and then he hastened to give his sanction. As soon as the decree was sanctioned, the Assembly determined to put it in execution, and required its ecclesiastical members to take the oath in their places. Men and women who had until then shown very little attachment to religion, all at once made themselves extremely busy in provoking the refusal of the ecclesiastics. (*See* Appendix G G.) Some of the bishops and some of the *curés* took the oath. The majority refused, with a feigned moderation and an apparent attachment to its principles. The Assembly nevertheless persisted in the nomination of new bishops and *curés*, and was cheerfully seconded by the administrations. The former ecclesiastical functionaries were at liberty to perform divine service apart, and those who were recognised by the state took their places in the churches. The dissenters at Paris hired the church of the Theatines for their place of worship. The Assembly permitted this, and the national guard protected them as much as possible from the fury of the populace, which did not always allow them to perform their devotions in quiet.

The Assembly has been condemned for having occasioned this schism, and for having added a new cause of division to those which before existed. In the first place, as to its rights, it must be evident to every just mind that the Assembly did not exceed them in directing its attention to the temporalities of the Church. As for considerations of prudence, we may affirm that it added little to the difficulties of its position. It is evident that the court, the nobility, and the clergy had lost enough, and the people had gained enough, to be irreconcilable enemies, and to impel the Revolution to its inevitable issue, even without the effects of the new schism. And, besides, when the Assembly was abolishing all abuses, could it suffer those of the ancient ecclesiastical organization to remain? Could it suffer idle persons to live in abundance, while pastors, the only useful members of the profession, had scarcely the necessaries of existence?

This last struggle completed the work of universal division. While the clergy excited the provinces of the West and South, the refugees at Turin made several attempts, which were frustrated by their weakness and their anarchy. A conspiracy was set on foot at Lyons. The arrival of the princes, and an abundant distribution of favours were there announced. Lyons was even promised to be made the capital of the kingdom, instead of Paris, which had incurred the displeasure of the court. The King was apprised of these schemes, and—not expecting success from them, perhaps not even desiring it, for he despaired of governing the victorious aristocracy—he did all that lay in his power to prevent it. This conspiracy was discovered about the end of 1790, and its principal agents were delivered up to justice.

This last reverse determined the emigrants to remove from Turin to Coblentz, where they settled in the territory of the Elector of Treves, and at the expense of his authority, which they almost entirely usurped. We have already seen that these nobles, who had fled from France, were divided into two parties. The one, consisting of old servants, pampered with favours, and composing what was called the court, would not, while supported by the provincial nobility, consent to share influence with the latter, and for this reason they meant to have recourse to foreigners alone. The others, men relying more upon their swords, proposed to raise the provinces of the South, by rousing their fanaticism. The former carried their point, and repaired to Coblentz, on the northern frontier, to wait there for the foreign aid. In vain did those who wished to fight in the South insist that aid ought to be sought from Piedmont, Switzerland, and Spain—faithful and disinterested allies—and that a distinguished leader should be left in their vicinity. The aristocracy, directed by Calonne, was adverse to this. That aristocracy had not changed since leaving France: frivolous, haughty, incapable and prodigal—at Coblentz as at Versailles—it displayed its vices still more conspicuously amidst the difficulties of exile and of civil war. "You must have citizens in your commission," it said to those gallant men who offered to fight in the South, and who asked under what title they were to serve. (*See* Appendix H H.) Some subordinate agents only were left at Turin; these, actuated by mutual jealousy, thwarted each others' efforts, and prevented the success of every attempt. The Prince of Condé (*See* Appendix I I.), who seemed to have retained all the energy of his branch of the royal family, was not in favour with part of the nobility; he took post near the Rhine, with all those who like himself were not disposed to intrigue, but to fight.

The emigration became daily more considerable, and the roads were covered with nobles, who imagined that they performed a sacred duty by hastening to take arms against their country. Even women deemed it incumbent on them to attest their horror of the Revolution by forsaking the soil of France. Among a nation which is so easily led away by example it became the fashion to emigrate. People hardly gave themselves the trouble to take leave, so short did they consider the journey, and so speedy their return.—(*See* Appendix J J.) The revolutionists of Holland, betrayed by their general, abandoned by their allies, had yielded in a few days; those of Brabant had not held out much longer: so too, according to these imprudent emigrants, would the French Revolution be quelled in one short campaign, and absolute power would once more flourish in subjugated France.

The Assembly, irritated rather than alarmed at such presumption, had proposed measures, but they had always been deferred. The King's aunts, finding their consciences compromised at Paris, thought to ensure their salvation by repairing to the Pope. They set out for Rome, and were stopped on the way by the municipality of Arnai-le-Duc. The people immediately thronged to the residence of Monsieur, who also was said to be preparing to depart. Monsieur appeared, and promised not to forsake the King. The people were pacified, and the Assembly took into consideration the departure of Mesdames. The deliberation had lasted a considerable time, when Menou put an end to it by this sally: "All Europe," said he, "will be astonished to learn that a great

Assembly has spent several days in deciding whether two old women shall hear mass at Paris or at Rome." The committee of constitution was nevertheless directed to present a law on the residence of the public functionaries and on emigration. This decree, adopted after warm discussions, rendered it obligatory on public functionaries to reside in the place of their functions. The King, as the highest of all, was required not to withdraw himself from the legislative body during the session, and at other times not to leave the kingdom. The penalty for all the functionaries, in case of their violating this law, was dismissal from office. Another decree relative to emigration was demanded from the committee.

Meanwhile the King, unable to endure the constraint imposed upon him, and the reductions of power to which he was subjected by the Assembly, enjoying moreover no peace of mind since the new decrees relative to priests, had resolved upon flight. The whole winter had been devoted to preparations for it: the zeal of Mirabeau was urged, and great promises were held out to him if he should succeed in setting the royal family at liberty. Mirabeau prosecuted his plan with the utmost activity. Lafayette had just broken with the Lameths. The latter thought him too much attached to the court; and his integrity being, unlike that of Mirabeau, above suspicion, they found fault with his understanding, and alleged that he suffered himself to be duped. The enemies of the Lameths accused them of being jealous of the military power of Lafayette, as they had envied the rhetorical power of Mirabeau. They joined, or seemed to join, the friends of the Duke of Orleans, and it was asserted that they wished to secure for one of them the command of the national guard. It was Charles Lameth who was said to be ambitious of obtaining this appointment. To this motive were attributed the incessantly recurring difficulties that were subsequently thrown in the way of Lafayette.

On the 28th of February the populace, instigated it is said by the Duke of Orleans, repaired to the castle of Vincennes, which the municipality had appropriated for the reception of prisoners, with whom the prisons of Paris were too much crowded. The castle was attacked as a new Bastille. Lafayette hastened to the spot in time, and dispersed the populace of the fauxbourg St. Antoine, who were led upon this expedition by Santerre. (*See* Appendix K K.) While he was restoring order in this quarter, other difficulties were preparing for him at the Tuileries. On the rumour of a commotion, the dependents of the palace, to the number of several hundred, had repaired thither. They carried concealed weapons, such as hunting-knives and daggers. The national guard, astonished at this concourse, took alarm, and disarmed and maltreated some of them. Lafayette having arrived, caused the palace to be cleared, and seized the weapons. The circumstance was immediately rumoured abroad. It was said that daggers had been found upon them, whence they were afterwards called knights of the dagger. They asserted that they had only come to defend the person of the King, which was threatened. In reply they were accused of an intention to carry off the King; and the affair ended, as usual, in reciprocal calumnies. This scene determined the real position of Lafayette. It was clearly shown on this occasion, that, placed between the most opposite parties, he was there to protect both the person of the King and the constitution. His double victory increased his popularity, his power, and the hatred of his enemies. Mirabeau, who wrongfully encouraged the distrust of the court towards him, represented his conduct as profoundly hypocritical. Under the appearance of moderation and hostility to all parties, it tended, according to him, to usurpation. In his spleen, he described the Lameths as wicked and senseless men, associated with the Duke of Orleans, and having no more than about thirty partisans in the Assembly. As for the right side, he declared that he could make nothing of it, but that he relied on the three or four hundred members who were bound by no engagements, but decided from the impression of reason and eloquence which he produced at the moment.

There was nothing true in this representation but his estimate of the respective force of the parties, and his opinions concerning the means of directing the Assembly. He virtually governed it, by influencing all who had not bound themselves by engagements. On this same day, the 28th of February, he exercised his sway almost for the last time, displayed his hatred to the Lameths, and brought his formidable power to bear against them.

The law relative to emigration was about to be discussed. Chapelier presented it in the name of the committee, which, he said, participated in the general indignation against those Frenchmen who were forsaking their country; but he declared that, after several days' consideration, the committee had satisfied itself that it was impossible to make any law concerning emigration. It was in reality a difficult thing to do. It was necessary, in the first place, to inquire if they had right to attach men to the soil. They certainly had a right to do so, if the welfare of the country demanded it. But it was requisite to make a distinction between the motives of travellers, which became inquisitorial. It was requisite to make a distinction between their quality as Frenchmen or foreigners, emigrants or mere mercantile men. Such a law then was extremely difficult, if not impossible. Chapelier added that the committee, in compliance with the directions of the Assembly, had nevertheless drawn up one, which he would read, if permitted, but which he had no hesitation in declaring violated all principles. From all quarters issued cries of "Bead!" "Don't read!" A great number of deputies asked leave to speak. Mirabeau demanded it in his turn, obtained permission, and, what is still more, commanded silence. He read a very eloquent letter, addressed some time before to Frederick William, in which he advocated the liberty of emigration as one of the most sacred rights of man, who, not being attached by roots to the soil, ought not to be attached to it by anything but by happiness. Mirabeau, perhaps to gratify the court, but still more from conviction, repelled as tyrannical every measure against the liberty of entering, or withdrawing from, the country. A bad use was no doubt made of this liberty at the moment; but the Assembly, confident in its strength, had winked at so many abuses of the press committed against itself, had encountered so many vain attempts, and so victoriously overthrown them, that one might safely advise it to persist in the same system.

Mirabeau's opinion was applauded, but the members continued to insist on the reading of the proposed law. Chapelier at length read it. It suggested, in case of disturbances, the appointment of a commission of three members, which should appoint by name, and at their pleasure, those who were to be at liberty to leave the kingdom. At this cutting irony, which denounced the impossibility of a law, murmurs arose. "Your murmurs have soothed me," exclaimed Mirabeau; "your hearts respond to mine, and oppose this absurd tyranny. As for me, I hold myself released from every oath towards those who shall be infamous enough to admit of a dictatorial commission."—Cries were raised on the left side. "Yes," he repeated, "I swear . . . ." He was again interrupted. "That popularity," he resumed in a voice of thunder, "to which I have aspired, and which I have enjoyed as well as others, is not a feeble reed; I will thrust it deep into the earth, and I will make it shoot up in the soil of justice and reason." Applauses burst forth from all quarters. "I swear," added the orator, "if a law against emigration is voted, I swear to disobey you."

He descended from the tribune, after astounding the Assembly, and overawing his enemies. The discussion nevertheless continued. Some were for adjournment, that they might have time for making a better law; others insisted that they should forthwith declare that none should be made, in order to pacify the people, and to put an end to the ferment. Murmurs, shouts, applauses, succeeded. Mirabeau asked, and seemed to require, to be heard. "What right of dictatorship is it," cried M. Groupil, "that M. De Mirabeau exercises here?"—Mirabeau, without heeding him, hurried to the tribune. "I have not given you permission to speak," said the president. "Let the Assembly decide." But the Assembly listened without deciding. "I beg my interrupters," said Mirabeau, "to remember that I have all my life combated tyranny, and that I will combat it wherever I find it." As he uttered these words he cast his eyes from the right to the left. Loud applause followed his words. He resumed. "I beg M. Goupil to recollect that he was under a mistake some time since in regard to a Catiline, whose dictatorship he this day attacks; I beg the Assembly to remark that the question of adjournment, though apparently simple, involves others: for example, it presupposes that a law is to be made." Fresh murmurs arose on the left. "Silence! ye thirty voices!" exclaimed the speaker, fixing his eyes on the place of Barnave and the Lameths. "However," added he, "if it is wished, I too will vote for the adjournment, on condition that it he decreed that, from this time until the expiration of the adjournment, there shall he no sedition." Unanimous acclamations followed the concluding words. The adjournment was nevertheless carried, but by so small a majority that the result was disputed, and a second trial demanded.

Mirabeau, on this occasion, was particularly striking by his boldness. Never, perhaps, had, he more imperiously overruled the Assembly. But these were his last triumphs. His end approached. Presentiments of death mingled with his vast projects, and sometimes subdued his nights of fancy. His conscience, however, was satisfied: the public esteem was joined with his own, and assured him that, if he had not yet done enough for the welfare of the state, he had at least done enough for his own glory. Philosophy and gaiety divided his last moments between them. Pale, and with his eyes deeply sunk in their orbits, he appeared quite different in the tribune. Moreover, he was subject to frequent and sudden fainting-fits. Excess in pleasure and in business, together with the excitement of the tribune, had in a short time undermined his vigorous constitution. Baths, containing a solution of sublimate, had produced that greenish tint which was attributed to poison. (*See* Appendix L L.) The court was alarmed; all parties were astonished, and, before his death, people inquired the cause of it. On his last public appearance he spoke five different times, left the Assembly exhausted, and never afterwards went abroad. The bed of death received him, and he left it only for the Pantheon. He had enjoined Cabanis not to call in any physicians: he was nevertheless disobeyed, and they found that death was approaching, and that it had already seized his lower extremities. His head was last attacked, as if nature had decreed that his genius should continue to shine till the very last moment. An immense crowd collected around his abode, and filled all the avenues in the deepest silence. The court sent messenger after messenger; the bulletins of his health were transmitted from mouth to mouth, and each progressive stage of his disorder excited fresh grief. He himself, surrounded by his friends, expressed some regret at the interruption of his labours, and some pride at what he had accomplished. "Support," said he to his servant, "support this head, the greatest in France." He was affected by the sympathy of the people; and the visit of his enemy, Barnave, who called upon him in the name of the Jacobins, excited in him a soothing emotion. He bestowed some more thoughts on public affairs. The Assembly was about to direct its attention to the right of making wills. He sent for M. De Talleyrand, and put into his hands a speech which he had just written. "It will be curious," said he, "to hear a man speaking against wills who is no more, and who has just made his own." The court had, in fact, requested him to do so, promising to pay all the legacies. Extending his views over Europe, and foreseeing the plans of England, "That Pitt," said he, "is the minister of preparations; he governs with threats: I would give him some trouble if I should live." The priest of his parish came to offer his attendance, which he politely declined, saying, with a smile, that he should gladly have accepted it, if he had not in his house his ecclesiastical superior, the Bishop of Autun. He desired the windows to be opened. "My friend," said he to Cabanis, "I shall die to-day. All that can now be done is to envelope oneself in perfumes, to crown oneself with flowers, to surround oneself with music, that one may sink quietly into everlasting sleep." Acute pains from time to time interrupted these calm and dignified observations. "You have promised," said he to his friends, "to spare me needless suffering." So saying, he earnestly begged for opium. As it was refused, he demanded it with his accustomed violence. To quiet him, they resorted to deception, and handed him a cup which they said contained opium. He took it with composure, swallowed the draught which he believed to be mortal, and appeared satisfied. In a moment afterwards he expired. This was on the 20th of April, 1791. The tidings soon reached the court, the city, and the Assembly. All parties had hope in him, and all, excepting the envious, were filled with grief. The Assembly suspended its proceedings; a general mourning was ordered, and a magnificent funeral prepared. A certain number of deputies was asked for. "We will all go!" they exclaimed. The church of St. Genevieve was converted into a Pantheon, with this inscription, which, at the moment that I record these facts, no longer exists:

AUX GRANDS HOMMES LA PATRIE RECONNAISSANTE.

Mirabeau was the first admitted into it, and placed by the side of Descartes. His funeral took place on the following day. All the authorities, the department, the municipalities, the popular societies, the Assembly, and the army, accompanied the procession. This mere orator obtained more honours than had ever been paid to the pompous coffins formerly conveyed to St. Denis. Such was the end of that extraordinary man, who, after boldly attacking and vanquishing the ancient race, dared to direct his efforts against the new, which had assisted him to conquer; who checked them with his voice, and made them respect him even while he employed his energies against them; that man, in short, who did his duty from reason, and from the promptings of genius, but not for the sake of a handful of gold; and who had the singular honour, when the popularity of all other statesmen terminated in the disgust of the people, to see his yield to death alone. But would he have infused resignation into the heart of the court, moderation into the hearts of the ambitious?—would he have said to the popular tribunes, who sought to shine in their turn, "Remain in these obscure fauxbourgs?"—would he have said to Danton, that second Mirabeau of the populace, (*See* Appendix M M.) "Stop in this section, and ascend no higher?" We cannot tell: but in that case all wavering interests would have placed themselves in his hands and have relied upon him. Long was the want of his presence felt, la the confusion of the disputes which followed, the eye would turn to the place which he had occupied, and seemed to seek him who had been accustomed to terminate them with a victorious word. "Mirabeau is no longer here," exclaimed Maury one day, in ascending the tribune, "I shall not be prevented from speaking."

The death of Mirabeau deprived the court of all courage. Fresh events occurred to accelerate the flight of the royal family which it had resolved upon. On the 18th of April the King intended to go to St. Cloud. A report was spread, that, as he did not choose to employ a priest who had taken the oath for the duties of Easter, he had resolved to keep away during the Passion week. Others alleged that his intention was flight. The populace immediately collected and stopped the horses. Lafayette hastened to the spot, besought the King to remain in his carriage, assuring him that he would have a passage cleared for him. The King nevertheless alighted, and would not permit any attempt to be made. It was his old policy not to appear to be free. By the advice of his ministers, he repaired to the Assembly to complain of the insult which he had just received. The Assembly greeted him with its ordinary warmth, promising to do every thing that depended on it to ensure his liberty. Louis XVI. withdrew, applauded by all sides excepting the right side.

On the 23rd of April, agreeably to the advice given to him, he ordered a letter to be written to the foreign ambassadors by M. De Montmorin, in which he contradicted the intentions imputed to him of leaving the country, declaring to the powers that he had taken an oath to the constitution which he was determined to keep, and proclaiming as his enemies all who should insinuate the contrary. The expressions of this letter were voluntarily exaggerated, that it might appear to have been, extorted by violence. This the King himself acknowledged to the envoy of the Emperor Leopold. That prince was then travelling in Italy, and was at this moment in Mantua. Calonne was in negotiation with him. An envoy, M. Alexandre de Durfort, came from Mantua to the King and Queen, to learn their real disposition. He first questioned them concerning the letter addressed to the ambassadors, and they replied that he might see from the language that it was wrung from them. He then inquired what were their hopes, and they answered that they had none since the death of Mirabeau; lastly, he wished to know their disposition towards the Count d'Artois, and they assured him that it could not be more favourable.

In order to comprehend the motive of these questions, it should be known that the Baron de Breteuil was the declared enemy of Calonne; that his enmity had not ceased at the time of the emigration; and that, charged with the full powers of Louis XVI. to the court of Vienna, he crossed all the proceedings of the princes. He assured Leopold that the King would not consent to be saved by the emigrants, because he dreaded their rapacity, and that the Queen personally had quarrelled with Count d'Artois. He always proposed for the welfare of the throne, the very contrary to what Calonne proposed, and he neglected nothing to destroy the effect of this new negotiation. The Count de Durfort returned to Mantua, and on the 20th of May, 1791, Leopold promised to set in motion thirty-five thousand men in Flanders, and fifteen thousand in Alsace. He declared that a like number of Swiss should march upon Lyons, as many Piedmontese upon Dauphiné, and that Spain should assemble twenty thousand men. The Emperor promised the co-operation of the King of Prussia and the neutrality of England. A protest was to be drawn up in the name of the house of Bourbon, and signed by the King of Naples, the King of Spain, the Infant of Palma, and the expatriated princes. Until then the utmost secrecy was to be observed. It was recommended to Louis XVI, not to think of withdrawing, though he had expressed a desire to do so. Breteuil, on the contrary, advised the King to set out. It is possible that this advice was well meant on both sides. Still it must be remarked, that it was given with an eye to the interests of each. Breteuil, with a view to counteract Calonne's negotiation at Mantua, recommended departure; and Calonne, whose rule would have been at an end if Louis XVI. had removed beyond the frontiers, caused it to be intimated to him that he ought to remain. Be this as it may, the King resolved to set out, and he frequently said with displeasure, "It is Breteuil who insists on it." Accordingly he wrote to Bouillé, that he was determined to wait no longer. It was not his intention to leave the kingdom, but to retire to Montmedy, where he might, in case of need, be supported by Luxemburg, and receive foreign aid. The Chalons road, by Clermont and Varennes, was preferred, contrary to the advice of Bouillé. All the preparations were made for starting on the 20th of June. The general assembled the troops on which he could place most reliance, prepared a camp at Montmedy, collected forage, and alleged movements which he perceived on the frontiers as a pretext for all these dispositions. The Queen took upon herself all the preparations from Paris to Chalons, and Bouillé from Chalons to Montmedy. Small detachments of cavalry, upon pretext of escorting money, were to proceed to different points, and receive the King on his passage. Bouillé himself purposed to advance to some distance from Montmedy. The Queen had secured a private door for quitting the palace. The royal family was to travel by a foreign name, and with a fictitious passport. Everything was arranged for the 20th, but some alarm caused the journey to be deferred until the 21st, a delay which proved fatal to this unfortunate family. M. De Lafayette knew nothing whatever of the plan, nay, even M. De Montmorin, though possessing the confidence of the court, was entirely ignorant of it: the secret was entrusted to those persons only who were indispensable for its execution. Rumours of flight had been circulated, either because the scheme had transpired, or because it was one of those alarms which are so frequently raised. At any rate, the committee of research had been apprized of it, and the vigilance of the national guard had been in consequence increased.

In the evening of the 21st of June, the King, the Queen, Madame Elizabeth, and Madame de Tourzel, governess of the royal children, disguised themselves, and successively quitted the palace. Madame de Tourzel proceeded with the children to the Petit Carrousel, and got into a carriage driven by M. de Fersen, a young foreign gentleman, disguised as a coachman. The King soon joined them. But the Queen, who had gone away with a life-guardsman, occasioned them all the utmost anxiety. Neither herself nor her guide was acquainted with the streets of Paris; she lost her way, and it was an hour before she found the Petit Carrousel. On her way thither she met the carriage of M. De Lafayette, whose attendants walked by it with torches. She concealed herself beneath the wickets of the Louvre, and, having escaped this danger, reached the carriage, where she was awaited with extreme impatience. The whole family, being now together, lost no time in setting out. They arrived, after a long ride, at the Porte St. Martin, and mounted a berline with six horses, stationed there to wait for them. Madame de Tourzel, by the name of Madame de Korff, was to pass for a mother travelling with her children; and the King for her valet-de-chambre. Three of the life-guards, in disguise, were to precede the carriage as couriers, or to follow it as servants. At length they started, attended by the good wishes of M. de Fersen, who returned to Paris, with the intention of setting out for Brussels. Meanwhile Monsieur proceeded with his consort towards Flanders, travelling a different road to prevent suspicions, and lest there should be a want of horses at the different stations.

They travelled all night, during which Paris knew nothing of the matter. M. de Fersen hastened to the municipality to ascertain what was known there. At eight o'clock people were still unacquainted with the circumstance. But the report soon got abroad and spread with rapidity. (*See* Appendix N N.) Lafayette sent for his aides-de-camp and ordered them to set out immediately, saying that though there was little hope of their overtaking the fugitives, still they must try what they could do. He issued this order on his own responsibility, and in drawing it up he expressed his presumption that the royal family had been carried off by enemies of the public welfare. This respectful supposition was admitted by the Assembly, and invariably adopted by all the authorities. At this moment the people, in commotion, reproached Lafayette with having favoured the King's escape. The aristocratic party, on the contrary, has since accused him of having winked at his flight, with the intention of stopping him afterwards, and thus ruining him by this vain attempt. If, however, Lafayette had chosen to wink at the King's flight, would he have sent two aides-de-camp in pursuit of him, before any order was issued by the Assembly? And if, as the aristocrats have surmised, he had permitted his flight merely with a view to retake him, would he have allowed the carriage a whole night's start? The populace was soon convinced of its mistake, and Lafayette reinstated in its good opinion.

The Assembly met at nine in the morning. Its attitude was as majestic as it had been in the first days of the Revolution. The supposition adopted was that Louis XVI. had been carried off. The utmost calmness and harmony prevailed during the whole of this sitting. The measures spontaneously taken by Lafayette were approved of. The people had stopped his aides-de-camp at the barriers. The Assembly, universally obeyed, ordered the gates to be opened to them. One of them, young Romeuf, was the bearer of the decree confirming the orders already issued by the general, and enjoining the public functionaries to stop, by all the means in their power, *the progress of the said abduction, and to prevent the continuance of the journey*. At the suggestion of the people, and upon the information furnished by them, Romeuf took the road to Chalons, which was the right one, as the appearance upon it of a carriage and six sufficiently indicated. The Assembly then summoned the ministers, and passed a decree that they should receive orders from it alone. At his departure Louis XVI. had commanded the minister of justice to send him the seal of state. The Assembly directed that the seal should be retained for the purpose of being affixed to its decrees: it decided at the same time that the frontiers should be put in a state of defence, and that the minister for foreign affairs should be charged to assure the powers that the dispositions of the French nation in regard to them remained unchanged.

M. De la Porte, intendant of the civil list, was then heard. He had received several messages from the King; among others, a note, which he begged the Assembly not to open, and a memorial stating the reasons for departure. The Assembly, ready to pay due regard to all rights, returned, unopened, the note which M. De la Porte was unwilling to make public, and ordered the memorial to be read. It was listened to with the utmost calmness. It produced scarcely any impression. The King complained of his loss of power without sufficient dignity, and he seemed as much mortified at the reduction of the civil list to thirty millions as at the loss of all his other prerogatives. The Assembly listened to the complaints of the monarch, pitied his weakness, and proceeded to the consideration of other matters.

At this moment very few persons wished for the apprehension of Louis XVI. The aristocrats beheld in his flight the realization of the oldest of their wishes, and flattered themselves with the prospect of a speedy civil war. The most vehement members of the popular party, who already began to be tired of the King, found in his absence an occasion to dispense with him, and indulged the idea and the hope of a republic. The whole moderate party, which at this moment governed the Assembly, wished that the King might arrive safely at Montmedy; and, relying upon his equity, it nattered itself that an accommodation between the throne and the nation would be thereby facilitated. Few persons, at this time, were apprehensive, as formerly, of seeing the monarch threatening the constitution from amidst an army. The populace alone, into whom this apprehension had been studiously instilled, continued to retain it when it was no longer felt by the Assembly, and ardently wished for the recapture of the royal family. Such was the state of things at Paris.

The carriage, which set out in the night between the 21st and 22nd, had performed great part of the journey, and arrived without impediment at Chalons about five o'clock the next afternoon. There the King, who had been imprudent enough to put his head frequently out at the window, was recognised. The person who made this discovery would at once have divulged the secret, but he was prevented by the mayor, who was a stanch royalist. On reaching Pont de Sommeville, the royal family did not find the detachments which ought to have received it there; those detachments had been waiting for several hours; but the excitement of the people, alarmed at this movement of troops, had obliged them to retire.

The King, meanwhile, arrived at St. Menehould. There, still showing himself at the window, he was perceived by Drouet, the postmaster's son, a violent revolutionist. This young man, not having time to cause the carriage to be detained at St. Menehould, posted off to Varennes. A worthy quartermaster, who had observed his haste, and suspected his motives, flew after to stop him, but could not overtake him. Drouet used such speed that he arrived at Varennes before the unfortunate family. He immediately gave information to the municipality, and caused all the necessary measures for apprehending the fugitives to be taken forthwith. Varennes is situated on the bank of a narrow but deep river. A detachment of hussars was on the watch there, but the officer, not seeing the treasure arrive which he had been directed to wait for, had left his men in their quarters. The carriage at length drove up and crossed the bridge. No sooner was it beneath an archway through which it was obliged to pass, than Drouet, assisted by another person, stopped the horses. "Your passport!" he exclaimed, and with a musket he threatened the travellers if they persisted in proceeding. The order was complied with, and the passport handed to him. Drouet took it, and said that it must be examined by the solicitor of the commune. The royal family was then conducted to the house of this solicitor, named Sausse. The latter, after examining the passport, and pretending to find it quite right, very politely begged the King to wait; he accordingly waited a considerable time When Sausse had at length ascertained that a sufficient number of the national guards had assembled, he threw off all disguise, and informed the prince that he was recognised and apprehended. An altercation ensued Louis declared that he was not what he was taken to be, and the dispute growing too warm, "Since you acknowledge him to be your King," exclaimed the Queen, angrily, "speak to him with the respect that you owe him."

The King, seeing that further denial was useless, took no more trouble to disguise himself. The little room was full of people. He spoke, and expressed himself with a warmth that was unusual with him. He protested his good intentions, asserted that he was going to Montmedy, merely that he might listen more freely to the wishes of his people, by withdrawing from the tyranny of Paris; lastly, he insisted on continuing his journey, and being conducted to the end of it. The unfortunate prince, with deep emotion, embraced Sausse, and implored him to save his wife and his children. The Queen joined him, and, taking the dauphin in her arms, besought Sausse to release them. Sausse was affected, but withstood their entreaties, and advised them to return to Paris, to prevent a civil war. The King, on the contrary, having a dread of returning, persisted in proceeding to Montmedy.

At this moment Messrs. de Damas and de Goquelas arrived with the detachments which had been stationed at different points. The royal family considered itself as saved; but the hussars were not to be relied on. The officers assembled them, informed them that the King and his family were apprehended, and that they must release them. The men replied that they were for the nation. At the same instant the national guards, called together from all the environs, arrived and filled Varennes. The whole night was passed in this state. At six in the morning, young Romeuf arrived with the decree of the Assembly. He found the carriage with six horses harnessed to it, and turned towards Paris. He went up stairs and delivered the decree with pain. A general outcry burst from the whole family against M. de Lafayette, who caused them to be apprehended. The Queen even expressed her astonishment that he had not been put to death by the people. Romeuf replied that his general and himself had only done their duty in pursuing them, but that they had hoped not to overtake them. The Queen took up the decree, threw it on the bed of her children, then snatched it up again, saying that it would pollute them. "Madame," said Romeuf, who was attached to her, "would you rather have any one but me to witness these passions?" The Queen then came to herself, and resumed all her dignity. At the same moment the arrival of different corps, stationed in the environs by Bouillé, was announced. The municipality then gave orders for starting. The royal family was of course obliged to enter the carriage, and to take the road to Paris, that fatal and deeply dreaded course!

Bouillé, roused in the middle of the night, had mounted a regiment of horse, and set out with shouts of "*Long live the King!*" This brave general, urged by anxiety, marched with all speed, and proceeded nine leagues in four hours. He arrived at Varennes, where he found several corps already collected. But the King had been gone an hour and a half; Varennes was barricaded, and judicious arrangements had been made for its defence; the bridge was broken down, and the river was not fordable. Thus, after a first combat to carry the barricades, it would have been necessary to seek the means of crossing the river, and, after such a loss of time, to overtake the carriage, which had got the start by an hour and a half. These obstacles rendered any attempt at rescue impossible; and it required nothing short of such an impossibility to deter a man so loyal and so enterprising as Bouillé. He retired, therefore, overwhelmed with grief and mortification.

When news of the King's apprehension arrived in Paris, he was believed to be beyond reach. The people manifested extraordinary joy. The Assembly deputed three commissioners, selected from the three sections of the left side, to accompany the monarch, and to conduct him back to Paris. These commissioners were Barnave, Latour-Maubourg, and Petion. They repaired to Chalons, and, from the moment that they joined the court, all orders emanated from them alone. Madame de Tourzel removed into a second carriage with Latour-Maubourg; Barnave and Petion entered that of the royal family. Latour-Maubourg, a person of distinction, was a friend of Lafayette, and, like him, was as strongly attached to the King as to the constitution. In yielding to his two colleagues the honour of being with the royal family, it was his intention to interest them in behalf of fallen greatness. Barnave sat at the back, between the King and Queen; Petion in front, between Madame Elizabeth and Madame Royale; the young dauphin on the lap, first of one and then of another. Such had been the rapid course of events! A young advocate of some twenty years, remarkable only for his abilities, and another, distinguished by his talents, but, above all, by the sternness of his principles, were seated beside a prince lately the most absolute in Europe, and commanded all his movements. The journey was slow, because the carriage followed the pace of the national guards. It took eight days to return from Varennes to Paris. The heat was excessive; and a scorching dust, raised by the multitude, half-suffocated the travellers. At first a deep silence prevailed. The Queen could not conceal her vexation. The King at length entered into conversation with Barnave. It turned upon all sorts of subjects, and lastly upon the flight to Montmedy. Both were surprised to find the others what they were. The Queen was astonished at the superior understanding and the delicate politeness of young Barnave. (See Appendix O O.) She soon threw up her veil and took part in the conversation. Barnave was touched by the good-nature of the King and the graceful dignity of the Queen. Petion displayed more rudeness; he showed and received less respect. By the time they reached Paris, Barnave was strongly attached to the unfortunate family, and the Queen, charmed with the merits and the good sense of the young tribune, had granted him all her esteem. Hence it was that, in all the intercourse which she afterwards had with the constitutional deputies, it was in him that she placed the greatest confidence. Parties would forgive, if they could see and hear one another. (*See* Appendix P P.)

In Paris, the reception to be given to the royal family had been decided upon. A public notice was distributed and posted everywhere: *Whoever applauds the King shall be flogged; whoever insults him shall be hanged.* The order was punctually obeyed. Neither applauses nor insults were heard. The carriage made a circuit, that it might not be obliged to traverse Paris. It entered by the Champs Elysées, which lead directly to the palace. An immense crowd received it in silence, and with hats on. Lafayette, followed by a numerous guard, had taken all possible precautions. The three life-guardsmen who had assisted the King's flight were on the box, exposed to the gaze and the wrath of the people; they nevertheless experienced no violence. (*See* Appendix Q Q.) The moment the carriage arrived at the palace, it was surrounded. The royal family hastily alighted, and passed between a double file of national guards, drawn up for its protection. The Queen, who was the last to alight, was almost borne along in the arms of Messrs. de Noailles and d'Aiguillon, enemies of the court, but generous friends of misfortune. On observing them approach, she had at first some doubts respecting their intentions; but she resigned herself to them, and arrived safe and unarmed at the palace.

Such was that journey, the fatal issue of which cannot fairly be attributed to any of those by whom it was planned. An accident thwarted it. An accident might have crowned it with success. If, for instance, Drouet had been overtaken and stopped by his pursuer, the carriage would have escaped. Perhaps too, the King was deficient in energy when he was recognised. Be that as it may, this journey cannot be matter of reproach to any one, either to those who advised, or to those who executed it. It was the result of that fatality which pursues weakness amidst revolutionary crises.

The journey to Varennes had the effect of destroying all respect for the King, of habituating men's minds to do without him, and of exciting a wish for a republic. On the very morning of his arrival, the Assembly had provided for everything by a decree. Louis XVI. was suspended from his functions; a guard was placed over his person, and that of the Queen and the dauphin. That guard was made responsible for their safe custody. Three deputies, D'André, Tronchet, and Duport, were commissioned to take the declarations of the King and Queen. The utmost delicacy was observed in the expressions; for never was this Assembly deficient in decorum; but the result was evident, and the King was for the time being dethroned.

The responsibility imposed on the national guard rendered it strict and frequently annoying in its duty about the royal persons. Sentinels were constantly stationed at their door, and never lost sight of them. The King, wishing one day to ascertain if he was really a prisoner, went up to a door: the sentinel opposed his passage. "Do you know me?" said Louis XVI. "Yes, sire," replied the sentinel. All the liberty the King had left to him was to walk in the Tuileries in the morning, before the garden was opened to the public.

Barnave and the Lameths then did what they had so severely reproached Mirabeau for doing—they lent their aid to the throne and reconciled themselves with the court. It is true that they received no money: but it was not so much the price of the alliance, as the alliance itself, that they had flung in the teeth of Mirabeau; and, after having formerly been so severe, they now followed the custom of all popular chiefs, which is, to ally themselves successively with power, as soon as they arrive at it. However, nothing could be more praiseworthy in the state of affairs at that moment, than the service rendered to the King by Barnave and the Lameths; and never did they display more address, energy, and talent. Barnave dictated the answer of the King to the commissioners appointed by the Assembly. In this answer, Louis XVI. assigned as the motive for his flight a desire to make himself better acquainted with the state of public opinion; he declared that he had learned much on that head during his journey, and proved by a variety of facts that it had not been his intention to leave France. As for the protestations contained in his memorial transmitted to the Assembly, he justly alleged that they bore not upon the fundamental principles of the constitution, but upon the means of execution that were left him. Now, he added, that the general will was clearly manifested to him, he did not hesitate to submit to it, and to make all the sacrifices requisite for the public welfare. (*See* Appendix R R.)

Bouillé, in order to draw upon himself the indignation of the Assembly, addressed to it a letter, which might be called mad, but for the generous motive which dictated it. He avowed himself the sole author of the King's journey, though, on the contrary, he had opposed it. He declared, in the name of the sovereigns, that Paris should be responsible for the safety of the royal family, and that the slightest injury offered to them should be signally avenged. He added, what he knew to be otherwise, that the military means of France were nearly null; that he was well acquainted with the points where an invading force might enter, and that he would himself lead the hostile armies into the heart of the country. The Assembly winked at this generous bravado, and threw the whole blame on Bouillé, who had nothing to fear, for he was already abroad.

The Court of Spain, apprehending that the slightest movement might produce irritation and expose the royal family to still greater dangers, prevented an attempt that was about to be made on the southern frontier, in which the Knights of Malta were to assist with two frigates. It then declared to the French government that its good disposition towards it remained unchanged. The north behaved with much less moderation. On that side, the powers, instigated by the emigrants, began to threaten. Envoys were despatched by the King to Brussels and Coblentz, to come to an understanding with the emigrants in those places, to acquaint them with the favourable disposition of the Assembly, and the hopes entertained of an advantageous arrangement. But, no sooner had they arrived than they were treated with indignity, and immediately returned to Paris. The emigrants raised troops in the name of the King, and thus obliged hiin to give them a formal contradiction. They pretended that Monsieur, who had by this time joined them, was regent of the kingdom; that the King, being a prisoner, had no will of his own, and that that which he expressed was only the will of his oppressors. The peace, concluded by Catherine with the Turks in the month of August, heightened their senseless joy, and they fancied that they had all the powers of Europe at their disposal. Considering the disarming of the fortresses, and the disorganisation of the army, which all the officers were leaving, they could not suppose the result of the invasion to be doubtful, or the fitting time for it far distant.

They had, nevertheless, been out of France nearly two years, and, though daily flattering themselves with the prospect, they had not yet returned victorious. The powers seemed to promise much, but Pitt hung back; Leopold, exhausted by the war, and displeased with the emigrants, wished for peace; the King of Prussia promised a great deal, but had no interest in keeping his word; Gustavus was anxious to command an expedition against France, but he was at a great distance; and Catherine, who was to second him, had scarcely got rid of the Turks, and still had Poland to reduce. Besides, in order to effect this coalition, it would be necessary to reconcile so many conflicting interests, that it was scarcely possible to entertain any hope of success.

The declaration of Pilnitz ought more especially to have enlightened the emigrants respecting the zeal of the sovereigns. This declaration, issued jointly by the King of Prussia and the Emperor Leopold, purported that the situation of the King of France was a subject of general interest to all the sovereigns, and that they would undoubtedly unite to furnish Louis XVI. with the means of establishing a government suitable to the interests of the throne and of the people; that, in this case, the King of Prussia and the Emperor would join the other princes, to attain the same end. Meanwhile their troops should be put into a condition for active service. It was afterwards known that this declaration contained secret articles. They purported that Austria would not oppose any obstacle to the claims of Prussia to part of Poland. It required this concession to induce Prussia to neglect her more ancient interests by connecting herself with Austria against France. What could be expected from a zeal that it was necessary to excite by such means? And if it was so reserved in its expressions, what was it likely to be in its acts? France, it is true, was in a disarmed state; but a whole nation aroused is soon armed: and, as the celebrated Carnot observed at a later period, what is impossible to twenty-five millions of men? It is true that the officers were retiring, but, being generally young, and owing their appointment to favour, they were inexperienced and disliked by the army. Besides, the impetus given to all the resources of war was on the point of speedily producing officers and generals. Still, it must be confessed that, even without the presumption of Coblentz, one might fairly have doubted the resistance which France opposed somewhat later to her invaders.

Meanwhile, the Assembly sent commissioners to the frontiers and ordered great preparations. All the national guards offered to march. Several generals tendered their services, and among others Dumouriez (*See* Appendix S S.), who subsequently saved France in the denies of Argonne.

The Assembly, while attending to the external safety of the State, hastened to complete its constitutional labours, to restore to the King his functions, and if possible some of his prerogatives.

All the subdivisions of the left side, excepting the men who had just assumed the new name of republicans, had rallied around one and the same system of moderation. Barnave and Malouet went hand in hand and laboured in concert. Petion, Robespierre, Buzot, and some others, had adopted the republic; but their number was small. The right side persisted in its imprudent conduct, and protested, instead of joining the moderate majority. This majority, however, governed the Assembly. Its enemies, who would have accused it, if it had dethroned the King, nevertheless reproached it for having brought him back to Paris and replaced him on a tottering throne. But what could it do? To supersede the King by a republic would have been too hazardous. To change the dynasty would have been useless; for if they meant to give themselves a King, they might as well keep the one they had. Besides, the Duke of Orleans did not deserve to be preferred to Louis XVI. In either case, to dispossess the reigning King would have been to infringe acknowledged rights, and to send to the emigrants a chief of inestimable value to them, since he would have brought them titles which they did not possess. On the contrary, to give back to Louis XVI. his authority, to restore to him as many of his prerogatives as they could, would he fulfilling their constitutional task, and taking away all pretext for civil war. In a word, it would he doing their duty; for the duty of the

Assembly, according to all the engagements by which it had bound itself, was to establish a free, but a monarchical government.

The Assembly did not hesitate, but it had great obstacles to surmount. The new term, republic, had piqued minds already somewhat tired of those of monarchy and constitution. The absence and the suspension of the King had, as we have seen, taught them to do without him. The journals and the clubs instantly threw off the respect which had hitherto been paid to his person. His departure, which, according to the terms of the decree relative to the residence of public functionaries, rendered deposition imminent, caused it to be asserted that he was deposed. Nevertheless, according to the same decree, before he could incur the penalty of dethronement, he must have left the kingdom and resisted the summons of the legislative body. But these conditions were of little consequence to overheated minds, and they declared the King guilty and dethroned. The Jacobins and the Cordeliers were violently agitated, and could not conceive how it was that, after people had got rid of the King, they could burden themselves with him again, and that of their own accord. If the Duke of Orleans had ever entertained hopes, it was now that they might have been awakened. But he must have seen how little influence his name possessed, and, above all, how ill a new sovereign, however popular he might be, would harmonise with the state of people's minds. Some pamphleteers, devoted to his interest, endeavoured, perhaps without his knowledge, to place the crown on his head, as Antony did by Caesar; they proposed to give him the regency, but he found himself obliged to decline the offer in a declaration, which was thought as lightly of as himself. "*No King!*" was the general cry at the Jacobins, at the Cordeliers, in the streets, and in the public papers.

Numberless addresses were published. One of these was posted on all the walls of Paris, and even on those of the Assembly. It was signed with the name of Achille Duchâtelet, a young colonel. He addressed himself to the French: he reminded them of the tranquillity which had prevailed during the journey of the King, and thence concluded that his absence was more beneficial than his presence: he added that his flight was an abdication; that the nation and Louis XVI. were released from all engagements towards one another; finally, that history was full of the crimes of kings, and that the people ought to renounce all intention of giving themselves another.

This address, attributed to young Duchâtelet, was written by Thomas Paine, an Englishman, and a principal actor in the American Revolution. (*See* Appendix T T.) It was denounced to the Assembly, which, after a warm debate, deemed it right to pass to the order of the day, and to reply by indifference to advice and to abuse, as it had hitherto invariably done.

At length, the commissioners charged to make their report on the affair of Varennes presented it on the 16th of July. In the journey, they said, there was nothing culpable; and even if there were, the King was inviolable. Dethronement could not result from it, since the King had not staid away long enough, and had not resisted the summons of the legislative body.

Robespierre, Buzot, and Petion, repeated all the well-known arguments against the inviolability. Duport, Barnave, and Salles, answered them, and it was at length resolved that the King could not be brought to trial on account of his flight. Two articles were merely added to the decree of inviolability. No sooner was this resolution passed, than Robespierre rose, and protested strongly against it, in the name of humanity.

On the evening preceding this decision, a great tumult had taken place at the Jacobins. A petition to the Assembly was there drawn up, praying it to declare that the King was deposed as a perfidious traitor to his oaths, and that it would seek to supply his place by all the constitutional means. It was resolved that this petition should be carried on the following day to the Champ de Mars, where every one might sign it on the altar of the country. Next day, it was accordingly carried to the place agreed upon, and the crowd of the seditious was reinforced by that of the curious, who wished to be spectators of the event. At this moment the decree was passed, so that it was now too late to petition. Lafayette arrived, broke down the barricades already erected, was threatened and even fired at, but, though almost close to the muzzle of the weapon, he escaped without injury. The municipal officers having joined him, at length prevailed on the populace to retire. National guards were posted to watch their retreat, and for a moment it was hoped that they would disperse. But the tumult was soon renewed. Two invalids, who happened to be, nobody knows for what purpose, under the altar of the country, were murdered, and then the uproar became unbounded. The Assembly sent for the municipality, and charged it to preserve public order. Bailly repaired to the Champ de Mars, ordered the red flag to be unfurled, and, by virtue of martial law, summoned the seditious to retire. This summons, whatever has been said of it, was just. People either agreed or did not agree to the new laws. If they agreed to them, it was requisite that they should be executed, that there should be something fixed, that insurrection should not be perpetual, and that the will of the Assembly should not be modified by the decisions of the mob. It was Bailly's duty, therefore, to carry the law into execution. He advanced, with that unshrinking courage which he had always displayed, was fired at several times without being hit, and at length read the customary summons. Lafayette at first ordered a few shots to be fired in the air: the crowd quitted the altar of the country, but soon rallied. Thus driven to extremity, he gave the word *Fire!* The first discharge killed some of the rioters. Their number has been exaggerated. Some have reduced it to thirty, others have raised it to four hundred, and others to several thousand. The last statement was believed at the moment, and the consternation became general. This severe example quieted the agitators for a short time. As usual, all the parties were accused of having excited the commotion, and it is probable that several of them had a hand in it, for to several tumult was desirable. The King, the majority of the Assembly, the national guard, the municipal and departmental authorities, were then unanimous for the establishment of constitutional order; but they had to combat the democracy at home, and the aristocracy abroad. The Assembly and the national guard composed that middle class—wealthy, intelligent, and prudent—which wished well to order and the laws; and they could not at the moment but naturally ally themselves with the King, who, for his part, seemed to resign himself to a limited power. But, if it suited them to stop at the point at which they had arrived, it did not suit either the aristocracy, which desired a convulsion, or the people, who sought to gain and to raise themselves still more. Barnave was, as Mirabeau had been before him, the mouthpiece of this wise and moderate middle class; and Lafayette was its military chief. Danton and Camille Desmoulins (*See* Appendix U U.) were the spokesmen, Santerre the general of the rabble, that wished to reign in its turn. A few ardent or fanatic spirits represented this rabble either in the Assembly or in the new administrations, and hastened its rule by their declamations.

Lafayette and Bailly were vehemently reproached for the proceedings in the Champ de Mars; but both of them, considering it their duty to observe the law, and to risk popularity and life in its execution, felt neither regret nor fear for what they had done. The factions were overawed by the energy which they displayed. The most conspicuous began already to think of recoiling from the blows which they conceived to be aimed at them. Robespierre, whom we have hitherto seen supporting the most extravagant propositions, trembled in his obscure habitation; and, notwithstanding his inviolability as a deputy, applied to all his friends for an asylum. Thus the example had the desired effect, and for a moment all the turbulent spirits were quieted by fear.

About this time the Assembly came to a determination which has since been censured, but the result of which did not prove so mischievous as it has been supposed. It decreed that none of its members should be re-elected. Robespierre was the proposer of this resolution, and it was attributed to the envy which he felt against his colleagues, among whom he had not shone. It was at least natural that he should bear them a grudge, having always been opposed by them;

and in his sentiments there might have been at once conviction, envy, and hatred. The Assembly, which was accused of a design to perpetuate its powers, and which, moreover, displeased the rabble by its moderation, was anxious to reply to all censures by a disinterestedness that was perhaps exaggerated; and it decreed that its members should be excluded from the next legislature. The new Assembly was thus deprived of men whose enthusiasm was somewhat abated, and whose legislative science was matured by an experience of three years. However, when we see by and by the cause of the subsequent revolutions, we shall be able to judge what was the importance of that measure which has been so frequently condemned.

This was the moment for completing the constitutional labours of the Assembly, and for bringing its stormy career to a calm conclusion. The members of the left side intended, by means of an agreement among themselves, to amend certain parts of the constitution. It had been resolved that it should be read throughout, in order to judge of the whole together, and to have an opportunity of making its different parts harmonize. This was called the revision, which was afterwards, in the days of the republican fervour, considered as most calamitous. Barnave and the Lameths had agreed with Malouet to modify certain articles, which trenched upon the royal prerogative and what was termed the stability of the throne. It was even said that the plan was to re-establish the two chambers. It was arranged that, the moment the reading was finished, Malouet should make his attack; that Barnave should then reply with vehemence, in order the better to disguise his intentions; but that, in defending most of the articles, he should give up some as evidently dangerous, and condemned by known experience.

Such were the conditions agreed upon when the ridiculous and dangerous protests of the right side, which had resolved to vote no more, transpired. Accommodation then became impossible. The left side would hear no more, and, when the concerted attempt was made, the cries which burst from all quarters, prevented Malouet and his partisans from proceeding. (*See* Appendix V V.) The constitution wad therefore completed with some haste, and submitted to the King for his acceptance. From that moment his freedom was restored to him; or, if that expression be objected to, the strict watch kept over the palace ceased, and he had liberty to retire whithersoever he pleased, to examine the constitutional act and to accept it freely. What was Louis XVI. to do in this case? To reject the constitution would have been to abdicate in favour of a republic. The safest way, even according to his own system, was to accept it, and to expect from time those restitutions of power which he considered as due to him. Accordingly, after a certain number of days, he declared that he accepted the constitution. An extraordinary joy burst forth at this intelligence, as if in fact some obstacle had been anticipated on the part of the King, and his assent had been an unhoped-for concession. He repaired to the Assembly, where he was received as in the most brilliant times. Lafayette, who never forgot to repair the inevitable evils of political troubles, proposed a general amnesty for all acts connected with the devolution, which was proclaimed amidst shouts of joy, and the prisons were instantly thrown open. At length, on the 30th of September, Thouret, the last president, declared that the. Constituent Assembly had terminated its sittings.

THE NATIONAL LEGISLATIVE ASSEMBLY.

THE Constituent Assembly had now terminated its long and laborious career; and, notwithstanding its noble courage, its perfect equity, and its immense toils, it was hated as revolutionary at Coblentz, and as aristocratic at Paris. In order to form a proper judgment of this memorable Assembly, which combined talents so great and so diversified, the resolutions of which were so bold and so persevering, and in which were seen, perhaps for the first time, all the enlightened men of a nation assembled with the will and the power to realize the wishes of philosophy, we must consider the state in which it had found France, and that in which it left her.

In 1789 the French nation knew and felt all evils it suffered under, but it did not conceive the possibility of curing them. All at once, on the unforeseen demand of the parliaments, the States-general were convoked, the Constituent Assembly was formed and came into the presence of the throne, proud of its ancient power, and disposed at most to put up with a few complaints. Thoroughly impressed with its rights, it then declared itself to be the nation, and dared to declare this to the astonished government. Threatened by the aristocracy, by the court, and by an army, not yet foreseeing the popular commotions, it declared itself inviolable, and forbade power to touch it. Convinced of its rights, it addressed itself to enemies who were not convinced of theirs, and, by the mere expression of its determination, gained the ascendancy over a power of several centuries, and an army of thirty thousand men. Such was the Revolution. Such was its first and noblest act. It was just—it was heroic; for never did nation act with greater propriety, or amid greater dangers.

Power being vanquished, it became necessary to reconstitute it in a just and suitable manner. But, at the sight of that social ladder, on the summit of which there is a superabundance of everything—power, honours, wealth; whilst at the bottom everything is wanting, even to the bread that is indispensable for life—the Constituent Assembly experienced a violent reaction in its ideas, and was for reducing all to one level. It decided, therefore, that the mass of the citizens, placed on a complete equality, should express their will, and that the King should be charged only with its execution.

Its error here consists, not in having reduced royalty to a mere magistracy, for the King had still sufficient power to uphold the laws, and more than magistrates possess in republics, but in having imagined that a king, with the recollection of what he had been, could resign himself to be what he was; and that a nation, scarcely awakened, which had recovered part of the popular power, would not, determine to conquer it entirely.

History proves, in fact, that it is necessary to divide magistracies to infinity, or that, if a single chief be appointed, he must be so well endowed as to have no temptation to usurp.

When nations, engrossed by their private interests, find, it necessary to transfer the cares of government to a chief, they do right to give themselves one; but in this case, that chief must, like the kings of England, possess in reality the greatest part of the sovereignty, and the power of convoking and dissolving the national assemblies, without being compelled to obey their mandates, sanctioning them only when he thinks fit, and being prevented only from doing what is mischievous. The dignity of man can still be preserved under such a government, when the law is strictly observed, when every citizen feels his own value, and knows that powers so extensive left to the prince have only been granted as a concession to human weakness.

But it is not at the moment when a nation suddenly bethinks itself of its rights that it can renounce all its prerogatives, submit to take a secondary part, and yield the supreme power to a chief, lest he should feel an inclination to usurp it. The Constituent Assembly was equally incapable with the nation itself of consenting to such an abdication.

It reduced the King, therefore, to a mere hereditary magistrate, hoping that the nation would leave him that, and that he would himself be content with this magistracy, still resplendent with honours, wealth, and power.

But, whether the Assembly hoped this or not, could it, in such a state of uncertainty, evade the question? Could it abolish royalty, or could it confer on it all the power that England grants to her monarchs?

It could not, on the one hand, depose Louis XVI.; for if it is always necessary to introduce a spirit of justice into a government, it is not so to change its form, when that spirit exists in it, and suddenly to convert a monarchy into a republic. Moreover, possession carries with it authority, and if the Assembly had despoiled the reigning dynasty, what would not its enemies have said, who accused it of violating property because it attacked feudal rights?

On the other hand, it could not confer on the King the absolute veto, the appointment of the judges, and other similar prerogatives, because public opinion was adverse to such concessions; and, as this opinion constituted its only strength, the Assembly was obliged to defer to it.

With regard to the establishment of a single chamber, its error was, perhaps, more real, but just as inevitable. If it was dangerous to leave nothing but the remembrance of power to a king who had possessed it entire, while legislating for a people desirous of wresting from him the last remnant of it; much more false was it in principle not to recognise social inequalities and gradations, when they are admitted by republics themselves, and when in all of them there is a senate either hereditary or elective. But we must not require of men and minds more than they are capable of at the time. How can the necessity of ranks be recognised at the moment of a revolt against their injustice? How is it possible to constitute an aristocracy at the moment when war is proclaimed against aristocracy? To constitute royalty would have been an easier task, because, placed apart from the people, it would have been less oppressive, and because it moreover performs functions which seem more necessary.

But, I repeat it, if these errors had not existed in the Assembly, they existed in the nation; and the course of events will prove that, if the

Assembly had left the King and the aristocracy all the powers which it did not leave them, the Revolution would, nevertheless, have taken place, even to its greatest excesses.

To be convinced of this, we must make a distinction between the revolutions which have taken place among nations long in a state of subjection, and those which have taken place among free people, that is to say, people in possession of a certain political activity. At Rome, at Athens, and elsewhere, we see the people and their chiefs disputing for the greater or less share of authority. Among modern nations entirely stripped of it, the course is different. Completely subjected, their slumber is long. The more enlightened classes are the first to awake. These rouse themselves and recover a portion of power. The awakening is progressive. Ambition is progressive too, and keeps spreading to the lowest classes, till the whole mass is in motion. Presently, satisfied with what they have obtained, the enlightened classes wish to stop; but they can no longer do so, and are incessantly pushed forward by those behind them. Those who stop, were they in the very last rank but one, if they pretend to oppose the last, are to it an aristocracy, and are stigmatised with the name. The mere tradesman is called aristocrat by the artisan, and hated as such.

The Constituent Assembly represented that class which first awakes and cries out against power while yet all-powerful. Sagacious enough to perceive what was due to those who had everything and to those who had nothing, it wished to leave the former part of what they possessed, because they had always possessed it, and to procure for the latter, above all things, knowledge, and the rights which it confers. But regret sways the one, ambition the other. Regret wishes to recover all, ambition to conquer all, and a war of extermination commences. The Constituents then, are those first good men, who shaking off slavery, attempt to establish a just system, try it without apprehension, nay, accomplish this immense task, but fail in endeavouring to persuade the one to yield something, the other not to grasp at everything.

The Constituent Assembly, in its equitable allotments, had shown forbearance towards the former possessors of power. Louis XVI., with the title of King of the French, an income of thirty millions, the command of the armies, and the right of suspending the national decrees, still possessed extensive prerogatives. The recollection of absolute power alone can excuse him for not having been content with so brilliant a remnant of absolute power.

The clergy, stripped of the immense possessions which had formerly been given to it, on condition of relieving the poor whom it did not relieve, and of performing that divine worship which it left to be performed by poor curates, was no longer a political order. But its ecclesiastical dignities were preserved, its dogmas respected, its scandalous wealth changed into a sufficient, nay, we may say, an abundant revenue, for it still possessed considerable episcopal luxury. The nobility was no longer an order; it no longer possessed the exclusive right of killing game and the like; it was no longer exempt from taxes; but could it make these things a subject of reasonable regret? Its immense possessions were left to it. Instead of the favour of the court, it had a certainty of the distinctions conferred on merit. It had the privilege of being elected by the people, and of representing it in the state, if it could but show the slightest good-will and resignation. The robe and the sword were ensured to its talents: why then was it not all at once inspired with a generous emulation? What an avowal of incapacity did it not make in regretting the favours of former times!

The old pensioners had been spared; the ecclesiastics had received indemnities; every one had been treated with indulgence: was then the lot which the Constituent Assembly had assigned to all so intolerable?

The constitution being completed, the King had no hope left of recovering, by means of the legislation, the prerogatives which he regretted. He had but one course to pursue, to be resigned and to uphold the constitution, unless he reckoned upon the foreign powers. But he hoped very little from their zeal, and distrusted the emigrants. He decided, therefore, in favour of the former line of conduct, and what proves his sincerity is, that he meant frankly to point out to the Assembly the defects which he found in the constitution. But he was dissuaded from doing so, and he resolved to trust to time for those restitutions of power which he deemed his due. The Queen was not less resigned. "Courage!" said she to Bertrand the minister, who waited upon her, "all is not yet lost. The King is determined to adhere to the constitution; that course is certainly the best." And there is every reason to believe that, if she had had other thoughts to utter, she would not have hesitated to express them before Bertrand de Molleville. (*See* Appendix W W.)

The old Assembly had broken up. Its members had returned to the bosom of their families, or were scattered throughout Paris. Some of the most conspicuous, such as Lameth, Duport, Barnave, communicated with the court, and gave it their advice. But the King, resolved as he was to observe the constitution, could not make up his mind to follow the advice that he received; for not only was it recommended to him not to violate that constitution, but by all his acts to induce the belief that he was sincerely attached to it. These members of the late Assembly, joined by Lafayette since the revision, were the chiefs of that first revolutionary generation, which had laid down the first rules of liberty, and desired that they should be adhered to. They were supported by the national guard, whom long service under Lafayette had strongly attached to him and to his principles. The constituents then fell into an error—that of disdaining the new Assembly, and frequently irritating it by their contempt. A sort of aristocratic vanity had already seized these first legislators; and it seemed as though all legislative science had disappeared along with them.

The new Assembly was composed of different classes of men. It included enlightened partisans of the first Revolution: Ramond, Girardin, Vaublanc, Dumas, and others, who called themselves constitutionalists, and occupied the right side, where not one of the late privileged class was to be found. Thus, by the natural and progressive march of the Revolution, the left side of the first Assembly was destined to become the right of the second. Next to the constitutionalists came many distinguished men, whose heads were heated and whose expectations were exaggerated by the Revolution. Witnesses of the labours of the Constituent Assembly, and impatient as lookers-on, they were of opinion that enough had not yet been done. They durst not avow themselves republicans, because, on all sides, people mutually exhorted one another to be faithful to the constitution; but the experiment of a republic which had been made during the journey of Louis XVI., and the suspicious intentions of the court, were incessantly leading their minds back to that idea; and they could not but attach themselves to it more and more from their continual hostilities with the government.

Among this new generation of talents, the most remarkable were the deputies of La Gironde, from whom the whole party, though composed of men from all the departments, derived the name of Girondins. Condorcet (*See* Appendix X X.), a writer celebrated for the comprehensiveness of his ideas, and for an extreme austerity of mind and character, was its writer; and Vergniaud (*See* Appendix Y Y.), a pure and persuasive extempore speaker, was its orator. This party, increased continually by all who despaired of the court, did not want such a republic as fell to it in 1793. It dreamt of one with all its fascinations, with its severe virtues and manners. Enthusiasm and vehemence were of course its principal characteristics.

Such a party could not but have its extremes. There were Bazire, Merlin de Thionville, and others, who though its inferiors in talent, were its superiors in boldness. They became the party of the Mountain, when after the overthrow of the throne, they separated from the Girondins. This second Assembly had also, like the first, a middle mass, which, without being bound to any party, voted first with the one and then with the other. Under the Constituent Assembly, when real liberty still prevailed, this mass had remained independent; but, as it was not so from energy but from indifference, in the subsequent Assemblies, and during the reign of violence, it became cowardly and contemptible, and received the trivial and ignominious name of *belly* (*ventre*).

The clubs gained at this period a very different kind of importance. Agitators under the Constituent, they became rulers under the Legislative, Assembly. The National Assembly could not contain all the ambitious; they betook themselves therefore to the clubs, where they found a theatre for their declamations and passions. Thither resorted all who longed to speak, to take an active part, to agitate themselves, that is to say: almost the whole nation. The people ran to this new sight, they filled the tribunes of all the Assemblies, and there found, from this time forward, a lucrative employment, for they began to be paid for their applause. Bertrand, the minister, confesses that he paid them himself.

The oldest of the clubs, that of the Jacobins, had acquired extraordinary importance. A church was scarcely sufficient to hold the crowd of its members and auditors. An immense amphitheatre rose in the form of a circus and occupied the whole great nave of the church of the Jacobins. A desk was placed in the centre, at which sat the president and the secretaries. Here the votes were collected, and here reports of the deliberations were entered in a register. An active correspondence kept up the zeal of the societies which were scattered over the entire surface of France, and were called affiliated societies. This club, from its seniority and persevering violence, had constantly maintained an ascendancy over all those that had desired to show themselves more moderate or even more vehement. After the journey to Varennes, the Lameths, with all its most distinguished members, left it and joined the Feuillans. In this latter were blended all the attempts at moderate clubs, attempts which had never succeeded, because they ran counter to the feeling which caused people to frequent the clubs—the desire of agitation. It was at the Feuillans that the constitutionalists, or partisans of the first Revolution, now met. Hence the name of Feuillant became a ground of proscription, when that of moderate was unpopular.

Another club, that of the Cordeliers, endeavoured to rival in violence that of the Jacobins. Camille Desmoulins was its secretary, and Danton its president. The latter, who had not been successful at the bar, had gained the adoration of the multitude, which he powerfully excited, by his athletic figure, his sonorous voice, and his popular passions. The Cordeliers however were not able, even with the aid of exaggeration, to eclipse their rivals, to whom habit brought a concourse of auditors. But almost all of them belonged to the Jacobin club, and when occasion required, they repaired thither in the train of Danton, to swell the majority in his favour.

Robespierre, whom we have seen, in the time of the Constituent Assembly, distinguishing himself by the severity of his principles, was excluded from the Legislative Assembly by the decree of non-re-election, to the passing of which he had himself contributed. He had intrenched himself at the Jacobins, where he ruled without partner, by the dogmatism of his opinions and by a reputation for integrity which had gained him the epithet of incorruptible. Panic-struck, as we have seen, at the moment of the revision, he had since taken courage, and continued the work of his popularity. Robespierre had found, two rivals whom he began to hate—Brissot (*See* Appendix Z Z.) and Louvet. Brissot, mixed up with all the men of the first Assembly, a friend of Mirabeau and Lafayette, known to be a republican, and one of the most distinguished members of the legislature, was fickle in character, but remarkable for certain qualities of mind. Louvet, with an ardent spirit, an excellent understanding, and great boldness, was one of those, who, having outstripped the Constituent Assembly, dreamt of a republic. Hence they naturally approximated to the Girondins. His contests with Robespierre soon attached him still more to them. This party of the Gironde, formed by degrees, without design, by men possessing too much merit to ally themselves to the populace, and distinction enough to be envied by it and its leaders, and who were united rather by their situation than by any concert, was destined to be brilliant but weak, and to fall before the more resolute factions which sprang up around it.

Such then was the state of France. The lately privileged persons had retired beyond the Rhine. The partisans of the constitution comprehended the right of the Assembly, the national guard, and the club of the Feuillans. The Girondins had the majority in the Assembly, but not in the clubs, where low violence had greater sway. Lastly, the hotheaded democrats of this new epoch, seated on the highest benches of the Assembly, and thence denominated *the Mountain*, were all-powerful in the clubs and among the populace.

Lafayette had resigned all military rank and had been accompanied to his country-seat by the homage and regret of his companions in arms. The command had not been conferred on a new general, but six chiefs of legions commanded by turns the whole national guard. Bailly, the faithful ally of Lafayette during those three arduous years, likewise resigned the mayoralty. The voices of the electors were divided between Lafayette and Petion; but the court, which would not at any rate have Lafayette, who was nevertheless favourably disposed towards it, preferred Petion, though a republican. It hoped more from his coldness, which it mistook for stupidity, but which was quite the reverse, and it incurred considerable expense in order to secure him a majority. He was accordingly appointed mayor. Petion, with an enlightened understanding, a cold but settled conviction, and considerable address, constantly served the republicans against the court, and found himself allied to the Gironde by conformity of views, and by the envy which his new dignity excited among the Jacobins.

If, however, notwithstanding these dispositions of the parties, the King could have been relied upon, it is possible that the distrust of the Girondins might have worn off, and that, the pretext for disturbances no longer existing, the agitators would thenceforward have found no pretexts for urging the populace to commotion.

The intentions of the King were formed; but he was so weak that they were never irrevocable. It was requisite that he should prove them before they could gain belief; and till he could afford proof, he was liable to more than one outrage. His disposition, though good, was not without a certain tendency to ill-humour. His resolutions were in consequence easily shaken by the first faults of the Assembly. This Assembly having been constituted, took the oath with pomp on the book of the constitution. Its first decree relative to the ceremonial, abolished the titles of *sire* and *majesty*, usually given to the King. It ordered moreover that, whenever he appeared in the Assembly, he should sit in an arm-chair exactly similar to that of the president.

Such were the first results of the republican spirit, and the pride of Louis XVI. was cruelly wounded by them. To spare himself what he regarded as an humiliation, he resolved not to attend the Assembly, but to send his ministers to open the legislative session. The Assembly, repenting this first hostility, revoked its decree on the following day, and thus gave a rare example of recantation. The King then went and was warmly received. Unluckily, it had been decreed that, if the King continued sitting, the members should likewise keep their seats. They did so, and Louis XVI. considered this as a fresh insult. The applause with which he was greeted could not heal the wound. He returned home pale and with agitated looks. No sooner was he alone with the Queen than he threw himself into a chair, sobbing. "Ah! madam," he exclaimed, "you witnessed this humiliation! What! come to France to see. . . . . . ." The Queen strove to comfort him; but his heart was too deeply lacerated, and his good intentions must have been shaken by this treatment.

If, however, he henceforth thought only of having recourse to foreigners, the dispositions of the powers were not such as to give him much hope. The declaration of Pilnitz had remained inoperative, either from want of zeal on the part of the sovereigns, or perhaps on account of the danger which Louis XVI. would have incurred, having been ever since his return from Varennes the prisoner of the Constituent Assembly. The acceptance of the constitution was an additional motive for the sovereigns to await the results of experience before they proceeded to action. This was the opinion of Leopold and of Kaunitz, the minister. Accordingly, when Louis XVI. had notified to all the courts that he had accepted the constitution, and that it was his intention to observe it faithfully, Austria returned a most pacific answer. Prussia and England did the same, and protested their amicable intentions. It is to be observed that the neighbouring powers acted with more reserve than the remote powers, such as Sweden and Russia, because they were more immediately compromised by a war. Gustavus, who dreamt of some brilliant expedition against France, replied to the notification that he did not consider the King as free. Russia deferred the explanation of her sentiments. Holland, the Italian principalities, and Switzerland in particular, gave satisfactory answers. The electors of Treves and Mentz, in whose territories the emigrants resided, used evasive expressions. Spain, also, importuned by the emigrants of Coblentz, abstained from speaking out; alleging that she wished for time to ensure the liberty of the King. She nevertheless declared that she had no intention of disturbing the tranquillity of the kingdom.

Such answers, not one of which was hostile, the assured neutrality of England, the hesitation of Frederick William, the pacific and well-known disposition of Leopold, all seemed to promise peace. It is impossible to tell what passed in the vacillating mind of Louis XVI.; but his evident interest, and the very fears with which the war subsequently filled him, must induce a belief that he too was desirous of the maintenance of peace. Amidst this general concert, the emigrants alone continued to be obstinately bent on war, and to prepare for it.

They still kept thronging to Coblentz; where, with great activity, they armed themselves, prepared magazines, contracted for accoutrements, and formed skeletons of regiments, which however were not filled up, for none of them would become soldiers. Moreover, they instituted ranks which were sold; and, if they attempted nothing really dangerous, they nevertheless made great preparations, which they themselves deemed formidable, and by which they expected to strike terror into the imagination of the French people.

The grand point was to ascertain whether Louis XVI. were favourable to them or not; and it was difficult to suppose that he could be otherwise than well-disposed towards kinsmen and servants who were taking up arms to restore to him his former powers. It would have required nothing less than the utmost sincerity and continual demonstrations to produce a contrary conviction. The letters of the King to the emigrants contained invitations, nay, even orders, to return; but he kept up, it was said (*see* Appendix A A A.), a secret correspondence, which contradicted his public correspondence, and destroyed its effect. That secret communications took place with Coblentz cannot indeed be denied, but I cannot believe that Louis XVI. made use of them to contradict the injunctions which he had publicly addressed to the emigrants. His most evident interest was that they should return. Their presence at Coblentz could not be serviceable so long as they entertained the design of fighting: and Louis XVI. dreaded civil war above all things.

Not desiring then that the emigrants should employ their swords on the Rhine, it was better that he should have them about him, that he might employ them as occasion required, and combine their efforts with those of the constitutionalists for the protection of his person and his throne. Moreover, their presence at Coblentz provoked severe laws, which he would not sanction—a refusal which compromised him with the Assembly; and we shall see that it was the use which he now made of the veto that completely stripped him of popularity, and caused him to be considered as an accomplice of the emigrants. It would be strange if he had not perceived the cogency of these reasons, which was felt by all his ministers, who were unanimously of opinion that the emigrants ought to return and to keep near the person of the King, in order to defend him, to put an end to alarms, and to deprive agitators of every pretext. This was the opinion of Bertrand de Molleville himself, whose principles were anything but constitutional. "It was necessary," says he, "to use all possible means to increase the popularity of the King. The most efficacious and the most useful of all, at this moment, was to recall the emigrants. Their return, generally desired, would have revived in France the royalist party, which the emigration had completely disorganised. This party, strengthened by the unpopularity of the Assembly, and recruited by numerous deserters from the constitutional party, and by all the discontented, would soon have become powerful enough to render decisive in favour of the King the explosion, more or less speedy, which there was every reason to expect."

Louis XVI., conformably with this advice of his ministers, addressed exhortations to the principal officers of the army and navy, to recall them to their duty, and to keep them at their posts. His exhortations, however, were useless, and the desertion continued without intermission. The minister at war reported that nineteen hundred officers had deserted. The Assembly could not moderate its wrath, and resolved to take vigorous measures. The Constituent Assembly had gone no further than to decree that public functionaries who were out of the kingdom should be superseded, and that the property of emigrants should be burdened with a triple contribution, to indemnify the state for the services of which they deprived it by their absence. The new Assembly proposed more severe penalties.

Several plans were presented. Brissot distinguished three classes of emigrants: the leaders of the desertion, the public functionaries who abandoned their duties, and lastly, those who out of fear had fled from their country. They ought, he said, to deal severely with the former, to despise and pity the others.

It is certain that the liberty of man does not allow him to be chained down to the soil, but when a certainty is obtained, from a multitude of circumstances, that the citizens who forsake it are going to assemble abroad for the purpose of declaring war against it, then, indeed, it is justifiable to take precautions against such dangerous projects.

The debate was long and warm. The constitutionalists condemned all the measures proposed, and asserted that they ought to despise useless attempts, as their predecessors had invariably done. The opposite party, however, carried their point; and a first decree was passed, enjoining Monsieur, the King's brother, to return within two months, in default of which he should lose his eventual right to the regency. A second and more severe decree was levelled against the emigrants in general: it declared that the French assembled beyond the frontiers of the kingdom were suspected of conspiring against France; that, if on the 1st of

January next they still continued assembled, they should he declared guilty of conspiracy, prosecuted as such, and punished with death; and that the revenues of those who refused to comply should be levied during their lives for the benefit of the nation, without prejudice to the rights of wives, children, and lawful creditors.

The act of emigration not being in itself reprehensible, it is difficult to characterise the case in which it becomes so. All that the law could do was to apprize people that they would become culpable in such and such cases; and all who wished not to be so had only to obey. Those who, when apprized of the term beyond which absence from the kingdom became a crime, should not return, would consent by this very circumstance to pass for criminals. It was incumbent on those who, without any hostile or political motive, were out of the kingdom, to hasten their return: in fact, it is a very trifling sacrifice to the safety of a state to abridge a journey of pleasure or profit.

Louis XVI., in order to satisfy the Assembly and public opinion, assented to the decree requiring Monsieur to return upon pain of losing his right to the regency; but he affixed his veto to the law against the emigrants. The ministers were directed to go in a body to the Assembly, for the purpose of communicating the pleasure of the King. They first read several decrees to which the sanction was given. When they came to that relative to the emigrants, profound silence pervaded the Assembly; and when the keeper of the seals pronounced the official formula, *The King will examine it*, great discontent was expressed on all sides. He would have entered into a development of the forms of the veto, but a great number of voices were raised, and told the minister that the constitution granted to the King the right of opposing, but not that of assigning motives for opposition. The minister was therefore obliged to withdraw, leaving behind him a deep irritation. This first resistance of the King to the Assembly was a definitive rupture; and though he had sanctioned the decree which deprived his brother of the regency, yet people could not help discovering in his rejection of the second decree an affection for the insurgents at Coblentz. They considered that he was their kinsman, their friend, and in some degree their copartner; and thence concluded that it was impossible for him not to make common cause with them against the nation.

The very next day, Louis XVI. published a proclamation to the emigrants, and two separate letters to his two brothers. The reasons which he stated to both were excellent, and appeared to be sincerely urged. He exhorted them to put an end by their return to the distrust which evil-disposed persons took delight in spreading. He besought them not to compel him to employ severe measures against them; and, as to his want of liberty, which was made a pretext for not obeying him, he adduced as an evidence of the contrary the veto which he had just affixed in their favour. (*See* Appendix B B B.) Be this as it might, those reasons produced neither at Coblentz nor at Paris the effect which they were, or appeared to be, intended to produce. The emigrants did not return; and in the Assembly the tone of the proclamation was deemed too mild; nay, the power of the executive to issue one was called in question. That body was in fact too much irritated to be content with a proclamation, and above all to suffer the King to substitute a useless measure for the vigorous resolutions which had just been adopted.

A similar trial was at the same moment imposed upon the King, and produced an equally unfortunate result. The first religious disturbances had broken out in the West; the Constituent Assembly had sent thither two commissioners, one of whom was Gensonné, afterwards so celebrated in the party of the Gironde. Their report had been made to the Legislative Assembly, and, though very moderate, this report had filled it with indignation. It will be recollected that the Constituent Assembly, in depriving the nonjuring priests of their functions, had nevertheless left them a pension, and liberty to perform religious service apart. They had ever since endeavoured to excite the people against their colleagues who had taken the oath, and inveighed against them as impious wretches, whose ministry was null and dangerous. They drew the peasants after them to great distances for the purpose of saying mass to them. The latter were irritated to see their churches occupied by a worship which they were taught to consider as bad, and to be obliged to go so far in quest of that which they looked upon as good. Civil war was imminent. (*See* Appendix C C C.) Fresh information communicated to the Assembly proved that the danger had become still greater. It then determined to adopt measures against these new enemies of the constitution, similar to those which it had taken against the armed enemies beyond the Rhine, and to put the disposition of the King to a new test.

The Constituent Assembly had required all priests to take the civic oath. Those who refused to comply, though they lost the character of ministers of public worship paid by the state, retained their pensions as mere ecclesiastics and the liberty of exercising their ministry in private. Nothing could be milder or more moderate than such a restriction. The Legislative Assembly required the oath to be taken anew, and deprived those who refused of any salary whatever. As they abused their liberty by exciting civil war, it ordered that, according to their conduct, they should be removed from one place to another, and even sentenced to imprisonment if they refused to obey. Lastly, it forbade them the free exercise of their private worship, and directed the administrative bodies to transmit to it a list, with notes, relative to the conduct of each of them.

This measure, as well as that which had just been taken against the emigrants, originated in the anxiety which seizes governments that are threatened to surround themselves with excessive precautions. It is not the ascertained fact which they punish, but the presumed attack against which they proceed, and their measures become as arbitrary and cruel as they are suspicious.

The bishops and the priests who had remained in Paris, and who had kept up a correspondence with the King, immediately sent to him a memorial against the decree. The King, who was already full of scruples, and had always reproached himself for having sanctioned the decree of the Constituent Assembly, needed no encouragement for this refusal. "As for this," said he, speaking of the new plan, "they shall take my life before they shall oblige me to sanction it." The ministers were nearly all of the same opinion. Barnave and Lameth, whom the King occasionally consulted, advised him to refuse his sanction; but to this counsel they added other recommendations, which the King could not make up his mind to follow. These were, that, in opposing the decree, he should not leave any doubt respecting his disposition, and for this purpose he should remove from about his person all priests who refused to take the oath, and compose his chapel of none but constitutional ecclesiastics.

But of all the counsels which they gave him, the King adopted only such as harmonised with his weakness or his devotion. Duport-Dutertre, keeper of the seals, and the organ of the constitutionalists with the ministry, procured its approbation of their advice; and when the council had decided, to the great satisfaction of Louis XVI., that the veto should be affixed, he added, as his opinion, that it would be well to surround the person of the King with priests who were not liable to suspicion. To this proposal Louis XVI., usually so flexible, manifested invincible obstinacy, and said that the freedom of religious worship, decreed for every body, ought to be allowed to him as well as to his subjects, and that he ought to have the liberty of appointing about him such priests as he approved. The ministers did not insist, and, without as yet communicating the circumstance to the Assembly, the veto was decided upon.

The constitutional party, to which the King seemed to consign himself at this moment, brought him a fresh reinforcement. This was the directory of the department, which was composed of the most esteemed members of the Constitutional Assembly. Among them were the Duke De Larouchefoucault, the Bishop of Autun, Baumetz, Desmeuniers, Ansons, &c. It presented a petition to the King, not as an administrative body, but as a meeting of petitioners, and called for the affixing of the veto to the decree against the priests.

"The National Assembly," they said, "certainly meant well; we love to avenge it here on its guilty detractors; but so laudable a design has propelled it towards measures of which neither the constitution, justice, nor prudence can approve. It makes the payment of the pensions of all ecclesiastics not in office depend on the taking of the civic oath, whereas the constitution has expressly and literally classed those pensions with the public debts. Now, can the refusal to take any oath whatever destroy the title of an acknowledged credit? The Constituent Assembly has done what it could do on behalf of the nonjuring priests; they refused to take the prescribed oath, and it has deprived them of their functions; in dispossessing them, it has reduced them to a pension. The Legislative Assembly proposes that the ecclesiastics who have not taken the oath, or who have retracted it, may, during religious disturbances, be temporarily removed, and imprisoned if they fail to obey the order which shall be intimated to them. Is not this renewing the system of arbitrary orders, since it permits the punishing with exile, and soon afterwards with imprisonment, one who has not yet been convicted of having offended against any law? The National Assembly refuses all those who shall not take the civic cath the free exercise of their religious worship. Now, this liberty cannot be wrested from any person. It is guaranteed for ever in the declaration of rights."

These reasons were certainly excellent, but it is impossible to allay with arguments either the animosities or the fears of parties. How persuade an Assembly that it ought to permit refractory priests to excite disturbance and civil war? The directory was abused, and its petition to the King was combated by a multitude of others addressed to the legislative body. Camille Desmoulins presented a very bold petition at the head of a section; in which might be already perceived an increasing violence of language, and a renunciation of all the respect hitherto paid to the authorities and to the King. Desmoulins told the Assembly that a signal example was required; that the directory ought to be tried; that it was the leaders who ought to be prosecuted; that it ought to strike at the head, and launch thunderbolts at the conspirators; that the power of the royal veto had a limit, and that a veto would not prevent the taking of a Bastille.

Louis XVI., though determined to refuse his sanction, hesitated to acquaint the Assembly with his resolution. He wished first, by certain acts, to conciliate the public opinion. He selected his ministers from among the constitutional party. Montmorin, weary of his laborious career under the Constituent Assembly, and of his arduous negotiations with all the parties, could not be induced to encounter the storms of a new legislature, and had retired in spite of the entreaties of the King. The ministry for foreign affairs, refused by several persons, was accepted by Delessart, who, in order to assume it, relinquished that of the interior. Delessart, an upright and enlightened man, was under the influence of the Constitutionalists, or Feuillans; but he was too weak to fix the will of the King and to overawe foreign powers and domestic factions. Cahier de Gerville, a decided patriot, but rather rough than persuasive, was appointed to the interior, to gratify public opinion. Narbonne, a young man, full of activity and ardour, a zealous constitutionalist, and who understood the art of making himself popular, was placed at the head of the war department by the party which then composed the ministry. He might have had a beneficial influence upon the council, and reconciled the Assembly with the King, if he had not had an adversary in Bertrand de Molleville, a counter-revolutionary minister, who was preferred by the court to all the others. Bertrand de Molleville, detesting the constitution, artfully wrapped himself up in the letter for the pin-pose of attacking its spirit, and sincerely desired that the King would attempt to execute it, "merely," as he said, "to prove that it was not practicable." The King could not make up his mind to dismiss him, and with this mixed ministry he endeavoured to pursue his course. After he had endeavoured to gratify public opinion by these appointments, he tried other means for attaching it to him still more; and he appeared to accede to all the diplomatic and military measures proposed against the assemblages formed upon the Rhine.

The last repressive laws had been prevented by the veto, and yet every day fresh denunciations apprised the Assembly of the preparations and the threats of the emigrants. The reports (*procès-verbaux*) of the municipalities and departments on the frontiers, and the accounts given by commercial men coming from beyond the Rhine, attested that the Viscount de Mirabeau, brother of the celebrated member of the Constituent Assembly, was at the head of six hundred men in the bishopric of Strasburg: that, in the territory of the Elector of Mentz, and near Worms, there were numerous corps of emigrants, under the command of the Prince of Condé; that the same was the case at Coblentz and throughout the whole electorate of Treves; that outrages and acts of violence had been committed upon Frenchmen; and lastly, that a proposal had been made to General Wimpfen to deliver up New Brisach.

These accounts, in addition to many other circumstances that were matter of public notoriety, drove the Assembly to the last degree ot irritation. A decree was immediately proposed, to require of the electors the disarming of the emigrants. The decision was deferred for two days, that it might not appear to be too much hurried. After this delay the discussion commenced.

Isnard (*see* Appendix D D D) was the first speaker. He insisted upon the necessity of ensuring the tranquillity of the kingdom, not in a temporary, but in a durable manner; of overawing by prompt and vigorous measures, which should attest to all Europe the patriotic resolutions of France. "Fear not," said he, "to bring upon yourselves a war with the great powers. Interest has already decided their intentions. Your measures will not change them, but will oblige them to explain themselves. The conduct of the Frenchman ought to correspond with his new destiny. A slave under Louis XVI., he was nevertheless intrepid and great. Now that he is free, ought he to be weak and timid? They are mistaken, said Montesquieu, who imagine that a people in a state of revolution are disposed to be conquered. They are ready, on the contrary, to conquer others. (*Applause.*)

"Capitulations are proposed to you. It is proposed to increase the power of the King—of a man whose will can paralyse that of the whole nation, of a man who receives thirty millions, while thousands of citizens are perishing from want! (*Fresh applause.*) It is proposed to bring back the nobility. Were all the nobles on earth to attack us, the French, holding their gold in one hand and the sword in the other, would combat that haughty race, and force it to endure the punishment of equality.

"Talk to the ministers, to the King, and to Europe, the language befitting the representatives of France. Tell the ministers that, so far, you are not satisfied with their conduct, and that by responsibility you mean death. (*Prolonged applause.*) Tell Europe that you will respect the constitutions of all other countries, but that, if a war of kings is raised against France, you will raise a war of people against kings." The applause was here renewed. "Say," he added, "that the battles which nations fight at the command of despots are like the blows which two friends, excited by a perfidious instigator, strike at each other in the dark. The moment a light appears they embrace, and take vengeance on him who deluded them. In like manner, if, at the moment when the hostile armies shall be engaged with ours, the light of philosophy bursts upon their sight, the nations will embrace one another before the face of dethroned tyrants, of consoled earth, and of delighted Heaven!"

The enthusiasm excited by these words was such that the members thronged around the speaker to embrace him. The decree which he supported was instantly adopted. M. de Vaublanc was directed to carry it to the King, at the head of a deputation of twenty-four members. By this decree the Assembly declared that it considered it indispensably necessary to require the electors of Treves and Mentz, and the other princes of the empire, to break up the assemblages formed on the frontiers. At the same time, it prayed the King to accelerate the negotiations commenced respecting the indemnities due to the princes who had possessions in Alsace.

M. de Vaublanc accompanied this decree with a firm and respectful address, which was highly applauded by the Assembly. "Sire," said he, "if the French, driven from their country by the revocation of the edict of

Nantes, had assembled in arms on the frontiers, and had been protected by German princes, we ask you, sire, what would have been the conduct of Louis XIV.? Would he have suffered these assemblages? What he would have done for the sake of his authority, your Majesty cannot hesitate to do for the maintenance of the constitution."

Louis XVI., having determined, as we have said, to counteract the effect of the veto by acts which should gratify public opinion, resolved to go to the Assembly and personally reply to its message in a speech likely to give it satisfaction.

On the 14th of December, in the evening, the King accordingly went, after having announced his intention in the morning by a mere note. He said that the message of the Assembly deserved mature consideration, and that, in a circumstance in which French honour was involved, he deemed it right to come in person; that, sharing the intentions of the Assembly, but dreading the scourge of war, he had endeavoured to bring back the misled French; that, friendly remonstrances having proved ineffectual, he had anticipated the message of the representatives, and signified to the electors that, if before the 15th of January the assemblage of troops should not have ceased, they should be considered as enemies of France; that he had written to the emperor to claim his interference as head of the empire; and that, in case satisfaction were not obtained, he should propose war. He concluded with saying that it would be vain to attempt to surround the exercise of his authority with disgust; that he would faithfully guard the deposit of the constitution; and that he deeply felt how glorious it was to be King of a free people.

Applause succeeded the silence, and made the King amends for the reception which he had experienced on entering. The Assembly, having resolved in the morning that he should be answered by a message, could not immediately express its satisfaction, but gave orders that his speech should be sent to the eighty-three departments. Narbonne soon afterwards entered, to communicate the means which had been adopted to ensure the effect of the intimations addressed to the empire. One hundred thousand men were to be assembled on the Rhine; and this he added was not impossible. Three generals were appointed to command them, Luckner, Rochambeau, and Lafayette (*See* Appendix E E E.). The last name was received with applause. Narbonne added that he should set out immediately to inspect the frontiers, to ascertain the state of the fortresses, and to give the greatest activity to defensive operations; that no doubt the Assembly would grant the necessary funds, and not cheapen liberty. Cries of "No, no," burst from all sides. Lastly, he asked the Assembly if, though the legal number of marshals was complete, it would not permit the King to confer that rank on the two generals, Luckner and Rochambeau, who were charged to save liberty. Acclamations testified the consent of the Assembly and the satisfaction caused by the activity of the young minister. It was by persevering in such conduct that Louis XVI. might have succeeded in gaining popularity and reconciling the republicans, who wished for a republic solely because they believed the King to be incapable of loving and defending liberty.

Advantage was taken of the satisfaction produced by these measures to notify the veto affixed to the decree against the priests. Care was taken to publish in the journals of the same morning the dismissal of the former diplomatic agents accused of aristocracy, and the appointment of new ones. Owing to these precautions, the message was received without a murmur. The Assembly, indeed, expected it, and the sensation was not so unfavourable as might have been apprehended. We see how extremely cautious the King was obliged to be in making use of his prerogative, and what danger he incurred in employing it. Had the Constituent Assembly, which is accused of having ruined by stripping him of his authority, conferred on him the absolute veto, would he have been more powerful on that account? Had not the suspensive veto in this case all the effect of the absolute veto? "Was it legal power that the King lacked, or the power of opinion? We see, from the effect itself, that it was not the want of sufficient prerogatives which ruined Louis XVI., but the indiscreet use of those which were left him.

The activity promised to the Assembly was not delayed. The propositions for the expenses of the war and for the nomination of the two marshals, Luckner and Rochambeau, followed without interruption. Lafayette, forced from the retirement which he had sought, in order to recruit himself after three years' fatigues, presented himself before the Assembly, where he was cordially received. Battalions of the national guard escorted him on leaving Paris, and everything proved to him that the name of Lafayette was not forgotten, but that he was still regarded as one of the founders of liberty.

Meanwhile Leopold, naturally peaceful, was not desirous of war, for he knew that it was not consistent with his interests; but he wished for a congress backed by an imposing force, in order to bring about an accommodation and some modifications in the constitution. The emigrants wished not to modify but to destroy it. More prudent and better informed, the Emperor knew that it was necessary to concede a great deal to the new opinions, and that the utmost that could be expected was to restore to the King certain prerogatives, and to modify the composition of the legislative body by the establishment of two chambers instead of one. (*See* Appendix F F F.)

This last measure was the most dreaded, and it was with the plan of it that the Remnant or constitutional party was most frequently reproached. It is certain that, if this party had, in the early time of the Constituent Assembly, opposed the upper chamber, because it justly apprehended that the nobility would there entrench themselves, it had not now the same fears. On the contrary, it had just hopes of filling such a chamber almost of itself. Many constituents, reduced to mere ciphers, would there have found occasion to appear again on the political stage. If then this upper chamber did not accord with their views, still less did it accord with their interests. It is certain that the newspapers frequently adverted to it, and that this report was universally circulated. How rapid had been the progress of the Revolution! The right side at this time was composed of members of the former left side; and the plan so dreaded and condemned, was not a return to the old system, but the establishment of an upper chamber. What a difference from 1789! How swiftly a foolish resistance had hurried on events!

Leopold perceived then no other possible amelioration for Louis XVI. Meanwhile, his object was to protract the negotiations, and, without breaking with France, to awe her by his firmness. But this aim he thwarted by his answer. This answer consisted in a notification of the resolutions of the diet of Ratisbon, which refused to accept any indemnity for the princes who had possessions in Alsace. Nothing could be more absurd than such a decision; for the whole territory subject to one and the same rule ought also to be subject to the same laws. If princes of the empire had estates in France, it was right that they should be comprehended in the abolition of feudal rights, and the Constituent Assembly had done a great deal in granting indemnities for them. Several of those princes having already treated on this point, the diet annulled their agreements, and forbade them to accept any composition. The empire thus pretended not to recognise the Revolution in as far as itself was concerned. With regard to the assemblages of emigrants, Leopold, without entering into explanation on the subject of their dispersion, answered Louis XVI. that, as the Elector of Treves might, according to the intimations of the French government, be exposed to speedy hostilities, he had ordered General Bender to give him prompt assistance.

Nothing could have been more injudicious than this answer. It obliged Louis XVI., in order that he might not compromise himself, to adopt vigorous measures and to propose war. Delessart was immediately sent to the Assembly to communicate this answer, and to express the astonishment which the King felt at the conduct of Leopold. The minister alleged that the Emperor had probably been deceived, and that he had been falsely persuaded that the Elector had performed all the duties of a friendly neighbour. Delessart communicated also the reply returned to Leopold. It was intimated to him that, notwithstanding his answer and the orders given to Marshal Bender, if the electors had not, by the time prescribed, namely, the 15th of

January, complied with the requisition of France, arms would be employed against them.

"If," said Louis XVI., in his letter to the Assembly, "this declaration fails to produce the effect which I have reason to hope from it, if it is the destiny of France to be obliged to fight her own children, and her allies, I will make known to Europe the justice of our cause: the French people will uphold it by their courage, and the nation will see that I have no other interest but its interests, and that I shall ever consider the maintenance of its dignity and safety as the most essential of my duties."

These words, in which the Fung seemed in the common danger to unite with the nation, were warmly applauded. The papers were delivered to the diplomatic committee, with directions to make a speedy report upon them to the Assembly.

The Queen was once more applauded at the Opera as in the days of her splendour and her power, and, quite overjoyed, she told her husband on her return that she had been received as formerly. But this was the last homage paid to her by a people which had once idolised her royal graces. That feeling of equality, which remains so long dormant in men, and which is so capricious when it does awake, began already to manifest itself on all sides. It was very near the conclusion of the year 1791; the Assembly abolished the ancient ceremonial of New-year's day, and decided that the homage paid to the King on that solemn day should thenceforth cease. Just about the same time, a deputation complained that the folding-doors of the council chamber had not been opened for it. The discussion was scandalous, and the Assembly, in writing to the King, suppressed the titles of sire and majesty. On another occasion, a deputy entered the King's apartment with his hat on, and in a very unsuitable dress. This conduct was frequently provoked by the rude reception given by the courtiers to the deputies; and, in these reprisals, the pride of both was determined not to be outdone.

Narbonne prosecuted his tour with extraordinary activity. Three armies were formed on the threatened frontier. Rochambeau, a veteran general, who had formerly displayed ability in war, but who was now ailing, ill-humoured, and discontented, commanded the army stationed in Flanders, and called the army of the North. Lafayette had the army of the centre, and was encamped near Metz. Luckner, an old warrior, an ordinary general, a brave soldier, and very popular in the army for his exclusively military manners, commanded the corps which occupied Alsace. These were all the generals that a long peace and a general desertion had left us.

Rochambeau, dissatisfied with the new system, and irritated with the want of discipline which prevailed in the army, was constantly complaining and held out no hope to the ministers. Lafayette, young, active, and anxious to distinguish himself forthwith in the defence of the country, re-established discipline among his troops, and overcame all the difficulties raised by the ill-will of the officers, who were the aristocrats of the army. He called them together, and addressing them in the language of honour, he told them that they must quit the camp if they would not serve loyally; that, if any of them wished to retire, he would undertake to procure them either pensions in France, or passports for foreign countries; but that, if they persisted in serving, he expected from them zeal and fidelity. In this manner he contrived to introduce into his army better order than that which prevailed in any of the others. As for Luckner, having no political opinion, and being consequently indifferent to all systems, he promised the Assembly a great deal, and actually succeeded in gaining the attachment of the soldiers.

Narbonne travelled with the greatest expedition, and returned to give an account of his rapid journey to the Assembly. He reported that the repair of the fortresses was already considerably advanced; that the army, from Dunkirk to Besancon, presented a mass of two hundred and forty battalions, and one hundred and sixty squadrons, with artillery requisite for two hundred thousand men, and supplies for six months.

He bestowed the highest encomiums on the patriotism of the volunteer national guards, and declared that in a short time their equipment would be complete. The young minister no doubt gave way to the illusions of zeal, but his intentions were so noble, and his operations so prompt, that the Assembly loaded him with applause, held forth his report to the public gratitude, and sent it to all the departments—the usual way of expressing esteem for those with whom it was satisfied.

War then was the great question of the moment. For the Revolution it was a question of existence itself. Its enemies being now abroad, it was there that it became necessary to seek and to conquer them. Would the King, as chief of the armies, act cordially against his relatives and his former courtiers? Such was the doubt which it was of importance to clear up to the satisfaction of the nation. This question of war was discussed at the Jacobins, which suffered none to pass without pronouncing a sovereign decision upon it. What will appear singular is, that the outrageous Jacobins, and Robespierre, their leader, were in favour of peace, and the moderate Jacobins, or Girondins, for war. Brissot and Louvet were at their head. Brissot advocated war with his talents and influence. He thought with Louvet and all the Girondins that it was desirable for the nation, because it would put an end to a dangerous uncertainty, and unveil the real intentions of the King. These men, judging of the result by their own enthusiasm, could not believe that the nation would be conquered; and they thought that if, through the fault of the King, it experienced any transient check, it would instantly be enlightened and depose an unfaithful chief. How happened it that Robespierre and the other Jacobins opposed a determination which must produce so speedy and so decisive a denouement? In answer to this question nothing but conjectures can be offered. Was the timid Robespierre afraid of war? Or did he oppose it only because Brissot, his rival at the Jacobins, supported it, and because young Louvet had defended it with ability? Be this as it may, he fought with extreme obstinacy for peace. The Cordeliers, who were Jacobins, attended the discussion, and supported Robespierre. They seemed more especially afraid lest war should give too many advantages to Lafayette, and soon procure for him the military dictatorship. This was the continual fear of Camille Desmoulins, who never ceased to figure him to himself at the head of a victorious army, as in the Champ de Mars, crushing Jacobins and Cordeliers. Louvet and the Girondins attributed a different motive to the Cordeliers, and supposed them to be hostile to Lafayette, because he was an enemy of the Duke of Orleans, with whom they were said to be secretly united.

The Duke of Orleans, now again brought before the public by the suspicions of his enemies rather than by the Revolution, was then nearly eclipsed. At the commencement, his name might have had some weight, and he himself might have conceived some hope of those to whom he lent it; but everything had since greatly changed. Feeling himself how much he was out of his place in the popular party, he had endeavoured to obtain the pardon of the court during the latter days of the Constituent Assembly, and had been repulsed. Under the Legislative, he had been retained in the list of admirals, and he had made fresh solicitations to the King. On this occasion he was admitted to his presence, had a long conversation with him, and was not unfavourably received. He was to return to the palace. He repaired thither. The Queen's dinner was served, and numerous courtiers were in attendance. No sooner was he perceived than the most insulting expressions were uttered. "Take care of the dishes!" was the general cry, as though they had been afraid that he would throw poison into them. They pushed him, trod on his toes, and obliged him to retire. As he went down stairs, he received fresh insults, and departed in deep indignation, conceiving that the King and Queen had prepared for him this humiliating scene. They, however, were totally ignorant of it, and were extremely shocked at the imprudence of the courtiers. (*See* Appendix G G G.) That prince had a right to be more exasperated than ever, but he certainly became neither a more active nor a more able party-leader than before. His friends at the Jacobins and in the Assembly, no doubt, thought fit to make a little more noise; hence it was supposed that his faction was again raising its head, and it was thought that his pretensions and his hopes were renewed by the dangers of the throne.

The Girondins imagined that the extreme Cordeliers and Jacobins advocated peace with no other view than to deprive Lafayette, the rival of the Duke of Orleans, of the reputation which war might give him. Be this as it may, war, deprecated by the Jacobins, but supported by the Girondins, could not fail to be adopted by the Assembly, in which the latter had the ascendency. The Assembly began by putting under accusation, from the 1st of January, Monsieur, the King's brother, the Count d'Artois, the Prince of Condé, Calonne, Mirabeau the younger, (*see* Appendix H H H.), and Lequeille as charged with the commission of hostilities against France. As a decree of accusation was not submitted to the King for his sanction, no veto was in this case to be apprehended. The sequestration of the property of the emigrants, and the application of their revenues to the benefit of the state, enacted by the unsanctioned decree, were prescribed anew by another decree, to which the King made no opposition. The Assembly took possession of the revenues as indemnities for the war. Monsieur was deprived of the regency by virtue of the resolution previously adopted.

The report on the last despatch of the emperor was at length presented to the Assembly by Gensonné. He represented that France had always lavished her treasures and her troops for Austria without ever obtaining any return; that the treaty of alliance concluded in 1756 had been violated by the declaration of Pilnitz, and the subsequent declarations, the object of which was to raise up an armed coalition of sovereigns; that this had likewise been done by the arming of the emigrants, permitted and even seconded by the princes of the empire. Gensonné, moreover, insisted that, though orders had recently been given for the dispersion of such assemblages, those apparent orders had not been executed; that the white cockade had not ceased to be worn beyond the Rhine, the national cockade to be insulted, and French travellers maltreated: that, in consequence, it behoved the Assembly to demand of the emperor a final explanation relative to the treaty of

1756. The report was ordered to be printed, and the consideration of it adjourned.

On the same day, January 14, 1792, Guadet ascended the tribune. "Of all the facts," said he, "communicated to the Assembly, that by which it has been most struck is the plan of a congress to be assembled for the purpose of obtaining the modification of the French constitution—a plan long suspected, and at length denounced as possible by the committees and the ministers. If it be true," added Guadet, "that this intrigue is conducted by men who fancy that they discover in it the means of emerging from that political nonentity into which they have just sunk; if it be true that some of the agents of the executive power are seconding with all the influence of their connexions this abominable plot; if it be true that they think to bring us by delay and discouragement to accept this ignominious mediation—ought the National Assembly to shut its eyes to such dangers? Let us swear," exclaimed the speaker, "to die, all of us, on this spot, rather . . . ." He was not allowed to finish: the whole Assembly rose, crying, "Yes, yes, we swear it;" and with enthusiasm it declared every Frenchman who should take part in a congress, the object of which was to modify the constitution, infamous and a traitor to his country. It was more especially against the members of the late Constituent Assembly, and Delessart, the minister, that this decree was directed. It was Delessart who was accused of protracting the negotiations. On the 17th, the discussion on Gensonné's report was resumed, and it was resolved that the King should not treat further, unless in the name of the French nation, and that he should require of the emperor a definitive explanation before the 1st of March ensuing. The King replied that it was more than a fortnight since he had demanded positive explanations from Leopold.

During this interval, news arrived that the Elector of Treves, alarmed at the urgency of the French cabinet, had issued fresh orders for the dispersion of the assemblages of troops, for the sale of the magazines formed in his dominions, and for prohibiting recruiting and military exercises; and that these orders were, in fact, carried into execution. In the then prevailing disposition, this intelligence was coldly received. The Assembly would not regard these measures in any other light than as empty demonstrations without result; and persisted in demanding the definitive answer of Leopold.

Dissensions existed in the ministry between Bertrand de Molleville and Narbonne. Bertrand was jealous of the popularity of the minister at war, and found fault with his condescension to the Assembly. Narbonne complained of the conduct of Bertrand de Molleville and of his unconstitutional sentiments, and wished that the King would dismiss him from the ministry. Cahier de Gerville held the balance between them, but without success. It was alleged that the constitutional party was desirous of raising Narbonne to the disunity of prime minister; it would even appear that the King was imposed upon, that the popularity and the ambition of Narbonne were employed as bugbears to frighten him, and that he was represented to him as a presumptuous young man who wanted to govern the cabinet. The newspapers were informed of these dissensions. Brissot and the Gironde warmly defended the minister who was threatened with disgrace, and as warmly attacked his colleagues and the King. A letter, written by the three generals of the north to Narbonne, in which they expressed their apprehensions respecting his dismissal, which was said to be near at hand, was published. The King, irritated at this, immediately dismissed him; but to counteract the effect of this dismissal, he declared his determination to remove Bertrand de Molleville also. The effect of the first, however, was not weakened by the latter step. It excited an extraordinary sensation, and the Assembly resolved to declare, agreeably to the form previously adopted in Necker's case, that Narbonne carried with him the confidence of the nation, and that the entire ministry had lost it. From that condemnation, however, it proposed to except Cahier de Gerville, who had always been hostile to Bertrand de Molleville, and who had even just had a violent quarrel with him. After much agitation, Brissot offered to prove that Delessart had betrayed the confidence of the nation. This minister had communicated to the diplomatic committee his correspondence with Kaunitz. It was without dignity, and even gave Kaunitz a very unfavourable notion of the state of France, and seemed to have authorized the conduct and the language of Leopold. It should be observed that Delessart and his colleague, Dupont-Dutertre, were the two ministers who belonged more particularly to the Feuillans, and who were most disliked, because they were accused of favouring the plan of a congress.

In one of the most stormy sittings of the Assembly, the unfortunate Delessart was accused by Brissot of having compromised the dignity of the nation, of having neglected to apprise the Assembly of the concert of the powers and the declaration of Pilnitz; of having professed unconstitutional doctrines in his notes; of having given Kaunitz a false notion of the state of France; of having protracted the negotiation, and conducted it in a manner contrary to the interests of the country. Vergniaud joined Brissot, and added new grievances to those imputed to Delessart. He reproached him for having, when minister of the interior, kept too long in his portfolio the decree which incorporated the Comtat with France, and thus having caused the massacres at Avignon. "From this tribune from which I address you," added Vergniaud, "may be seen the palace where perverse advisers mislead and deceive the King whom the constitution has given us. I see the windows of the palace where they are hatching counter-revolution, where they are combining the means of plunging us back into slavery. In ancient times terror has often stalked forth in the name of despotism from this famous palace; let it now return thither, in the name of the law; let it there seize every heart; let all those who dwell in it know that our constitution grants inviolability to the King alone."

The decree of accusation was immediately put to the vote and carried. Delessart was sent to the high national court, established at Orleans, which was empowered by the constitution to try crimes against the state. The King felt the greatest pain at his departure. He had given him his confidence, and been delighted with his moderate and pacific sentiments. Duport-Dutertre, minister of the constitutional party, was also threatened with accusation, but he anticipated it, demanded permission to justify himself, was absolved by the order of the day, and immediately afterwards resigned. Cahier de Gerville also gave in his resignation, and thus the King found himself deprived of the only one of his ministers who had a reputation for patriotism with the Assembly.

Separated from the ministers whom the Feuillans had given him, and not knowing to whom to cling amidst this storm, Louis XVI., who had dismissed Narbonne because he was too popular, thought of connecting himself with the Gironde, which was republican. It is true that it was so only from distrust of the King; and it was possible that, when he had once committed himself to this party, it might attach itself to him. But it would have been requisite that he should give himself up sincerely; and that everlasting question of sincerity arose here as on all other occasions. No doubt Louis XVI. was sincere when he consigned himself to a party, but it was not without ill-humour and regret. Thus when this party imposed upon him a difficult but necessary condition, he rejected it. Distrust instantly sprang up, animosity followed, and very soon a rupture was the consequence of those unhappy alliances between hearts which were exclusively occupied by two opposite interests. Thus it was that Louis XVI., after admitting the Feuillant party to his presence, had, in a fit of ill-humour, dismissed Narbonne, who was its most conspicuous chief, and now found himself reduced to the necessity of giving himself up to the Gironde, in order to allay the storm. The example of England, where the King frequently takes his ministers from the opposition, was one of the motives of Louis XVI. The court then conceived a hope—for people cannot help forming hopes, even in the most gloomy conjectures—that Louis XVI., by taking incapable and ridiculous demagogues, would ruin the reputation of the party from which he should have selected them. This hope, however, was not realised; and the new ministry was not such as the malice of the courtiers would have desired.

Above a month before this time, Delessart and Narboune had selected a man whose talents they held in high estimation, and placed him near them for the purpose of availing themselves of his abilities. This was Dumouriez, who, having successfully commanded in Normandy and in La Vendée, had everywhere displayed extraordinary firmness and intelligence. He had first offered himself to the court, and then to the Constituent Assembly, because all parties were the same to him, provided he had opportunities to exercise his activity and his superior talents. Dumouriez, kept down by the times in which he lived, had spent part of his life in diplomatic intrigues. With his bravery, and his military and political genius, he was still, at the age of fifty, and at the commencement of the Revolution, only a brilliant military adventurer. He had nevertheless retained the fire and the hardihood of youth, and, as soon as there appeared a prospect of a war or a revolution, he formed plans and addressed them to all the parties, ready to act for any, provided he could but act. He was thus accustomed not to take any account of the nature of the cause; but, though too little swayed by conviction, he was generous, sensible, and capable of attachment, if not for principles, at least for persons. Yet, with such a graceful, prompt, and comprehensive mind, and courage alternately calm and impetuous, he was admirable for serving, but incapable of directing. He had neither the dignity of a profound conviction nor the pride of a despotic will, and he could command none but soldiers. If, with his genius, he had possessed the passions of a Mirabeau, or the resolution of a Cromwell, or merely the dogmatism of a Robespierre, he might have directed the course of the Revolution, and France.

No sooner was Dumouriez connected with Narbonne, than he formed a vast military plan. He was at once for offensive and defensive war. Wherever France extended to her natural limits, the Rhine, the Alps, the Pyrenees, and the sea, he proposed that she should confine herself to the defensive. But in the Netherlands, where our territory did not extend to the Rhine, and in Savoy, where it did not extend to the Alps, he proposed that we should attack immediately, and that, on reaching the natural limits, we should resume the defensive. This would have been reconciling at once our interests with our principles, as it would have been profiting by a war which we had not provoked, to return on the score of boundaries to the genuine laws of nature. Dumouriez proposed a fourth army, destined to occupy the South, and applied for the command of it, which was promised him.

Dumouriez had gained the good-will of Gensonné, one of the civil commissioners sent into La Vendée by the Constituent Assembly, afterwards a deputy to the Legislative Assembly, and one of the most influential members of the Gironde. He had remarked, moreover, that the Jacobins were the predominating power. He had attended their club and read several memorials, which had been highly applauded, but had nevertheless kept up his former intimacy with Delaporte, intendant of the civil list, and a devoted friend of Louis XVI. Connected thus with the different powers which were on the point of uniting, Dumouriez could not fail to carry all before him and to be called to the ministry. Louis XVI. offered him the portfolio of foreign affairs, which the decree of accusation against Delessart had just rendered vacant; but, still attached to the accused minister, the King offered it only *ad interim*. Dumouriez, feeling that he was powerfully supported, and disliking to appear to keep the place for a Feuillant minister, refused the portfolio, and obtained it without an *ad interim* stipulation. He found only Cahier de Gerville and Degraves in the ministry. Cahier de Gerville, though he had given in his resignation, had not yet relinquished duties. Degraves had succeeded Narbonne. He was young, easy, and inexperienced. Dumouriez contrived to gain him, and thus he held in his hands the foreign relations and the military administration of the war. Nothing less would have satisfied his enterprising spirit.

No sooner had he attained the ministry than Dumouriez put on the red cap at the Jacobins—a new distinction borrowed from the Phrygians, and which had become the emblem of liberty. He promised to govern for them and by them. On being presented to Louis XVI., he pacified him respecting his conduct at the Jacobins. He removed the prejudices which that conduct had excited; he had the art to touch him by testimonies of attachment, and to dispel his gloomy melancholy by his wit. He persuaded him that if he sought popularity it was only for the benefit of the throne and for the purpose of strengthening it. But, notwithstanding all his deference, he took care to make the prince sensible that the constitution was inevitable, and endeavoured to console him by striving to prove that with it a King might still be very powerful. His first despatches to the powers, full of sound reason and firmness, changed the nature of the negotiations, and gave France quite a new attitude, but rendered war imminent. It was natural that Dumouriez should desire war, since he had a genius for it, and had meditated thirty-six years on that great art; but it must also be admitted that the conduct of the cabinet of Vienna, and the irritation of the Assembly, had rendered it inevitable.

Dumouriez, from his conduct at the Jacobins and his known connexion with the Gironde, could not, even without any hatred against the Feuillans, help embroiling himself with them. Besides, he had displaced them. He was, therefore, in continual opposition to all the chiefs of that party. Braving the sarcasms and the contempt which they levelled against the Jacobins and the Assembly, he determined to pursue his career with his accustomed assurance.

It was necessary to complete the ministry. Petion, Gensonné, and Brissot, were consulted respecting the persons to be selected. According to the law, the ministers could not be taken either from the present or from the last Assembly: the choice, therefore, was extremely limited. Dumouriez proposed for the marine, Lacoste, who had formerly been employed in that department, an industrious and experienced man, an obstinate patriot, who nevertheless was attached to the King, was esteemed by him, and remained about him longer than all the others. It was further proposed to give the ministry of justice to young Louvet, who had recently distinguished himself at the Jacobins, and who had won the favour of the Gironde, since he had so ably supported the opinion of Brissot in favour of war. The envious Robespierre caused him to be immediately denounced. Louvet successfully justified himself; but, as it was not deemed right to take one whose popularity was contested, Duranthon (*see* Appendix I I I.), an advocate of Bordeaux, an enlightened, upright, but weak man, was sent for. The ministry of the finances and of the interior yet remained to be filled up. The Gironde again proposed Clavières (*see* Appendix K K K.), who was known by some highly esteemed works on finance. The minister appointed to the interior was Roland (*see* Appendix L L L.), formerly inspector of manufactories, who had distinguished himself by some excellent publications on industry and the mechanical arts. This man, with austere manners, inflexible opinions, and a cold, forbidding look, yielded, without being aware of it, to the superior ascendancy of his wife. Madame Roland was young and beautiful. Bred in the depths of retirement, and imbued with philosophic and republican ideas, she had conceived notions superior to those of her sex, and had formed a severe religion out of the then prevailing principles. Living in the closest friendship with her husband, she lent him her pen, communicated to him a portion of her own vivacity, infused her own ardour not only into him but into all the Girondins, who, enthusiasts for liberty and philosophy, admired her beauty and intelligence, and were influenced by her opinions, which were in fact their own opinions. (*See* Appendix M M M.)

The new ministry comprehended abilities great enough for its prosperity; but it behoved it not to displease Louis XVI., and to keep up its alliance with the Gironde. It might then prove adequate to its task; but if blunders of individuals were to be added to the incompatibility of the parties which had united, all would be lost—and this was what could not fail to happen very speedily. Louis XVI., struck by the activity of his ministers, by their good intentions, and by their talent for business, was for a moment delighted, especially with their economical reforms; for he had always been fond of that kind of improvement which required no sacrifice either of power or of principle. If he could always have felt the confidence which he did then, and have separated himself from the hangers-on of the court, he might easily have reconciled himself to the constitution. This he repeated with sincerity to the ministers, and succeeded in convincing the two most difficult, Roland and Clavières. The persuasion was complete on both sides. The Gironde, which was republican solely from distrust of the King, ceased then to be so; and Vergniaud, Gensonné, and Gaudet, entered into correspondence with Louis XVI., which was subsequently one of the charges in the accusation preferred against them. The inflexible wife of Roland was alone doubtful, and kept back her friends, who were too ready, as she said, to surrender themselves. The reason of her distrust is natural. She never saw the King. The ministers, on the other hand, had daily interviews with him, and honest men, when they meet, soon feel satisfied with one another. But this confidence could not last, because inevitable questions were on the point of displaying the wide difference of their opinions.

The court strove to throw ridicule on the somewhat republican simplicity of the new ministry, and on the unpolished rudeness of Roland, who appeared at the palace without buckles to his shoes. Dumouriez returned these sarcasms, and, mingling mirth with the most serious business, pleased the King, charmed him by his wit, and perhaps too suited him better than the others, from the flexibility of his opinions. The Queen, perceiving that he had more influence over the mind of the monarch than any of his colleagues, was desirous of seeing him. He has recorded in his memoirs this extraordinary interview, which shows the agitation of that princess, worthy of another reign, other friends, and another fate.

On being ushered into the Queen's apartment, he found her, he says, alone, her face much flushed, walking hastily to and fro, with an agitation which seemed to betoken a warm explanation. He was going to post himself at the corner of the fire-place, painfully affected at the state of this princess, and the terrible sensations from which she was suffering. She advanced towards him with a majestic air and angry look, and said, "Sir, you are all-powerful at this moment, but it is through the favour of the people, who soon break their idols in pieces. Your existence depends on your conduct. It is said that you possess great abilities. You must be aware that neither the King nor myself can endure all these innovations on the constitution. This I tell you frankly: choose your side."

"Madam," he replied, "I am deeply pained by the secret which your majesty has just imparted to me. I will not betray it; but I stand between the King and the nation, and I belong to my country. Permit me to represent to you that the welfare of the King, your own, and that of your august children, is linked with the constitution, as well as the re-establishment of legitimate authority. I should do you disservice and the King too, if I were to hold any other language. You are both surrounded by enemies, who are sacrificing you to their private interest. The constitution, when once it shall be in vigour, so far from bringing misery upon the King, will constitute his happiness and his glory. It is absolutely necessary that he should concur in establishing it solidly and speedily." The unfortunate Queen, shocked at this contradiction of her opinions, raising her voice, angrilv exclaimed, "That will not last. Take care of yourself!"

Dumouriez rejoined with modest firmness, "Madame, I am past fifty; my life has been crossed by many perils, and, in accepting the ministry I was thoroughly sensible that responsibility is not the greatest of my dangers."—"Nothing more was wanting." she cried, with deep chagrin, "but to calumniate me. You seem to think me capable of causing you to be murdered," and tears trickled from her eyes.

"God preserve me," said Dumouriez, as much agitated as herself, "from doing you so cruel an injury! The character of your majesty is great and noble; you have given heroic proofs of it, which I have admired, and which have attached me to you." At this moment she became more calm and drew nearer to him. He continued: "Believe me, madame, I have no interest in deceiving you. I abhor anarchy and crime as much as you do. This is not a transient popular movement, as you seem to think. It is an almost unanimous insurrection of a mighty nation against inveterate abuses. Great factions fan this flame. In all of them there are villains and madmen. In the Revolution I keep in view only the King and the entire nation; all that tends to part them leads to their mutual ruin; I strive as much as possible to unite them; it is for you to assist me. If I am an obstacle to your designs, if you persist in them tell me so; I will instantly send my resignation to the King, and hide myself in some corner, to mourn over the fate of my country and over yours."

The concluding part of this conversation entirely restored the confidence of the Queen. They reviewed together the different factions; he pointed out to her the blunders and crimes of all; he proved to her that she was betrayed by those about her; and repeated the language held by persons in her most intimate confidence. . The princess appeared in the end to be entirely convinced, and dismissed him with a serene and affable look. She was sincere; but those around her and the horrible excesses of the papers written by. Marat (*See* Appendix N N N.) and the Jacobins soon drove her back to her baneful resolutions.

On another occasion she said to Dumouriez, in the presence of the King, "You see me very sad. I dare not approach the window which looks into the garden. Yesterday evening, I Went to the window towards the court, just to take a little air, a gunner of the guard addressed me in terms' of vulgar abuse, adding, 'How I should like to see your head on the point of my bayonet! 'In this horrid garden you see on one side a man mounted on a chair, reading aloud the most abominable calumnies against us; on the other, a military man or an abbé, dragged through one of the basins, overwhelmed with abuse, and beaten; whilst others are playing at ball or quietly walking about. What an abode! What a people!" (*See* Appendix O O O.)

Thus, by a kind of fatality, the supposed intentions of the palace excited the distrust and the fury of the people, and the uproar of the people increased the anxiety and the imprudence of the palace. Despair therefore reigned within and without. But why, it may be asked, did not a candid explanation put an end to so many evils? Why did not the palace comprehend the fears of the people? Why did not the people comprehend the afflictions of the palace? But, why are men men? At this last question we must pause, submissively resign ourselves to human nature, and pursue our melancholy story.

Leopold II. was dead. The pacific dispositions of that prince were to be regretted for the tranquillity of Europe, and the same moderation could not be hoped for from his successor and nephew, the Tung of Bohemia and Hungary. Gustavus, King of Sweden, had just been assassinated during an entertainment. The enemies of the Jacobins attributed this murder to them; tut it was fully proved to be the crime of the nobility, humbled by Gustavus in the last Swedish Revolution. Thus the nobility, who in France cried out against the revolutionary fury of the people, gave in the north an example of what it had formerly been itself, and of what it still was in countries where civilization was least advanced. What an example for Louis XVI., and what a lesson, if at the moment he could have comprehended it! The death of Gustavus thwarted the enterprise which he had meditated against France—an enterprise for which Catherine was to furnish soldiers and Spain subsidies. It is doubtful, however, if the perfidious Catherine would have performed her promise, and the death of Gustavus, from which most important consequences were anticipated, was in reality a very insignificant event. (*See* Appendix P P P.)

Delessart had been impeached on account of the feeble tone of his despatches. It was not consonant either with the disposition or the interest of Dumouriez to treat feebly with the powers. The last despatches appeared to satisfy Louis XVI. on account of their aptness and their firmness. M. de Noailles, ambassador at Vienna, and by no means a sincere servant, sent his resignation to Dumouriez, saying that he had no hope of making the head of the empire listen to the language that had just been dictated to him. Dumouriez lost no time in communicating the circumstance to the Assembly, which, indignant at this resignation, immediately passed a decree of accusation against M. de Noailles. A new ambassador was instantly sent with fresh despatches. Two days afterwards, Noailles recalled his resignation, and sent the categorical answer which he had required from the court of Vienna.

Among all the faults committed by the powers, this note of M. de Cobentzel's is one of the most impolitic. M. de Cobentzel insisted, in the name of his court, on the re-establishment of the French monarchy on the bases fixed by the royal declaration of the 23rd of June, 1789. This was equivalent to requiring the re-establishment of the three orders, the restitution of the property of the clergy, and that of the Comtat-Venaissin to the Pope. The Austrian minister moreover demanded the restoration of the domains in Alsace, with all their feudal rights, to the princes of the empire. In order to propose such conditions, a man must have known nothing of France unless through the medium of the passions of Coblentz. It was demanding at once the destruction of a constitution sworn to by the King and the nation, and the repeal of a decisive determination in regard to Avignon. Lastly, it was imposing the necessity of bankruptcy by the restitution of the possessions of the clergy, already sold. Besides, what right had the emperor to claim such a submission? What right had he to interfere in our affairs? What complaint had he to make for the princes of Alsace, since their domains were enclosed by the French territory, and must of course submit to the same laws as that?

The first movement of the King and Dumouriez was to hasten to the Assembly and to communicate to it this note. The Assembly was indignant, and justly so. The cry for war was universal. But Dumouriez did not inform the Assembly that Austria, which he had threatened with a fresh revolution at Liege, had sent an agent to treat with him on that subject; that the language of this agent was totally different from that held at this moment by the Austrian ministry; and that this note was evidently the effect of a sudden and suggested resolution. The Assembly annulled the decree of accusation passed against Noailles, and demanded a speedy report. The King could no longer recede. That fatal war was at length on the point of being declared. In no case could it be favourable to his interests. If victorious, the French would become more urgent and more inexorable relative to the observance of the new law. If vanquished, they would find fault with the government and accuse it of having feebly carried on the war.

Louis XVI. was perfectly aware of this double danger, and this resolution was one of those which were most painful to him. (*See* Appendix Q Q Q.) Dumouriez drew up his report with his usual celerity, and carried it to the King, who kept it three days. It became a question whether the King, obliged to take the initiative with the Assembly, would urge it to declare war, or whether he would content himself with consulting it on this subject, in announcing that, agreeably to the injunctions given, France was in a state of war. The ministers Roland and Clavières were in favour of the former procedure. The orators of the Gironde likewise supported it, and were for dictating the speech from the throne. Louis XVI. felt repugnance to declare war, and preferred declaring the country in a state of war. The difference was unimportant, yet to his mind the one was preferable to the other. Dumouriez, whose mind was more easily made up, listened to none of the ministers; and, supported by Degraves, Lacoste, and Duranthon, caused the King's opinion to be adopted. This was his first quarrel with the Gironde. The King composed his speech himself, and repaired in person to the Assembly, followed by all his ministers. A considerable concourse of spectators added to the effect of this sitting, which was about to decide the fate of France and of Europe. The King's features appeared careworn, and indicated deep thought. Dumouriez read a detailed report of the negotiations of France with the Empire; he showed that the treaty of 1756 was *de facto* broken, and that, according to the last ultimatum, France was in a *state of war*. He added that the King, having no other legal medium for consulting the Assembly but the *formal proposal of war*, submitted to consult in that manner. Louis XVI. then spoke with dignity but with a faltering voice. "Gentlemen," said he, "you have just heard the result of the negotiations in which I have been engaged with the court of Vienna. The conclusions of the report have been unanimously approved by my council: I have myself adopted them. They are conformable with the wish which the National Assembly has several times expressed, and with the sentiments communicated to me by a great number of citizens in different parts of the kingdom: all would rather have war than see the dignity of the French people any longer insulted, and the national security threatened.

"Having previously, as it was my duty, employed all possible means to maintain peace, I now come, agreeably to the terms of the constitution, to propose to the National Assembly war against the King of Hungary and Bohemia."

This proposal was most warmly received: shouts of "*Vive le Roi!*" resounded on all sides. The Assembly answered that it would deliberate, and that the King should be apprised by a message of the result of the deliberation. A most stormy discussion immediately commenced, and continued till the night was far advanced. The reasons already given pro and con were here repeated; the decree was at length passed, and war resolved upon by a great majority.

"Considering," said the Assembly, "that the court of Vienna, in contempt of treaties, has not ceased to grant open protection to French rebels; that it has provoked and formed a concert with several powers of Europe against the independence and the safety of the French nation;

"That Francis I., King of Hungary and Bohemia, has, by his notes of the 18th of March and the 7th of April last, refused to renounce this concert;

"That, notwithstanding the proposal made to him by the note of the 11th of March, 1792, to reduce the troops upon the frontiers, on both sides, to the peace establishment, he has continued, and augmented his hostile preparations;

"That he has formally attacked the sovereignty of the French nation, by declaring his determination to support the pretensions of the German princes holding possessions in France, to whom the French nation has not ceased to offer indemnities;

"That he has sought to divide the French citizens and to arm them, one against the other, by offering to support the malcontents in concert with the other powers;

"Considering, lastly, that the refusal to answer the last despatches of the King of the French leaves no hope of obtaining an amicable redress of these various grievances by means of an amicable negotiation, and is equivalent to a declaration of war, the Assembly declares that it is compelled," &c. &c.

It must be admitted that this cruel war, which for so long a period afflicted Europe, was not provoked by France but by the foreign powers. France, in declaring it, did no more than recognise by a decree the state in which she had been placed. Condorcet was directed to draw up an exposition of the motives of the nation. History ought to preserve this paper, an admirable model of reasoning and moderation. (*See* Appendix R R R.)

The war occasioned general joy. The patriots beheld in it the end of those apprehensions which they felt on account of the emigration and the wavering conduct of the King. The moderates, alarmed by divisions, hoped that the common danger would put an end to them, and that the fields of battle would absorb all the turbulent spirits generated by the Revolution. Some Feuillans alone, glad to find faults in the Assembly, reproached it with having violated the constitution, according to which, France ought never to be in a state of aggression. It is but too evident that here France was not the assailant. Thus, war was the general wish of all excepting the King and a few discontented persons.

Lafayette prepared to serve his country bravely in this new career. It was he who was more particularly charged with the execution of the plan conceived by Dumouriez and apparently ordered by Degraves. Dumouriez had justly flattered himself, and given all the patriots reason to hope, that the invasion of the Netherlands would be an easy task. That country, recently agitated by a revolution, which Austria had suppressed, might naturally be expected to be disposed to rise on the first appearance of the French, and then would be fulfilled the warning of the Assembly to the sovereigns—"If you send us war, we will send you back liberty." It was, moreover, the execution of the plan conceived by Dumouriez, which consisted in extending the French territory to its natural frontiers.

Rochambeau commanded the army close to the scene of action, but he could not be charged with this operation on account of his peevish and discontented disposition, and more especially because he was less fitted than Lafayette for an invasion half military, half popular. It was wished that Lafayette might have the general command, but Dumouriez refused to comply, no doubt from ill-will. He alleged, as a reason, that it was impossible, in the presence of a marshal, to give the chief command of that expedition to a mere general. He said, moreover, and this reason was not quite so bad, that Lafayette was suspected by the Jacobins and by the Assembly. It is certain that, young, active, the only one of all the generals who was beloved by his army, Lafayette was a terror to overheated imaginations, and furnished occasion, by his influence, to the calumnies of the malignant. Be this as it may, he cheerfully offered to execute the plan of the ministry, at once diplomatic and military: he demanded fifty thousand men, with whom he proposed to push forward by Namur and the Meuse to Liege, the possession of which would make him master of the Netherlands.

This plan was judicious, and it was approved by Dumouriez. War had been declared only a few days. Austria had not had time to cover her possessions in the Netherlands, and success appeared certain. Accordingly, Lafayette was ordered at first to advance with ten thousand men from Givet to Namur, and from Namur to Liege or Brussels. He was to be followed immediately by his whole army. While he was executing this movement, Lieutenant-Greneral Biron was to set out from Valenciennes with ten thousand men, and to march upon Mons. Another officer had orders to proceed to Tournay, and to take possession of it immediately. These movements, conducted by officers of Rochambeau's, were intended to support and mask the real attack committed to Lafayette.

The orders given to this effect were to be executed between the 20th of April and the 2nd of May. Biron commenced his march, left Valenciennes, made himself master of Quievrain, and found a few hostile detachments near Mons. All at once, two regiments of dragoons, though not in presence of the enemy, cried out, "We are betrayed!" betook themselves to flight, and were followed by the whole army. In vain the officers strove to stop the fugitives, they threatened to shoot them, and continued their flight. The camp was given up, and all the military effects fell into the hands of the Imperialists.

While this event was occurring at Mons, Theobald Dillon left Lille, according to a preconcerted plan, with two thousand infantry and a thousand horse. In the very same hour that Biron's disaster happened, the cavalry, at the sight of some Austrian troops, gave way, crying out that it was betrayed. It hurried the infantry along with it, and again the whole of the baggage was abandoned to the enemy. Theobald Dillon and an officer of engineers, named Berthois, were murdered by the soldiers and the populace of Lille, who insisted that they were traitors.

Meanwhile Lafayette, apprised too late of these circumstances, had proceeded from Metz to Givet, after encountering extreme difficulties, and by roads that were scarcely passable. Nothing but the ardour of his troops enabled him to perform, in so short a time, the considerable distance which he had traversed. There, learning the disasters of Rochambeau's officers, he thought it right to halt.

This intelligence produced a general agitation. It was natural to suppose that these two events had been concerted, judging from their coincidence and their simultaneous occurrence. All the parties accused one another. The Jacobins and the furious patriots insisted that there was a design to betray the cause of liberty. Dumouriez, not accusing Lafayette, but suspecting the Feuillans, conceived that there had been a scheme to thwart his plan, in order to make him unpopular. Lafayette complained, but less bitterly than his party, that he had been directed too late to commence his march, and that he had not been furnished with all the means necessary for accomplishing it. The Feuillans, moreover, reported that Dumouriez had designed to ruin Rochambeau and Lafayette by chalking out a plan for them, without giving them the means of executing it. Such an intention was not to be supposed; for Dumouriez, in stepping beyond the duty of minister for foreign affairs in order to form a plan of campaign, incurred a grievous risk in case of its failure. Besides, the project of gaining Belgium for France and liberty formed part of a plan which he had long meditated: how then could it be imagined that he wished to make it miscarry? It was evident that in this case neither the minister nor the generals could be insincere, because they were all interested in succeeding. But parties always put persons in the place of circumstances, that they may throw upon some one the blame of the disasters which befal them.

Degraves, alarmed at the tumult excited by the recent military events, determined to resign an office which had long been too arduous for him, and Dumouriez was wrong in not undertaking it. Louis XVI., still under the sway of the Gironde, gave that department to Servan, an old soldier, known for his patriotic opinions. This choice gave increased strength to the Gironde, which found itself almost in a majority in the council, having Servian, Clavières, and Roland, at its disposal. From that moment, discord began to prevail among the ministers. The Gironde daily became more distrustful, and consequently more urgent for demonstrations of sincerity on the part of Louis XVI. Dumouriez, who was but little guided by opinions, and who was touched by the confidence of the King, always took his part. Lacoste, who was strongly attached to the prince, did the same. Duranthon was neuter, and had no preference but for the weakest parties. Servan, Clavières, and Roland, were inflexible. Filled with the fears of their friends, they daily showed themselves more impracticable and inexorable at the council.

Another circumstance completed the rupture between Dumouriez and the principal members of the Gironde. Dumouriez, on accepting the ministry for foreign affairs, had demanded six millions for secret services, and insisted that he should not be called upon to account for the expenditure of that sum. The Feuillans had opposed this, but, through the influence of the Gironde, his demand proved triumphant, and the six millions were granted. Petion had applied for funds for the police of Paris; Dumouriez had allowed him thirty thousand francs per month; but, ceasing to be a Girondin, he permitted only one payment to be made. On the other hand, it was learnt or suspected that he had just spent one hundred thousand francs upon his pleasures. Roland, around whom rallied the Gironde, was, with all his friends, highly indignant at this circumstance. The ministers dined with one another by turns, for the purpose of conversing on public affairs. When they met at the house of Roland, it was in the presence of his wife and all his friends; and we may say that the council was then held by the Gironde itself. It was at such a meeting that remonstrances were made to Dumouriez on the nature of his secret expenses. At first he replied with gaiety and good-humour, afterwards lost his temper, and quarrelled decidedly with Roland and the Girondins. He ceased to attend at these accustomed parties, and alleged as his reason that he would not talk of public affairs either before a woman or before Roland's friends. He nevertheless went occasionally to Roland's, but either said very little, or nothing at all, concerning business. Another discussion widened still further the breach between him and the Girondins. Guadet, the most petulant of his party, read a letter, proposing that the ministers should induce the King to choose for his spiritual director a priest who had taken the oath. Dumouriez maintained that the ministers could not interfere in the religious exercises of the King. He was supported, it is true, by Vergniaud and Gensonné; but the quarrel was not the less violent, and a rupture became inevitable.

The newspapers commenced the attack upon Dumouriez. The Feuillans, who were already leagued against him, then found themselves aided by the Jacobins and the Girondins. Dumouriez, assailed on all sides, firmly confronted the storm, and caused severe measures to be taken against some of the journalists.

A decree of accusation had already been directed against Marat, author of the *Ami du Peuple*; an atrocious work, in which he openly advocated murder, and heaped the most audacious insults on the royal family, and on all who were objects of suspicion to his frenzied imagination. To counterbalance the effect of this measure, a decree of accusation was obtained against Royou, who was the author of the *Ami du Roi*, and who inveighed against the republicans with the same violence that Marat displayed against the royalists.

For a long time past, a great deal had been said concerning an Austrian committee. The patriots talked of it in the city, as the Orleans faction was talked of at court. To this committee a secret and mischievous influence was attributed, which was exercised through the medium of the Queen. If any thing resembling an Austrian committee had existed in the time of the Constituent Assembly, there was nothing of the kind under the Legislative. At the former period an illustrious personage, who held an appointment in the Netherlands, communicated to the Queen, in the name of her family, some very prudent advice, which was still more prudently commented upon by the French intermediate agent. But under the Legislative Assembly these private communications had ceased; the Queen's family had continued its correspondence with her, but never omitted to recommend patience and resignation to her. It is true that Bertrand de Molleville and Montmorin still paid visits to the palace after their removal from the ministry. It was against them that all suspicions were directed, and they were, in fact, the agents of all the secret commissions. They were publicly accused by Carra, the journalist. Determined to prosecute him as a calumniator, they summoned him to produce documents in support of his denunciation. The journalist backed himself by three deputies, and named Chabot, Merlin, and Bazire, as the authors of the particulars which he had published. Larivière, justice of the peace, who was devoted to the cause of the King, prosecuted this affair with great courage, and had the boldness to issue a summons against the three above-mentioned deputies. The Assembly, indignant at this attack on the inviolability of its members, replied to the justice of peace by a decree of accusation, and sent the unfortunate Larivière to Orleans. (*See* Appendix S S S.)

This unlucky attempt served only to increase the general agitation, and the hatred which prevailed against the court. The Gironde no longer considered itself as guiding Louis XVI., since Dumouriez had established his influence over him, and it had resumed its part of violent opposition.

The new constitutional guard of the King had been recently formed. Agreeably to the law, the civil establishment also ought to have been composed; but the nobility would not enter into it, that they might not recognise the constitution by filling posts which it had created. On the other hand, there was a determination not to compose it of new men, and it was abandoned. "How will you, madam," wrote Barnave to the Queen, "continue to raise the least doubt in those people concerning your sentiments? When they decree you a military and a civil establishment, like young Achilles among the daughters of Lycomedes, you eagerly grasp the sword and put away mere ornaments." The ministers, and Bertrand himself, remonstrated on their part to the same purpose as Bar-nave, but they could not carry their point, and the composition of the civil establishment was abandoned.

The military establishment, formed agreeably to a plan proposed by Delessart, had been composed, one-third of troops of the line, and two-thirds of young citizens selected from the national guards. This composition could not but appear satisfactory. But the officers and the soldiers of the line had been chosen in such a manner as to alarm the patriots. Combined against the young men taken from the national guards, they had rendered the situation of the latter so disagreeable, that most of them had been obliged to retire. The vacancies had soon been filled up by trusty men: the number of this guard had been singularly increased; and, instead of eighteen hundred men fixed by the law, the number had been swelled, it is said, to nearly six thousand. Dumouriez had apprised the King of this circumstance, and he always replied that the old Duke de Brissac, who commanded these troops, could not be regarded as a conspirator.

Meanwhile, the conduct of the new guard at the palace and at other places was such, that suspicions were expressed in all quarters, and the clubs took up the subject. At the same period, twelve Swiss hoisted the white cockade at Neuilly; a considerable quantity of paper was burned at Sèvres (*See* Appendix T T T.), and these proceedings gave rise to serious suspicions. The alarm then became general; the Assembly declared itself permanent, as though it was still the time when thirty thousand men threatened Paris. It is true, however, that the disturbances were general; that the nonjuring priests were exciting the people in the southern provinces, and abusing the secrecy of confession to kindle fanaticism; that the concert of the powers was manifest; that Prussia was on the point of joining Austria; that the foreign armies became threatening, and that the recent disasters of Lille and Mons was the general topic of conversation. It is, moreover, true that the power of the people excites little confidence, that it is never believed till it has been exercised, and that an irregular multitude, how numerous soever it may be, cannot counterbalance the force of six thousand men, armed and disciplined.

The Assembly therefore lost no time in declaring itself permanent, and it caused an accurate report to be drawn up respecting the composition of the King's military establishment, and the number, choice, and conduct of those who composed it. After deciding that the constitution had been violated, it issued a decree for disbanding the guard, and another of accusation against the Duke de Brissac, and sent both these decrees for the royal sanction. The King was disposed at first to affix his veto. Dumouriez reminded him of the dismissal of his life-guards, who had been much longer in his service than his new military household, and exhorted him to make this second and much less difficult sacrifice. He recapitulated, besides, the positive faults committed by his guard, and obtained the execution of the decree. But he immediately insisted on its recomposition; and the King, either returning to his former policy of appearing to be oppressed, or relying upon this disbanded guard, whose pay he secretly continued, refused to replace it, and was thus exposed, without protection, to the popular fury.

The Gironde, despairing of the King's sincerity, followed up its attack with perseverance. It had already issued a new decree against the priests, instead of that which the King had refused to sanction. As reports of their factious conduct were continually arriving, it pronounced the sentence of banishment upon them. The designation of the culprits was difficult; and as this measure, like all those of safety, rested upon suspicion, it was according to their notoriety that the priests were judged and banished. On the denunciation of twenty active citizens, and with the approbation of the directory of the district, the directory of the department pronounced sentence. The condemned priest was obliged to leave the canton in twenty-four hours, the department in three days, and the kingdom in a month. If he was indigent, three livres a day were granted him till he reached the frontiers.

This severe law proved the increasing irritation of the Assembly. It was immediately followed by another. Servan, the minister, without having received any orders from the King, or consulting his colleagues, proposed that, on the approaching anniversary of the Federation of the 14th of July, there should be formed a camp of twenty thousand federalists, destined to protect the Assembly and the capital. It may easily be conceived with what enthusiasm this plan was hailed by the majority of the Assembly, consisting of Girondins. At this moment the power of the latter was at its height. They governed the Assembly, where the constitutionalists and the republicans were in a minority, and where those who called themselves impartial were, as at all times, but indifferent persons, ever more complying the more powerful the majority became. Moreover, they had Paris at their beck, through Petion, the mayor, who was wholly devoted to them. Their plan was by means of the proposed camp, without personal ambition, but from ambition of party and of opinion, to make themselves masters of the King, and to forestall his suspicious intentions.

No sooner was Servan's proposal known, than Dumouriez asked him, in full council, and with the strongest emphasis, in what character he made such a proposition. He replied, that it was in the character of a private individual. "In that case," replied Dumouriez, "you should not put after the name of Servan the title of minister at war." The dispute became so warm, that, but for the King's presence, blood would probably have been spilt in the council. Servan offered to withdraw his motion; but this would have been useless, as the Assembly had taken it up; and the King, instead of gaining anything by it, would have appeared to exercise a violence upon his minister. Dumouriez, therefore, opposed this; the motion was persevered in, and was combated by a petition signed by eight thousand of the national guard, who were offended because it seemed to be thought that their service was insufficient for the protection of the Assembly. It was nevertheless carried, and sent to the King. Thus there were two important decrees awaiting his sanction, and it was already surmised that the King would refuse his adhesion to them. In this case, the Assembly was prepared to pass a definitive resolution against him.

Dumouriez maintained, in full council, that this measure would be fatal to the throne, but still more so to the Girondins, because the new army would be formed under the influence of the most violent Jacobins. He nevertheless added that it ought to be adopted by the King, because, if he refused to convoke twenty thousand men regularly chosen, forty thousand would spontaneously rise and make themselves masters of the capital. Dumouriez, moreover, declared that he had an expedient for annulling this measure, and which he would communicate at the fitting time. In like manner, he insisted that the decree respecting the banishment of the priests ought to be sanctioned, because they were culpable, and besides, exile would withdraw them from the fury of their enemies. Still Louis XVI. hesitated, and replied that he would consider farther of it. At the same council, Roland insisted on reading, in the

King's presence, a letter which he had already addressed to him, and which it was consequently superfluous to communicate to him a second time viva voce. This letter had been determined upon at the instigation of Madame Roland, and it was her composition. It had been previously proposed that one should be written in the name of all the ministers. They had refused; but Madame Roland continued to urge the point upon her husband, till he resolved to take the step in his own name. To no purpose did Duranthon, who was weak but discreet, object with reason that the tone of his letter, so far from persuading the King, would only sour him against his ministers, who possessed the public confidence, and that a fatal rupture between the throne and the popular party would be the result of it. Roland persisted, agreeably to the advice of his wife and his friends. The Gironde, in fact, was bent on coming to an explanation, and preferred a rupture to an uncertainty.

Roland, therefore, read this letter to the King, and made him listen in full council to the harshest remonstrances. This famous letter was as follows:

"Sire,—The present state of France cannot last long. It is a state of crisis, the violence of which has nearly attained the highest degree; it must terminate in a catastrophe which cannot but interest your Majesty as deeply as it concerns the whole empire.

"Honoured by your confidence, and placed in a post which renders truth an imperative duty, I will venture to tell the whole truth: it is an obligation which is imposed upon me by yourself.

"The French have given themselves a constitution, which has made malcontents and rebels: nevertheless, the majority of the nation is determined to uphold that constitution. It has sworn to defend it at the price of its blood, and it has hailed with joy the war which presented a powerful medium for securing it. The minority, however, supported by hopes, has united all its efforts to gain the advantage. Hence that intestine struggle against the laws, that anarchy which good citizens deplore, and of which the malevolent eagerly avail themselves to calumniate the new system. Hence that division everywhere diffused and everywhere excited, for nowhere does indifference exist. People desire either the triumph, or a change, of the constitution. They act either to maintain or to alter it. I shall abstain from examining what it is of itself, in order to consider only what circumstances require; and, expressing myself as dispassionately as possible, I will seek what we are authorised to expect and what it is right to favour.

"Your majesty possessed great prerogatives, which you considered as pertaining to royalty. Brought up in the idea of retaining them, you could not see them taken from you with pleasure. The desire of recovering them was therefore as natural as regret on seeing them annihilated. These sentiments, inherent in the nature of the human heart, must have entered into the calculation of the enemies of the Revolution; they reckoned, therefore, upon a secret favour, till circumstances should admit of a declared protection. This disposition could not escape the nation, nor fail to excite its jealousy.

"Your majesty has therefore been constantly under the alternative of yielding to your first habits, to your private affections, or of making sacrifices dictated by philosophy, and required by necessity; consequently of encouraging rebels by alarming the nation, or of appeasing the latter by uniting yourself with it. Everything has its time, and that of uncertainty has at length arrived.

"Can your majesty at the present day ally yourself openly with those who pretend to reform the constitution, or ought you generously to strive without reserve to render it triumphant? Such is the real question, the solution of which the present state of affairs renders inevitable. As for that highly metaphysical one, whether the French are ripe for liberty, its discussion is not to the purpose here, for it is not the point to judge what we shall become in a century, but to discover what the present generation is capable of.

"Amidst the agitations in which we have been living for four years past, what has happened? Privileges burdensome to the people have been abolished. Ideas of justice and equality have been universally diffused. The opinion of the rights of the people has justified the feelings of its rights. The recognition of the latter, solemnly proclaimed, has become a sacred doctrine; the hatred, inspired for ages by feudalism, has been exasperated by the manifest opposition of most of the nobles to the constitution, which destroys that system.

"During the first year of the Revolution, the people beheld in those nobles men odious for the oppressive privileges which they had possessed, but whom they would have ceased to hate after the suppression of those privileges, if the conduct of the nobility since that time had not strengthened every possible reason for dreading it, and for combating it as an irreconcileable enemy.

"Attachment to the constitution has increased in the like proportion. Not only are the people indebted to it for manifest benefits, but they have judged that it was preparing for them still greater; since those who were accustomed to make them bear all the burdens were striving so powerfully to overthrow or to modify it.

"The declaration of rights is become a political gospel, and the French constitution a religion for which the people are ready to perish.

"Thus zeal has sometimes proceeded so far as to take the place of the law, and when the latter was not sufficiently restrictive to repress disturbers, the citizens have ventured to punish them themselves.

"Thus it is that the property of emigrants has been exposed to ravages instigated by revenge. Hence, too, so many departments have deemed themselves constrained to pursue severe measures against the priests whom public opinion had proscribed, and of whom it would have made victims.

"In this collision of interests the sentiments of all have taken the tone of passion. The country is not a word which the imagination has delighted to embellish. It is a being to which people have made sacrifices, to which they are becoming daily more and more strongly attached on account of the anxieties which it occasions, which they have created with mighty efforts, which rises from amidst alarms, and which is loved as much for what it has cost as for what is hoped from it. All the attacks made upon it are but means of kindling enthusiasm in its behalf. To what a height will this enthusiasm attain, at the moment when hostile forces, assembled without, combine with internal intrigues for the purpose of striking the most fatal blows! In all parts of the empire the ferment is extreme; it will burst forth in a terrible manner, unless a well-founded confidence in the intentions of your majesty can at length allay it: but this confidence cannot be established upon protestations; it can no longer have anything but facts for its basis.

"It is evident to the French nation that its constitution can go alone, that the government will have all the strength that is necessary for it, the moment that your majesty, absolutely bent on the triumph of that constitution, shall support the legislative body with all the power of the executive, shall remove all pretext for the alarm of the people, and take away all hope from the discontented.

"For example, two important decrees have been passed. Both essentially concern the public tranquillity and the welfare of the state. The delay in their sanction excites distrust. If it be further prolonged it will cause discontent; and I am obliged to confess that, in the present effervescence of opinions, discontent may lead to any consequences.

"It is too late to recede, and there are no longer any means of temporising. The Revolution is accomplished in people's minds. It will be consummated at the expense of their blood, and cemented with it, if prudence does not prevent the calamities which it is yet possible to avoid.

"I know that it may be imagined that everything may be effected and everything repressed by extreme measures; but when force has been employed to overawe the Assembly, when terror has been spread throughout Paris, and dissension and stupor in its environs, all France will rise with indignation, and, tearing herself in pieces amidst the horrors of a civil war, will develop that stern energy, which is the parent alike of virtues and of crimes, and is always fatal to those by whom it has been called forth.

"The welfare of the state and the happiness of your majesty are intimately connected. No power is capable of separating them. Cruel pangs and certain calamities will environ your throne, if it is not placed by yourself upon the bases of the constitution, and strengthened by the peace which its maintenance must at length procure us. Thus the state of opinion, the course of events, motives for any particular line of policy, the interest of your majesty, render indispensable the obligation of uniting yourself with the legislative body and responding to the wish of the nation, who make a necessity of that which principles present as a duty. But the sensibility natural to this affectionate people is ready to find in that necessity a motive for gratitude. You have been cruelly deceived, sire, when you have been filled with aversion or distrust for a people so easily touched. It is by being kept in perpetual uneasiness that you yourself have been led to a conduct calculated to alarm. Let them see that you are determined to aid the progress of that constitution to which they have attached their felicity, and you will soon become the object of their thanksgiving.

"The conduct of the priests in many places, and the pretexts with which fanaticism furnished the discontented, have caused a wise law to be enacted against the disturbers. Be pleased, sire, to give it your sanction. The public tranquillity claims it. The safety of the priests solicits it. If this law be not put in force, the departments will be constrained to substitute for it, as they do in every instance, violent measures, and the incensed people will, for want of it, have recourse to outrages.

"The attempts of our enemies, the commotions which have broken out in the capital, the extreme uneasiness excited by the conduct of your guard, and which is still kept up by the testimonies of satisfaction which your majesty has been induced to bestow upon it, in a proclamation truly impolitic under existing circumstances, and the situation of Paris, and its proximity to the frontiers, have caused the want of a camp in its vicinity to be felt. This measure, the prudence and urgency of which have struck all well-meaning persons, is still waiting only for your majesty's sanction. Why should delays be allowed to produce the appearance of reluctance, when celerity would deserve gratitude?

"Already have the proceedings of the staff of the national guard of Paris against this measure, awakened a suspicion that it was acting from superior instigation. Already are the declamations of certain furious demagogues raising surmises of their connection with the parties concerned for the overthrow of the constitution. Already is public opinion compromising the intentions of your majesty. A little longer delay, and the disappointed people will imagine that in their King they behold the friend and accomplice of the conspirators.

"Gracious Heaven! hast thou stricken with blindness the powers of the earth, and are they never to have any counsels but such as shall lead them to perdition?

"I know that the austere language of truth is seldom relished near the throne. I know, too, that it is because it is scarcely ever proclaimed there that Revolutions are become necessary; and, above all, I know that it is my duty to hold such language to your majesty, not only as a citizen subject to the laws, but as a minister honoured by your confidence, or clothed with functions which suppose it; and I know nothing that can prevent me from performing a duty of which I am conscious.

"It is in the same spirit that I shall repeat my representations to your majesty on the utility of executing the law which directs that there shall be a secretary to the council. The mere existence of the law speaks so powerfully that it would seem that the execution ought to follow without delay; but it is of importance to employ all the means of ensuring to the deliberations the necessary gravity, discretion, and maturity; and for the responsible ministers there ought to be a medium of recording their opinions. Had such a medium existed, I should not on this occasion have addressed myself in writing to your majesty.

"Life is not a consideration with the man who prizes his duties above all things; but, next to the happiness of having performed them, the highest satisfaction he can enjoy is that of thinking that he has performed them faithfully; which is an obligation incumbent on the public man.

(Signed) ROLAND.

"Paris, June 10, 1792, the fourth year of liberty."

The King listened to this lecture with the utmost patience and withdrew, saying that he would communicate his intentions.

Dumouriez was summoned to the palace. The King and Queen were together. "Ought we," said they, "to endure any longer the insolence of these three ministers?"—"No," replied Dumouriez. "Will you undertake to rid us of them?" asked the King. "Yes, sire," answered the bold minister; "but in order to succeed, your majesty must consent to one condition. I have become unpopular, and I shall make myself still more so, by dismissing three colleagues, the leaders of a powerful party. There is but one way of persuading the public that they are not dismissed on account of their patriotism." "What is that?" inquired the King. "It is," replied Dumouriez, "to sanction the two decrees;" and he repeated the reasons which he had already given in full council. The Queen exclaimed that the condition was too hard: but Dumouriez represented to her that the twenty thousand men were not to be feared; that the decree did not mention the place where they were to be encamped; that they might be sent to Soissons, for instance; that there they might be employed in military exercises, and afterwards marched off by degrees to the armies, when the want of them began to be felt. "But then," said the King, "it is necessary that you should be minister at war."—"Notwithstanding the responsibility I consent to it," replied Dumouriez, "but your majesty must sanction the decree against the priests. I cannot serve you unless at that price. This decree, so far from being injurious to the ecclesiastics, will place them beyond the reach of the popular fury. Your majesty could do no other than oppose the first decree of the Constituent Assembly which prescribed the oath; now you can no longer recede."—"I was wrong then," exclaimed Louis XVI.; "I must not commit a second fault." The Queen, who did not share the religious scruples of her husband, joined Dumouriez, and for a moment the King appeared to comply.

Dumouriez pointed out the new ministers to supply the places of Servan, Clavières, and Roland. These were Mourgues, for the interior, and Beaulieu for the finances. The war was consigned to Dumouriez, who, for the moment, held two departments, till that of foreign affairs should be filled. The ordinance was immediately issued, and on the 13th, Roland, Clavières, and Servan received their official dismission. Roland, who possessed all the nerve necessary for executing what the bold spirit of his wife was capable of conceiving, repaired immediately to the Assembly, and read to it the letter which he had written to the King, and for which he was dismissed. This stop was certainly allowable when once hostilities were declared; but as a promise had been given to the King to keep the letter secret, it was by no means generous to read it publicly.

The Assembly bestowed the greatest applause on Roland's letter, and ordered it to be printed and sent to the eighty-three departments. It declared, moreover, that the three displaced ministers carried with them the confidence of the nation. It was at this very moment that Dumouriez, nothing daunted, ventured to appear in the tribune with his new title of minister at war. He had drawn up in the utmost haste a circumstantial report of the state of the army, of the faults of the administration and of the Assembly. He did not spare those whom he knew to be disposed to give him the most unfavourable reception. The moment he appeared, he was assailed with violent hootings by the Jacobins. The Feuillans maintained the most profound silence. He first gave an account of a slight advantage gained by Lafayette and of the death of Gouvion, an officer, a deputy, and an upright man, who, driven to despair by the calamities of the country, had purposely sought death. The Assembly bestowed its regrets on the loss of this generous citizen; but listened coldly to those of Dumouriez, and, above all, to the wish that he expressed to escape the same calamities by the same fate. But when he announced his report as minister at war, a refusal to listen to him was manifested on all sides. He coolly desired to be heard, and at length obtained silence. His remonstrances irritated some of the deputies. "Do you hear him?" exclaimed Guadet; "he is lecturing us!" "And why not?" coldly replied the intrepid Dumouriez. Quiet was restored; he finished reading, and was by turns hooted and applauded. As soon as he had done, he folded up the paper for the purpose of taking it with him. "He is running away!" cried one. "No," rejoined he, and boldly laying his memorial upon the desk again, he calmly signed it, and walked through the Assembly with unshaken composure. Some of the members, who thronged round him as he passed, said, "You will be sent to Orleans."—"So much the better," he replied; "for I shall then take baths and curds, and get a little rest, which I stand in need of."

His firmness cheered the King, who expressed his satisfaction; but the unhappy prince was already shaken and tormented with scruples. Beset by false friends, he had already taken up his former determinations, and refused to sanction the two decrees.

The four ministers met in council, and entreated the King to give his double sanction, which he had seemed to promise. The King drily replied, that he could assent only to the decree relative to the twenty thousand men; that, as for that concerning the priests, he was determined to oppose it; that his mind was made up; and that threats could not frighten him. He read the letter communicating his determination to the President of the Assembly. "One of you," said he to his ministers, "will countersign it;" and these words he uttered in a tone which he had never been known to use before.

Dumouriez then wrote to him, soliciting his dismissal. "That man," exclaimed the King, "has made me dismiss three ministers because they wanted to oblige me to adopt the decrees, and now he insists on my sanctioning them!" This reproach was unjust, for it was only on condition of the double sanction that Dumouriez had consented to remain in office after his colleagues. Louis XVI. saw him, and asked him if he persisted. "In that case," said he, "I accept your resignation." The other ministers had given in theirs also. The King, however, detained

Lacoste and Duranthon, and prevailed on them to remain. Messrs. Lajard, Chambonas, and Terrier de Mont-Ciel, selected from among the Feuillans, were appointed to the vacant ministerial departments.

"The King," says Madame Campan, "sunk about this time into a despondency that amounted even to physical debility. He was for ten days together without uttering a word even in the midst of his family, excepting at a game at backgammon, which he played with Madame Elizabeth after dinner, when he merely pronounced the words which are used in that game. The Queen roused him from this state, so ruinous in a crisis when every minute brought with it the necessity for acting, by throwing herself at his feet, and sometimes by employing images calculated to terrify him, at others, expressions of her affection for him. She also urged the claims which he owed to his family; and went so far as to say that, if they must perish, they ought to perish with honour, and not wait to be both stifled on the floor of their own apartment."

It is not difficult to guess the disposition of Louis XVI. when he recovered his spirits and returned to business. After having once forsaken the party of the Feuillans to throw himself into the arms of the Girondins, he could not go back to the former with much cordiality and hope. He had made the twofold experiment of his incompatibility with both, and, what was still worse, he had caused them all to make it too. Thenceforward he could not but think more than ever of foreign powers, and rest all his hopes upon them. This disposition became evident to all, and it alarmed those who beheld in the invasion of France the fall of liberty, the execution of its defenders, and perhaps the partition and dismemberment of the kingdom. Louis XVI. saw none of these things, for we always shut our eyes to the inconveniences of the course that we prefer.

Alarmed at the tumult produced by the rout of Mons and Tournay, he had sent Mallet du Pan to Germany, with instructions in his own handwriting. He there recommended to the sovereigns to advance cautiously, to treat the inhabitants of the provinces through which they should pass with the utmost indulgence, and to send forth before them a manifesto professing their pacific and conciliatory intentions. (*See* Appendix U U U.) Moderate as was this plan, it was nevertheless an invitation to advance into the country; and, besides, if such was the wish of the King, was that of the foreign princes and rivals of France and of the inveterately hostile emigrants the same? Was Louis XVI. assured that he should not be hurried away beyond his intentions? The ministers of Prussia and Austria themselves expressed to Mallet du Pan the apprehensions which they felt on account of the violence of the emigrants, and it appears that he had some difficulty to satisfy them on this head. (*See* Appendix V V V.) The Queen felt equally strong apprehensions on the same subject. She dreaded Calonne in particular, as the most dangerous of her enemies; but she nevertheless conjured her family to act with the greatest celerity for her deliverance. From that moment the popular party could not help considering the court as an enemy so much the more dangerous, because it had at its disposal all the forces of the state; and the combat that was commencing became a combat for life and death. The King, in composing his new ministry, did not select any conspicuous man. In expectation of his speedy deliverance, he had only to wait a few days more, and for that interval the most insignificant ministry was sufficient.

The Feuillans thought to profit by the occasion to unite themselves again to the court, less, it must be confessed, from personal ambition of party than from the interest which they felt for the King. They were far from reckoning upon an invasion. Most of them regarded it as a crime, and pregnant, moreover, with equal danger to the court and the nation. They rightly foresaw that the King must succumb before succour could arrive; and they dreaded lest the invasion should be followed by the atrocities of revenge, perhaps the dismemberment of the territory, and certainly the abolition of all liberty.

Lally Tollendal, who, as we have seen, quitted France as soon as the formation of the two chambers became impossible; Malouet, who had made a last attempt in their favour at the time of the revision; Duport,

Lameth, Lafayette, and others, who were desirous that things should remain as they were, united to make a last effort. This party, like all the other parties, was not in perfect harmony with itself. It united with one view only, that of saving the King from his errors, and of saving the constitution with him. Every party, obliged to act in secret, is forced to resort to proceedings which are termed intrigues when they are not successful. In this sense the Feuillans intrigued. As soon as they saw the dismissal of Servan, Clavières, and Roland, effected by Dumouriez, they sought the latter, and offered him their alliance, on condition that he would sign the veto to the decree against the priests. Dumouriez, perhaps from spleen, perhaps from want of confidence in their means, and no doubt also on account of the engagement he had made to obtain the King's sanction of the decree, refused this alliance, and repaired to the army, wishing, as he wrote to the Assembly, that some cannon-ball might reconcile all the opinions respecting him.

The Feuillans still had Lafayette left. Without taking part in their secret proceedings, he had shared their dislike of Dumouriez, and was, above all, desirous of saving the King, without injuring the constitution. Their means were feeble. In the first place, the court which they strove to save would not be saved by them. The Queen, who cheerfully confided in Barnave, had always adopted the greatest precautions in her interviews with him, and had never admitted him except in secret. The emigrants and the court would not have forgiven her for seeing constitutionalists. They recommended to her, in fact, not to treat with them, and rather to prefer the Jacobins, because, as they said, it would be necessary to make concessions to the former, but it would not be bound to any terms with the latter. If to this oft-repeated advice be added the personal hatred of the Queen for M. de Lafayette, it will be easy to conceive that the court would be very reluctant to accept the services of constitutionalists and Feuillans. Besides this aversion of the court to them, we must also consider the feebleness of the means which they had to employ against the popular party. Lafayette, it is true, was adored by his soldiers, and could rely upon his army; but he was in front of the enemy, and he could not leave the frontier uncovered for the purpose of marching into the interior. Old Luckner, by whom he was supported, was weak, fickle, and easily intimidated, though very brave in the field. But could they even have reckoned upon their military resources, the constitutionalists possessed no civil means. The majority of the Assembly belonged to the Gironde. The National Guard was in part devoted to them, but it was disunited and disorganized. In order to employ their military forces, they would therefore have been compelled to march from the frontiers upon Paris—that is to say, to attempt an insurrection against the Assembly; and insurrections, however advantageous for a violent party which adopts the offensive side, are unsuitable and ruinous to a moderate party, which, in resisting, supports itself by the laws.

Many, nevertheless, rallied round Lafayette, and concerted with him the plan of a letter to the Assembly. This letter, written in his name, was intended to express his sentiments relative to the King and the constitution, and his disapprobation of everything that tended to attack either. His friends were divided. Some excited, others restrained his zeal. But thinking only of what was likely to serve the King, to whom he had sworn fidelity, he wrote the letter, and defied all the dangers which were about to threaten his life. The King and Queen, though determined not to make use of him, allowed him to write, because they beheld in this step only an exchange of reproaches between the friends of liberty. The letter reached the Assembly on the 18th of June. Lafayette, disapproving in the first place of the late minister, whom, he said, he meant to denounce at the moment when he was informed of his dismissal, proceeded in these terms:—

"It is not enough that this branch of the government be delivered from a baneful influence; the public weal is in danger; the fate of France depends chiefly on her representatives—from them the nation expects its salvation; but, in giving itself a constitution, it has marked out for them the only route by which they are to save it."

Then, protesting his inviolable attachment to the law which had been sworn to, he expatiated on the state of France, which he saw placed between two kinds of enemies—those abroad and those at home:—

"Both must be destroyed. But you will not have the power to destroy them, unless you be constitutional and just. Look around you; can you deny that a faction—and, to avoid every vague denomination, that the Jacobin faction—has caused all these disorders? It is to this faction that I loudly attribute them. Organized like a separate empire, in its principal society and its affiliations, blindly directed by a few ambitious leaders, this party forms a distinct corporation amongst the French people, whose powers it usurps, by overawing its representatives and its functionaries.

"It is there that, in the public sittings, love of the laws is called aristocracy and their violation patriotism; there the assassins of Desilles receive triumphs, the crimes of Jourdan find panegyrists; there the account of the murder which has sullied the city of Metz has but just now excited infernal acclamations.

"Will they expect to escape from these reproaches by bragging of an Austrian manifesto in which these sectaries are mentioned? Have they become sacred since Leopold has pronounced their name? And, because we must combat foreigners who interfere in our quarrels, are we to dispense with the duty of delivering our country from a domestic tyranny?"

Then, recapitulating his former services for liberty, and enumerating the guarantees which he had given to the country, the general answered for himself and his army, and declared that the French nation, if it was not the vilest in the world, could and ought to resist the conspiracy of the kings who had coalesced against it. "But," added he, "in order that we, soldiers of liberty, should fight with efficacy, and die with benefit for her, it is requisite that the number of the defenders of the country should be speedily proportioned to that of its adversaries; that supplies of all kinds be multiplied to facilitate our movements; that the well-being of the troops, their equipments, their pay, and the arrangements relative to their health, be no longer subject to fatal delays." Then followed other advice, the principal and last of which was this: "Let the reign of the clubs annihilated by you give place to the reign of the law—their usurpations, to the firm and independent exercise of the constituted authorities; their disorganizing maxims, to the genuine principles of liberty; their frantic fury, to the calm and persevering courage of a nation which knows its rights and defends them; and, lastly, their sectarian combinations to the true interests of the country, which, in this moment of danger, ought to rally around them all those to whom its subjugation and ruin are not objects of atrocious satisfaction and infamous speculation!"

This was saying to exasperated passions, "Stop!"—to the parties themselves, "Put an end to your own existence!"—to a torrent, "Cease to flow!" But though the advice was useless, it was not the less a duty to give it. The letter was highly applauded by the right side; the left was silent. No sooner was the reading of it finished, than it was proposed to print and send it to the departments.

Vergniaud asked and obtained permission to speak. According to him, it was of importance to that liberty which M. de Lafayette had hitherto so ably defended, to make a distinction between the petitions of private citizens, who offered advice or claimed an act of justice, and the lectures of an armed general. The latter ought never to express his sentiments unless through the medium of the Ministry, otherwise liberty would be undone. It was, therefore, expedient to pass to the order of the clay. M. Thevenot replied, that the Assembly ought to receive from the lips of M. de Lafayette truths which it had not dared to tell itself. This last observation excited a great tumult. Some members denied the authenticity of the letter. "Even if it were not signed," exclaimed M. Coubé, "none but M. de Lafayette could have written it." Gaudet demanded permission to speak upon a matter of fact, and asserted that the letter could not be that of M. de Lafayette, because it adverted to the dismissal of Dumouriez, which had not taken place till the 16th, and it was dated the very same day. "It is therefore impossible," he added, "that the person whose name is signed to it should have made mention of a fact which could not have been known to him. Either the signature is not his, or it was attached to a blank, which was left for a faction to fill up at its pleasure."

A great uproar followed these words. Guadet resumed: he said that M. de Lafayette was incapable, according to his known sentiments, of having written such a letter. "He must know," added he, "that when Cromwell . . ." Dumas, the deputy, unable to contain himself, at this last word desired to be heard. Agitation prevailed for a considerable time in the Assembly. Guadet, however, regained possession of the tribune, and began: "I was saying . ." Again he was interrupted. "You were at Cromwell," said some one to him. "I shall return to him," he replied. "I was saying that M. de Lafayette must know that when Cromwell held a similar language, liberty was lost in England. It is expedient either that we ascertain whether some coward has not sheltered himself beneath the name of M. de Lafayette, or prove by a signal example to the French people that we have not taken a vain oath in swearing to maintain the constitution."

A great number of members attested the signature of M. de Lafayette. The letter was, nevertheless, referred to the committee of twelve, for the purpose of ascertaining its authenticity. It was thus deprived of the honour of being printed and sent to the departments.

This generous procedure then proved absolutely useless, and could not be otherwise in the existing state of the public mind. From that moment, the general became almost as unpopular as the court; and if the leaders of the Gironde, more enlightened than the populace, did not believe M. de Lafayette capable of betraying his country because he had attacked the Jacobins, the mass nevertheless believed him to be so, because it was constantly repeated in the clubs, in the newspapers, and in the public places, that he was.

Thus the alarm which the court had excited in the popular party was heightened by that which M. de Lafayette had just added to it by a step of his own. This party then became absolutely desperate, and resolved to strike a blow at the court before it could carry into execution the plots of which it was accused.

We have already seen how the popular party was composed. In speaking out more decidedly, it also manifested a more decided character, and several additional persons rendered themselves conspicuous in it. Robespierre has already been mentioned at the Jacobins, and Danton at the Cordeliers. The clubs, the municipality, and the sections, comprised many men who, from the ardour of their disposition and opinions, were ready for any enterprise. Among these were Sergent and Panis, whose names, at a later period, were connected with a terrible event. In the fauxbourgs were remarked several commanders of battalions, who had rendered themselves formidable. The principal of these was a brewer named Santerre. By his stature, his voice, and a certain fluency of speech, he pleased the people, and had acquired a kind of sway in the fauxbourg St. Antoine, the battalion of which he commanded. Santerre had already distinguished himself in the attack on Vincennes, repulsed by Lafayette in February, 1791; and, like all men who are too easily wrought upon, he was capable of becoming very dangerous, according to the excitement of the moment. (*See* Appendix W W W.) He attended all the factious meetings held in the distant fauxbourgs. There, too, were to be found Carra, the journalist, prosecuted for an attack on Bertrand de Molleville and Montmorin; Alexandre, commandant of the fauxbourg St. Marceau; a person well known by the name of Fournier the American; Legendre (*See* Appendix X X X.), the butcher, who was afterwards a deputy to the Convention; a journeyman goldsmith, named Rossignol; and several others, who, by their communications with the populace, set all the fauxbourgs in commotion. By the most conspicuous among them they communicated with the chiefs of the popular party, and were thus able to conform their movements to a superior direction.

It is impossible to designate in a precise manner such of the deputies as contributed to this direction. The most distinguished of them were strangers to Paris, and possessed no other influence there but that of their eloquence. Guadet, Isnard, Vergniaud, were all natives of the provinces, and communicated more with their departments than with Paris. Besides, though extremely ardent in the tribune, they were not at all active out of the Assembly, and were not capable of exciting the multitude. Condorcet and Brissot, deputies of Paris, were not more active than those just mentioned, and, by the conformity of their opinions with those of the deputies of the West and South, they had become Girondins. Poland, since the dismissal of the patriot ministry, had returned to private life. He occupied an humble and obscure dwelling in the Rue St. Jacques. Persuaded that the court entertained the design of delivering up France and liberty to foreigners, he deplored the calamities of his country in conjunction with some of his friends, who were members of the Assembly. It does not, however, appear that any plans were formed in his society for attacking the court. He merely promoted the printing of a paper entitled *La Sentinelle*, which was conducted in a patriotic spirit by Louvet, already known at the Jacobins by his controversy with Robespierre. Roland, during his ministry, had allowed funds for the purpose of enlightening the public opinion by means of the press, and it was with a remnant of these funds that *La Sentinelle* was carried on.

About this period there was, at Paris, a young native of Marseilles, full of ardour, courage, and republican illusions, and who, on account of his extraordinary beauty, was called the Antinous. He had been deputed by his commune to the Legislative Assembly, to complain of the directory of his department; for this division between the inferior and superior authorities, between the municipalities and the directories of departments, was general throughout all France. The name of this young man was Barbaroux. Possessing intelligence and great activity, he was likely to become very serviceable to the popular cause. He met Poland, and deplored with him the dangers with which the patriots were threatened. They agreed that, as the danger was daily growing greater in the north of France, they ought, if driven to the last extremity, to retire to the south, and there found a republic, which they might some day extend, as Charles VII. had formerly extended his kingdom from Bourges. They examined the map with Servan, the ex-minister, and said to each other that Liberty, if beaten upon the Rhine and beyond it, ought to retire behind the Vosges and the Loire; that, driven from these intrenchments, she would still have left, in the east, the Doubs, the Ain, and the Rhone; in the west, the Vienne and the Dordogne; in the centre, the rocks and the rivers of the Limousin. "And beyond these," added Barbaroux, "we have the Auvergne, its steep hills, its ravines, its aged forests, and the mountains of the Velay, laid waste of old by fire, now covered with pines; a wild country, where men plough amidst snow, but where they live independently. The Cevennes would offer us another asylum too celebrated not to be formidable to tyranny; and in the extreme south, we should find for barriers the Isere, the Durance, the Rhone from Lyons to the sea, the Alps, and the ramparts of Toulon. Lastly, if all these points were forced, we should have Corsica left—Corsica, where neither Genoese nor French have been able to naturalise tyranny; which needs but hands to be fertile, and philosophers to be enlightened."

It was natural that the natives of the South should think of betaking themselves to their provinces in case the North should be invaded. They did not, however, neglect the North, for they agreed to write to their departments, to induce them to form spontaneously a camp of twenty thousand men though the decree relative to this camp had not yet been sanctioned. They reckoned much upon Marseilles, an opulent city, with a numerous population, and extremely democratic. It had sent Mirabeau to the States-general, and it had since diffused over all the South the spirit with which it was itself animated. The mayor of that city was a friend of Barbaroux, and held the same opinions as he did. Barbaroux wrote, desiring him to provide supplies of corn, to send trusty persons into the neighbouring departments as well as to the armies of the Alps, of Italy, and of the Pyrenees, in order to prepare the public opinion there; to sound Montesquiou, the commander of the army of the Alps, and to turn his ambition to the advantage of liberty; lastly, to concert with Paoli, and the Corsicans, so as to secure a sure aid and a last asylum. It was also recommended to the same mayor to retain the produce of the taxes in order to deprive the executive government of it, and in case of need to employ it against the latter. What Barbaroux did for Marseilles, others did for their departments, and thought of ensuring a refuge for themselves. Thus distrust, converted into despair, paved the way for a general insurrection, and, in the preparations for insurrection, there was already a marked difference between Paris and the departments.

Petion, the mayor, connected with all the Girondins and subsequently classed and proscribed with them, had from his functions much intercourse with the agitators of Paris. He had great composure, an appearance of coldness which his enemies mistook for stupidity, and an integrity which was extolled by his partisans and never attacked by his slanderers. The people, who give distinct appellations to all those who engage their attention, called him *Virtue Petion*. We have already mentioned him on occasion of the journey to Varennes, and of the preference given him by the court to Lafayette for the mayoralty of Paris. The court hoped to bribe him, and certain swindlers promised to accomplish this matter. They demanded a sum of money, which they kept, without having even made overtures to Petion, whose well-known character would have rendered them useless. The joy felt by the court at the prospect of gaining a supporter and corrupting a popular magistrate, was of short duration. It soon discovered that it had been cheated, and that its adversaries were not so venal as it had imagined.

Petion had been one of the first to take for granted that the propensities of a King, born to absolute power, are not to be modified. He was a republican before any one ever dreamt of a republic; and in the Constituent Assembly he was from conviction, what Robespierre was from the acerbity of his temper. Under the Legislative Assembly, he became still more convinced of the incorrigibleness of the court. He was persuaded that it would call in foreigners, and, as he had before been a republican from system, he now became so for the sake of safety.

Thenceforward he resolved in his mind, as he said, how to promote a new revolution. He checked ill-directed movements, favoured on the contrary such as were judicious, and strove above all things to reconcile them with the law, of which he was a strict observer, and which he was determined not to violate but at the last extremity.

Though we are not well acquainted with the extent of the participation of Petion in the movements which were preparing, and know not whether he consulted his friends of the Gironde for the purpose of promoting them, we are authorized by his conduct to assert that he did nothing to impede them. It is alleged that, in the latter part of June, he went to the house of Santerre with Robespierre, Manuel, *procureur syndic* of the commune, Sillery, ex-constituent, and Chabot, ex-capuchin and deputy; that the latter harangued the section of the Quinze-Vingts, and said that the Assembly was waiting for it. Whether these circumstances be true or not, it is certain that clandestine meetings were held; and from the well-known opinions and subsequent conduct of the persons above named, it is not to be believed that they had any scruple to attend them. (*See* Appendix Y Y Y.) From that moment a, fete for the 20th of June, the anniversary of the oath at the Tennis Court, was talked of in the fauxbourgs. It was said that a tree of liberty was to be planted on the terrace of the Feuillans, and a petition presented to the Assembly as well as to the King. This petition, moreover, was to be presented in arms. It is obvious that the real intention of this scheme was to strike terror into the palace by the sight of forty thousand pikes.

On the 16th of June, a formal application was addressed to the general council of the commune that the citizens of the fauxbourg St. Antoine should be authorised to meet on the 20th in arms, and to present a petition to the Assembly and to the King. The general council of the commune passed to the order of the day, and directed that its resolution (*arrêté*) should be communicated to the directory and to the municipal body. The petitioners did not regard this proceeding as a condemnation of their purpose, and declared loudly that they would meet in spite of it. It was not till the 18th that Petion, the mayor, made the communications ordered on the 16th; he made them, moreover, to the department only and not to the municipal body.

On the 19th, the directory of the department, which we have seen exerting itself on all occasions against agitators, passed a resolution (*arrêté*) forbidding armed assemblages, and enjoining the commandant-general and the mayor to employ the measures necessary for dispersing them. This resolution was notified to the Assembly by the minister of the interior, and a discussion immediately arose on the question whether it should be read or not.

Vergniaud opposed its being read, but unsuccessfully. The reading of the resolution was immediately followed by the order of the day.

Two circumstances of considerable importance had just occurred in the Assembly. The King had signified his opposition to the two decrees, one of which related to the nonjuring priests, and the other to the formation of a camp of twenty thousand men. This communication had been received in profound silence. At the same time, some persons from Marseilles had appeared at the bar for the purpose of reading a petition. We have just seen what kind of correspondence Barbaroux: kept up with them. Excited by his counsels, they had written to Petion, offering him all their forces, and this offer was accompanied with a petition to the Assembly. In this petition they said among other things:

"French liberty is in danger, but the patriotism of the South will save France. . . . The day of the people's wrath is arrived. . . . Legislators, the power of the people is in your hands; make use of it: French patriotism demands your permission to march with a more imposing force towards the capital and the frontiers. . . . You will not refuse the sanction of the law to those who would cheerfully perish in its defence."

This petition gave rise to long debates in the Assembly. The members of the right side maintained that, to send such a decree to the departments, would be inviting them to insurrection. Its transmission was nevertheless decreed, in spite of these remarks, which were certainly very just but unavailing, since people were persuaded that nothing but a new revolution could save France and liberty.

Such had been the occurrences of the 19th. Notwithstanding the resolution of the directory, the movements continued in the fauxbourgs, and it is affirmed that Santerre said to his trusty partisans, who were somewhat intimidated by that resolution, "What are you afraid of? The national guard will not have orders to fire, and M. Petion will be there."

At midnight the mayor, whether he conceived that the movement was irresistible, or that he ought to favour it, as he did that of the 10th of August, wrote to the directory, soliciting it to authorize the assemblage, by permitting the national guard to receive the citizens of the fauxbourgs into its ranks. This expedient fully accomplished the views of those who, without wishing for any disturbance, were nevertheless desirous of overawing the King; and everything proves that such were in fact the views of Petion and the popular chiefs.

At five o'clock on the morning of the 20th of June, the directory replied that it persisted in its preceding resolutions. Petion then ordered the commandant-general on duty to keep up all the posts to their full complement, and to double the guard of the Tuileries. But he did nothing more: and, unwilling either to renew the scene in the Champ de Mars, or to disperse the assemblage, he waited till nine o'clock for the meeting of the municipal body. As soon as it met, it came to a decision contrary to that of the directory, and the national guard was enjoined to open its ranks to the armed petitioners. Petion did not oppose a resolution which violated the administrative subordination, and was thus guilty of a species of inconsistency, with which he was afterwards reproached. But, whatever was the character of that resolution, its objects were rendered useless, for the national guard had not time to assemble, and the concourse soon became so considerable, that it was no longer possible to change either its form or its direction.

It was eleven o'clock in the forenoon. The Assembly had just met in expectation of some great event. The members of the department hastened to it for the purpose of acquainting it with the inutility of their efforts. Rœderer, the *procureur syndic*, obtained permission to speak. He stated that an extraordinary assemblage of citizens had met, in spite of the law and various injunctions of the authorities; that the object of this assemblage appeared to be to celebrate the anniversary of the 20th of June, and to pay a new tribute of respect to the Assembly; but that, if this was the intention of the greater number, it was to be feared that evil-disposed persons were desirous of availing themselves of this concourse to carry an address to the King, to whom none ought to be presented but in the peaceful form of a mere petition.

Then, referring to the resolutions of the directory and of the general council of the commune, the laws enacted against armed assemblages, and those which limit to twenty the number of citizens who could present a petition, he exhorted the Assembly to enforce them; "for," added he, "armed petitioners are to-day thronging hither by a civic movement; but to-morrow a crowd of evil-disposed persons may collect, and then, I ask you, gentlemen, what should we have to say to them?"

Amidst the applause of the right and the murmurs of the left, which, by disapproving the apprehensions and the foresight of the department, evidently approved the insurrection, Vergniaud ascended the tribune, and observed that the abuse with which the *procureur syndic* was alarming the Assembly for the future, had already taken place; that, on several occasions, armed petitioners had been received, and even permitted to file through the hall; that this was perhaps wrong, but that the petitioners of that day would have reason to complain if they were treated differently from others; that if, as it was said, they purposed to present an address to the King, no doubt they would send to him unarmed petitioners; and, at any rate, if any danger was apprehended for the King, they had but to send him a deputation of sixty members for a safeguard.

Dumolard admitted all that Vergniaud had asserted, confessed that the abuse had taken place, but declared that a stop ought to be put to it, and more especially on this occasion, if they did not wish the Assembly and the King to appear in the eyes of all Europe the slaves of a destructive faction. He proposed, like Vergniaud, the sending of a deputation; but he required, moreover, that the municipality and the department should be responsible for the measures taken for the maintenance of the laws. The tumult became more and more violent. A letter was brought from Santerre. It was read amidst the applause of the tribunes. It purported that the inhabitants of the fauxbourg St. Antoine were celebrating the 20th of June; that they were calumniated, and begged to be admitted to the bar of the Assembly, in order that they might confound their slanderers, and prove that they were still the men of the 14th of July.

Vergniaud then replied to Dumolard that, if the law had been violated, the example was not new; that to attempt to oppose the violation of it this time would be to renew the sanguinary scene in the Champ de Mars; and that, after all, there was nothing reprehensible in the sentiments of the petitioners. Justly anxious about the future, added Vergniaud, they wish to prove that, in spite of all the intrigues carried on against liberty, they are still ready to defend it.

Here, as we see, the true sentiment of the day was disclosed by an ordinary eifect of the discussion. The tumult continued. Ramond desired permission to speak, but a decree was required before he could obtain it. At this moment it was stated that the petitioners were eight thousand. "Eight thousand!" exclaimed Calvet, "and we are but seven hundred and forty-five. Let us adjourn." Cries of "Order! order!" arose on all sides. Calvet was called to order, and Ramond was urged to speak, because eight thousand citizens were waiting. "If eight thousand citizens are waiting," said he, "twenty-four millions of French are waiting for me too." He then repeated the reasons urged by his friends of the right side. All at once, the petitioners rushed into the hall. The Assembly, indignant at the intrusion, rose; the president put on his hat, and the petitioners quietly withdrew. The Assembly, gratified by this mark of respect, consented to admit them.

This petition, the tone of which was most audacious, expressed the prevailing idea of all the petitions of that period. "The people are ready.

They wait but for you. They are disposed to employ great means for carrying into execution Article 2 of the declaration of rights—*resistance to oppression*. . . . . Let the minority among you, whose sentiments do not agree with ours, cease to pollute the land of liberty, and betake yourselves to Coblentz. Investigate the cause of the evils which threaten us. If it proceeds from the executive, let the executive be annihilated!"

The president, after a reply in which he promised the petitioners the vigilance of the representatives of the people, and recommended obedience to the laws, granted them, in the name of the Assembly, permission to file off before it. The doors were then thrown open, and the mob, amounting at that moment to at least thirty thousand persons, passed through the hall. It is easy to conceive what the imagination of the populace, abandoned to itself, is capable of producing. Enormous tables, upon which lay the declaration of rights, headed the procession. Around these tables danced women and children, hearing olive-branches and pikes, that is to say, peace or war, at the option of the enemy. They sang in chorus the famous *Ca ira*. Then came the porters of the markets, the working men of all classes, with wretched muskets, swords, and sharp pieces of iron fastened to the ends of thick bludgeons. Santerre and the Marquis de St. Hurugues, who had already attracted notice on the 5th and 6th of October, marched with drawn swords at their head. Battalions of the national guard followed in good order, to prevent tumult by their presence. After them came women and more armed men. Waving flags were inscribed with the words. "The constitution or death." Bagged breeches were held up in the air with shouts of *Vivent les sans-culottes!* Lastly, an atrocious sign was displayed to add ferocity to the whimsicality of the spectacle. On the point of a pike was borne a calf's heart with this inscription: "Heart of an aristocrat."

Grief and indignation burst forth at this sight. The horrid emblem instantly disappeared, but was again exhibited at the gates of the Tuileries. The applause of the tribunes, the shouts of the people passing through the hall, the civic songs, the confused uproar, and the silence of the anxious Assembly, composed an extraordinary scene, and at the same time an afflicting one to the very deputies who viewed the multitude as an auxiliary. Why, alas! must reason prove so insufficient in such times of discord? Why did those who called in the disciplined barbarians of the north oblige their adversaries to call in those other undisciplined barbarians, who, by turns merry and ferocious, abound in the heart of cities, and remain sunk in depravity amid the most polished civilisation!

This scene lasted for three hours. At length Santerre again came forward to express to the Assembly the thanks of the people, and presented it with a flag in token of gratitude and attachment.

The mob at this moment attempted to get into the garden of the Tuileries, the gates of which were closed. Numerous detachments of the national guard surrounded the palace, and, extending in line from the Feuillans to the river, presented an imposing front. By order of the King, the garden-gate was opened. The people instantly poured in, and filed off under the windows of the palace and before the ranks of the national guard, without any hostile demonstration, but shouting, "Down, with the veto! The *sansculottes* for ever!" Meanwhile some persons, speaking of the King, said, "Why does he not show himself? . . . We mean to do him no harm."—The old expression, *He is imposed upon*, was occasionally, but rarely, heard. The people, quick at catching the opinions of its leaders, had, like them, despaired.

The crowd, moving off by the garden-gate leading to the Pont Royal, proceeded along the quay and through the wickets of the Louvre to the Place du Carrousel. This place, now so spacious, was then intersected by numerous streets. Instead of that immense court, extending from the body of the palace to the gate and from one wing to the other, there were small courts separated by walls and houses. Ancient wickets opened from each of them into the Carrousel. All the avenues were crowded with people, and they appeared at the royal gate. They were refused admittance. Some of the municipal officers addressed them, and appeared to have prevailed upon them to retire. It is asserted that at this moment Santerre, coming from the Assembly, where he had stayed till the last moment to present a flag, whetted the almost blunted purpose of the people, and caused the cannon to be drawn up to the gate.

It was nearly four o'clock. Two municipal officers all at once ordered the gate to be opened. The troops, which were in considerable force at this point, and consisted of battalions of the national guard and several detachments of gendarmerie, were then paralyzed. The people rushed headlong into the court, and thence into the vestibule of the palace. Santerre, threatened, it is said, by two "witnesses, on account of this violation of the royal residence, exclaimed, turning to the assailants, "Bear witness that I refuse to go into the King's apartments." This apostrophe did not stop the mob, which had received a sufficient stimulus. They poured into every part of the palace, took possession of all the staircases, and by main force dragged a piece of cannon up to the first floor. At the same instant, the assailants commenced an attack with swords and hatchets upon the doors which were closed against them.

Louis XVI. had just at this moment sent away a great number of his dangerous friends, who, without possessing the power to save, had so often compromised him. They had hastened to him, but he had made them leave the Tuileries, where their presence would only have served to exasperate, without repressing, the people. He had with him the old Marshal de Mouchy Acloque, *chef de bataillon*, some of the servants of his household, and several trusty officers of the national guard. It was at this moment that the cries of the people and the strokes of the hatchets were heard. The officers of the national guard immediately surrounded him and implored him to show himself, vowing to die by his side. Without hesitation, he ordered the door to be opened. At that instant, the panel, driven in by a violent blow, fell at his feet. It was at length opened, and a forest of pikes and bayonets appeared. "Here I am!" said Louis XVI., showing himself to the furious rabble. Those who surrounded bun kept close to him and formed a rampart of their bodies.

"Pay respect to your King," they exclaimed; and the mob, which certainly had no definite purpose, relaxed its intrusion.

Several voices announced a petition, and desired that it might be read. Those about the King prevailed upon him to retire to a more spacious room to hear this petition. The people, pleased to see their desire complied with, followed the prince, whom his attendants had the good sense to place in the embrasure of a window. He was made to mount a small bench; several others were set before him, and a table was added. All who had accompanied him were ranged around. Some grenadiers of the guard and officers of the household arrived to increase the number of his defenders, who formed a rampart, behind which, he could listen with less danger to this terrible lecture of the rabble. Amidst uproar and shouts were heard the oft-repeated cries of "No veto! No priests! No aristocrats! The camp near Paris!" Legendre, the butcher, stepped up, and in popular language demanded the sanction of the decree. "This is neither the place nor the moment," replied the King with firmness; "I will do all that the constitution requires." This resistance produced its effect. "*Vive la nation! vive la nation!*" shouted the assailants. "Yes," resumed Louis XVI., "Vive la nation! I am its best friend." "Well, prove it then," said one of the rabble, holding before him a red cap at the point of a pike. A refusal might have been dangerous; and certainly in the situation of the King, dignity did not consist in throwing away his life by rejecting a vain sign, but in doing as he did, in bearing with firmness the assault of the multitude. He put the cap upon his head, and the applause was general. As he felt oppressed by the heat of the weather and the crowd, one of the half-drunken fellows, who had brought with him a bottle and a glass, offered him some of his drink. The King had long been apprehensive lest he should be poisoned; he nevertheless drank without hesitation, and was loudly applauded.

Meanwhile, Madame Elizabeth, who was fondly attached to her brother, and who was the only one of the royal family that could get to him, followed him from window to window, to share his danger. The people, when they saw her, took her for the Queen. Shouts of "There's the Austrian!" were raised in an alarming manner. The national grenadiers, who had surrounded the princess, endeavoured to set the people right. "Leave them," said that generous sister, "leave them in their error, and save the Queen!"

The Queen, with her son and her daughter, had not been able to join her royal consort. She had fled from the lower apartments, hurried to the council-chamber, and could not reach the King on account of the crowd, which filled the whole palace. She was anxious to rejoin him, and earnestly begged to be led to the room where he was. On being dissuaded from this attempt, standing behind the council-table, with some grenadiers, she watched the people file off with a heart full of horror, and eyes swimming in tears, which she repressed. Her daughter was weeping by her side; her young son, frightened at first, had soon recovered his cheerfulness, and smiled in the happy ignorance of his age. A red cap had been handed to him, and the Queen had put it on his head. Santerre recommended respect to the people, and spoke cheeringly to the princess. He repeated to her the accustomed and unfortunately useless expression, "Madam, you are imposed upon; you are imposed upon." Then, seeing the young prince encumbered with the red cap, "The boy is stifling," said he, and relieved him from that ridiculous head-dress.

Some of the deputies, on receiving intelligence of the danger of the palace, had hastened to the King, addressed the people, and enjoined respect. Others had repaired to the Assembly, to inform it of what was passing, and the agitation there was increased by the indignation of the right side, and the efforts of the left to palliate this invasion of the palace of the monarch. A deputation had been decreed without discussion, and twenty-four members had set out to surround the King. It had been moreover decreed that the deputation should be renewed every half-hour, in order that the Assembly might be instantly apprised of everything that might occur. The deputies who were sent spoke alternately, hoisted upon the shoulders of the grenadiers. Petion afterwards made his appearance, and was accused of having come too late. He declared that it was half-past four before he heard of the attack made at four; that it had taken him half an hour to get to the palace, and that it was not till a long time after this that he could overcome the obstacles which separated him from the King, so that he had been prevented from reaching his presence earlier than half-past five. On approaching the prince, "Fear nothing, sire," said he, "you are in the midst of your people." Louis XVI., taking the hand of a grenadier, placed it upon his heart, saying "Feel whether it beats quicker than usual." This noble answer was warmly applauded. Petion at length mounted an armchair, and addressing the crowd, said that, after laying its remonstrances before the King, it had now nothing further to do but to retire peaceably and in such a manner as not to sully that day. Some persons who were present assert that Petion said its just remonstrances. This expression, however, would prove nothing but the necessity for not offending the mob. Santerre reinforced him with his influence, and the palace was soon cleared. The rabble retired in a peaceful and orderly manner. It was then about seven in the evening.

The King was immediately joined by the Queen, his sister, and his children, shedding a flood of tears. Overcome by the scene, the King had still the red cap on his head. He now perceived it for the first time during several hours, and flung it from him with indignation. At this moment, fresh deputies arrived to learn the state of the palace. The Queen, going over it with them, showed them the shattered doors and the broken furniture, and expressed keen vexation at such outrages. Merlin de Thionville, one of the stanchest republicans, was one of the deputies present. The Queen perceived tears in his eyes. "You weep," said she to him, "to see the King and his family treated so cruelly by a people whom he has always wished to render happy."—"It is true, madam," replied Merlin; "I weep over the misfortunes of a beautiful, tender-hearted woman and mother of a family; but do not mistake; there is not one of my tears for the King or the Queen—I hate Kings and Queens."

Next day, general indignation prevailed among the partisans of the court, who considered it as outraged, and among the constitutionalists, who regarded this invasion as a violation of the laws and of the public tranquillity. The disturbance had been alarming, but now it was greatly exaggerated. It was alleged to have been a plan for murdering the King, and it was even asserted that this plan had miscarried solely from the effect of a lucky accident. Hence, by a natural reaction, the popular opinion of the day was in favour of the royal family, who on the preceding, had been exposed to so many dangers and outrages; and the supposed authors of the assault became the objects of unqualified censure.

Sad faces were seen in the Assembly. Several deputies inveighed strongly against the events of the preceding day. M. Bigot proposed a law against armed petitions, and against the custom of suffering bodies of men to file off through the hall. Though there already existed laws on this head, they were renewed by a decree. M. Daveirhoult moved for proceedings against the disturbers. "Proceedings," exclaimed one of the members, "against forty thousand men!"—"Well then," he replied, "if it is impossible to distinguish among forty thousand men, punish the guard, which did not defend, itself; or, at least, do something."

The ministers then entered, to present a report on what had happened, and a discussion arose on the nature of the circumstances. A member of the right, observing that Vergniaud's testimony was above suspicion, and that he had been an eye-witness of the affair, called upon him to relate what he had seen. Vergniaud, however, declined to rise at this appeal, but maintained silence. The boldest of the left side, nevertheless, shook off constraint and took courage towards the conclusion of the sitting. They even ventured to propose that an examination should be instituted whether the veto was necessary in certain peculiar circumstances; but this motion was thrown out by a great majority.

Towards evening, a fresh scene similar to that of the preceding day was apprehended. The people, on retiring, had said that they should come again, and it was believed that they would keep their word. But, whether this was only a remnant of the agitation of the day before, or whether for the moment this new attempt was disapproved of by the leaders of the popular party, it was very easily stopped; and Petion repaired in great haste to the palace, to inform the King that order was restored, and that the people, having laid their remonstrances before him, were now tranquil and satisfied. "That is not true," said the King.—"Sire." . . .—"Be silent."—"It befits not the magistrate of the people to be silent when he does his duty and speaks the truth."—"The tranquillity of Paris rests on your head."—"I know my duty; I shall perform it."—"Enough; go and perform it. Retire."

The King, notwithstanding his extreme good-nature, was liable to fits of ill-humour, which the courtiers termed *coups de boutoir*. The sight of Petion, who was accused of having encouraged the scenes of the preceding day, exasperated him, and produced the conversation which we have just quoted. It was soon known to all Paris. Two proclamations were immediately issued, one by the King, the other by the municipality; and hostilities seemed to be commencing between these two authorities.

The municipality told the citizens to be peaceable, to pay respect to the King, to respect the National Assembly and *to make it be respected*; not to assemble in arms, because it was forbidden by the laws, and, above all, to be aware of evil-disposed persons who were striving to excite fresh commotions.

It was actually rumoured that the court was endeavouring to excite a second insurrection of the people, that it might have occasion to sweep them away with artillery. Thus the palace supposed the existence of a plan for a murder—the fauxbourgs that a plan existed for a massacre.

The King said, "The French will not have learned without pain that a multitude, led astray by certain factious persons, has entered by force of arms the habitation of the King. . . . The King has opposed to the threats and the insults of the factious nothing but his conscience and his love for the public weal.

"He knows not where will be the limit at which they will stop; but to what excesses soever they proceed, they shall never wring from him a consent to anything that he deems contrary to the public interest.

"If those who wish to overthrow the monarchy have need of another crime, they have it in their power to commit it.

"The King enjoins all the administrative bodies and municipalities to provide for the safety of persons and property."

These opposite sentiments corresponded with the two opinions which were then formed. All those whom the conduct of the court had driven to despair were but the more exasperated against it, and the more determined to thwart its designs by all possible means. The popular societies, the municipalities, the pikemen, a portion of the national guard, and the left side of the Assembly, were influenced by the proclamation of the mayor of Paris, and resolved to be prudent no farther than was necessary to avoid being mowed down by grape-shot without any decisive result. Still, uncertain as to the means to be employed, they waited full of the same distrust, and even aversion. Their first step was to oblige the ministers to attend the Assembly, and give account of the precautions which they had taken on two essential points:

1. On the religious disturbances excited by the priests;

2. On the safety of the capital, which the camp of twenty thousand men, refused by the King, was destined to cover.

Those who were called aristocrats, the sincere constitutionalists, part of the national guards, several of the provinces, and especially the departmental directories, spoke out on this occasion, and in an energetic manner. The laws having been violated, they had all the advantage of speech, and they used it without reserve. A great number of addresses were sent to the King. At Rouen and at Paris a petition was drawn up and supported by twenty thousand signatures. This petition was associated in the minds of the people with that already signed by eight thousand Parisians against the camp below Paris. Lastly, legal proceedings were ordered by the department against

Petion, the mayor, and Manuel, *procureur* of the commune, who were both accused of having favoured, by their dilatory conduct, the irruption of the 20th of June. At this moment, the behaviour of the King during that trying day was spoken of with admiration. There was a general change of opinion respecting his character, and people reproached themselves for having charged it with weakness. But it was soon perceived that the passive courage which resists is not that which anticipates dangers, instead of awaiting them with resignation.

The constitutional party fell anew to work with the utmost activity. All those who had surrounded Lafayette, to concert with him the letter of the 16th of June, again united for the purpose of taking some signal step. Lafayette had felt deep indignation on learning what had occurred at the palace; and he was found to be quite willing to assist. Several addresses from his regiments, expressing similar indignation, were sent to him. Whether these addresses were concerted or spontaneous, he put a stop to them by an order of the day, in which he promised to express, in person, the sentiments of the whole army. He resolved, therefore, to go to Paris, and to repeat to the legislative body what he had written to it on the 16th of June. He arranged the matter with Luckner, who was as easily led as an old warrior who has never been out of his camp. He induced him to write a letter addressed to the King, expressing the same sentiments that he was himself about to proclaim viva voce at the bar of the legislative body. He then took all requisite measures so that his absence might not be detrimental to the military operations, and, tearing himself from his attached soldiers, he hastened to Paris to confront the greatest dangers.

Lafayette reckoned upon his faithful national guard, and on imparting a new impulse by means of it. He reckoned upon the court, which he could not believe to be his foe, when he came to sacrifice himself for it. Having proved his chivalrous love of liberty, he was now resolved to prove his sincere attachment to the King; and, in his heroic enthusiasm, it is probable that his heart was not insensible to the glory of this twofold self-devotion. He arrived on the morning of the 28th of

June. The news soon spread, and it was everywhere repeated with surprise and curiosity that General Lafayette was in Paris.

Before his arrival, the Assembly had been agitated by a great number of contrary petitions. Those of Rouen, Havre, the Ain, the Seine and Oise, the Pas de Calais, and the Aisne, condemned the outrages of the 20th of June. Those of Arras and of L'Herault seemed almost to approve of them. There had been read, on the one hand, Luckier' s letter to the King, and, on the other, atrocious placards against him. The reading of these different papers had produced excitement for several preceding days.

On the 28th, a considerable concourse had repaired to the Assembly, hoping that Lafayette, whose intentions were yet a secret, would make his appearance there. About half-past one o'clock, a message was actually brought, stating that he desired to be admitted to the bar. He was received with plaudits by the right side, but with silence by the tribunes and the left side.

"Gentlemen," said he, "I must in the first place assure you that, in consequence of arrangements concerted between Marshal Luckner and myself, my presence here cannot in any way compromise either the success of our arms, or the safety of the army which I have the honour to command."

The general then explained the motive of his coming. It had been asserted that his letter was not written by himself. He came to avow it, and, to make this avowal, he came from amidst his camp, where he was surrounded by the love of his soldiers. A still stronger reason had urged him to this step. The 20th of June had excited his indignation and that of his army, which had presented to him a multitude of addresses. He had put a stop to them, and solemnly engaged to be the organ of its sentiments to the National Assembly. "The soldiers," he added, "are already asking themselves if it is really the cause of liberty and of the constitution that they are defending." He besought the National Assembly—

1. To prosecute the instigators of the 20th of June;

2. To suppress a sect which grasps at the national sovereignty, and whose public debates leave no doubt respecting the atrocity of its designs;

3. Lastly, to enforce respect for the authorities, and to give the armies the assurance that the constitution shall suffer no injury at home, while they are spilling their blood to defend it abroad.

The president replied that the Assembly would uphold the law which had been sworn to, and that it would examine his petition. He was invited to the honours of the sitting.

The general proceeded to take his seat on the benches of the right. Kersaint, the deputy, observed that his proper place was on the petitioners' bench. Cries of "Yes!" "No!" burst from all parts. The general modestly rose and removed to the petitioners' bench. Numerous plaudits accompanied him to this new place. Guadet was the first who spoke, and, resorting to a clever circumlocution, he asked if the enemy was vanquished, and the country delivered, since M. de Lafayette was in Paris. "No," he exclaimed in reply, "the country is not delivered; our situation is not changed; and yet the general of one of our armies is in Paris! "He should not inquire, he continued, whether M. de Lafayette, who saw nothing in the French people but a factious mob surrounding and threatening the authorities, was not himself surrounded by a staff which was circumventing him; but he should observe to M. de Lafayette that he was trespassing against the constitution by making himself the organ of an army legally incapable of deliberating, and that probably he was also trespassing against the authority of the military powers by coming to Paris without being authorized by the minister at war.

Guadet, in consequence, proposed that the minister at war should be called upon to state whether he had given leave of absence to M. de Lafayette, and that, moreover, the extraordinary commission should report upon the question whether a general had a right to address the Assembly on purely political subjects.

Ramond came forward to answer Guadet. He set out with a very natural observation, and one that is very frequently applicable, that the interpretation of the laws is liable to great variations according to circumstances. "Never," said he, "have we been so scrupulous relative to the existence of the right of petition. "When, but very lately, an armed multitude presented itself, it was not asked what was its errand; it was not reproached with infringing by the parade of arms the independence of the Assembly; but when M. de Lafayette, who is for America and for Europe the standard of liberty—when he presents himself, suspicions are awakened! . . . If there are two weights and two measures, if there are two ways of considering things, let it be allowable to make some distinction in favour of the eldest son of liberty!"

Ramond then moved to refer the petition to the extraordinary commission, for the purpose of examining, not the conduct of Lafayette, but the petition itself. After a great tumult and two divisions, Ramond's motion was carried. Lafayette left the Assembly surrounded by a numerous train of deputies and soldiers of the national guard, all of them his partisans and his old companions in arms.

This was the decisive moment for the court, for himself, and for the popular party. He repaired to the palace. The most abusive expressions were repeated around him among the groups of the courtiers. The King and Queen received with coldness the man who came to devote himself for them. Lafayette withdrew, mortified at the disposition which he had perceived, not for his own sake but for the sake of the royal family. On leaving the Tuileries, a numerous concourse escorted him to his residence, shouting, "Long live Lafayette!" and even planted a May before his gate. These demonstrations of old attachment touched the general and intimidated the Jacobins. But it was requisite to take advantage of these feelings of attachment and to rouse them still more, in order to render them efficacious. Some officers of the national guard, particularly devoted to the court, applied to it inquiring how they ought to act. The King and Queen were both of opinion that they ought not to second M. Lafayette. He thus found himself forsaken by the only portion of the national guard from which he could still have expected support. Anxious, nevertheless, to serve the King, in spite of himself, he consulted his friends. But these were not agreed. Some, and particularly Lally Tollendal, were for acting promptly against the Jacobins, and attacking them by main force in their club. Others, all members of the department and of the Assembly, supporting themselves constantly by the authority of the law, and having no resources but in it, would not advise its violation, and opposed any open attack.

Lafayette, nevertheless, preferred the boldest of these two courses and appointed a rendezvous for his partisans, for the purpose of going with them to drive the Jacobins from their place of meeting, and walling up the doors. But though the place for assembling was fixed, few attended, and Lafayette found it impossible to act. Whilst, however, he was deeply mortified to perceive that he was so ill supported, the Jacobins, ignorant of the defection of his partisans, were seized with a panic and abandoned their club. They ran to Dumouriez, who had not yet set out for the army, and urged him to put himself at their head, and to march against Lafayette; but their application was not complied with. Lafayette stayed another day in Paris, amidst denunciations, threats, and hints of assassination, and at length departed, lamenting the uselessness of his self-devotion and the fatal obstinacy of the court. And yet this same man, so completely forsaken when he had come to expose his own life to save the King, has been accused of having betrayed him! The writers of the court have asserted that his means were ill combined. No doubt it was easier and safer, at least in appearance, to employ eighty thousand Prussians; but in Paris, and with the determination not to call in foreigners, what more could he do than put himself at the head of the national guard, and overawe the Jacobins by dispersing them!

Lafayette set out with the design of still serving the King, and contriving, if possible, means for his quitting Paris. He wrote a letter to the Assembly, in which he repeated with still greater energy all that he had himself said against what he called the factious.

No sooner was the popular party relieved from the fears occasioned by the presence and the plans of the general, than it continued its attacks upon the court, and persisted in demanding a strict account of the means which it was adopting for preserving the territory. It Avas already known, though the executive power had not yet made any communication on the subject to the Assembly, that the Prussians had broken the neutrality, and that they were advancing by Coblentz, to the number of eighty thousand men, all old soldiers of the great Frederick, and commanded by the Duke of Brunswick, a celebrated general. Luckner, who had too few troops and could not fully rely on the Belgians, had been obliged to retire upon Lille and Valenciennes. An officer, in retreating from Courtray, had burned the suburbs of the town, and it was conceived that the aim of this cruel measure was to alienate the Belgians. The government did nothing to reinforce the armies, which amounted at the utmost, on the three frontiers, to two hundred and thirty thousand men. It resorted to none of those mighty schemes which rouse the zeal and the enthusiasm of a nation. The enemy, in short, might he in Paris in six weeks.

The Queen reckoned upon this result, and mentioned it in confidence to one of her ladies. She had the route of the emigrants and the King of Prussia. She knew that on such a day they would be at Verdun, on such a one at Lille, and that they were to lay siege to the latter place. That unfortunate princess hoped, she said, to be delivered in a month. Why alas! did she not believe the sincere friends who represented to her the inconveniences of foreign aid, and told her that this aid would be useless; that it would arrive soon enough to compromise, but not soon enough to save her! Why did she not believe her own fears on this point, and the gloomy forebodings which sometimes overwhelmed her! Why, in short, did she not spare herself a fault, and many misfortunes!

We have seen that the measure to which the national party clung most tenaciously was a reserve of twenty thousand men below Paris. The King, as we have shown, was adverse to this plan. He was summoned, in the person of his ministers, to state what precautions had been taken in the place of those proposed in the decree to which he had refused his sanction. He answered by proposing a new project, which consisted in directing upon Soissons a reserve of forty-two battalions of national volunteers, to supply the place of the old reserve, which had been exhausted in completing the two principal armies. This was as nearly as possible the first decree; with this difference, that the camp of reserve should be formed between Paris and the frontiers, and not near Paris itself. This plan was received with murmurs and referred to the military committee.

Several departments and municipalities, excited by their correspondence with Paris, had subsequently resolved to carry into execution the decree for a camp of twenty thousand men, though it was not sanctioned. The departments of the Bouches du Rhône, la Gironde, and L'Herault, set the first example; which was soon followed by others. Such was the commencement of the insurrection.

As soon as intelligence of these spontaneous levies was received, the Assembly, modifying the plan of the forty-two new battalions proposed by the King, decreed that the battalions, whose zeal should have led them to march before they were legally called upon, should pass through Paris, for the purpose of being inscribed at the municipality of that city; that they should then proceed to Soissons, to be there encamped; and lastly, that those who should happen to be in Paris on the 14th of July, the anniversary of the Federation, should attend that national solemnity. It had not been held in 1791, on account of the flight to Varennes, and it was determined that it should be celebrated in 1792 with *éclat*. The Assembly added that, immediately after this festival, the federalists should march off to the place of their destination.

This was at once authorising insurrection, and reviving, with some trifling variation, the unsanctioned decree. The only difference was that the federalists should merely pass through Paris. But the grand point was to bring them thither; and, when once there, a thousand circumstances might arise to detain them. The decree was immediately sent to the King, and sanctioned on the following day.

To this important measure was added another. A distrust was felt of part of the national guards, and particularly of the staffs, which, after the example of the departmental directories, the nearer they approached in rank to superior authority the more they were disposed in its favour. It was especially the national guard of Paris at which the blow was aimed; but it could not be struck directly, and therefore it was decreed that all the staffs in towns containing upwards of fifty thousand inhabitants should be dissolved and re-elected. In the agitated state in which France then was, with the constantly increasing influence which this agitation ensured to the most ardent spirits, this re-election could not fail to bring forward persons devoted to the popular and republican party.

These were important measures, carried by main force, in opposition to the right side and to the court. Yet all this did not appear to the patriots to fortify them sufficiently against the imminent dangers by which they conceived themselves to be threatened. Forty thousand Prussians, and as many Austrians and Sardinians, were approaching our frontiers. A court, apparently in concert with the enemy, resorted to no means for augmenting the armies and exciting the nation, but on the contrary employed the veto to thwart the measures of the legislative body, and the civil list to secure partisans in the interior. Lastly, there was a general, who was not supposed to be capable of uniting with the emigrants to deliver up France, but who was seen to be disposed to support the court against the people. All these circumstances alarmed and deeply agitated the public mind. "The country is in danger!" was the general cry. But how was that danger to be prevented? There lay the difficulty. People were not even agreed respecting the causes. The constitutionalists and the partisans of the court, as much terrified as the patriots themselves, imputed the dangers to the factious only. They trembled only for royalty, and saw no peril but in discussion. The patriots, trembling for a contrary reason, beheld this peril in invasion alone, and laid the whole blame of it on the court, its refusals, its tardiness, and its underhand proceedings. Petitions continued to pour in. Some attributed everything to the Jacobins, others to the court, designated alternately by the appellations of the *palace*, the *executive power*, and the *veto*. The Assembly listened to and referred them all to the extraordinary commission of twelve, appointed long before to seek and propose means for saving the country.

Its plan was awaited with impatience. Meanwhile all the walls were covered with threatening placards; the public papers, not less bold than the posting bills, talking of nothing but forfeiture of the crown and dethronement. This was the topic of general conversation, and no moderation seemed to be observed but in the Assembly. There the attacks against royalty were yet only indirect. It had been proposed, for example, to suppress the veto for decrees of circumstance; observations had several times been made oh the civil list and on the culpable use that was made of it; and it had been suggested that it should either be reduced, or that a public account of its expenditure should be demanded.

At length, the commission of twelve proposed its measures. The court had never refused to comply with the recommendations of the Assembly materially to augment the means of defence. It could not have done so without compromising itself too openly; and, besides, it could not much dread the numerical increase of armies which it believed to be in a state of complete disorganization.

The popular party desired, on the contrary, some of those extraordinary means, which indicate a great resolution, and which frequently confer victory on the most desperate cause. The commission of twelve devised such, and proposed to the Assembly the following plan:

When the danger should become extreme, the legislative body was itself to declare it by this solemn form of expression: *The country is in danger*.

After this declaration, all the local authorities, the councils of the communes, those of the districts and departments, and the Assembly itself, as the highest of the authorities, were to be permanent and to sit without interruption. All the citizens, under the severest penalties, were to deliver to the authorities the arms which they possessed, with a view to their suitable distribution. All the men, old and young, fit for service, were to be enrolled in the national guards. Some were to proceed to the seats of the different authorities of districts or departments; others to march whither soever the exigencies of the country required, either at home or abroad. Those only should be expected to appear in uniform who were able to defray the expense of it. The pay of volunteers was to be given to all the national guards who should be removed from their homes. The authorities were to be directed to provide themselves with military stores. Any sign of rebellion, wilfully displayed, was to be punished with death. Every cockade, every flag, was to be reputed seditious, excepting the tricoloured cockade and flag.

According to this plan, the whole nation would be on the alert and in arms. It would possess the means of deliberating and fighting at every point and at every moment: and would be able to dispense with the government and to make amends for its inactivity. That aimless agitation of the popular masses would be regulated and directed. If, in short, after this appeal, the French should fail to respond to it, the Assembly could not be expected to do any more for a nation which would not do anything for itself. This plan gave rise, as might naturally be expected, to a most vehement discussion.

Pastoret, the deputy, read the preliminary report. It satisfied no one; imputing faults to all, balancing some by others; and not fixing in a positive manner the means of parrying the public dangers. After him, Jean de Bry explained clearly and with moderation the plan of the commission. The discussion, once commenced, soon became a mere exchange of recriminations. It afforded scope for those impetuous imaginations, which rush headlong into extreme measures. The great law of the public welfare, that is to say the dictatorship—in other words, the power of doing everything, with the chance of using it cruelly but energetically—that power which could by right be decreed only in the Convention, was nevertheless proposed in the Legislature.

M. Delaunay of Angers proposed to the Assembly to declare that, till the removal of the danger, it would *consult only the imperative and supreme law of the public welfare.* This would have been, by an abstract and mysterious formula, evidently to abolish royalty and to declare the Assembly absolute sovereign. M. Delaunay said that the Revolution was not completed; that people were mistaken if they thought so; and that it was right to keep fixed laws for the Revolution saved and not the Revolution to be saved. He said, in short, all that is usually said in favour of the dictatorship, the idea of which always presents itself in moments of danger. The answer of the deputies of the right side was natural. "They should violate," they said, "the oaths taken to the constitution, by creating an authority that would absorb the regulated and established powers." Their adversaries replied by saying that the example of violation was already given, and that they ought not to suffer themselves to be anticipated and surprised without defence. "But, prove then," rejoined the partisans of the court, "that this example has been given, that the constitution has been betrayed." This challenge was answered by fresh accusations against the court, and these charges were repelled in their turn by recriminations against agitators. "You are factious men."—"You are traitors." Such was the reciprocal and everlasting reproach—such the question to be resolved.

So violent did M. Jaucour deem the proposal, that he was for referring it to the Jacobins. M. Isnard, with whose ardour it harmonized, urged that it should be taken into consideration, and that the speech of M. Delaunay should be sent to the departments, to counterpoise that of M. Pastoret, which was but *a dose of opium given to a patient in the agonies of death.*

M. de Vaublanc succeeded in obtaining a hearing. He said that the constitution could save itself by the constitution; that the plan of M. Jean de Bry was a proof of this; that it was right to print the speech of M. Delaunay, if they so pleased, but at any rate not to send it to the departments; and that they ought to return to the proposal of the commission. The discussion was accordingly adjourned till the 3rd of July.

One deputy had not yet spoken. This was Vergniaud. A member of the Gironde, and its most eloquent orator, he was nevertheless independent. Whether from thoughtlessness or from real elevation, he seemed to be above the passions of his friends; and, in sharing their patriotic ardour, he did not always share their prepossessions and their vehemence. When he had made up his mind upon a question, he carried along with him by his eloquence and a certain acknowledged impartiality, that floating portion of the Assembly which Mirabeau had formerly hurried away by his reasoning and Jus warmth. Wavering masses are everywhere decided by talents and reason.

It had been announced that he would speak on the 3rd of July. An immense concourse had assembled to hear this distinguished orator on a question which was regarded as decisive. Accordingly, he did speak, and first drew a sketch of the state of France. "If," said he, "one did not believe in the imperishable love of the people for liberty, one would doubt whether the Revolution retrogrades or whether it is reaching its term. Our armies of the North advanced into Belgium, and all at once they fell back. The theatre of war is transferred to our territory, and we shall have left the unfortunate Belgians nothing but the remembrance of the conflagrations that lighted our retreat. At the same time, a formidable army of Prussians is threatening the Rhine, though we had been taught to hope that their progress would not be so rapid.

"How happens it that this moment should have been chosen for the dismissal of the popular ministers, for breaking the chain of their labours, for committing the empire to inexperienced hands, and for rejecting the useful measures which we have deemed it our duty to propose? . . . . Can it be true that a dread is felt of our triumphs? Is it the blood of Coblentz or yours, that there is a desire to spare? Is there a wish to reign over forsaken towns and devastated fields? . . . . In short, where are we? . . . . And you, gentlemen, what grand work are you about to undertake for the public weal?

"You, whom some flatter themselves that they have intimidated: you, whose consciences they flatter themselves that they have alarmed by stigmatizing your patriotism as the spirit of faction, as if those who took the oath in the Tennis Court had not also been called factious: you, who have been so slandered, because you belong not to a proud caste which the constitution has thrown down in the dust: you, to whom are imputed guilty intentions, as if, invested with a, power different from that of the law, you had a civil list: you, whose concern for the dangers of the people a hypocritical moderation hoped to cool: you, whom means have been found to divide, but who, in this moment of danger, will lay aside your animosities, your paltry dissensions, and not find it so delightful to hate one another as to prefer that infernal pleasure to the welfare of the country;—you, finally, hearken to me! What are your resources? What does necessity command you? What does the constitution permit you to do?"

During this exordium, loud applause drowned the voice of the speaker. He continued his speech, and exhibited two kinds of dangers, the one internal, the other external.

"To remove the former, the Assembly has proposed a decree against the priests, and, whether the spirit of a Medicis still flits beneath the vaults of the Tuileries, or a Lachaise or a Letellier still disturbs the heart of the prince, the decree has been rejected by the throne. It is not possible to believe, without doing the King injustice, that he wishes for religious disturbances! He fancies himself then sufficiently powerful—he has then ancient laws enough—to ensure the public tranquility. Let his ministers then answer for it with their heads, since they have the means of ensuring it!

"To provide against eternal dangers, the Assembly conceived the idea of a camp of reserve. The King rejected it. It would be doing him injustice to suppose that he wishes to deliver up France to the enemy; he must therefore have forces sufficient to protect it; his ministers therefore ought to answer to us with their heads for the salvation of the country."

Thus far the speaker confines himself, as we see, to the ministerial responsibility, and strives to exhibit it under the most threatening aspect. "But," added he, "to throw the ministers into the abyss which their malice or their imbecility has opened, is not all . . . . Listen to me calmly; be in no hurry to anticipate what I am about to say."

At these words the attention of his auditors was redoubled. Profound silence pervaded the Assembly. "It is in the name *of the King*" said he, "that the French princes have endeavoured to raise Europe against us. It is to avenge the *dignity of the King* that the treaty of Pilnitz has been concluded. It is to come *to the aid of the King* that the sovereign of Hungary and Bohemia makes war upon us, that Prussia is marching towards our frontiers. Now, I read in the constitution: 'If the King puts himself at the head of an army and directs its forces against the nation, or if he does not oppose by a formal act an enterprise of this kind that may be executed in his name, he shall be considered as having abdicated royalty.'

"What is a formal act of opposition? If one hundred thousand Austrians were marching towards Flanders, and one hundred thousand Prussians towards Alsace, and the King were to oppose to them ten or twenty thousand men, would he have done a formal act of opposition?

"If the King, whose duty it is to notify imminent hostilities, apprised of the movements of the Prussian army, were not to communicate any information on the subject to the National Assembly; if a camp of reserve, necessary for stopping the progress of the enemy into the interior, were proposed, and the King were to substitute in its stead an uncertain plan which it would take a long time to execute; if the King were to leave the command of an army to an intriguing general, of whom the nation was suspicious; if another general, bred afar from the corruption of courts and familiar with victory, were to demand a reinforcement, and the King were by a refusal to say to him: *I forbid thee to conquer*—could it be asserted that the King had committed a formal act of opposition?

"I have exaggerated several circumstances," resumed Vergniaud, "to take away every pretext for explanations purely hypothetical. But if, while France was swimming in blood, the King were to say to you, 'It is true that the enemies pretend to be acting for me, for my dignity, for my rights, but I have proved that I am not their accomplice. I have sent armies into the field; these armies were too weak, but the constitution does not fix the degree of their force. I have assembled them too late, but the constitution does not fix the time for collecting them. I have stopped a general who was on the point of conquering, but the constitution does not order victories. I have had ministers, who deceived the Assembly, and disorganised the government, but their appointment belonged to me. The Assembly has passed useful decrees which I have not sanctioned, but I had a right to act so. I have done all that the constitution enjoined me. It is, therefore, impossible to doubt my fidelity to it.' Vehement applause here burst from all quarters.

"If then," continued Vergniaud, "the King were to hold this language, should you not have a right to reply: 'King, who, like Lysander, the tyrant, have believed that truth was not worth more than falsehood—who have feigned a love for the laws merely to preserve the power which enabled you to defy them—was it defending us to oppose to the foreign soldiers forces whose inferiority left not even uncertainty as to their defeat? Was it defending us, to thwart plans tending to fortify the interior? Was it defending us, not to check a general who violated the constitution, but to enchain the courage of those who were serving it? Did the constitution leave you the choice of the ministers for our prosperity or for our ruin? Did it make you the head of the army for our glory or our disgrace? Did it, finally, confer on you the right of sanction, a civil list, and so many prerogatives, in order constitutionally to undo the constitution of the empire? No! no! Man, in whom the generosity of the French has excited no corresponding feeling, insensible to everything but the love of despotism, you are henceforth nothing to that constitution which you have so unworthily violated—to that people whom you have so basely betrayed! '

"But no," resumed the speaker, "if our armies are not complete, the King assuredly is not to blame for this; no doubt he will take the necessary measures for saving us; no doubt the march of the Prussians will not be so triumphant as they hope; but it was requisite to foresee everything and to say everything, for frankness alone can save us."

Vergniaud concluded by proposing a message to Louis XVI., firm but respectful, which should oblige him to choose between France and foreigners, and teach him that the French were resolved to perish or triumph with the constitution. He wished also that the Assembly should declare the country in danger, in order to awaken in hearts those mighty affections which have animated mighty nations, and which no doubt would be found in the French; "for," said he, "it will not be in the regenerated French of '89 that Nature will show herself degenerated." He wished, finally, that an end should be put to dissensions which began to assume a sinister character, and that they should reunite those who were in Rome and on Mount Aventine.

As he uttered these last words, the voice of the speaker faltered, and the emotion was general. The tribunes, the left side, in short, all applauded. Vergniaud left the tribune, and was surrounded by a crowd, who thronged to congratulate him. He alone had dared to speak to the Assembly concerning the forfeiture of the crown, which was a general topic of conversation in public; but he had presented the subject only in an hypothetical manner, and clothed in forms still respectful, when compared with the language suggested by the passions of the time.

Dumas came forward to reply. He attempted to speak extempore after Vergniaud, before auditors still full of the feelings that he had excited. He several times claimed silence and an attention which it was not in his power to grain. He animadverted on the reproaches urged against the executive power. "The retreat of Luckner," said he, "is owing to the chance of battles, which cannot be governed in the recesses of cabinets. Assuredly you have confidence in Luckner?" Cries of "Yes! yes!" were the answer: and Kersaint proposed a decree, declaring that Luckner had retained the national confidence. The decree was passed, and Dumas proceeded. He observed very justly that, if they had confidence in that general, they could, not consider the intention of his retreat as culpable or suspicious; that, as for the want of forces which was complained of, the marshal himself knew that all the troops then disposable were assembled for this enterprise; that, moreover, everything must have been already prepared by the old Girondin ministry, the author of the offensive warfare; and that, if the menus were inadequate, that ministry alone was to blame; that the new ministers could not possibly repair all that was defective by a few couriers; and, lastly, that they had given *carte blanche* to Luckner, and had left him the power to act according to circumstances and local situation.

"The camp of twenty thousand men has been rejected," added Dumas, "but, in the first place, the ministers are not responsible for the veto, and, in the next, the plan which they substituted in its stead was far preferable to that proposed by the Assembly, because it did not paralyse the means of recruiting. The decree against the priests has been rejected, but there is no need of new laws to ensure the public tranquillity. Nothing is wanting but quiet, security, respect for individual liberty, and liberty of conscience. Wherever these liberties have been respected, the priests have not been seditious." Dumas concluded with justifying the King, by objecting that he had not wished for war, and Lafayette by reminding the Assembly that he had always been a lover of liberty.

The decree proposed by the commission of twelve, for arranging the forms according to which the country should be declared in danger, was passed amidst the most vehement applause. But the declaration of danger was adjourned, because it was not thought right as yet to proclaim it. The King, no doubt excited by all that had been said, notified to the Assembly the imminent hostilities with Prussia, which he grounded on the convention of Pilnitz, on the favourable reception given to the rebels, on the acts of violence committed upon French mercantile men, on the dismissal of our minister, and the departure of the Prussian ambassador from Paris; lastly, on the march of the Prussian troops to the number of fifty-two thousand men. "Everything proves to me," added the King's message, "an alliance between Vienna and Berlin. (There was a laugh at these words.) Agreeably to the terms of the constitution, I give this intimation of it to the legislative body."—"Yes," replied several voices, "when the Prussians are at Coblentz." The message was referred to the commission of twelve.

The discussion relative to the forms of the declaration *of the country in danger* was continued. It was decreed that this declaration should be considered as a simple proclamation, and that consequently it should not be subject to the royal sanction, which was not quite just, since it comprehended legislative clauses, but, without meaning to proclaim it, the Assembly already followed the law of the public welfare.

The discussions were daily increasing in violence. The wish of Vergniaud to unite those who were in Rome and on Mount Aventine was not fulfilled: the fear which each excited in the other was changed into irreconcilable hatred.

There was in the Assembly a deputy named Lamourette, constitutional Bishop of Lyons, who had never considered liberty in any other light than as a return to primitive fraternity, and who was as much grieved as astonished at the divisions of his colleagues. He did not believe that the one harboured any real hatred against the others. He supposed that all of them merely entertained unjust suspicions. On the 7th of July, at the moment when the discussion on the country in danger was about to be resumed, he asked leave to speak for the purpose of a motion to order; and, addressing his colleagues in the most persuasive tone and with the noblest aspect, he told them that terrible measures were every day proposed to them in order to put an end to the danger of the country; that, for his part, he had faith in milder and more efficacious means. It was the disunion among the representatives that was the cause of all the evils, and to this disunion it behoved them to apply a remedy. "Oh!" exclaimed the worthy prelate, "he who should succeed in reconciling you, that man would be the real conqueror of

Austria and of Coblentz. It is daily alleged that, at the point to which things have been carried, your reunion is impossible. Ah! I tremble at the thought . . . but this is a calumny. There is nothing irreconcilable but guilt and virtue. Good men dispute warmly, because they are impressed with the sincere conviction of the correctness of their opinions, but they cannot hate one another. Gentlemen, the public weal is in your hands. Why do you delay carrying it into operation?

"What is it that the two portions of the Assembly charge each other with? One accuses the other of wishing to modify the constitution by the hands of foreigners; and the latter accuses the former of striving to overthrow the monarchy for the purpose of establishing a republic. Well, gentlemen, hurl one and the same anathema against a republic and the two chambers. Devote them to general execration by a last and irrevocable oath! Let us swear to have but one spirit, but one sentiment. Let us swear everlasting fraternity! Let the enemy know that what we will, Ave all will, and the country is saved!"

Scarcely had the speaker finished these concluding words, when both sides of the Assembly rose, applauding his generous sentiments, and eager to rid themselves of the burden of their reciprocal animosities. Amidst universal acclamations, they devoted to public execration any project for changing the constitution either by two chambers or by a republic; and the members rushed from the opposite benches to embrace one another. Those who had attacked and those who had defended Lafayette, the veto, the civil list, the *factions*, and the *traitors*, were clasped in each others' arms. All distinctions ceased, and Messrs. Pastoret and Condorcet, who the day before were loading one another with abuse in the public papers, were seen locked in each other's embrace. There was no longer any right or left side, and all the deputies sat indiscriminately together. Dumas was beside Basire, Jaucourt next to Merlin, and Ramond by Chabot.

It was immediately decided that they should inform the provinces, the army, and the King, of this happy event. A deputation, headed by Lamourette, repaired to the palace. Lamourette returned, announcing the intention of the King to come, as on the 4th of February, 1790, to express his satisfaction to the Assembly, and to assure it that he was sorry he had to wait for a deputation, for he was most anxious to hasten into the midst of it.

The enthusiasm was increased to the highest pitch by these words, and if the unanimous cry might be credited, the country was saved. Was it, then, that a King and eight hundred hypocritical deputies had suddenly formed the plan of deceiving each other, and feigning an oblivion of injuries, that they might afterwards betray one another with the greater certainty? No, assuredly not. Such a plan is not formed among so great a number of persons, and all at once, without premeditation. But hatred is burdensome; it is a relief to get rid of the weight of it: and, moreover, at the prospect of the most threatening events, which party was it that, in the uncertainty of victory, would not gladly have consented to keep the present as it was, provided that it were ensured to them? This fact demonstrates that distrust and fear produced all the animosities, that a moment of confidence allayed them, and that, if the party called republican thought of a republic, it was not from system but from despair. Why did not the King, on returning to his palace, write immediately to Prussia and Austria? Why did he not combine with these secret measures some grand public measure? Why did he not say, like his ancestor Louis XIV., on the approach of the enemy, *Let us all go*!

But in the evening the Assembly was informed of the result of the proceedings instituted by the department against Petion and Manuel; and this result was the suspension of those two magistrates. From what has since been learned from the lips of Petion himself, it is probable that he could have prevented the commotion of the 20th of June, since he afterwards prevented others. In fact, his real sentiments were not then known, but it was strongly presumed that he had connived with the agitators. There were moreover some infringements of the law to lay to his charge. He was reproached, for instance, with having been extremely dilatory in his communications to the different authorities, and with having suffered the council of the commune to pass a resolution (*arrêté*) contrary to that of the department, in deciding that the petitioners should be admitted into the ranks of the national guard. The suspension pronounced by the department was, therefore, legal and courageous, but impolitic. After the reconciliation of the morning, was it not, in fact, the height of imprudence to signify, in the evening of the very same day, the suspension of two magistrates enjoying the greatest popularity? The King, indeed, referred the matter to the Assembly; but, without betraying its dissatisfaction, it sent back the decision to him that he might himself pronounce upon it. The tribunes recommenced their usual cries; a great number of petitions were presented, demanding *Petion or death*; and Grangeneuve, the deputy, who had been personally insulted, insisted on a report against the perpetrator of the outrage. Thus the reconciliation was already forgotten. Brissot, to whose turn it had come to speak on the question of the public danger, solicited time to modify the expressions of his speech, on account of the reconciliation which had since taken place. Nevertheless, he could not abstain from enumerating all the instances of neglect and tardiness laid to the charge of the court; and, in spite of the pretended reconciliation, he concluded with proposing that the question of the forfeiture of the crown should be solemnly discussed; that ministers should be impeached for having so long delayed to notify the hostilities of Prussia; that a secret commission of seven members should be appointed and charged to attend to the public welfare; that the property of the emigrants should be sold; that the organization of the national guards should be accelerated; and, lastly, that the Assembly should forthwith declare *the country* to be *in danger*.

Intelligence was at the same time received of the conspiracy of Dessaillant, one of the late noblesse, who, at the head of a party of insurgents, had gained possession of the fort of Pannes, in the department of the Ardèche, and thence threatened the whole surrounding country. The disposition of the powers was also reported to the Assembly by the ministers. The house of Austria, influencing

Prussia, had induced it to march against France; the pupils of the great Frederick nevertheless murmured against this impolitic alliance. The electorates were all our open or concealed enemies. Russia had been the first to declare against the Revolution; she had acceded to the treaty of Pilnitz; she had flattered the projects of Gustavus and seconded the emigrants; and all to deceive Prussia and Austria, and to urge them both on against France, whilst she acted against Poland. At that moment she was treating with MM. de Nassau and d'Esterhazy, leaders of the emigrants; but, notwithstanding her magnificent promises, she had merely furnished them with a frigate, to rid herself of their presence at St. Petersburg. Sweden was immovable since the death of Gustavus, and admitted our ships. Denmark promised a strict neutrality. We might consider ourselves as being at war with the court of Turin. The Pope was preparing his thunderbolts. Venice was neutral, but seemed disposed to protect Trieste with its navy. Spain, without entering openly into the coalition, appeared not unwilling to adhere to the family compact, and to return to France the aid which she had received from her.

England promised neutrality and gave fresh assurances of it. The United States would gladly have assisted us with all their means; but those means were then null, on account of their distance and their thin population.

Immediately after the communication of this report, the Assembly was for declaring the country in danger: but that declaration was postponed till after the presentation of a new report from all the committees united. On the 11th, after this report had been read, amidst profound silence, the president pronounced the solemn formula, CITIZENS, THE COUNTRY IS IN DANGER.

From that moment the sittings were declared permanent. The discharge of cannon, fired from moment to moment, proclaimed this important crisis. All the municipalities, all the district and departmental councils, sat without interruption. All the national guards put themselves in motion. Amphitheatres were erected in the public places, and there the municipal officers received, upon a table borne by drummers, the names of those who came voluntarily to enrol themselves. The number enrolled amounted to fifteen thousand in one day.

The reconciliation of the 7th of July and the oath which followed, had not, as we have just seen, dispelled any distrust. People were still devising means to protect themselves against the designs of the palace, and the idea of declaring that the King had forfeited the crown, or of forcing him to abdicate, presented itself to every mind as the only possible remedy for the evils which threatened France. Vergniaud had merely pointed hypothetically to this idea; but others, especially Torne, the deputy, were desirous that this supposition of Vergniaud should be considered as a reality. Petitions poured in from every part of France, to lend the aid of public opinion to this desperate scheme of the patriotic deputies.

The city of Marseilles had previously presented a threatening petition, read to the Assembly on the 19th June, and the substance of which has been already given. At the moment when the country was declared in danger, several others were received. One of them proposed to accuse Lafayette, to suppress the veto in certain cases, to reduce the civil list, and to reinstate Manuel and Petion in their municipal functions. Another demanded, together with the suppression of the veto, the publicity of the councils. But the city of Marseilles, which had set the first example of these acts of boldness, soon carried them to the utmost excess. It presented an address, recommending to the Assembly to abolish royalty in the reigning branch, and to substitute in its stead a merely elective royalty and without veto, that is to say, a purely *executive magistracy*, as in republics. The stupor produced by the reading of this address was soon followed by the applause of the tribunes; and a motion for printing it was made by a member of the Assembly. The address was, nevertheless, referred to the commission of twelve, that the law declaring infamous every plan for altering the constitution might be applied to it.

Consternation pervaded the court. It pervaded also the patriotic party, which hold petitions were far from cheering. The King conceived that violence was intended against his person. He attributed the events of the 20th of June to a scheme for murdering him, which had miscarried; but he was assuredly wrong, for nothing would have been easier than the consummation of that crime, if it had been projected. He was fearful of being poisoned, and himself and his family took their meals with a lady in the Queen's confidence, where they ate of different dishes from those which were prepared in the offices of the palace. (*See* Appendix Z Z Z.) As the anniversary of the Federation was approaching, the Queen caused a kind of breastplate, composed of several folds of stuff, capable of resisting a first thrust of a dagger, to be made for the King. However, as time passed away, and the popular audacity increased, without any attempt at assassination being made, the King began to form a more correct notion of the nature of his danger; and he already perceived that it was not the point of a dagger, but a judicial condemnation, that he had to dread; and the fate of Charles I. continually haunted his tortured imagination.

Lafayette, though repulsed by the court, had nevertheless resolved to save the King. He therefore caused a plan of flight, that was very boldly conceived, to be submitted to him. He had first gained over Luckner, and had even extorted from the easy disposition of the old marshal a promise to march towards Paris. Lafayette proposed that the King should send for him and Luckner, upon pretext of attending the Federation. The presence of two generals might, he thought, overawe the people, and prevent the dangers which were apprehended from that day. Lafayette further proposed that, the day after the ceremony, Louis XVI. should publicly leave Paris, professedly with the intention of going to Compiègne, in order to exhibit a proof of his liberty to all Europe. In case of opposition, he asked for no more than fifty trusty horse, to carry him off from Paris. From Compiègne, squadrons kept in readiness were to conduct him to the French armies, where Lafayette would depend on his sincerity for the maintenance of the new institutions. Lastly, in case none of these schemes should succeed, the general had determined to march with all his troops to Paris.

Whether this plan required too great boldness, and Louis XVI. had not enough of that quality, or whether the dislike of the Queen to Lafayette, prevented him from accepting his aid, he again refused it, and directed a very cold answer, and one very unworthy of the zeal which the general manifested for him, to be returned. "The best advice," to use the words of that answer, "which can be given to M. Lafayette is to continue to serve as a bugbear to the factious, by the able performance of his duty as a general."

The anniversary of the Federation approached. The people and the Assembly were desirous that Petion should be present at the solemnity of the 14th. The King had already endeavoured to throw upon the Assembly the responsibility of approving or disapproving the resolution of the department; but the Assembly had, as we have seen, constrained him to speak out himself; urging him daily to communicate his decision, that this matter might be settled before the 14th. On the 12th, the King confirmed the suspension. The Assembly lost no time in taking its own course. What that was may easily be conceived. Next day, that is, on the 13th, it reinstated Petion. But, from a shadow of delicacy, it postponed its decision respecting Manuel, who, amidst the tumult of the 20th of June, had been seen walking about in his scarf, without making any use of his authority.

The 14th of July, 1792, at length arrived. How times had changed since the 14th of July, 1790! There was neither that magnificent altar, with three hundred officiating priests, nor that extensive area, covered by sixty thousand national guards, richly dressed and regularly organized, nor those lateral tiers of seats, crowded by an immense multitude, intoxicated with joy and delight; nor lastly, that balcony, where the ministers, the royal family, and the Assembly, were accommodated at the first Federation. Everything was changed. People hated each other as after a hollow reconciliation, and all the emblems indicated war. Eighty-three tents represented the eighty-three departments. Beside each of these stood a poplar, from the top of which waved flags of the three colours. A large tent was destined for the Assembly and the King, and another for the administrative bodies of Paris. Thus all France seemed to be encamped in the presence of the enemy. The altar of the country was but a truncated column, placed at the top of those tiers of seats which had been left in the Champ de Mars, ever since the first ceremony. On one side was seen a monument for those who had died or who were destined soon to die, on the frontiers; on the other an immense tree, called the tree of feudalism. It rose from the centre of a vast pile, and bore on its branches crowns, blue ribbons, tiaras, cardinals' hats, St. Peter's keys, ermine mantles, doctors' caps, bags of law proceedings, titles of nobility, escutcheons, coats of arms, &c. The King was to be invited to set fire to it.

The oath was to be taken at noon. The King had repaired to the apartments of the Military School, where he waited for the national procession, which had gone to lay the first stone of a column destined to rise upon the ruins of the ancient Bastille. The King displayed a calm dignity. The Queen strove to conquer a grief that was but too visible. His sister, his children, surrounded him. Some touching expressions excited emotion in those who were in the apartments, and tears trickled from the eyes of more than one. At length the procession arrived. Until then the Champ de Mars had been almost empty. All at once the multitude rushed into it. Beneath the balcony where the King was placed, a confused mob of women, children, and drunken men was seen to pass, shouting "Petion for ever! Petion or death!" and bearing on their hats the words which they had in their mouths; federalists, arm in arm, and carrying a representation of the Bastille and a press, which stopped from time to time, for the purpose of printing and distributing patriotic songs. Next came the legions of the national guard, and the regiments of the troops of the line, preserving with difficulty the regularity of their ranks amidst the moving populace; and lastly, the authorities themselves, and the Assembly. The King then went down, and, placed amidst a square of troops, moved on with the procession towards the altar of the country. The concourse in the centre of the Champ de Mars was immense, so that they could advance but slowly. After great exertions on the part of the regiments, the King reached the steps of the altar. The Queen, stationed on the balcony, which she had not quitted, watched this scene with a glass. The confusion seemed to increase about the altar, and the King to descend a step. At this sight, the Queen uttered a shriek, and filled all around her with alarm. The ceremony, however, passed off without accident.

As soon as the oath was taken, the people hastened to the tree of feudalism. They were for hurrying the King along with them, that he might set fire to it; but he declined, saying very pertinently that there was no longer any such thing as feudalism. He then set out on his return to the Military School. The troops, rejoiced at having saved him, raised reiterated shouts of *Vive le Roi!* The multitude, which always feels constrained to sympathize, repeated these shouts, and was as prompt to pay him homage as it had been to insult him a few moments before. For a few hours longer the unfortunate Louis XVI. appeared to be beloved; for an instant the people and himself believed this to be the case; but even illusion had ceased to be easy, and they began already to find it impossible to deceive themselves. The King returned to the palace, glad at having escaped the dangers which he conceived to be great, but alarmed at those which he beheld approaching.

The news which arrived daily from the frontiers increased the alarm and agitation. The declaration of *the country in danger* had set all France in motion, and had occasioned the departure of a great number of federalists. There were only two thousand at Paris on the day of the Federation; but they kept continually arriving, and the way in which they conducted themselves there justified both the fears and the hopes that had been conceived of their presence in the capital. All voluntarily enrolled, they comprised the most violent spirits in the clubs of France. The Assembly ordered them an allowance of thirty sous per day, and reserved the tribunes for them exclusively. They soon gave law to it by their shouts and their applause. Connected with the Jacobins, and united in a club which in a few days surpassed all the others in violence, they were ready for insurrection at the first signal. They even made a declaration to this effect in an address to the Assembly. They would not set out, they said, till the enemies in the interior were overthrown. Thus the scheme of assembling an insurrectional force at Paris was completely accomplished, in spite of the opposition of the court.

In addition to this engine, other means were resorted to. The old soldiers of the French guards were dispersed among the regiments. The Assembly ordered them to be collected into a corps of gendarmerie. There could be no doubt respecting their disposition, since it was they who had begun the Revolution. To no purpose was it objected that these men, almost all of them subalterns in the army, constituted its principal force. The Assembly would not listen to any representation, dreading the enemy at home more than the enemy abroad. After composing forces for itself, it resolved to decompose those of the court. To this end, the Assembly ordered the removal of all the regiments. Thus far it had kept within the limits appointed by the constitution; but, not content with removing, it enjoined them to repair to the frontier, and by so doing, it usurped the disposal of the public force, which belonged to the King.

The principal aim of this measure was to get rid of the Swiss, whose fidelity could not be doubted. To parry this blow, the ministers instigated M. d'Affry, their commandant, to remonstrate. He appealed to his capitulations in justification of his refusal to leave Paris. The Assembly appeared to take into consideration the reasons which he urged, but ordered for the moment the departure of two Swiss battalions.

The King, it is true, had his veto to resist these measures, but he had lost all influence, and could no longer exercise his prerogative. The Assembly itself could not always withstand the propositions brought forward by certain of its members, and invariably supported by the applause of the tribunes. It never failed to declare itself in favour of moderation, when that was possible; and, whilst it assented on the one hand to the most insurrectional measures, it was seen on the other receiving and approving the most moderate petitions.

The measures that were adopted, the petitions that were daily read, and the language that was used in all conversations, indicated a speedy revolution. The Girondins foresaw and wished for it; but they did not clearly distinguish the means, and dreaded the issue of it. Among the people complaints were made of their listlessness. They were accused of indolence and incapacity. All the leaders of clubs and sections, weary of eloquent speeches without result, loudly demanded an active and concentrated direction, that the popular efforts might not be unavailing.

There was at the Jacobins a room appropriated to the business of correspondence. Here had been formed a central committee of federalists, for the purpose of concerting and arranging their proceedings. In order that their resolutions might be the more secret and energetic, this committee was limited to five members, and was called among themselves the *insurrectional committee.* These five members were Vaugeois, grand vicar; Debesse of La Drome; Guillaume, professor at Caen; Simon, journalist at Strasburg; and Galissot of Langres. To these were soon added Carra, Gorsas, Fournier the American, Westermann, Kienlin of Strasburg, Santerre, Alexandre, commandant of the fauxbourg St. Marceau, a Pole named Lazouski, captain of the gunners in the artillery of St. Marceau, Antoine of Metz, an ex-constituent, and Lagrey and Garin, two electors. It was joined by Manuel, Camille Desmoulins, and Danton; and these exercised the greatest influence over it. (*See* Appendix A A A A.) They entered into arrangements with Barbaroux, who promised the co-operation of his Marseillais, whose arrival was impatiently expected. They placed themselves in communication with Petion, the mayor, and obtained from him a promise not to prevent the insurrection. In return they promised him to protect his residence and to place a guard upon it, in order to justify his inaction by an appearance of constraint, if the enterprise should miscarry.

The plan definitively adopted was to repair in arms to the palace, and to depose the King. But it was requisite to set the people in motion, and, to succeed in this purpose, some extraordinary exciting cause was indispensably necessary. Endeavours were made to produce one, and the subject was discussed at the Jacobins. Chabot, (*see* Appendix B B B B.) the deputy, expatiated with all the ardour of his disposition on the necessity for a great revolution, and he said that, in order to bring about such a one, it was desirable that the court should attempt the life of a deputy. Grangeneuve, himself a deputy, heard this speech. He was a man of limited understanding but resolute disposition. He took Chabot aside, "You are right," said he; "it is expedient that a deputy should perish, but the court is too cunning to give us so fair an occasion. You must make amends, the put me to death as soon as possible in the environs of and palace. Prepare the means and keep your secret." Chabot, seized with enthusiasm, offered to share his fate. Grangeneuve assented, observing that two deaths would produce a greater effect than one. They agreed upon the day, the hour, and the means, of putting an end to their lives, without maiming themselves, as they said; and they separated, resolved to sacrifice themselves for the success of the common cause. Grangeneuve, determined to keep his word, put his domestic affairs in order, and proceeded at half-past ten o'clock at night to the place of meeting. Chabot was not there. He waited. As Chabot did not come, he conceived that he had changed his mind, but he hoped that, in regard to himself at least, the execution would take place. He walked to and fro several times in expectation of the mortal blow, but was obliged to return, safe and sound, without enjoying the satisfaction of immolating himself for the sake of a calumny.

The occasion so impatiently looked for did not occur, and the parties began mutually to accuse each other of want of courage, intelligence, and unity. The Girondin deputies, Petion, the mayor, and, in short, all persons of any eminence, and who were obliged, either in the tribune or in the performance of their official duties, to speak the language of the law, kept themselves more and more aloof, and condemned these incessant agitations, which compromised them without producing any result. They reproached the subaltern agitators with exhausting their strength in partial and useless movements, which exposed the people without leading to any decisive event. The latter, on the contrary, who did in their respective spheres all that they could do, reproached the deputies and Petion, the mayor, for their public speeches, and accused them of repressing the energy of the people.

Thus the deputies reproached the mass with not being organised, and the latter complained that the deputies themselves were not. The want most sensibly felt was that of a leader. We need a man, was the general cry; but who is it to be? No fit person was to be found among the deputies. They were all of them rather orators than conspirators; and, besides, their elevated situation and their mode of life removed them too far from the multitude, on whom it was necessary to act. In the same predicament were Roland, Servan, and all those men whose courage was undoubted, but whose rank lifted them too high above the populace.

Petion might, from his office, have had opportunity to communicate easily with the multitude; but he was cold, passionless, and capable of dying rather than acting. By means of his system of checking petty agitations, for the benefit of a decisive insurrection, he thwarted the daily movements, and lost all favour with the agitators, whom he impeded without controlling. They wanted a leader who, not having yet issued from the bosom of the multitude, had not lost all power over it, and who had received from nature the spirit of persuasion.

A vast field had been opened in the clubs, the sections, and the revolutionary papers. Many had there distinguished themselves, but none had yet gained a marked superiority. Camille Desmoulins had acquired notice by his energy, his cynical spirit, his audacity, and his promptness in attacking all those who seemed to flag in the revolutionary career. He was known to the lower classes; but he had neither the lungs of a popular speaker, nor the activity and powers of persuasion of a party-leader.

Another public writer had gained a frightful celebrity. This was Marat, known by the name of the Friend of the People, and who, by his instigations to murder, had become an object of horror to all those who yet retained any moderation. A native of Neufchatel, and engaged in the study of the physical and medical sciences, he had boldly attacked the most firmly-established systems, and had shown an activity of mind that might be termed convulsive. He was physician to the stables of Count d'Artois, when the Revolution commenced. He rushed without hesitation into a new career, and soon acquired distinction in his section. He was of middle height, with a large head, strongly-marked features, livid complexion, a piercing eye, and careless in his personal appearance. It was necessary, he asserted, to strike off several thousand heads, and to destroy all the aristocrats, who rendered liberty impossible. Horror and contempt were alternately excited by him. People ran against him, trod upon his toes, made game of his wretched-looking figure; but, accustomed to scientific squabbles and the most extravagant assertions, he had learned to despise those who despised him, and he pitied them as incapable of comprehending him.

Thenceforward he diffused in his papers the horrid doctrine with which he was imbued. The subterraneous life to which he was doomed in order to escape justice had heated his temperament, and the public horror served still more to excite it. Our polished manners were, according to his notions, but vices which were hostile to republican equality; and, in his ardent hatred for the obstacles, he saw but one means of safety—extermination. His studies and his observations on the physical man must have accustomed him to conquer the sight of pain; and his ardent mind, unchecked by any instinct of sensibility, proceeded directly to its goal by ways of blood. That same idea of operating by destruction had gradually become systematised in his head. He proposed a dictator, not for the purpose of conferring on him the pleasure of omnipotence, but of imposing upon him the terrible task of purifying society. The dictator was to have a cannon-ball attached to his leg, that he might always be in the power of the people. He was to have but one faculty left him, that of pointing out victims and ordering death as their only chastisement. Marat knew no other penalty, because he was not for punishing but for suppressing the obstacle.

Perceiving aristocrats on all sides conspiring against liberty, he collected here and there all the facts that gratified his passion. He denounced with fury, and with a levity which was the result of that very fury, all the names mentioned to him, and which frequently had no existence. He denounced them without personal hatred, without fear, nay even without danger to himself; because he was out of the pale of human society, and because the relations between the injured and the injurer no longer existed between him and his fellow-men.

Being recently included in a decree of accusation with Royou, the King's friend, he had concealed himself in the house of an obscure and indigent advocate, who had afforded him an asylum. Barbaroux was requested to call upon him. Barbaroux had cultivated the physical sciences, and had formerly been acquainted with Marat. He could not refuse to comply with this request, and conceived, when he heard him, that his mind was deranged. The French, according to this atrocious man, were but paltry revolutionists. "Give me," said he, "two hundred Neapolitans, armed with daggers, and bearing on the left arm a muff, by way of buckler; with them I will traverse France and produce a revolution." He proposed that, in order to mark the aristocrats, the Assembly should order them to wear a white ribbon on the arm, and that it should be lawful to kill them when three were found together. Under the name of aristocrats, he included the royalists, the Feuillans, and the Girondins; and when, by chance, the difficulty of recognising and distinguishing them was mentioned, he declared that it was impossible to mistake; that it was only necessary to fall upon those who had carriages, servants, silk clothes, and who were coming out of the theatres. All such were assuredly aristocrats.

Barbaroux: left him horror-struck. Marat, full of his atrocious system, concerned himself but little about the means of insurrection, and was moreover incapable of preparing them. In his murderous reveries, he feasted himself on the idea of retiring to Marseilles. The republican enthusiasm of that city led him to hope that there he should be better understood and more cordially received. He had thoughts, therefore, of seeking refuge there, and begged Barbaroux; to send him thither with his recommendation. But the latter, having no desire to make such a present to his native city, left that insensate wretch, whose apotheosis he was then far from foreseeing, where he found him.

The systematic and bloodthirsty Marat was not therefore the active chief who could have united these scattered and confusedly fermenting masses. Robespierre would have been more capable of doing so, because he had gained at the Jacobins a patronising circle of auditors, usually more active than a patronising circle of readers. But neither did he possess the requisite qualities. Robespierre, an advocate of little repute at Arras, had been sent by that city as its deputy to the States-general. There he had connected himself with Petion and Buzot, and maintained with bitterness the opinions which they defended with a deep and calm conviction. At first, he appeared ridiculous, from the heaviness of his delivery and the mediocrity of his eloquence; but his obstinacy gained him some attention, especially at the epoch of the revision. When it was rumoured, after the scene in the Champ de Mars, that the persons who had signed the petition of the Jacobins were to be prosecuted, his terror and his youth excited the pity of Buzot and Roland. An asylum was offered to him, but he soon recovered from his alarm: and, the Assembly having broken up, he intrenched himself at the Jacobins, where he continued his dogmatic and inflated harangues. Being elected public accuser, he refused that new office, and thought only how to acquire the double reputation of an incorruptible patriot and an eloquent speaker. (*See* Appendix C C C C.)

His first friends, Petion, Buzot, Brissot, and Roland, admitted him to their houses, and observed with pain his mortified pride, which was betrayed by his looks and by his every motion. They felt an interest for him, and regretted that, thinking so much of the public welfare, he should also think so much of himself. He was, however, a person of too little importance for people to be angry with him for his pride; and it was forgiven on account of his mediocrity and his zeal. It was particularly remarked that, silent in all companies, and rarely expressing his sentiments, he was the first on the following day to retail in the tribune the ideas of others which he had thus collected. This observation was mentioned to him, but unaccompanied with any reproach; and he soon began to detest this society of superior men, as he had detested that of his constituents. He then betook himself entirely to the Jacobins, where, as we have seen, he differed in opinion from Brissot (*see* Appendix D D D D.) and Louvet on the question of war, and called them, nay, perhaps believed them to be, bad citizens, because their sentiments did not coincide with his, and they supported their opinions with eloquence. Was he sincere, when he immediately suspected those who had opposed him, or did he slander them wilfully? These are the mysteries of minds. But, with a narrow and common intellect, and with extreme susceptibility, it was easy to give him unfavourable impressions and difficult to correct them. It is therefore not impossible that a hatred from pride may have changed in him to a hatred from principle, and that he soon believed all those to be wicked who had offended him.

Be this as it may, in the lower sphere in which he moved, he excited enthusiasm by his dogmatism and by his reputation for incorruptibility. He thus founded his popularity upon blind passions and moderate understandings. Austerity and cold dogmatism captivate ardent characters, nay, often superior minds. There were actually men who were disposed to discover in Robespierre real energy and talents superior to those which he possessed. Camille Desmoulins called him his Aristides, and thought him eloquent.

Others, without talents, but subdued by his pedantry, went about repeating that he was the man who ought to be put at the head of the Revolution, and that without such a dictator it could not go on. For his part, winking at all these assertions of his partisans, he never attended any of the secret meetings of the conspirators. He complained even of being compromised, because one of them, dwelling in the same house as himself, had occasionally brought thither the insurrectional committee. He kept himself, therefore, in the back-ground, leaving the business of acting to his panegyrists, Panis, Sergent, Osselin, and other members of the sections and of the municipal councils.

Marat, who was looking for a dictator, wished to ascertain if Robespierre was fit for the office. The neglected and cynical person of Marat formed a striking contrast to that of Robespierre, who was particularly attentive to external appearance. In the retirement of an elegant cabinet, where his image was repeated in all possible ways, in painting, in engraving, and in sculpture, he devoted himself to assiduous study, and was continually reading Rousseau, in order to glean ideas for his speeches. Marat saw him, found in him nothing but petty animosities, no great system, none of that sanguinary audacity which he himself derived from his monstrous convictions—in short, no genius. He departed, filled with contempt for this *little man*, declared him incapable of saving the state, and became more firmly persuaded than ever that he alone possessed the grand social system.

The partisans of Robespierre surrounded Barbaroux, and wished to conduct the latter to him, saying that *a man* was wanted, and that Robespierre alone could be that man. This language displeased Barbaroux, whose bold spirit could not brook the idea of a dictatorship, and whose ardent imagination was already seduced by the virtue of Roland and the talents of his friends. He called nevertheless on Robespierre. They talked during the interview of Petion, whose popularity threw Robespierre into the shade, and who, it was alleged, was incapable of serving the Revolution. Barbaroux: replied with warmth to the reproaches urged against Petion, and as warmly defended a character which he admired. Robespierre talked of the Revolution, and repeated, according to his custom, that he had accelerated its march. He concluded, as everybody else did, by saying that a leader was wanted. Barbaroux replied that he wanted neither dictator nor King. Freron observed that Brissot was desirous of being dictator. Thus reproaches were bandied from one to the other, and they could not agree. As they went away, Panis, wishing to counteract the bad effect of this interview, said to Barbaroux: that he had mistaken the matter; that it was but a momentary authority that was contemplated, and that Robespierre was the only man on whom it could be conferred. It was these vague expressions, these petty rivalries, which falsely persuaded the Girondins that Robespierre designed to act the usurper. An ardent jealousy was mistaked in him for ambition. But it was one of those errors which the confused vision of parties is continually committing. Robespierre, capable at the utmost of hating merit, had neither the strength nor the genius of ambition, and his partisans raised pretensions for him which he himself would not have dared to conceive.

Danton was more capable than any other of being the leader whom all ardent imaginations desired, for the purpose of giving unity to the revolutionary movements. He had formerly tried the bar, but without success. Poor and consumed by passions, he then rushed into the political commotions with ardour, and probably with hopes. He was ignorant, but endowed with a superior understanding and a vast imagination. His athletic figure, his flat and somewhat African features, his thundering voice, his eccentric but grand images, captivated his auditors at the Cordeliers and the sections. His face expressed by turns the brutal passions, jollity, and even good-nature. Danton neither envied nor hated any body, but his audacity was extraordinary; and, in certain moments of excitement, he was capable of executing all that toe atrocious mind of Marat was capable of conceiving.

A Revolution, the unforeseen but inevitable effect of which had been to set the lower against the upper classes of society, could not fail to awaken envy, to give birth to new systems, and to let loose the brutal passions. Robespierre was the envious man, Marat the systematic man, and Danton the impassioned, violent, fickle, and by turns cruel and generous man. If the two former, engrossed, the one by a consuming envy, the other by mischievous systems, could not have many of those wants which render men accessible to corruption, Danton, on the contrary, the slave of his passions, and greedy of pleasure, must have been nothing less than incorruptible. Under pretext of compensating him for the loss of his former place of advocate to the council, the court gave him considerable sums. But, though it contrived to pay, it could not gain him. He continued, nevertheless, to harangue and to excite the mob of the clubs against it. When he was reproached with not fulfilling his bargain, he replied that, in order to retain the means of serving the court, he was obliged in appearance to treat it as an enemy.

Danton was therefore the most formidable leader of those bands which were won and guided by public oratory. But, audacious and fond of hurrying forward to the decisive moment, he was not capable of that assiduous toil which the thirst of rule requires; and, though he possessed great influence over the conspirators, he did not yet govern them. He was merely capable, when they hesitated, of rousing their courage and propelling them to the goal by a decisive plan of operation.

The different members of the insurrectional committee had not yet been able to agree. The court, apprised of their slightest movements, took, on its part, some measures for screening itself against a sudden attack, so that it might be enabled to await in safety the arrival of the coalesced powers. It had formed a club, called the French club, which met near the palace, and was composed of artisans and soldiers of the national guard. They had all their arms concealed in the very building in which they assembled; and they could, in case of emergency, hasten to the aid of the royal family. This single association cost the civil list ten thousand francs per day. A Marseillais, named Lieutaud, kept moreover in pay a band which alternately occupied the tribunes, the public places, the coffee-houses, and the public-houses, for the purpose of speaking in favour of the King, and opposing the continual tumults of the patriots. Quarrels occurred, in fact, everywhere, and from words the parties almost always came to blows; but, in spite of all the efforts of the court, its adherents were thinly scattered, and that portion of the national guard which was attached to it was reduced to the lowest state of discouragement.

A great number of faithful servants, who had till then been at a distance from the throne, had come forward to defend the King, and to make a rampart for him with their bodies. Their meetings at the palace were numerous, and they increased the public distrust. After the scene in February, 1790, they were called knights of the dagger. Letters had been delivered for the purpose of calling secretly together the constitutional guard, which, though disbanded, had always received its pay. During this time, conflicting opinions were maintained around the King, which produced the most painful perplexities in his weak and naturally wavering mind. Some intelligent friends, among others, Malesherbes, advised him to abdicate. Others, and these constituted the majority, recommended flight. For the rest, they were far from agreeing either upon the means, or the place, or the result of the invasion. In order to reconcile these different plans, the King desired Bertrand de Molleville to see and to arrange matters with Duport, the constituent. The King had great confidence in the latter, and he was obliged to give a positive order to Bertrand, who alleged that he disliked to have any communication with a constitutionalist such as Duport. To this committee belonged also Lally-Tollendal, Mallouet, Clermont-Tonnerre, Gouvernet, and others, all devoted to Louis XVI., but otherwise differing widely as to the part which royalty ought to be made to act, if they could contrive to save it.

The flight of the King and his retreat to the castle of Gaillon, in Normandy, were then resolved upon. The Duke de Liancourt, a friend of the King, and possessing his unlimited confidence, commanded that province. He answered for his troops and for the inhabitants of Rouen, who had, in an energetic address, declared themselves against the 20th of June. He offered to receive the royal family, and to conduct it to Gaillon, or to consign it to Lafayette, who would convey it into the midst of his army. He offered, moreover, his whole fortune for the purpose of seconding this project, asking permission to reserve for his children merely an annuity of one hundred louis. This plan was liked by the constitutional members of the committee, because, instead of placing the King in the hands of the emigrants, it put him under the care of the Duke de Liancourt and Lafayette. For the same reason it displeased others, and was likely to displease the Queen and the King. Still, the castle of Gaillon possessed the important advantage of being only thirty-six leagues from the sea, and of offering an easy flight to England through Normandy, a favourably disposed province. It had also another, namely, that of being only twenty leagues from Paris. The King could therefore repair thither without violating the constitutional law; and this had great weight with him, for he was extremely tenacious of not committing any open infringement of it.

M. de Narbonne and Necker's daughter, Madame de Stael, likewise devised a plan of flight. The emigrants, on their part, proposed another. This was to carry the King to Compiègne, and thence to the banks of the Rhine, through the forest of the Ardennes. Every one is eager to offer advice to a weak King, because every one aspires to impart to him a will which he has not. So many contrary suggestions added to the natural indecision of Louis XVI.; and this unfortunate prince, beset by conflicting counsels, struck by the reason of some, hurried away by the passion of others, tortured by apprehensions concerning the fate of his family, and disturbed by scruples of conscience, wavered between a thousand projects, and beheld the popular flood approaching without daring either to flee from or to confront it. (*See* Appendix E E E E.)

The Girondin deputies, who had so boldly broached the question of the forfeiture of the crown, continued, nevertheless, undecided on the eve of an insurrection; and, though the court was almost disarmed, and the supreme power was on the side of the people, still the approach of the Prussians, and the dread always excited by an old authority, even after it is disarmed, persuaded them that it would be better to come to terms with the court than to expose themselves to the chances of an attack. In case this attack should even prove successful, they feared lest the arrival of the Prussians, which was very near at hand, should destroy all the results of a victory over the palace, and cause a momentary success to be followed by terrible vengeance.

Notwithstanding, however, this disposition to treat, they opened no negotiations on the subject, and durst not venture to make the first overtures; but they listened to a man named Boze, painter to the King, and very intimate with Thierry, valet-de-chambre of Louis XVI. Boze, alarmed at the dangers which threatened the public weal, exhorted them to write what they thought proper, in this extremity, to save the King and liberty. They accordingly drew up a letter, which was signed by Guadet, Gensonné, and Vergniaud, and which began with these words: "You ask us, sir, what is our opinion respecting the present situation of France." This exordium sufficiently proves that the explanation had been called for. It was no longer time, said the three deputies to Boze, for the King to deceive himself, and he would do so most egregiously, if he did not perceive that his conduct was the cause of the general agitation, and of that violence of the clubs of which he was continually complaining. New protestations on his part would be useless, and appear derisory, for at the point to which things had come, decisive steps were absolutely necessary to give confidence to the people. Every body, for instance, was persuaded that it was in the power of the King to keep the foreign armies away. He ought, therefore, to begin by making them draw back. He should then choose a patriotic ministry, dismiss Lafayette, who, in the existing state of affairs, could no longer serve him usefully, issue a law for the constitutional education of the young dauphin, submit to the public accountability of the civil list, and solemnly declare that he would not accept any increase of power without the free consent of the nation. On these conditions, added the Girondins, it was to be hoped that the irritation would subside, and that, in time and by perseverance in this system, the King would recover the confidence which he had then entirely lost.

Assuredly, the Girondins were very near the attainment of their aim, if a republic had been a system for which they had long and steadily conspired. And, when so near this goal, would they have stopped short, and even have renounced it, to obtain the ministry for three of their friends? This was not likely, and it becomes evident that a republic was desired only from despair of the monarchy, that it never was a fixed plan, and that, on the very eve of attaining it, those who are accused of having long paved the way to it would not sacrifice the public weal for its sake, but would have consented to a constitutional monarchy, if it were accompanied with sufficient safeguards. The care taken by the Girondins, to demand the removal of the foreign troops, plainly proves that they were wholly engrossed by the existing danger; and the attention which they paid to the education of the dauphin affords as strong a proof that monarchy was not to them an insupportable prospect for the future.

It has been asserted that Brissot, on his part, had made offers to prevent the dethronement of the King, and that the payment of a very large sum was one of the conditions. This assertion is advanced by Bertrand de Molleville, who always dealt in calumny for two reasons—malignity of heart, and falseness of mind. But he adduces no proof of it; and the known poverty of Brissot and his enthusiastic principles ought to answer for him. It is, to be sure, not impossible that the court might have consigned money to the care of Brissot; but this would not prove that the money was either asked for or received by him. The circumstance already related respecting Petion, whom certain swindlers undertook to bribe for the court—this circumstance, and many others of the same kind, sufficiently prove what credit ought to be attached to these charges of venality, so frequently and so easily hazarded. Besides, let matters stand as they will in regard to Brissot, the three deputies, Guadet, Gensonné, and Vergniaud, have not even been accused, and they were the only persons who signed the letter delivered to Boze.

The deeply wounded heart of the King was less capable than ever of listening to their prudent advice. Thierry handed him the letter, but he harshly pushed it back, and returned his two accustomed answers, that it was not he but the patriotic ministry who had provoked the war; and that, as for the constitution, he adhered to it faithfully, whilst others were exerting all their efforts to destroy it. (*See* Appendix F F F F.) These reasons were not the most just; for though he had not provoked the war, it was not the less his duty to carry it on with vigour; and, as for his scrupulous fidelity to the letter of the law, the observance of that letter was of little consequence. It behoved him not to compromise the thing itself by calling in foreigners.

To the hopes entertained by the Girondins that their counsels would be followed must no doubt be attributed the moderation which they displayed when it was proposed to take up the question of the forfeiture of the crown—a question daily discussed in the clubs, among the groups out of doors, and in petitions. Whenever they came, in the name of the commission of twelve, to speak of the danger of the country and the means of preventing it, they were met by the cry of "Go back to the cause of the danger."—"To the cause," repeated the tribunes. Vergniaud, Brissot, and the Girondins, replied that they had their eyes upon the cause, and that in due time it should be unveiled; but for the moment it behoved them not to throw down a fresh apple of discord.

In consequence of an entertainment given to the federalists, the insurrectional committee resolved that its partisans should meet on the morning of the 26th of July, for the purpose of proceeding to the palace, and chat they should march with the red flag, bearing this inscription: "*Those who fire upon the columns of the people shall instantly he put to death.*" The intention was to make the King prisoner, and to confine him at Vincennes. The national guard of Versailles had been requested to second this movement; but the application had been made so late, and there was so little concert with that corps, that its officers came on the very same morning to the mayor's residence at Paris, to inquire how they were to act. The secret was so ill kept that the court was already apprized of it. All the royal family was stirring, and the palace was full of people. Petion, perceiving that the measures had not been judiciously taken, fearful of some treachery, and considering moreover that the Marseillais had not yet arrived, repaired in the utmost haste to the fauxbourg, to stop a movement which must have ruined the popular party if it had not succeeded.

The tumult in the fauxbourgs was tremendous. The tocsin had been ringing there all night. The rumour spread for the purpose of exciting the people was that a quantity of arms had been collected in the palace, and they were urged to go and bring them away. Petion succeeded, with great difficulty, in restoring order, and Champion de Cicé, keeper of the seals, who also repaired to the spot, received several sabre strokes. At length the people consented to stay, and the insurrection was deferred.

The petty quarrels and wranglings which are the usual prelude to a definitive rupture, continued without intermission. The King had caused the garden of the Tuileries tp be closed ever since the 20th of June. The Terrace of the Feuillans, leading to the Assembly, was alone open; and the sentries had directions not to suffer any person to pass from that terrace into the garden. D'Esprémenil was there met conversing loudly with a deputy. He was hooted, pursued into the garden, and carried to the Palais Royal, where he received several wounds. The prohibition to penetrate into the garden having been violated, a motion was made for supplying its place by a decree. The decree, however, was not passed. It was merely proposed to set up a board with the words, "*It is forbidden to trespass on these grounds.*" The board was accordingly erected, and it was sufficient to prevent the people from setting foot in the garden, though the King had caused the sentries to be removed. Thus courtesy ceased to be any longer observed. A letter from Nancy, for instance, reported several civic traits which had occurred in that city. The Assembly immediately sent a copy of it to the King.

At length, on the 30th of July, the Marseillais arrived. They were five hundred in number, and their, ranks comprised all the most fiery spirits that the South could produce, and all the most turbulent characters that commerce brought to the port of Marseilles. Barbaroux went to Charenton to meet them. On this occasion a new scheme was concerted with Santerre. It was proposed, upon pretext of going to meet the Marseillais, to collect the people of the fauxbourgs, and afterwards to repair in good order to the Carrousel, and there encamp without tumult, until the Assembly had suspended the King, or till he had abdicated of his own accord.

This project pleased the philanthropists of the party, who would fain have terminated the Revolution without bloodshed. It failed, however, because Santerre did not succeed in assembling the fauxbourg, and could lead only a small number of men to meet the Marseillais. Santerre immediately offered them a repast, which was served up in the Champs Elysées. On the same day, and at the same moment, a party of the national guards of the battalion of the Filles St. Thomas, and of other persons, clerks or military men, wholly devoted to the court, were dining near the spot where the Marseillais were being entertained. Most assuredly this dinner had not been prepared with the intention of disturbing that of the Marseillais, since the offer made to the latter was unexpected, for, instead of an entertainment, it was an insurrection that had been contemplated. It was, nevertheless, impossible for neighbours so adverse to finish their repast quietly. The populace insulted the royalists, who put themselves upon the defensive. The patriots, summoned to the aid of the populace, hastened with ardour to the place, and a battle ensued. It was not long, for the Marseillais, rushing upon their adversaries, put them to flight, killing one, and wounding several others. In a moment all Paris was in commotion. The federalists paraded the streets, and tore off the cockades of ribbon, saying that they ought to be made of woollen.

Some of the fugitives arrived, covered with blood, at the Tuileries, where they were kindly received and attentions were paid to them which were perfectly natural, since they were regarded as friends who had suffered for their attachment. The national guards on duty at the palace related these particulars, perhaps added to them, and this furnished occasion for fresh reports, and fresh animosity against the royal family and the ladies of the court, who, it was said, had wiped off the perspiration and the blood of the wounded. It was even concluded that the scene had been prepared, and this was the motive for a new accusation against the court.

The national guard of Paris immediately petitioned for the removal of the Marseillais; but it was hooted by the tribunes, and its petition proved unsuccessful.

Amidst these proceedings, a paper attributed to the Prince of Brunswick, and soon ascertained to be authentic, was circulated. We have already adverted to the mission of Mallet du Pan. He had furnished, in the name of the King, the idea and model of a manifesto; but this idea was soon distorted. Another manifesto, inspired by the passions of Coblentz, was signed with the name of Brunswick, and distributed in advance of the Prussian army. This paper was couched in the following terms:—

"Their Majesties the Emperor and the King of Prussia having intrusted me with the command of the combined armies assembled by their orders on the frontiers of France, I am desirous to acquaint the inhabitants of that kingdom with the motives which have determined the measures of the two sovereigns, and the intentions by which they are guided.

"After having arbitrarily suppressed the rights and possessions of the German princes in Alsace and Lorraine; deranged and overthrown good order and the legitimate government in the interior; committed against the sacred person of the King, and his august family, outrages and attacks of violence which are still continued and renewed from day to day; those who have usurped the reins of the administration have at length filled up the measure by causing an unjust war to be declared against his Majesty the Emperor, and attacking his provinces situated in the Netherlands: some of the possessions of the Germanic empire have been involved in this oppression, and several others have escaped the same danger solely by yielding to the imperative menaces of the predominant party and its emissaries.

"His Majesty the King of Prussia, united with his imperial Majesty by the bonds of a close and defensive alliance, and himself a preponderating member of the Germanic body, has therefore not been able to forbear marching to the aid of his ally and his co-states; and it is in this twofold relation that he takes upon himself the defence of that monarch and of Germany.

"With these great interests an object equally important is joined, and which the two sovereigns have deeply at heart, namely, to put an end to the anarchy in the interior of France, to stop the attacks directed against the throne and the altar, to re-establish the legal power, to restore to the King the security and liberty of which he is deprived, and to place him in a condition to exercise the legitimate authority which is his due.

"Convinced that the sound part of the French nation abhors the excesses of a faction which domineers over it, and that the majority of the inhabitants await with impatience the moment of succour, to declare themselves openly against the odious enterprises of their oppressors, his Majesty the Emperor, and his Majesty the King of Prussia, call upon and invite them to return without delay to the ways of reason and justice, of order and peace. Agreeably to these views, I, the undersigned, commander-in-chief of the two armies, declare—

"1. That the two allied courts, forced into the present war by irresistible circumstances, propose to themselves no other aim than the happiness of France, without pretending to enrich themselves by conquests;

"2. That they intend not to interfere in the internal government of France, but are solely desirous to deliver the King, the Queen, and the royal family from their captivity, and to procure for his most Christian Majesty the safety necessary to enable him to make without danger, without impediment, such convocations as he shall think proper, and labour to insure the happiness of his subjects, agreeably to his promises and in as far as it shall depend upon him;

"3. That the combined armies will protect the cities, towns, and villages, and the persons and property of all those who shall submit to the King, and that they will concur in the instantaneous re-establishment of order and police throughout France;

"4. That the national guards are summoned to watch *ad interim* over the tranquillity of the towns and of the country, and over the safety of the persons and property of all the French, till the arrival of the troops of their imperial and royal Majesties, or till it shall be otherwise ordained, upon penalty of being held personally responsible; that, on the contrary, such of the national guards as shall have fought against the troops of the two allied courts, and who shall be taken in arms, shall be treated as enemies and punished as rebels to their Fung, and as disturbers of the public peace;

"5. That the generals, officers, subalterns, and soldiers of the French troops of the line, are in like manner summoned to return to their ancient fidelity, and to submit forthwith to the King, their legitimate sovereign;

"6. That the members of the departments, districts, and municipalities, shall, in like manner be responsible with their lives and property for all misdemeanors, fires, murders, pillage, and acts of violence which they shall suffer to be committed, or which they shall notoriously not strive to prevent, in their territory; and they shall, in like manner, be required to continue their functions *ad interim*, till his most Christian Majesty, restored to full liberty, shall have made ulterior provisions, or till it shall have been otherwise ordained in his name, in the mean time;

"7. That the inhabitants of the cities, towns, and villages, who shall dare to defend themselves against the troops of their imperial and royal Majesties, and to fire upon them, either in the open field, or from the windows, doors, and apertures of their houses, shall be instantly punished with all the rigour of the law of war, and their houses demolished or burned. All the inhabitants, on the contrary, of the said cities, towns, and villages, who shall readily submit to their King, by opening the gates to the troops of their Majesties, stall be from that moment under their immediate safeguard. Their persons, their property, their effects, shall be under the protection of the laws; and provision shall be made for the general safety of all and each of them.

"8. The city of Paris and all its inhabitants without distinction are required to submit immediately and without delay to the King, to set that prince at full and entire liberty, and to ensure to him, as well as to all the royal personages, the inviolability and respect which the law of nature and nations renders obligatory on subjects towards their sovereigns; their imperial and royal Majesties holding personally responsible with their lives for all that may happen, to be tried militarily, and without hope of pardon, all the members of the National Assembly, of the department, of the district, of the municipality, and of the national guard of Paris, the justices of the peace, and all others whom it shall concern; their said Majesties declaring, moreover, on their faith and word, as emperor and king, that if the palace of the Tuileries is forced or insulted, that if the least violence, the least outrage, is offered to their Majesties the King and Queen, and to the royal family, if immediate provision is not made for their safety, their preservation, and their liberty, they will take an exemplary and ever-memorable vengeance by giving up the city of Paris to military execution and total destruction, and the rebels guilty of outrages, to the punishments which they shall have deserved. Their imperial and royal Majesties, on the other hand, promise the inhabitants of the city of Paris to employ their good offices with his most Christian Majesty to obtain pardon of their faults and misdeeds, and to take the most vigorous measures for the security of their persons and property, if they promptly and strictly obey the above injunctions.

"Lastly, their Majesties, unable to recognise as laws in France any but those which shall emanate from the King, enjoying perfect liberty, protest beforehand against the authenticity of all the declarations which may be made in the name of his most Christian Majesty, so long as his sacred person, that of the Queen, and of the whole royal family, shall not be really in safety; to the effect of which their imperial and royal Majesties invite and solicit his most Christian Majesty to name the city of his kingdom nearest to its frontiers, to which he shall think fit to retire with the Queen and his family, under a good and safe escort, which shall be sent to him for this purpose, in order that his most Christian Majesty may be enabled in complete safety to call around him such ministers and councillors as he shall please to appoint, make such convocations as shall to him appear fitting, provide for the re-establishment of good order, and regulate the administration of his kingdom.

"Finally, I again declare and promise in my own private name, and in my aforesaid quality, to make the troops placed under my command observe good and strict discipline, engaging to treat with kindness and moderation those well-disposed subjects who shall show themselves peaceful and submissive, and not to employ force unless against such as shall be guilty of resistance or hostility.

"For these reasons I require and exhort all the inhabitants of the kingdom, in the strongest and the most earnest manner, not to oppose the march and the operations of the troops which I command, but rather to grant them everywhere free entrance and all goodwill, aid, and assistance that circumstances may require.

"(Signed) CHATLES WILLIAM FERDINAND,

"Duke of Brunswick-Luneburg.

"Given at the head-quarters at Coblentz, the 25th of July, 1792."

What appeared surprising in this declaration was that, dated on the 25th of July, at Coblentz, it should be in Paris on the 28th, and be printed in all the royalist newspapers. It produced an extraordinary effect. Promises poured in from all quarters to resist an enemy whose language was so haughty and whose threats were so terrible. In the existing state of minds, it was natural that the King and the court should be accused of this new fault. Louis XVI. lost no time in disavowing the manifesto by a message, and he could no doubt do so with the utmost sincerity, since this paper was so different from the model which he had proposed; but he must already have seen, from this example, how far his intentions would be exceeded by his party, should that party ever be victorious. Neither his disavowal, nor the expressions with which it was accompanied, could satisfy the Assembly. Adverting to the people, whose happiness had always been so dear to him, he added, "How many sorrows might be dispelled by the slightest mark of its return to loyalty!"

These impressive words no longer excited the enthusiasm which they had in times past the gift of producing. They were regarded as the language of deceit, and many of the deputies voted for their being printed, in order, as they said, to render public the contrast which existed between the words and the conduct of the King. From that moment the agitation continued to increase, and circumstances became more and more aggravated. Intelligence was received of a resolution (*arrêté*) by which the department of the Bouches du Rhône withheld the taxes for the purpose of paying the troops which it had sent against the forces of Savoy, and charged the measures taken by the Assembly with insufficiency. This was the effect of the instigations of Barbaroux. The resolution was annulled by the Assembly, but its execution could not be prevented. It was rumoured, at the same time, that the Sardinians, who were advancing, amounted to fifty thousand. The minister for foreign affairs was obliged to repair in person to the Assembly, to assure it that the troops collected did not exceed at the utmost eleven or twelve thousand men. This report was followed by another. It was asserted that the small number of federalists who had at that time proceeded to Soissons had been poisoned with glass mixed up with the bread. It was even affirmed that one hundred and sixty were already dead, and eight hundred ill. Inquiries were made, and it was ascertained that the flour was kept in a church, the windows of which had been broken, and a few bits of glass had been found in the bread. There was, however, not one person either dead or ill.

On the 25th of July a decree had rendered all the sections of Paris permanent. They had met, and had directed Petion to propose in their name the dethronement of Louis XVI. On the morning of the 3d of August, the mayor of Paris, emboldened by this commission, appeared before the Assembly to present a petition in the name of the forty-eight sections of Paris. He reviewed the conduct of Louis XVI. ever since the commencement of the Revolution; he recapitulated, in the language of the time, the benefits conferred by the nation on the King, and the return which the King had made for them. He expatiated on the dangers by which all minds were struck, the arrival of the foreign armies, the total inadequacy of the means of defence, the revolt of a general against the Assembly, the opposition of a great number of the departmental directories, and the terrible and absurd threats issued in the name of Brunswick. In consequence, he concluded by proposing the dethronement of the King, and prayed the Assembly to insert that important question in the order of the day.

This important proposition, which had as yet been made only by clubs, federalists, and communes, assumed a very different character on being presented in the name of Paris, and by its mayor. It was received rather with astonishment than favour in the morning sitting. But in the evening the discussion commenced, and the ardour of one part of the Assembly was displayed without reserve. Some were for taking up the question forthwith, others for deferring it. It was, however, adjourned till Thursday, the 9th of August, and the Assembly continued to receive and to read petitions, expressing, with still greater energy than that of the mayor, the same wish and the same sentiments.

The section of Mauconseil, more violent than the others, instead of merely demanding the King's dethronement, pronounced it of its own authority. It declared that it no longer acknowledged Louis XVI. as King of the French, and that it should soon come to ask the legislative body if it at length meant to save France. Moreover, it exhorted all the sections of the empire—for it avoided the use of the term kingdom—to follow its example.

The Assembly, as we have already seen, did not follow the insurrectional movement so promptly as the inferior authorities, because, being specially charged with the maintenance of the laws, it was obliged to pay them more respect. Thus it found itself frequently outstripped by the popular bodies, and saw the power slipping out of its hands. It therefore annulled the resolution of the section of Mauconseil. Vergniaud and Cambon employed the most severe expressions against that act, which they called a usurpation of the sovereignty of the people. It appears, however, that it was not so much the principle as the precipitation which they condemned in this resolution, and particularly the indecorous language applied in it to the Assembly.

A crisis was now approaching. On the same day a meeting was held of the insurrectional committee of the federalists and of the King's friends, who were preparing for his flight. The committee deferred the insurrection till the day when the dethronement should be discussed, that is, till the evening of the 9th of August, or the morning of the 10th. The King's friends, on their part, were deliberating respecting his flight in the garden of M. de Montmorin. MM. de Liancourt and de Lafayette renewed their offers. Everything was arranged for departure. Money, however, was wanting. Bertrand de Molleville had uselessly exhausted the civil list by paying royalist clubs, spouters in tribunes, speakers to groups, pretended bribers, who bribed nobody, but put the funds of the court into their own pockets. The want of money was supplied by loans which generous persons eagerly offered to the King. The offers of M. de Liancourt have already been mentioned. He gave all the gold that he was able to procure. Others furnished as much as they possessed. Devoted friends prepared to accompany the carriage that was to convey the royal family, and, if it were necessary, to perish by its side.

Everything being arranged, the councillors who had met at the house of Montmorin decided upon the departure, after a conference which lasted a whole evening. The King, who saw them immediately afterwards, assented to this resolution, and ordered them to arrange with MM. de Montciel and de Sainte-Croix. Whatever might be the opinions of those who agreed to this enterprise, it was a great joy to them to believe for a moment in the approaching deliverance of the monarch. (*See* Appendix G G G G.)

But the next day everything was changed. The King directed this answer to be given, that he should not leave Paris, because he would not begin a civil war. All those who, with very different sentiments, felt an equal degree of anxiety for him, were thunderstruck. They learned that the real motive was not that assigned by the King. The real one was, in the first place, the arrival of Brunswick, announced as very near at hand; in the next, the adjournment of the insurrection; and, above all, the refusal of the Queen to trust the constitutionalists. She had energetically expressed her aversion, saying that it would be better to perish than to put themselves into the hands of those who had done them so much mischief.

Thus all the efforts made by the constitutionalists, all the dangers to which they had exposed themselves, were useless. Lafayette had seriously committed himself. It was known that he had prevailed on Luckner to march, in case of need, to the capital. The latter, summoned before the Assembly, had confessed everything to the extraordinary committee of twelve. Old Luckner was weak and fickle. When he passed out of the hands of one party into those of another, he suffered the avowal of all that he had heard or said on the preceding day to be wrung from him, and afterwards alleged, in excuse of these confessions, that he was unacquainted with the French language, wept, and complained that he was surrounded by factious persons only. Guadet had the address to draw from him a confession of Lafayette's proposals, and Bureau de Puzy, accused of having been the intermediate agent, was summoned to the bar. He was one of the friends and officers of Lafayette. He denied everything with assurance, and in a tone which persuaded the committee that the negotiations of his general were unknown to him. The question whether Lafayette should be placed under accusation was adjourned.

The day fixed for the discussion of the dethronement approached. The plan of the insurrection was settled and known. The Marseillais, whose barracks were at the farthest extremity of Paris, had repaired to the section of the Cordeliers, where the club of that name was held.

They were in the heart of Paris and close to the scene of action. Two municipal officers had had the boldness to order cartridges to be distributed among the conspirators. In short, everything was ready for the 10th.

On the 8th, the question concerning Lafayette was discussed. It was decided by a strong majority that there was not sufficient ground for an accusation. Some of the deputies, irritated at this acquittal, insisted on a division; and, on this new trial, four hundred and forty-six members and the courage to vote in favour of the general against two hundred and eighty. The people, roused by this intelligence, collected about the door of the hall, insulted the deputies as they went out, and particularly maltreated those who were known to belong to the right side of the Assembly, such as Vaublanc, Girardin, Dumas, &c. From all quarters abuse was poured forth against the national representation, and the people loudly declared that there was no longer any safety with an Assembly which could absolve the *traitor* Lafayette.

On the following day, August 9th, an extraordinary agitation prevailed among the deputies. Those who had been insulted the day before complained personally or by letter. When it was stated that M. Beaucaron had narrowly escaped being hanged, a barbarous peal of laughter burst from the tribunes; and when it was added that M. de Girardin had been struck, even those who knew how and where, ironically put the question to him. "What!" nobly replied M. de Girardin, "know you not that cowards never strike but behind one's back?" At length a member called for the order of the day. The Assembly, however, decided that Rœderer, the *procureur syndic* of the commune, should be summoned to the bar, and enjoined, upon his personal responsibility, to provide for the safety and the inviolability of the members of the Assembly.

It was proposed to send for the mayor of Paris, and to oblige him to declare, yes or no, whether he could answer for the public tranquillity. Guadet answered this proposition by another for summoning the King also, and obliging him in his turn to declare, yes or no, whether he could answer for the safety and inviolability of the territory.

Amidst these contrary suggestions, however, it was easy to perceive that the Assembly dreaded the decisive moment, and that the Girondins themselves would rather have brought about the dethronement by a deliberation, than recur to a doubtful and murderous attack. During these proceedings Rœderer arrived, and stated that one section had determined to ring the tocsin, and to march upon the Assembly and the Tuleries, if the dethronement were not pronounced. Petion entered, in his turn. He did not speak out in a positive manner, but admitted the existence of sinister projects. He enumerated the precautions taken to prevent the threatened commotions, and promised to confer with the department, and to adopt its measures, if they appeared to him better than those of the municipality.

Petion, as well as all his Girondin friends, preferred a declaration of dethronement by the Assembly to an uncertain combat with the palace. Being almost sure of a majority for the dethronement, he would fain have put a stop to the plans of the insurrectional committee. He repaired, therefore, to the committee of surveillance of the Jacobins, and begged Chabot to suspend the insurrection, telling him that the Girondins had resolved upon the dethronement and the immediate convocation of a national convention; that they were sure of a majority, and that it was wrong to run the risk of an attack, the result of which was doubtful. Chabot replied that nothing was to be hoped for from an assembly which had absolved the scoundrel Lafayette; that he, Petion, allowed himself to be deceived by his friends; that the people had at length resolved to save themselves; and that the tocsin would be rung that very evening in the fauxbourgs. "Will you always be wrongheaded, then?" replied Petion. "Woe betide us if there is a rising! . . . . I know your influence, but I have influence too, and will employ it against you."—"You shall be arrested and prevented from acting," rejoined Chabot.

People's minds were in fact too highly excited for the fears of Petion to be understood, and for him to be able to exercise his influence. A general agitation pervaded Paris. The drum beat the call in all quarters. The battalions of the national guard assembled and repaired to their posts, with very discordant dispositions. The sections were filled, not with the greater number, but with the most ardent of the citizens. The insurrectional committee had formed at three points. Fournier and some others were in the fauxbourg St. Marceau; Santerre and Westermann occupied the fauxbourg St. Antoine; lastly, Danton, Camille Desmoulins, and Carra, were at the Cordeliers with the Marseilles battalion. Barbaroux, after stationing scouts at the Assembly and the palace, had provided couriers ready to start for the south. He had also provided himself with a dose of poison, such was the uncertainty of success, and awaited at the Cordeliers the result of the insurrection. It is not known where Robespierre was. Danton had concealed Marat in a cellar belonging to the section, and had then taken possession of the tribune of the Cordeliers. Every one hesitated, as on the eve of a great revolution; but Danton, with a daring proportionate to the importance of the event, raised his thundering voice. He enumerated what he called the crimes of the court. He expatiated on the hatred of the latter to the constitution, its deceitful language, its hypocritical promises, always belied by its conduct, and lastly its evident machinations for bringing in foreigners. "The people," said he, "can now have recourse but to themselves, for the constitution is insufficient, and the Assembly has absolved Lafayette. You have, therefore, none left to save you but yourselves. Lose no time, then; for this very night, satellites concealed in the palace are to sally forth upon the people and to slaughter them, before they leave Paris to repair to Coblentz. Save yourselves, then! To arms! to arms!"

At this moment a musket was fired in the Cour du Commerce. The cry *To arms!* soon became general, and the insurrection was proclaimed. It was then half-past eleven. The Marseillais formed before the door of the Cordeliers, seized some pieces of cannon, and were soon reinforced by a numerous concourse, which ranged itself by their side. Camille Desmoulins and others ran out to order the tocsin to be rung; but they did not find the same ardour in the different sections. They strove to rouse their zeal. The sections soon assembled and appointed commissioners to repair to the Hôtel de Ville, for the purpose of superseding the municipality and taking all the authority into their own hands. Lastly, they ran to the bells, made themselves masters of them by main force, and the tocsin began to ring. This dismal sound pervaded the whole extent of the capital. It was wafted from street to street, from building to building. It called the deputies, the magistrates, the citizens, to their posts. At length it reached the palace, proclaiming that the terrible night was come; that fatal night, that night of agitation and blood, destined to be the last which the monarch should pass in the palace of his ancestors.

Emissaries of the court came to apprize it that the moment of the catastrophe was at hand. They reported the expression used by the President of the Cordeliers, who had told his people that this was not to be as on the 20th of June, a mere civic promenade; meaning that, if the 20th of June had been the threat, the 10th of August was the decisive stroke. On that point, in fact, there was no longer room for doubt. The King, the Queen, their two children, and their sister, Madame Elizabeth, had not retired to bed, but had gone after supper into the council-chamber, where all the ministers and a great number of superior officers were deliberating, in dismay, on the means of saving the royal family. The means of resistance were feeble and had been almost annihilated, either by decrees, of the Assembly, or by the false measures of the court itself.

The constitutional guard, dissolved by a decree of the Assembly, had not been replaced by the King, who had chosen rather to continue its pay to it than to form a new one. The force of the palace was thus diminished by eighteen hundred men.

The regiments whose disposition had appeared favourable to the King at the time of the last Federation had been removed from Paris by the accustomed expedient of decrees.

The Swiss could not be removed, owing to their capitulations, but their artillery had been taken from them; and the court, when it had, for a moment, decided upon flight to Normandy, had sent thither one of those faithful battalions, upon pretext of guarding supplies of corn that were expected. This battalion had not yet been recalled. Some Swiss only, in barracks at Courbevoie, had been authorized by Petion to come back, and they amounted altogether to no more than eight or nine hundred men.

The gendarmerie had recently been composed of the old soldiers of the French guards, the authors of the 14th of July.

Lastly, the national guard had neither the same officers, nor the same organization, nor the same attachment, as on the 6th of October, 1789. The staff, as we have seen, had been reconstituted. A great number of citizens had become disgusted with the service, and those who had not deserted their post were intimidated by the fury of the populace. Thus, the national guard was, like all the bodies of the state, composed of a new revolutionary generation. It was divided, with the whole of France, into constitutionalists and republicans. The whole battalion of the Filles St. Thomas, and part of that of the Petits Pères, were attached to the King. The others were either indifferent or hostile. The gunners, in particular, who composed the principal strength, were decided republicans. The fatigues incident to the duty of the latter had deterred the wealthy citizens from undertaking it. Locksmiths and blacksmiths were thus left in possession of the guns, and almost all of them, belonging to the populace, partook of its dispositions.

Thus the King had left him about eight or nine hundred Swiss, and rather more than one battalion of the national guard.

It will be recollected that the command of the national guard, after Lafayette's removal, had been transferred to six commanders of legions in rotation. It had fallen on that day to the commandant Mandat, an old officer, displeasing to the court for his constitutional opinions, but possessing its entire confidence, from his firmness, his intelligence, and his attachment to his duties. Mandat, general-in-chief on that fatal night, had hastily made the only possible dispositions.

The floor of the great gallery, leading from the Louvre to the Tuileries, had already been cut away for a certain space, to prevent the passage of the assailants. Mandat, in consequence, took no precautions for protecting that wing, but directed his attention to the side next to the courts and the garden. Notwithstanding the signal by drum, few of the national guards had assembled. The battalions remained incomplete. The most zealous of them proceeded singly to the palace, where Mandat had formed them into regiments ant posted them conjointly with the Swiss, in the courts, the garden, and the apartments. He had placed one piece of cannon in the court of the Swiss, three in the central court, and three in that of the princes.

These guns were unfortunately consigned to gunners of the national guard, so that the enemy was actually in the fortress. But the Swiss, full of zeal and loyalty, watched them narrowly, ready at the first movement to make themselves masters of their guns, and to drive them out of the precincts of the palace.

Mandat had moreover placed some advanced posts of gendarmerie at the colonnade of the Louvre and the Hôtel de Ville; but this gendarmerie, as we have already shown, was composed of old French guards.

To these defenders of the palace must he added a great number of old servants, whose age or whose moderation had prevented them from emigrating, and who, in the moment of danger, had come forward, some to absolve themselves for not having gone to Coblentz, others to die generously by the side of their prince. They had hastily provided themselves with all the weapons that they could procure in the palace. They were armed with swords, and pistols fastened to their waists by pocket-handkerchiefs. Some had even taken tongs and shovels from the fireplaces. Thus there was no want of jokes at this awful moment, when the court ought to have been serious at least for once. This concourse of useless persons, instead of rendering it any service, merely abstracted the national guard, which could not reckon upon it, and tended only to increase the confusion, which was already too great.

All the members of the departmental directory had repaired the palace. The virtuous Duke de Larochefoucauld was there. Rœderer, the *procureur syndic*, was there too. Petion was sent for, and he repaired thither with two municipal officers. Petion was urged to sign an order for repelling force by force, and he did sign it, that he might not appear to be an accomplice of the insurgents. Considerable joy was felt in having him at the palace, and in holding, in his person, an hostage so dear to the people. The Assembly, apprised of this intention, summoned him to the bar by a decree. The King, who was advised to detain him, refused to do so, and he therefore left the Tuileries without impediment.

The order to repel force by force once obtained, various opinions were expressed relative to the manner of using it. In this state of excitement, more than one silly project must necessarily have presented itself. There was one sufficiently bold, and which might probably have succeeded: this was to prevent the attack by dispersing the insurgents, who were not yet very numerous, and who, with the Marseillais, formed at most a few thousand men. At this moment, in fact, the fauxbourg St. Marceau was not yet formed; Santerre hesitated in the fauxbourg St. Antoine; Danton alone, and the Marseillais had ventured to form at the Cordeliers, and they were waiting with impatience at the Pont St. Michel for the arrival of the other assailants.

A vigorous sally might have dispersed them, and, at this moment of hesitation, a movement of terror would infallibly have prevented the insurrection. Another course, more safe and legal, was that proposed by Mandat, namely to await the march of the fauxbourgs; but as soon as they should be in motion, to attack them at two decisive points. He suggested, in the first place, that when one party of them should debouch upon the Place of the Hôtel de Ville, by the arcade of St. Jean, they should be suddenly charged; and that, at the Louvre, those who should come by the Pont Neuf, along the quay of the Tuileries, should be served in the same manner. He had actually ordered the gendarmerie posted at the colonnade to suffer the insurgents to file past, then to charge them in the rear, while the gendarmerie stationed at the Carrousel were to pour through the wickets of the Louvre, and attack them in front. The success of such plans was almost certain. The necessary orders had already been given by Mandat to the commandants of the different posts, and especially to that of the Hôtel de Ville.

We have already seen that a new municipality had just been formed there. Among the members of the former, Danton and Manuel only were retained. The order was shown to this insurrectional municipality. It immediately summoned the commandant to appear at the Hôtel de Ville. The summons was carried to the palace. Mandat hesitated; but those about him and the members of the department themselves, not knowing what had happened, and not deeming it right yet to infringe the law by refusing to appear, exhorted him to comply. Mandat then decided. He put into the hands of his son, who was with him at the palace, the order signed by Petion to repel force by force, and obeyed the summons of the municipality. It was about four o'clock in the morning. On reaching the Hôtel de Ville, he was surprised to find there a new authority. He was instantly surrounded and questioned concerning the order which he had issued. He was then dismissed, and in dismissing him the president made a sign which was equivalent to sentence of death. No sooner had the unfortunate commandant retired than he was seized and shot with a pistol. The murderers stripped him of his clothes, without finding about him the order, which he had delivered to his son, and his body was thrown into the river, whither it was soon to be followed by so many others.

This sanguinary deed paralyzed all the means of defence of the palace, destroyed all unity, and prevented the execution of the plan of defence. All, however, was not yet lost, and the insurrection was not completely formed. The Marseillais had impatiently waited for the fauxbourg St. Antoine, which did not arrive, and for a moment they concluded that the plan had miscarried. But Westermann had pointed his sword to the body of Santerre, and forced him to march. The fauxbourgs had then successively arrived, some by the Rue St. Honoré, others by the Pont Neuf, the Pont Royal, and the wickets of the Louvre. The Marseillais marched at the head of the columns, with the Breton federalists, and they had pointed their pieces towards the palace. The great number of the insurgents, which increased every moment, was joined by a multitude attracted by curiosity; and thus the enemy appeared stronger than they really were. While they were proceeding to the palace, Santerre had hurried to the Hôtel de Ville, to get himself appointed commander-in-chief of the national guard, and Westermann had remained on the field of battle to direct the assailants. Everything was therefore in the utmost confusion, so much so that Petion, who, according to the preconcerted plan, was to have been kept at home by an insurrectional force, was still waiting for the guard that was to screen his responsibility by an apparent constraint. He sent, himself, to the Hôtel de Ville, and at last a few men were placed at his door that he might seem to be in a state of arrest.

The palace was at this moment absolutely besieged. The assailants were in the Place; and by the dawning light they were seen through the old doors of the courts and from the windows. Their artillery was discovered pointed at the palace, and their confused shouts and threatening songs were heard. The plan of anticipating them had been anew proposed; but tidings of Mandat's death had just been received, and the opinion of the ministers, as well as of the department, was, that it was best to await the attack and suffer themselves to be forced within the limits of the law. Rœderer had just gone through the ranks of this little garrison, to read to the Swiss and the national guards the legal proclamation, which forbade them to attack, but enjoined them to repel force by force. The King was solicited to review in person the servants who were preparing to defend him. The unfortunate prince had passed the night in listening to the conflicting opinions that were expressed around him; and, during the only moments of relaxation, he had prayed to Heaven for his royal consort, his children, and his sister, the objects of all his fears. "Sire," said the Queen to him with energy, "it is time to show yourself." It is even asserted that, snatching a pistol from the belt of old D'Affry, she presented it angrily at the King. The eyes of the princess were inflamed with weeping; but her brow appeared lofty, her nostrils dilated, with indignation and pride. (*See* Appendixes H H H H and I I I I.)

As for the King, he feared nothing for his own person; nay, he manifested great coolness in this extreme peril; but he was alarmed for his family, and sorrow at seeing it thus exposed had altered his looks. He nevertheless went forward with firmness. He had on a purple suit of clothes, wore a sword, and his hair, which had not been dressed since the preceding day, was partly in disorder. On stepping out upon the balcony, he perceived, without agitation, many pieces of artillery pointed against the palace. His presence still excited some remains of enthusiasm. The caps of the grenadiers were all at once uplifted on the points of swords and bayonets; the old cry of "*Vive le Roi!*" rang for the last time beneath the walls of the paternal palace. A last spark of courage was rekindled. Dejected hearts were cheered. For a moment there was a gleam of confidence and hope, but at that instant some fresh battalions of the national guard arrived, which had been formed later than the others, and came agreeably to the order previously issued by Mandat. They entered at the moment when the cries of "*Vive le Roi!*" rang in the court. Some joined those who thus hailed the presence of the monarch; others, holding different sentiments, fancied themselves in danger, and, calling to mind all the popular fables that had been circulated, imagined that they were about to be given up to the knights of *the dagger*. They immediately cried out that they were betrayed by that villain Mandat, and raised a kind of tumult. The gunners, following their example, turned their pieces against the front of the palace. A quarrel instantly ensued with the loyal battalions. The gunners were disarmed and consigned to a detachment, and the new comers were despatched towards the gardens.

At this moment the King, after showing himself in the balcony, went down stairs to review the troops in the courts. His coming having been announced, every one had resumed his place in the ranks. He walked through them with a tranquil countenance, and cast upon them expressive looks which penetrated all hearts. Addressing the soldiers, he said, with a firm voice, that he was touched by their attachment, that he should be by their side, and that, in defending him, they were defending their wives and their children. He then proceeded through the vestibule, with the intention of going to the garden, but at that moment he heard shouts of "Down with the veto!" raised by one of the battalions which had just entered. Two officers, who were at his side, were then anxious to prevent him from continuing the review in the garden; others begged him to go and inspect the post at the Pont Tournant. He courageously complied. But he was obliged to pass along the Terrace of the Feuillans, which was crowded with people. During this walk, he was separated from the furious multitude merely by a tri-coloured ribbon. He nevertheless advanced, in spite of all sorts of insults and abuse; he even saw the battalions file off before his face, traverse the garden, and leave it with the intention of joining the assailants in the Place du Carrousel.

This desertion, that of the gunners, and the shouts of "Down with the veto!" had extinguished all hope in the King. At the same moment the gendarmes, assembled at the colonnade of the Louvre and other places, had either dispersed or joined the populace. The national guard, which occupied the apartments, and which could, it was conceived, be relied upon, was on its part dissatisfied at being with the gentlemen, and appeared to distrust them. The Queen strove to encourage it. "Grenadiers," cried she, pointing to those gentlemen, "these are your comrades; they are come to die by your side." In spite, however, of this apparent courage, her soul was overwhelmed with despair. The review had ruined everything, and she lamented that the King had shown no energy. That unfortunate prince, we cannot forbear repeating, feared nothing for himself. He had, in fact, refused to wear a buckler, as on the 14th of July, saying that on the day of battle it behoved him to be uncovered, like the meanest of his servants. He was not, therefore, deficient in courage, and he afterwards displayed a truly noble and elevated courage; but he lacked the boldness requisite for offensive operations. He lacked also consistency, and ought not, for example, to have dreaded the effusion of blood, when he consented to the invasion of France by foreigners. It is certain, as has frequently been observed, that, had he mounted a horse and charged at the head of his adherents, the insurrection would have been quelled.

At this moment, the members of the department, seeing the general confusion in the palace, and despairing of the success of resistance, went to the King and besought him to retire into the bosom of the Assembly. This advice, so frequently calumniated, like all that is given to kings, when not successful, recommended the only suitable course at the moment. By this retreat, all bloodshed was likely to be prevented, and the royal family preserved from a death that was almost certain if the palace should be taken by storm. In the existing state of things, the success of the assault was not doubtful, and, had it been, the very doubt was sufficient to make one avoid exposing oneself to it.

The Queen vehemently opposed this plan. "Madam," said Ecederer, "you endanger the lives of your husband and children. Think of the responsibility which you take upon yourself." The altercation grew very warm. At length the King decided to retire to the Assembly. "Let us go," said he, with a resigned look, to his family and to those around him. "Sir," said the Queen to Ecederer, "you answer for the lives of the King and of my children."—"Madam," replied the *procureur syndic*, "I answer for it that I will die by their side, but I promise nothing more."

They then set out, to proceed to the Assembly by the garden, the terrace of the Feuillans and the court of the Riding-house. All the gentlemen and servants rushed forward to follow the King, though it was possible that they might compromise him by irritating the populace and exciting the ill-will of the Assembly by their presence. Rœderer strove in vain to stop them, and loudly declared that they would cause the royal family to be murdered. He at length succeeded in keeping back a great number, and the royal party set out. A detachment of Swiss and of the national guard accompanied the royal family. A deputation of the Assembly came to receive and to conduct it into its bosom. At this moment the concourse was so great that the crowd was impenetrable. A tall grenadier took hold of the dauphin, and, lifting him up in his arms, forced his way through the mob, holding him over his head. The Queen, at this sight, conceived that her child was going to be taken from her, and gave a shriek; but she was soon set right; for the grenadier entered, and placed the royal infant on the bureau of the Assembly.

The King and his family then entered, followed by two ministers. "I come," said Louis XVI., "to prevent a great crime, and I think, gentlemen, that I cannot be safer than in the midst of you."

Vergniaud, who presided, replied to the monarch that he might rely on the firmness of the National Assembly, and that its members had sworn to die in defence of the constituted authorities.

The King seated himself beside the president; but on the observation of Chabot, that his presence might affect the freedom of deliberation, he was placed in the box of the writer appointed to report the proceedings. The iron railing was removed, that, in case a forcible entry should be made into the box, he might with his family take shelter without impediment in the Assembly. In this operation the prince assisted with his own hands. The railing was pulled down, and thus insults and threats could the more freely reach the dethroned monarch in his last asylum.

Rœderer then gave an account of what had happened. He described the fury of the multitude, and the danger which threatened the palace, the courts of which were already in the possession of the mob. The Assembly ordered twenty of its commissioners to go and pacify the populace. The commissioners departed. A discharge of cannon was all at once heard. Consternation pervaded the hall. "I assure you," said the King, "that I have ordered the Swiss to be forbidden to fire." But the report of cannon was again heard, mingled with the sound of musketry. The agitation was at its height. Intelligence was soon brought that the commissioners deputed by the Assembly had been dispersed. At the same moment the door of the hall was attacked, and rang with tremendous blows. Armed citizens appeared at one of the entrances. "We are stormed!" exclaimed a municipal officer. The president put on his hat; and a multitude of deputies rushed from their seats to keep hack the assailants. At length the tumult was appeased, and, amidst the uninterrupted reports of the musketry and cannon, the deputies shouted, "The nation, liberty, equality for ever!"

At this moment, in fact, a most sanguinary combat was racing at the palace. The King having left it, it was naturally supposed that the people would not persist in their attack on a forsaken dwelling; besides, the general agitation had prevented any attention from being paid to the subject, and no order had been issued for its evacuation. All the troops that were in the courts had merely been withdrawn into the interior of the palace, and they were confusedly mingled in the apartments with the domestics, the gentlemen, and the officers. The crowd at the palace was immense, and it was scarcely possible to move there, notwithstanding its vast extent.

The rabble, probably ignorant of the King's departure, after waiting a considerable time before the principal wicket, at length attacked the gate, broke it open with hatchets, and rushed into the Royal Court. They then formed in column, and turned against the palace the guns imprudently left in the court after the troops had been withdrawn. The assailants, however, yet forbore to attack. They made amicable demonstrations to the soldiers at the windows. "Give up the palace to us," said they, "and we are friends." The Swiss professed pacific intentions, and threw cartridges out of the windows. Some of the boldest of the besiegers, venturing beyond the columns, advanced beneath the vestibule of the palace. At the foot of the great staircase had been placed a piece of timber in the form of a barrier, and behind it were intrenched, pell-mell, some Swiss, and national guards. Those who from the outside had pushed in thus far, resolved to advance still farther and to gain possession of the barrier. After a struggle of considerable length, which however did not end in a battle, the barrier was taken. The assailants then forced their way up the staircase, repeating that the palace must be given up to them.

It is asserted that, at this moment, men armed with pikes, who had remained in the court, caught hold with hooks of the Swiss sentries stationed outside, and murdered them. It is added that a musket-shot was fired at a window, and that the Swiss, enraged at it, replied by a volley. A tremendous discharge immediately pealed in the palace, and those who had penetrated into it fled, crying that they were betrayed. It is difficult to ascertain, amidst this confusion, by which side the first shots were fired. The assailants have alleged that they advanced amicably, and that, when they had once entered the palace, they were treacherously surprised and fired upon. It is very improbable, for the Swiss were not in a situation to provoke a conflict. As, after the King's departure, it was no longer their duty to fight, they must naturally have thought only of saving themselves, and treachery was not the way to do that. Besides, if even aggression could change anything in the moral character of these events, it must be admitted that the first and real aggression, that is, the attack of the palace, proceeded from the insurgents. The rest was but an inevitable accident, to be imputed to chance alone.

Be this as it may, those who had succeeded in forcing their way into the vestibule and upon the great staircase suddenly heard the discharge, and, whilst retreating, and upon the staircase itself, they received a shower of balls. The Swiss then descended in good order, and, on reaching the last steps, debouched by the vestibule into the Royal Court. There they made themselves masters of one of the pieces of cannon which were in the court; and, in spite of a terrible fire, turned and discharged it at the Marseillais, killing a great number of them.

The Marseillais then fell back, and, the fire continuing, they abandoned the court. Terror instantly seized the populace, who fled on all sides and regained the fauxbourgs. If the Swiss had at this moment followed up their advantage; if the gendarmes stationed at the Louvre, instead of deserting their post, had charged the repulsed besiegers, the business would have been decided, and victory would have belonged to the palace.

But at this moment the King's order arrived, sent through M. d'Hervilly, forbidding the Swiss to fire. M. d'Hervilly had reached the vestibule at the moment when the Swiss had just repulsed the besiegers. He stopped them, and enjoined them, in the name of the King, to follow him to the Assembly. The Swiss, in considerable number, then followed M. d'Hervilly to the Feuillans amidst the most galling discharges. The palace was thus deprived of the greater portion of its defenders. Still, however, a considerable number were left, either on the staircase, or in the apartments. These the order had not reached, and they were soon destined to be exposed, without means of resistance, to the most awful dangers.

Meanwhile the besiegers had rallied. The Marseillais, united to the Bretons, were ashamed of having given way. They took courage again, and returned to the charge boiling with fury. Westermann, who afterwards displayed genuine talents, directed their efforts with intelligence. They rushed forward with ardour, fell in great numbers, but at length gained the vestibule, passed the staircase, and made themselves masters of the palace. The rabble, with pikes, poured in after them, and the rest of the scene was soon but one general massacre. The unfortunate Swiss in vain begged for quarter, at the same time throwing down their arms. They were butchered without mercy. The palace was set on fire; the servants who filled it were pursued; some escaped, others were sacrificed. (*See* Appendix J J J J.) Among the number there were generous conquerors. "Spare the women," cried one of them; "do not dishonour the nation!" and he saved the Queen's ladies, who were on their knees, with swords uplifted over their heads. There were courageous victims; there were others who displayed ingenuity in saving, when they had no longer the courage to defend themselves. Among those furious conquerors there were even feelings of honesty, and, either from popular vanity or from that disinterestedness which springs from enthusiasm, the money found in the palace was carried to the Assembly.

The Assembly had anxiously awaited the issue of the combat. At length, at eleven o'clock, were heard shouts of victory a thousand times repeated. The doors yielded to the pressure of a mob intoxicated with joy and fury. The hall was filled with wrecks that were brought thither, and with the Swiss who had been made prisoners, and whose lives had been spared, in order to do homage to the Assembly by this act of popular clemency. Meanwhile, the King and his family, confined within the narrow box of a reporter, witnessed the ruin of their throne and the joy of their conquerors. (*See* Appendix K K K K.) Vergniaud had for a moment quitted the chair, for the purpose of drawing up the decree of dethronement. He returned, and the Assembly passed that celebrated decree, to this effect:

Louis XVI. is, for the time being, suspended from royalty;

A plan of education is directed for the prince royal;

A national convention is convoked.

Was it, then, a plan long resolved upon to overthrow the monarchy, since they only suspended the King and provided an education for the prince? With what fear, on the contrary, did they not lay hands on that ancient power! With what a kind of hesitation did they not approach that aged tree, beneath which the French generations had been alternately fortunate or unfortunate, but under which at least they had lived!

The public mind, however, is prompt. It needed but a short interval to throw off the relics of an ancient veneration; and the monarchy suspended, was soon to become the monarchy destroyed. It was doomed to perish, not in the person of a Louis XI., a Charles IX., a Louis XIV., but in that of Louis XVI., one of the most honest kings that ever sat upon a throne.

Printed in Great Britain
by Amazon

27231351R00205